Introduction to Wide Area Networks

Protocols and Applications for Network-to-Network Connectivity

WestNet's Signature Series Courseware

Textbook   CD-ROM   Online Course

Visit the course companion Web site at:

http://www.westnetlearning.com/gateway/srs.asp

You will find **Web Based Support**, **Online Course Links**, and **Practice Quizzes**.

WestNet helps determine your certification path

WestNet courses map to more than 20 industry certifications

http://www.westnetlearning.com/mkt/certifications.asp

CREDITS

Author and Development Editor: Kenneth D. Reed

Editorial and Production Manager: Marilee E. Aust

Book Design and Composition, and Copy Editor Manager: D. Kari Luraas, Clairvoyance Design

Illustrator: Lynn Siefken

Proofreaders: Larry Beckett and Betty Reed

Technical Writer and Editor: David M. Watts

Indexer: Amy Casey

Copy Editors: Sheryl Shapiro and Michelle Hanson, Clairvoyance Design

Cover Design: David Jones

Printer: Johnson Printing

ISBN: 1-58676-144-7 (softcover)

Printed in the United States of America

Reed, Kenneth D.
Introduction to Wide Area Networks
608 pp., includes illustrations and index

1. Fundamentals of WANs 2. WAN Concepts and Components 3. Physical Layer WAN Protocols 4. Data Link Layer WAN Protocols 5. Higher-Layer WAN Protocols 6. WAN Solutions 7. Convergence of Communications Over WAN Technologies

WB47.0.1

For instructor-led training, self-paced courses,
turn-key curricula solutions, or more information contact:

WestNet Learning Technologies (dba: WestNet Inc.)
5420 Ward Road, Suite 150, Arvada, CO 80002 USA
E-mail: Info@westnetlearning.com

To access the WestNet student resource site, go to
http://www.westnetlearning.com/student

Preface

In the *Introduction to Wide Area Networks* course, students learn the concepts, technologies, components, and protocols used to move voice and data across long distances, and discover important technologies such as ATM that integrate voice, data, and video communications. Also reviewed are basic concepts of how information is transported over a wide area network (WAN), from the physical layer bits and bytes to the applications that WANs support.

This course is intended for individuals who desire a better understanding of the global telecommunications infrastructure and how it supports long-distance voice and data communications. When students complete this course, they will have a solid understanding of the fundamental concepts of WAN operations. Students develop a strong foundation in networking and communications systems and technologies, so that as they further target their studies toward administering specific network operating systems, they will carry with them a clear advantage over their peers.

Prerequisites

The *Introduction to Networking* course is the only prerequisite for this course. In addition, students will find that basic computer skills, such as using word processing applications, Internet browsers, and e-mail software are helpful in this course. Students may also find that studies in Local Area Networking technologies, Telecommunications Fundamentals, and Transmission Control Protocol/Internet Protocol concepts also aid understanding. Courses covering these topics are also available from WestNet Learning Technologies.

Key Topics

- Development of the telecommunications network
- The structure and function of the local loop PBX fundamentals, features, and functions
- Physical and virtual (logical) circuits
- Analog and digital voice circuits
- Wireless communications
- Voice digitization
- WAN devices such as CSU/DSUs, Multiplexers, and Channel Banks
- Physical WAN protocols such as T1, T3, and SONET
- Logical WAN protocols such as HDLC, PPP, ISDN-PRI, Frame Relay, X.25, ATM, and SMDS
- Internet access methods such as ADSL and cable modems
- Function and usage of ISDN, Frame Relay, ATM, X.25, and SMDS
- Voice over WAN technologies
- Introduction to Voice over Internet Protocol technologies
- Private VPNs
- Remote Network Access technologies

Course Objectives

- Describe the development and operation of today's telecommunications infrastructure
- Identify the physical and logical technologies used for WAN communications
- Apply physical layer technologies such as switched circuits, leased lines, T-carriers and Synchronous Optical Network (SONET)
- Apply Data Link Layer technologies such as High-Level Data Link Control (HDLC), Serial Line Internet Protocol (SLIP) and Point-to-Point Protocol (PPP)
- Apply higher layer protocols including Integrated Services Digital Network (ISDN), Frame Relay and Asynchronous Transfer Mode (ATM)

- Identify layered WAN protocols used to support networking applications such as remote access, VPNs, and Voice over technologies

- Combine WAN and LAN technologies to build an end-to-end, enterprise networking solution

Pedagogical Features

Several pedagogical features are included in this text to enhance the presentation of the materials so that you can easily understand the concepts and apply them. Throughout the book, emphasis is placed on applying concepts to real-world scenarios through end-of-lesson Activities, Extended Activities and other exercises and examples.

Learning Objectives, Unit Summaries, Discussion Questions, and Activities/Exercises

Learning objectives, unit summaries, discussion questions, and/or activities/exercises are designed to function as integrated study tools. Learning objectives reflect what you should be able to accomplish after completing each unit or chapter. Chapter summaries highlight the key concepts you should master. The discussion questions help guide critical thinking about those key concepts, and the Activities/Exercises provide you with opportunities to practice important techniques.

Key Terms

The information technology field includes many unique terms that are critical to creating a workable language when it is combined with the world of business. Definitions of key terms are provided in alphabetical order at the beginning of each unit and in a glossary at the end of the textbook.

Supplements

When this course is used in an academic or instructor-led setting, it is accompanied by an Instructor's Resource Tool Kit. The online-based kit includes an Instructor's Guide (also known as an "Answer Key") with the answers to Activities/Exercises, Lesson and Unit Quizzes and the End-of-Course Exam. It also includes PowerPoint presentations organized by lesson, unit, and course. The Instructor's Resource site may also include sample syllabi, labs, puzzles, cryptograms, and up-to-the-minute updates to the textbooks and supplemental course materials.

WestNet Learning Technologies' cutting edge Administrative Tools offer a unique online Windows-based exam software. The Online Course Exam engine includes lesson-, unit- and course-level questions. These exams can be accessed by individual students and is presented in randomized order, ensuring that no student ever gets the same question with the same sequence of answers. This feature allows you to create printed and online pre-tests, practice tests, and actual examinations.

Advancing Your Level of Technical Expertise

WestNet Learning Technologies envisions a new communications paradigm for the 21st century—a paradigm based on increased bandwidth and digital exchange. Moving forward, WestNet is integrating these capacities with data/telephony/IP educational solutions that will give its students a complete range of communications skills and knowledge.

Why Choose WestNet?

WestNet Learning Technologies develops and disseminates comprehensive information technologies (IT) certification and educational curricula to secondary schools, colleges and universities, as well as corporations, resellers and individual participants around the globe. These programs provide participants with the tools necessary to further their IT knowledge and skills and obtain hands-on experience. This unique, vendor-neutral experience helps prepare participants to pursue IT careers, earn secondary and post-secondary educational degrees and/or obtain industry certifications.

From distance learning to instructor-led courses, WestNet is unlike any other IT curriculum provider. All WestNet Signature Series courseware includes textbooks, CD-ROMs, and online courses—plus full instructor training and support. WestNet's IT curriculum is found in more than 1,000 institutions around the world, and is offered in five languages.

Contents at a Glance

Contents

INTRODUCTION

As discussed in the Preface, the only prerequisite to this course is *Introduction to Networking*. However, it is also recommended that you take *Introduction to Local Area Networks*, or have requisite local area network (LAN) experience/knowledge.

People communicate with other people in a variety of ways. For example, we talk to people face-to-face, or we write a letter and send it to someone and they write us a letter back. These are traditional forms of communication. When people use computers to communicate they use a computer network. This course is about computer networks and how they are used to transmit information between computers, and ultimately between people. The focus of this course is wide area networks (WANs).

Networks can be categorized into four major groups: LANs, campus networks, metropolitan area networks (MANs), and WANs. A WAN connects individual networks over long distances. A WAN typically connects two or more LANs using a particular type of service. There are many WAN services as we will see in this course. The principles covered in this course also apply to other types of networks; however, we will concentrate on aspects associated with wide area networking technology.

COURSE OVERVIEW

This course begins with a discussion of fundamental concepts related to WAN technologies and services. We should remember that the network used to provide many of the WAN data services today was originally developed to carry voice-grade traffic only. The analog network of old has been updated to a primarily digital network; however, analog local loops still connect home and many business users to the digital telephone network. Hence, Unit 1 discusses the basics of how analog and digital voice and data services are combined in WANs. Additional topics covered in Unit 1 include private branch exchange (PBX) fundamentals, features, and functions. PBX components, such as trunks, subscriber lines, equipment cabinets, and circuit cards, as well as adjunct devices, are introduced. We also briefly discuss PBX services that support call accounting, security, and convergence.

Unit 2 covers some of the basic concepts necessary for understanding how information is transported over a WAN. We look at analog versus digital transmission, circuit types, and different modes of communicating information from source to destination over a wide area. Devices such as modems, microwaves, satellites, and multiplexers (MUXs) are reviewed in both Units 1 and 2.

Unit 3 looks at the lowest layer of WAN technologies, the Physical Layer. The Physical Layer consists of the medium used to transmit bits, and the way bits are formatted for transmission across the physical media. Switched circuits, leased lines, T-carriers, and Synchronous Optical Network (SONET) technologies are presented, as are Asymmetric Digital Subscriber Line (ADSL) and cable modems.

Unit 4 discusses common Layer 2 WAN protocols, that is, protocols associated with the Open Systems Interconnection (OSI) model Data Link Layer. The Data Link Layer is concerned with moving frames from one piece of network hardware to another. This unit looks at such Layer 2 protocols as High-Level Data Link Control (HDLC), Serial Line Internet Protocol (SLIP), and Point-to-Point Protocol (PPP).

Units 5 and 6 discuss higher-layer WAN protocols used to move information across a network, not just a single link. Unit 5 covers the first two major protocols, Integrated Services Digital Network (ISDN) and frame relay.

Unit 6 introduces two cell-switching technologies, Asynchronous Transfer Mode (ATM) and Switched Multimegabit Data Service (SMDS). These technologies move information across networks in fixed-size cells, providing network devices with predictable performance and reliability.

Unit 7, the final unit, covers converged technologies and their supporting services, including Voice-over-IP (VoIP), ATM, and frame relay. We discuss VoIP network components and protocols and the factors motivating enterprises to implement their services. We finish by covering private public-switched telephone network (PSTN) virtual private networks (VPNs) and PSTN remote access services.

Unit 1
Fundamentals of WANs

This unit focuses on basic concepts that apply to the entire course. Some of the concepts covered in this unit were covered in greater detail in the *Introduction to Networking* course. They are presented here to prepare you for more detailed study of wide area networks (WANs).

Lessons

1. Classification of Networks
2. Telecommunications
3. Voice Networks
4. Voice Network Technology
5. PBX Fundamentals
6. PBX Features and Functions
7. Computer Data and the Voice Network
8. Digitizing the Voice
9. Integration of Services
10. Elements of the Telecommunications Business

Terms

amplitude modulation (AM)—AM imposes a signal pattern on a carrier wave (consistent electrical signal) by varying the height of the wave, or how far from the center it swings.

1

analog—Analog signals are waves of electrical current. Variations in the human voice, when mixed with an analog signal by means of a telephone handset, produce a new signal that represents the human voice as a unique electrical wave.

Asynchronous Transfer Mode (ATM)—ATM is a cell-switching network that consists of multiple ATM switches that forward each individual cell to its final destination. ATM can provide transport services for audio, data, and video.

automated attendant—An automated attendant is a device that automatically answers incoming calls and allows callers to route themselves to an extension in response to a recorded voice prompt.

Automatic Call Distributor (ACD)—An ACD is a programmable system that controls how inbound calls are received, held, delayed, treated, and distributed to call center agents.

Automatic Route Selection (ARS) —Also known as LCR, ARS is a switch software module the enables a user to program a system to route individual calls over the most appropriate selection of carrier and service offerings.

busy hour—Busy hour refers to the one hour during which a network or office telephone system carries its greatest traffic. A telephone network should be designed to provide enough transmission capacity to carry most busy-hour traffic, so that only some, but not many, callers are put on hold or receive busy signals.

Call Detail Report (CDR)—A CDR is an itemized report of all calls and their durations, used for call accounting purposes. A Call Detail Recording feature, as part of a PBX or provided by a carrier, collects the data presented in the report.

central office (CO)—A CO is a telephone company facility where local loops are terminated. The function of a CO is to connect individual telephones through a series of switches. COs are tied together in a hierarchy for efficiency in switching. Other terms for a CO are local exchange, wiring center, and end office.

channel—Generically speaking, a channel is a communications path between two or more communicating devices. Channels are also referred to as links, lines, circuits, and paths.

circuit—A circuit is the physical connection between two communicating devices.

class of restriction (CoR)—CoRs control call origination and termination on PBX trunks or trunk groups. CoRs control call routing, identification, and other trunk details.

class of service (CoS)—In the telecommunications world, CoS is the collection of privileges and services assigned to a particular extension. In the data world, CoS defines the prioritization or other differentiating treatment of particular data traffic classes, such as VoIP or video conferencing.

coder-decoder (codec)—A codec is a hardware device that takes an analog signal and converts it to a digital representation of the analog signal.

competitive access provider (CAP)—A CAP is a company that provides fiber optic links to connect urban business customers to IXCs, bypassing the LEC. Once these fiber optic links are in place in major metropolitan areas, CAPs can begin to expand their service offerings.

competitive local exchange carrier (CLEC)—CLECs are telecommunications resellers or brokers that sell services bought from ILECs. CLECs resell data service, such as Internet access and local toll calling, to business and residential customers.

Dataphone Digital Service (DDS)—DDS, also known as Digital Data Service, is a series of services, provided by a telephone company, that provide digital facilities for data communication. DDS is available in several speeds, including 2.4, 4.8, 9.6, and 56 Kbps.

dense wavelength-division multiplexing (DWDM)—DWDM uses multiple light wavelengths to transmit signals over a single optical fiber. Each wavelength, or channel, carries a stream of data at rates as high as 2.5 Gbps and higher. It can use over 50 channels.

Direct Inward Dialing (DID)—DID is a process by which a PBX routes calls directly to a particular extension (identified by the last four digits). Incoming trunks must be specifically configured to support DID.

Direct Inward System Access (DISA)—DISA is a method of dialing into a telephone system over either toll or toll-free lines, to gain access to internal telephone system services and features. For example, remote users can dial into a company PBX over a toll-free DISA line, and gain access to the company's long-distance service. Breaking into a PBX over DISA lines is one technique hackers use to commit toll fraud.

Direct Station Selector (DSS)—A DSS is a PBX auxiliary device that allows an operator to call an extension by merely touching a button. The operator can quickly observe an extension's status by looking at the state of the extension's indicator.

duplex—Duplex refers to the process of transmitting data in two directions simultaneously. This is also referred to as duplex transmission or full-duplex.

end office—An end office is a telephone company facility where local loops are terminated. The function of an end office is to connect individual telephones through a series of switches. End offices are tied together in a hierarchy for efficiency in switching. Other terms for end office are local exchange, wiring center, CO, and public exchange.

extension—Voice terminals connected to a PBX/switch by means of telephone lines are referred to as extensions. The term also defines the three-, four-, or five-digit numbers used to identify the voice terminal to the PBX/switch software for call routing purposes.

Federal Communications Commission (FCC)—The FCC is an independent U.S. government agency that was established by the Communications Act of 1934, and is directly responsible to Congress. The FCC is charged with regulating interstate and international communications carried by radio, television, wire, satellite, and cable. The FCC's jurisdiction covers the 50 states, the District of Columbia, and United States' possessions.

foreign exchange (FX)—An FX is a trunk service that lets businesses in one city operate in another city by allowing customers to call a local number. The number is connected, by means of a private line, to a telephone number in a distant city.

gate—A gate is a digital device designed to generate a binary output, that is a 1 or a 0, based on the state of one or more digital inputs.

guardband—A guardband is a band of unused frequencies that prevents overlap between adjacent transmissions. For example, the frequency bands assigned to two adjacent radio stations are separated by a transmission-free guardband.

half-duplex—Half-duplex transmission refers to the process of transmitting data in both directions, but not simultaneously.

hertz—One hertz is one cycle of a sine wave (electrical wave) in one second. One million hertz (megahertz) (1 MHz) is 1 million cycles per second.

hunt group—A group of trunks/agents selected to work together to provide specific routing of special-purpose calls is referred to as a hunt group.

Hypertext Markup Language (HTML)—HTML is a text-based language used to generically format text for Web pages. HTML tags different parts of a document in terms of their function rather than their appearance. A Web browser reads an HTML document and displays it as indicated by the HTML formatting tags and the browser's default settings.

incumbent local exchange carrier (ILEC)—An ILEC is the same as a LEC or RBOC.

Integrated Services Digital Network (ISDN)—ISDN is a digital multiplexing technology that can transmit voice, data, and other forms of communication simultaneously over a single local loop. ISDN-BRI provides two "bearer" channels (B channels) of 64 Kbps each, plus one control channel (D channel) of 16 Kbps. ISDN-PRI is also called "T1 service." It offers 23 B channels of 64 Kbps each, plus 1 D channel of 64 Kbps.

Interactive Voice Response (IVR) unit—See Voice Response Unit (VRU).

interexchange carrier (IXC)—An IXC is a long-distance company, such as AT&T or MCI, that provides telephone and data services between LATAs.

International Standards Organization (ISO)—ISO is a voluntary organization, chartered by the United Nations, that defines international standards for all fields other than electricity and electronics, which are handled by IEC.

International Telecommunication Union (ITU)—ITU is an international telecommunications standards-setting body based in Geneva, Switzerland. ITU is the United Nations agency responsible for adopting international treaties, regulations, and standards governing telecommunications.

leased line—Because of the noise associated with early analog telephone lines, it became common practice for telephone companies to "lease" lines to companies for continuous, unswitched use. These leased lines are also referred to as dedicated circuits or nailed lines.

least-cost routing—In data networks, least-cost routing describes the methods routers use to determine the lowest cost link between networks. Least-cost routing makes these determinations based on cost factors, such as bandwidth, delay, and cash costs.

local access and transport area (LATA)—LATAs are the geographic calling areas within which an RBOC may provide local and long-distance services. LATA boundaries, for the most part, fall within states and do not cross state lines, although, one state may have several LATAs.

local exchange carrier (LEC)—A LEC is a company that makes telephone connections to subscribers' homes and businesses, provides telephone services, and collects fees for those services. The terms LEC, ILEC, and RBOC are equivalent.

local loop—A local loop or subscriber line loop is the wiring that extends from a home or business to the CO. It is also referred to as the "last mile."

Local Number Portability (LNP)—LNP is an SS7 service, mandated by the Telecommunications Act of 1996, that allows a subscriber to change service providers while maintaining the same telephone number. LNP assigns each telephone number a network address, and network devices work together to quickly locate the destination, regardless of the carrier on which the address resides.

meet-me conference—A meet-me conference is a calling arrangement where conference members dial a specified number and enter a security access code, allowing them access to the conference.

modem—Short for modulator/demodulator, a modem is used to convert binary data into analog signals suitable for transmission across a telephone network.

multiplexer (MUX)—A MUX is computer equipment that allows multiple signals to travel over the same physical media.

packet switching—Packet switching is the process of sending data in packets over a network to some remote location. Frame relay and X.25 are examples of packet-switching networks.

pair gain—Pair gain is the multiplexing of a given number of telephone conversations over a lesser number of physical telephone lines. Lucent Technologies' SLC is one example of pair gain technology, where devices on each end of a line use multiplexing techniques to combine up to 96 analog local loops onto two wire pairs.

point of presence (POP)—A POP is the physical transfer point between two networks. In most cases, the POP is a CO switch located in the same building as the LEC CO; however, it also refers to an ISP's Internet access node for a city or area code.

port—There are two primary ways the term "port" is used in networking. Port can refer to a physical port in a device, such as a port on a switch or MUX. Port can also refer to a software port, a number typically used to identify a software process within a computer.

private branch exchange (PBX)—A PBX is a device that connects telephone users of a private network, such as a business, to outside lines available from a telephone company. Today's PBXs are fully digital, not only offering very sophisticated voice services, such as voice messaging, but also integrating voice and data.

Pulse Code Modulation (PCM)—PCM is a method of converting an analog voice signal to a digital signal that can be translated accurately back into a voice signal after transmission. A codec samples the voice signal 8,000 times per second, then converts each sample to a binary number that expresses the amplitude and frequency of the sample in a very compact form. These binary numbers are then transmitted to the destination. The receiving codec reverses the process, using the stream of binary numbers to re-create the original analog wave form of the voice.

queue—A queue is a collection point where calls are held until an agent or attendant can answer them. Calls are ordered as they arrive and are served in that order. Depending on the time delay in answering the call, announcements, music, or prepared messages may be employed until the call is answered.

RS-232-C—Also known as RS-232 and EIA/TIA-232-E, the RS-232-C specification details the electrical, functional, and mechanical interface between computers, terminals, and modems. The standard defines what the interface does, circuit functions, and their corresponding connector pin assignments.

signaling—Signaling is the method a telephone system uses to represent the status of a call. Signaling sets up and breaks down calls, and also represents call progression through the various switching offices and PBXs involved in the call's handling.

simplex—Simplex transmission refers to the process of transmitting data in only one direction.

slamming—Slamming is the illegal practice of switching a customer's long-distance service from one IXC to another, without the customer's knowledge or permission.

Station Message Desk Interface (SMDI)—SMDI is an integration protocol controlling integration information exchange over a serial interface. SMDI is typically used by CO switches.

Station Message Detail Reporter (SMDR)—Also known as Station Message Detail Recording, SMDR is a recording of all calls received or generated by a telephone switching system.

stutter tone—Stutter tone, also known as stutter dial tone, is a broken-up dial tone sent by a PBX or CO to indicate to a user that he or she has a voice mail message waiting to be heard. This is commonly used on telephones not equipped with a message waiting indicator.

Subscriber Line Carrier (SLC)—Lucent Technologies' SLC is a method of using T1 multiplexing technology to carry more lines over existing wires. See pair gain.

Systems Network Architecture (SNA)—SNA is IBM's architecture for computer networking. SNA was designed for transaction processing in mission-critical applications. SNA networks usually involve a large number of terminals communicating with a mainframe.

T1—In 1962, the Bell System installed the first "T-carrier" system for multiplexing digitized voice signals. The T-carrier family of systems, which now includes T1, T1C, T1D, T2, T3, and T4 (and their European counterparts E1, E2, etc.), replaced FDM systems, providing much better transmission quality.

tariff—Tariffs are documents filed by regulated telecommunications companies in accordance with FCC requirements. A tariff details the services, equipment, and pricing offered by a common carrier to all potential customers. A tariff is a public document, accessible by all.

telephony—Telephony refers to the transmission of voice signals over a distance (for example, using telephone equipment such as switches, telephones, and transmission media).

time-division multiplexing (TDM)—TDM is a multiplexing technology that transmits multiple signals over the same transmission link, by guaranteeing each signal a fixed time slot to use the transmission medium.

trunk—Trunk lines are the physical connections between the end offices of a telephone network.

uninterruptible power supply (UPS)—UPS is an emergency backup power source that instantly takes over when the regular electrical power fails.

Voice Response Unit (VRU)—Also known as an IVR unit, a VRU is an interface technology that allows outside callers to control a computer application and input information using their telephone keypads. All VRUs can speak back the results of the computer application, and some can also be programmed to fax back the results.

wavelength-division multiplexing (WDM)—WDM uses multiple light wavelengths to transmit signals over a single optical fiber. Each wavelength, or channel, carries a stream of data at rates as high as 2.5 Gbps and higher.

X.25—X.25 has been a long-time standard for packet switching. The X.25 interface lies at OSI Layer 3, rather than Layer 1. X.25 defines a protocol stack as having three layers.

X.400—X.400 is an ISO and ITU standard for addressing and transporting e-mail messages. It conforms to Layer 7 of the OSI model and supports several types of transport mechanisms, including Ethernet, X.25, TCP/IP, and dial-up lines.

Lesson 1—Classification of Networks

There are four classifications of computer networks. The classifications are designated by the distance the networks extend and type of facilities used to connect nodes and networks. This lesson looks at the four primary classifications of networks: local area networks (LANs), campus networks, metropolitan area networks (MANs), and WANs.

Objectives

At the end of this lesson you will be able to:

*   List the four terms commonly used to classify computer networks

*   Describe the differences between the different types of networks

 **Key Point**

LANs are connected over long distances with WAN technologies and services.

LANs

LANs range in size and number of connected computers; however, they typically consist of computers housed in a single building. A LAN can consist of a few nodes or up to several hundred nodes, or segments linked together in certain ways to form a larger, but still local, network. A segment is a portion of a network in which all nodes are directly connected. For example, all nodes may be connected by one piece of wire or, as shown on the LAN Diagram, connected to a central hub.

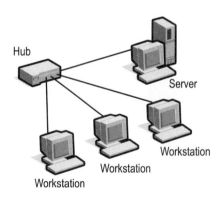

LAN

Campus Networks

When an organization includes computers connected across multiple buildings, the entire collection of computers is often referred to as a campus network. Therefore, a campus network consists of several LANs tied together in some way to form a larger campus network.

Campus networks are built by connecting LANs to other LANs within an organization's networking infrastructure. In other words, networking equipment used to connect LANs to form a campus network is owned and operated by the people within the organization. When all of the networking equipment belongs to the individual organization, the equipment is referred to as a private facility. The Campus Network Diagram illustrates a typical campus network.

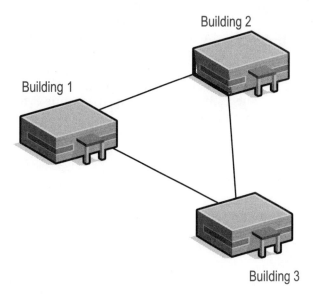

Campus Network

MANs

MANs continue to evolve and will be developed primarily by data carriers (telephone companies) in response to the demand to interconnect LANs across a metropolitan area. For example, a business might interconnect several offices over a citywide area using a service provided by the local telephone company.

One of the primary differences between a MAN and a campus network is that a campus network uses private facilities for interconnecting individual LANs, and a MAN uses public facilities for interconnecting individual LANs.

WANs

Still larger networks are formed by connecting LANs across a region or the world. These are referred to as WANs. To connect LANs across multiple cities, both local and long-distance public facilities are typically used. The WAN Diagram illustrates a typical WAN across multiple cities. Within each city, there may be LAN, campus, and MAN connectivity. The WAN portions of a network are the connections that provide communication between cities. Information travels across the WAN portion of a network only when the information is destined for another computer in another city.

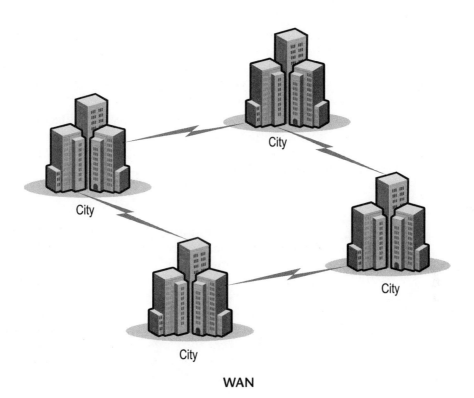

WAN

The WAN is often the most scrutinized part of a network, because it is typically the most expensive component. As with many aspects of networking, the faster the service, the more expensive. This is normally the case with WANs. With an increase in speed of a WAN circuit, the cost of the circuit increases as well. As we will see, there are many different options for connecting LANs to LANs using various WAN circuits and services.

Activities

1. A group of computers in the south side of a city are connected to another group of computers downtown. What type of network is this?

    a. WAN

    b. MAN

    c. LAN

    d. Campus network

2. A group of computers are connected in a multistory building. What type of network is this?

    a. WAN

    b. MAN

    c. LAN

    d. Campus network

3. A group of computers in Denver are connected to another group of computers in San Francisco. What type of network is this?

    a. WAN

    b. MAN

    c. LAN

    d. None of the above

4. Describe how a company might grow and require the four different types of networks described in this lesson.

    _____

    _____

    _____

    _____

    _____

    _____

5. Discuss the primary differences between the types of networks described in this lesson. Describe the type of network used at your organization.

_____

_____

_____

_____

_____

_____

Extended Activities

1. Determine the type, speeds, and topology of the LAN your school or organization is currently using. If possible, obtain a topology map.

_____

_____

2. What type of WAN service does your school or organization use?

_____

_____

3. What technology connects your organization's LANs? Does this connectivity use copper or fiber optic cabling? Does your organization own and maintain these connections, or are they owned and maintained by a service provider or vendor?

_____

_____

_____

4. Determine the MAN services available in your area. These can be found by using the Internet or a telephone book.

   _____

   _____

   _____

5. Determine the WAN services available in your area. These can be found by using the Internet or a telephone book.

   _____

   _____

   _____

Lesson 2—Telecommunications

The term "telecommunications" refers to "communication over a distance." This term was first used in reference to communicating a voice signal (conversation) over copper wires. The network originally designed to carry voice signals between two telephones is now used for a wide variety of purposes. This lesson looks at the development of the telecommunications network and some of the purposes it now serves.

Objectives

At the end of this lesson you will be able to:

- Describe the development of the telecommunications network
- Explain basic uses of the telecommunications network

 **Key Point**

The telecommunications network carries more than just conversations.

Development of the Telecommunications Network

Considered from the broadest perspective, there are four parts to the development of today's telecommunications network:

- Development of analog voice networks during a 75-year period beginning in the late nineteenth century
- Adaptation of analog voice networks to the transmission of digital data between computers
- Conversion of analog voice networks to digital voice transmission technology beginning in the 1960s
- Adaptation of digital voice networks to data communication, beginning in the early 1980s with the use of T1 for data and continuing today, with technologies such as Integrated Services Digital Network (ISDN) and Asynchronous Transfer Mode (ATM)

In 1874, Alexander Graham Bell determined that sound could be transmitted over a wire, by electricity, through variation of the intensity of an electrical current. This electrical current corresponded to variations in air density produced by sound from the human voice. Mr. Bell filed for a patent for the invention of the telephone on February 14, 1876. On March 10, 1876, he sent the first sentence ever transmitted by electricity over wires.

The telephone was of little use without some means of changing connections on an as-needed basis. In 1878 in New Haven, Connecticut, the first switching office was established. This was a precursor to all the offices that became known as central offices (COs), as shown on the CO Diagram. CO switches provide any-to-any connectivity between telephone service subscribers.

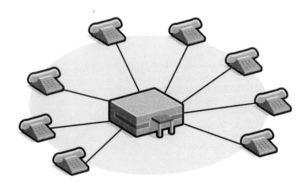

CO

Until the second half of the twentieth century, the telecommunications network was used exclusively for transmitting analog voice signals. With the advent of computers and voice digitization (discussed later), the telecommunications network began a migration from a strict analog network to a digital network. Today's telecommunications infrastructure is based on the transfer of digital information, whether the information is a digital representation of a voice signal or other types of information, such as computer data.

More Than Just Words

Today, communications systems that send voice, data, and video signals span the earth. Information is bounced off satellites and directed through cables that cross entire oceans. Computer-based systems operate in the dead of night, receiving messages from places where it is high noon. The network once used to carry voice conversations only, has become the infrastructure for many types of communication. Use of this network will continue to increase, and the services offered across it will continue to grow.

Activities

1. What types of information are carried over the telecommunications network?

    _____

    _____

    _____

    _____

2. In your opinion, how has the content of the information transferred over the telecommunications network changed over the past few years?

    _____

    _____

    _____

    _____

3. If voice communication (for example, telephone technology) did not exist, how would this impact your life?

    _____

    _____

    _____

    _____

4. Describe the development of the telecommunications network.

    _____

    _____

    _____

    _____

Extended Activities

1. Using the World Wide Web (Web), research the invention of the telephone and early developments of the telephone industry. Report your findings.

    _____

    _____

    _____

    _____

    _____

    _____

2. Research communication services available in your area that make use of the existing copper cable to your home or business. How have telecommunication service providers added high-bandwidth services to an infrastructure designed to only carry limited bandwidth analog voice signals?

    _____

    _____

    _____

    _____

    _____

    _____

Lesson 3—Voice Networks

The early telecommunications network was used to transfer voice calls only. It was entirely analog. Today's networks are primarily digital and carry all types of information for both home and business use. This lesson focuses on the analog voice network and associated technologies.

Objectives

At the end of this lesson you will be able to:

- Describe the basic use of the telecommunications network
- Explain the terms CO, local loop, and analog signaling
- Describe the purpose of a trunk line

 **Key Point**

Early voice networks were based on analog signaling.

Connectivity of the Analog Network

In the early days of telecommunications, voices were transmitted as a continuously varying electrical signal across a pair of wires (local loop or subscriber line loop) between the handset of a subscriber (telephone user) and a CO. The Analog Voice Circuits Diagram presents a typical analog circuit. Before digital dialing, COs had names such as Prospect or Elgin, and telephone numbers began with an abbreviation of the CO name (for example, PR6-6178 or EL3-1978).

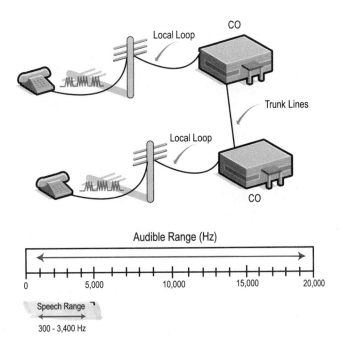

Audible Range (Hz)

Speech Range
300 - 3,400 Hz

Analog Voice Circuits

Speech Range

The frequency of the electrical signal varied from approximately 300 to 3,400 hertz (Hz) (cycles per second). Although humans can hear frequencies from approximately 20 to 20,000 Hz, most speech energy is concentrated in the range of 300 to 3,400 Hz. To ensure a quality circuit for voice signals, filters were placed on the lines to filter out frequencies above 4,000 Hz.

Early telephone COs performed switching with human operators, and in the 1930s, switching became automated. Before digital dialing, electromechanical rotary switches and crossbar switches connected subscriber lines. Telephones had rotary dials that generated electrical pulses for each digit dialed (1 pulse for "1," 2 pulses for "2," and so on through 10 pulses for "0"). The pulses "stepped" the switches to make the interconnection.

Trunk lines connected COs. As the number of COs grew, it quickly became necessary to organize the telephone system into a hierarchy. Too many trunk lines would have been required to interconnect all COs in even one metropolitan area, let alone the whole country. (Over 20,000 COs are in use today.) By connecting each CO to a toll center, and connecting toll centers with trunk lines, far fewer trunks were required, yet any subscriber could reach any other subscriber in the area. Over time, a hierarchy was developed to interconnect all COs in the United States.

Reduction of Trunk Lines

The number of trunk lines required to interconnect all COs in an area in a full "mesh" network rises geometrically, such that for even a small number of offices, many lines are required. Because the use of trunks between COs remote from one another is naturally relatively low, COs are also interconnected in a star to a toll center. This hierarchy was extended to four higher levels. The AT&T (United States) and International Telecommunication Union-Telecommunications Standardization Sector (ITU-T) (international) standard symbols and nomenclature are shown on the CO Hierarchy Diagram.

office of Last Resort

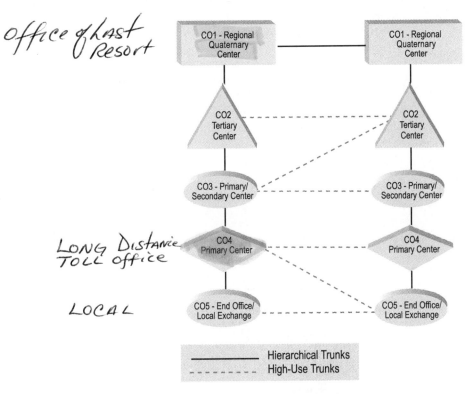

LONG DISTANCE TOLL office

LOCAL

CO Hierarchy

Although every center is connected to the next highest center, there is often a great deal of traffic between two centers (for example, two COs adjacent geographically). High-use trunks are installed to handle this traffic, rather than routing it through the hierarchy. These are shown as dashed lines on the diagram.

Activities

1. What is another name for the local loop? Can you think of any service that uses this term?

   _____

   _____

   _____

   _____

2. Why was it necessary to build a CO hierarchy?

   _____

   _____

   _____

   _____

3. Why is it hard to hear high-fidelity music over a telephone?

   _____

   _____

   _____

   _____

4. Describe the purpose of a trunk line and the role it plays in the CO hierarchy.

   _____

   _____

   _____

   _____

Extended Activities

1. Research and discuss how many types of telephone offices there are in the country. Where are the regional centers located?

   _____

   _____

   _____

   _____

2. If possible, tour a telephone company to learn how telephone switching occurs. If a visit is not possible, research the CO hierarchy for your local area. How many COs are there in your area, and how many sets of prefixes do they each service?

   _____

   _____

   _____

   _____

Lesson 4—Voice Network Technology

As the telecommunications network grew, methods of communication developed that increased the efficiency and decreased the cost of the physical circuitry. Two technologies are important for analog voice networks: duplexing and frequency-division multiplexing (FDM).

Objectives

At the end of this lesson you will be able to:

- Describe the basic operation of a frequency-division multiplexer (MUX)

- Explain the purpose of a trunk line

 **Key Point**

MUXs are used to combine multiple voice conversations.

Analog Technology

Because data communication takes place largely over the public telecommunications network, it is important to understand how these networks operate, not only for data communication but also for voice communication. The networks were designed for voice communication, not data communication, which affects their use for data. In any event, voice, data, and other media types will increasingly be transmitted on integrated facilities, such as ISDN.

Although analog technology is infrequently used for voice communication over trunks, an understanding of this technology is necessary as background information. In addition, some analog technology, such as FDM, is used elsewhere. For example, a type of FDM is used in modems.

In an analog network, the most basic telephone circuit consists of two wires, as presented on the Analog Diagram. This is the principle on which your home telephone circuit typically works.

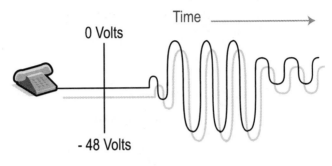

Analog

Voices are transmitted in both directions (simultaneously, if both parties spoke at the same time) by placing a -48-volt (V) potential on the circuit, and using the sound energy of the speaker's voice against the microphone to vary the current. The result is a pulsating direct current (DC) electrical current modulated within the range of frequencies necessary to reproduce human speech.

As mentioned earlier, the range was eventually standardized at 300 to 3,400 Hz. The amplitude of the pulsating current varies according to the loudness of the sound. For example, if we were to use a musical instrument to sound a continuous note at 500 Hz into the mouthpiece of a handset, a 500-Hz signal would be transmitted across the pair of wires. Its amplitude would vary between 0 and -48 V, with an average amplitude that depends on the loudness of the tone.

Voice is
DC - 48

Early Telephones

Early telephone systems connected each subscriber by means of a central switching office, where an operator provided manual switching between subscribers. The wire connecting a subscriber to the CO is referred to as a local loop. Because a major cost of a telephone system was the wire connecting the subscriber to the CO, COs covered relatively small geographic areas and were interconnected by "trunk" lines that could be shared by all subscribers, as illustrated on the Local Exchanges Diagram.

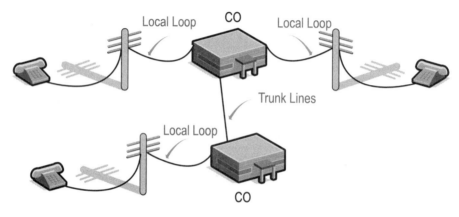

Local Exchanges

FDM

Long-distance trunk lines were expensive to build, yet even the simple copper wires used for the first long-distance lines were capable of carrying an electrical signal with a much wider bandwidth than was required for voice transmission. FDM was developed to allow a trunk line with only two pairs of wires to carry many voice conversations simultaneously. Because of limitations in the technology first developed for FDM, a voice channel was standardized at 4,000 Hz of bandwidth. An additional 600 Hz, between 3,400 and 4,000 Hz, were necessary to separate the channels on a multiplexed line, so one channel would not interfere with the next. This vacant frequency band is also known as a guardband.

FDM was developed to allow several voice signals to be transmitted (multiplexed) simultaneously over a single trunk, as presented on the Channel Bank Diagram. Although the operation of FDM is too detailed for a full explanation here, the basic principles are presented.

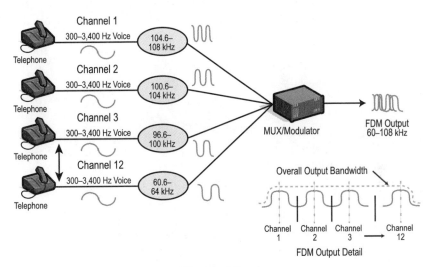

Channel Bank

Assume we want to multiplex 12 voice conversations, and the trunk onto which we want to multiplex the conversations is capable of carrying signals with frequencies between 60 and 108 kilohertz (kHz).

Devices that perform multiplexing for FDM transmission are called "channel banks." Similar devices for multiplexing digitized voice signals are also called channel banks. An overview of how analog channel banks multiplex voice signals with FDM is presented here.

A channel bank generates 12 carrier signals. Each carrier is a steady signal of a certain frequency. By convention, channel 1 is assigned the highest frequency band, 108 kHz. Channel 2 is 104 kHz, and so on, to channel 12, which is 64 kHz.

A channel bank mixes a voice signal for each channel with the carrier signal for that channel. The Channel Bank Diagram illustrates this process. The process translates the signal from one that varies from 0 to 4 kHz, into one that varies between the carrier frequency and the carrier frequency minus 4 kHz. For example, the signal for channel 12 varies between 64 kHz (assigned frequency) and 60 kHz (64 kHz minus 4 kHz). Or, if we do not include the guardband, it varies between 64 kHz and 60.6 kHz (64 kHz minus 3.4 kHz).

Finally, before transmission, the channel bank modulates the 12 output signals from the mixers simultaneously onto the output line. This is possible because each signal is confined to its own band. The frequency of the signal on the trunk then varies from 60 to 108 kHz (lowest frequency in channel 12 to the highest frequency in channel 1).

At the receiving end, the equipment demultiplexes the signal by using 12 filters. A type of electronic filter device, called a "band-pass filter," passes only signals of a certain range of frequencies. In this case, each filter passes signals that fall within the bandwidth for its channel. For example, the channel 12 filter passes only signals that fall within the 60 to 64 kHz range. Therefore, the output of a filter is a signal with frequencies only in its range.

The signal is then demodulated to produce the original voice signal. This is the reverse of the mixing process. For example, for channel 12, 60 kHz is subtracted from a signal that varies from 60 to 64 kHz to produce the original voice signal—0 to 4 kHz.

Duplexing

Although two-wire transmission is satisfactory for the relatively short distances, typical of local loops, problems occur over longer distances because of the need to transmit signals in both directions. Signals must be amplified, and amplification is much simpler if signals are transmitted in only one direction. For this and other reasons, trunk circuits are duplexed; that is, two pairs of wires (four wires) are used. Each pair transmits in one direction only; however, transmission can take place in both directions simultaneously. This process is shown on the Full Duplex Diagram.

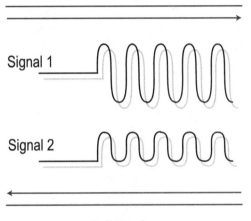

Full Duplex

A half-duplex circuit is one that provides transmission in two directions, but only in one direction at a time. A full-duplex circuit is one that provides transmission in both directions simultaneously. An end-to-end, four-wire circuit provides full-duplex capabilities. However, two-wire circuits can also be used for full-duplex communication by partitioning the available bandwidth into separate frequency bands for each direction of transmission (derived four wire). This technique is often used when a full-duplex data communication circuit is desired over dial-up (two-wire) facilities. On the other hand, the existence of four-wire circuits does not necessarily imply that full-duplex transmission can be achieved through simultaneous use of both pairs.

PBXs

When a large company or other organization had many telephones installed, it became desirable for a variety of reasons to locate a branch of an exchange at the site. These private branch exchanges (PBXs) were leased from the telephone company, in the days before deregulation, and were extensions of the same technology used in end offices. With a PBX, callers from outside could dial a single number to reach the organization, and their call would be switched by an operator to the appropriate individual. The PBX Diagram illustrates a PBX. A PBX can switch internal calls without going through the CO. When a telephone call is placed that is destined for another facility, a PBX routes the call to the local exchange. Your school or office uses a PBX to switch calls internally and route calls to outside facilities. Voice mail systems are typically part of a PBX.

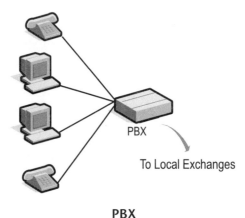

PBX

Activities

1. Full-duplex operation always requires the use of four wires. True or False

2. How does multiplexing reduce the number of physical wires in a network?

   _____

   _____

   _____

   _____

3. How does multiplexing reduce the cost of building telecommunications networks?

   _____

   _____

   _____

   _____

4. What is the purpose of a guardband?

   _____

   _____

   _____

5. Briefly describe the function of a channel bank.

   _____

   _____

   _____

   _____

6. How is a PBX related to the switching operation that occurs in a CO?

   _____

   _____

   _____

Extended Activities

1. Using the Web, determine the frequency range of each of the following frequency bands:

    a. Extremely low frequency (ELF)

    _____

    b. Infralow frequency (ILF)

    _____

    c. Very low frequency (VLF)

    _____

    d. Low frequency (LF)

    _____

    e. Medium frequency (MF)

    _____

    f. High frequency (HF)

    _____

    g. Very high frequency (VHF)

    _____

    h. Ultra high frequency (UHF)

    _____

    i. Super high frequency (SHF)

    _____

    j. Extremely high frequency (EHF)

    _____

    k. Tremendously high frequency (THF)

    _____

2. Using the Web, find out where the frequency ranges are used in communications.

_____

_____

_____

_____

_____

3. List the channel frequency ranges of a 12-channel, 108-kHz bandwidth FDM channel bank. Assume that each channel occupies 4 kHz with a guardband of 600 Hz per channel, and that the guardband resides at the bottom of the channel frequency range.

_____

_____

Lesson 5—PBX Fundamentals

PBXs are telephone switches that are, in many respects, similar to CO switches. A PBX controls access to outside lines. However, a PBX makes the connections invisible to the user. In other words, a user must specifically select an outside line by pushing a button; a PBX user simply dials an outside call and the PBX system handles the details of connecting to an outside line.

Like CO switches, PBXs are powerful, computerized systems that offer a wide range of sophisticated features. A PBX usually becomes cost-effective when a business grows to 20 to 50 lines. PBX systems are an economic necessity for businesses with thousands of lines in a campus environment.

Objectives

At the end of this lesson you will be able to:

- Describe the main components of a PBX

- Explain how a call is made through a PBX

- Define Direct Inward Dialing (DID)

- Name and briefly describe key PBX functions

- Name and briefly describe common auxiliary PBX equipment

Key Point

PBX systems are similar to CO switches.

PBX Components

Significant differences exist among the features in PBX products, and in the way the features are packaged and sold. However, the general structure of most PBXs is similar, and includes the following major components, shown on the PBX Components Diagram:

- Trunks to connect the PBX to the telephone company

- Extension lines to connect the PBX to internal telephones

- Equipment cabinet: main processor, trunk cards, and line cards
- Telephones and attendant console
- Administrative terminal

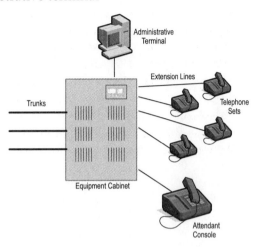

PBX Components

Trunks

The connections between a PBX and CO switch are called "trunks." Trunks are usually large-capacity connections, such as T1 or ISDN. (We will explain both of these in later units.) Each trunk can be configured for incoming calls, outgoing calls, or two-way calling.

Like any electronic system, a PBX requires a constant power source. If the system is not equipped with a backup power supply, certain trunks can be designated as Power Failure Transfer (PFT) trunks. If the power fails, these trunks are switched to standard, single-line telephones that draw their power from the telephone lines themselves (from the CO) and not from the PBX. This allows the business to continue answering incoming calls until power is restored.

Businesses configure their trunks depending on their telephone systems, business needs, and employee calling patterns. For example, a customer service center needs a higher number of incoming trunks, while a telemarketing business needs more outgoing trunks.

PBXs can connect to three types of external networks: local, interexchange, and private. In addition, many systems support special services, such as T1 lines and foreign exchange (FX) trunks to local calling areas in distant cities. The variety of interface circuits is a key distinguishing feature among PBX products and different generations of products.

A special system, called a "Subscriber Line Carrier (SLC) circuit," can reduce the number of physical wire pairs necessary to provide multiple trunks to a business. SLC uses multiplexing to allow one pair of wires to carry multiple call paths. SLC can provide from 2 to 96 separate trunks over a single physical connection. Because this approach effectively creates more connections, it is commonly referred to as "pair-gain" technology.

Extension Lines

The connections from individual telephone sets to the PBX are called "lines," or "extension lines." Each line is formed by a twisted pair of copper wire, and is assigned a telephone extension number by the PBX administrator.

A typical arrangement is to have more telephone extensions than trunks. However, the proportion of lines to trunks varies according to the needs of the business. Many customers configure their systems with 1 trunk for every 10 telephones, while businesses with heavy outside calling requirements may have 1 trunk for every 5 users or less. In general, however, most businesses need proportionally fewer outside trunks as the number of internal extensions grows.

Equipment Cabinet

The equipment cabinet, which is a large metal box in the main equipment room, is the heart of the PBX. It contains the computerized processors that perform telephone switching and other advanced features. The cabinet usually also contains the power supply, which converts 120-V alternating current (AC) (standard "household" electricity) into the low-voltage DC electrical current necessary to run the telephone system.

Much of the cabinet's circuitry is contained on electronic circuit cards that slide into slots and plug into a main processor board. Some of these cards allow the attachment of specialized accessory equipment. However, most of them are one of two main types:

- Trunk cards contain the circuitry necessary to communicate with the CO switch. Each trunk connects to a trunk card.

- Station cards contain the circuitry necessary to communicate with internal telephone extensions. Each line connects to a station card.

Trunks plug into one side of the equipment cabinet, attached to trunk cards. Lines plug into the other side, attached to station cards. The main processor board of the PBX makes connections between lines and trunks, and between lines. The portion of the processor that performs call switching is called the "switching fabric."

Older PBXs are analog systems; most of today's PBXs are digital switches that use Pulse Code Modulation (PCM) and time-division multiplexing (TDM) to switch voice calls within the switching fabric. Whether a PBX is analog or digital has significant implications for the connection between the customer's PBX and the CO, because a digital PBX requires digital transmission service, such as ISDN or T1.

Telephones and Attendant Console

Telephone sets are designed to work with a particular PBX system; they will not work when plugged into a "regular" telephone line. Each PBX telephone set includes programmable features that can be enabled or disabled by the company's telephone system administrator.

The attendant console, used by the office receptionist or a dedicated PBX operator, is essentially a larger telephone set. This console contains features and controls that perform the specialized operator-assisted functions we will discuss later.

Administrative Terminal

A computer workstation provides administrative access to the PBX system. The company's telephone administrator uses the system to configure the wide range of features and options available.

Making a Call on a PBX

Making a telephone call within a PBX environment is very similar to making a call from home using the public telephone network.

When you lift the receiver, placing the telephone in the off-hook position, the telephone signals the PBX that it needs a connection. The PBX then sends a dial tone to the extension telephone, and waits for incoming touchtones.

To call another extension within the same PBX system, the caller enters the digits of the extension number. When the PBX detects the tone that represents the first digit, it removes the dial tone from the line. When the complete extension number has been entered, the PBX sends a ringing signal to the called extension, and connects the two extensions when the called party answers.

To make an "outside" call, the caller must first signal the PBX, usually by dialing 9. This special number tells the PBX to seize an available outgoing trunk for the call. The PBX then signals the telephone company's CO switch to send a dial tone. The second dial tone confirms that the caller is now connected, through the PBX, to the public telephone network. The caller then enters the destination telephone number.

Call Routing

The primary function of a PBX is to provide internal access to telecommunications trunks provided by a telephone company. A PBX can also provide access to other PBXs, such as other company locations, by means of dedicated tie lines.

If necessary, a PBX can queue or hold calls until a trunk becomes available. PBXs can also provide custom routing options for each call, based on the called party number, caller's location, and other parameters. In other words, the PBX reviews these factors and decides whether to route the call over the internal network, a discount long-distance provider, or a specialized data service.

A feature called "Automatic Route Selection (ARS)" allows the telecommunications manager to program different trunks for use based on time of day, type of call, or any number of other factors. ARS is becoming increasingly important as more customers send voice calls by means of the Internet or public data networks.

Supplementary PBX Features

In addition to its core system features, a PBX can provide many supplementary services:

- Call hold—Callers can be placed on hold, or in parking orbits, where the call is left until the called party retrieves it by means of an access code.

- Music on hold—While callers are waiting, they can hear music or messages about new products and services. Tech-Data, a national computer distributor, even sells on-hold time to companies in the form of advertising.

- Hunting—Incoming calls can be routed to other extensions or lines if the first destination is busy. Hunting is commonly used in customer service centers and Help desks to distribute incoming calls among a group of representatives (called a "hunt group").

- Call restrictions or "class of restriction (CoR)"—A PBX can be programmed to restrict calls in various ways. This is usually done to prevent an extension, such as a lobby courtesy telephone, from making long-distance calls. You can program a PBX extension down to the smallest detail, even restricting access to specific numbers.

- Call tracking—By requiring callers to enter a numeric code, many aspects of a call can be tracked. For example, law firms use this feature to track the duration of calls attorneys make on behalf of their clients (for later billing).

DID

DID connects incoming callers directly to the employees they need to talk with. DID is an effective means of increasing customer contact while reducing the load on PBX operators.

In a traditional PBX, the console operator(s) or automated attendant must answer all incoming calls and connect them to destination extensions. However, with a PBX equipped for DID, coupled with DID service from the telephone company, incoming calls can be directly routed to individual extensions or departments served by the PBX.

DISA

A company can significantly reduce its telephone expenses by selecting the right long-distance carrier. However, it is often difficult for outside employees, such as salespeople or field service representatives, to access the low-priced carrier for work-related calls.

Direct Inward System Access (DISA) allows an outside caller to dial directly into the PBX system, then access the system's features and facilities remotely. DISA is typically used to allow employees to make long-distance calls from home or any remote area, using the company's less expensive long-distance service. To use DISA, an employee calls a special access number (usually toll-free), then enters a short password code.

Although DISA is a great convenience to remote employees, unauthorized people often acquire the toll-free access number and use it to steal long-distance telephone service. Changing the password codes from time to time can help prevent this. Still, it is best if the telephone administrator restricts DISA to only those employees who require it, and regularly checks the PBX call records to detect any unusual patterns.

Station Set Features

A PBX telephone set includes a large selection of features. Like programming a CO switch, programming the lines and features on each telephone set can be a complicated task.

There are literally hundreds of features in most PBX systems; however, most users cannot remember how to use more than two or three of the most common ones. Traditionally, a user must briefly press the telephone switchhook to access the set's features.

However, to make these features easier for users to understand and remember, many telephone sets now include special function keys to access popular functions such as:

- Call forwarding—An extension can be programmed to send incoming calls to another extension.

- Call transfer—After answering a call, an employee can transfer it to another extension.

- Speaker paging—By using an access code, employees can broadcast announcements from a telephone extension. Paging is commonly used in medical centers, manufacturing locations, and retail stores.

- Speed dialing—Commonly used telephone numbers can be programmed as abbreviated two- or three-digit access codes.

- Call pickup—If one person is away, any other person from the same defined workgroup (called a "pickup group") can enter an access code and answer a call that is ringing at the absent person's desk.

- Message waiting light—A light on the desk set glows when the user has voice mail. If a desk set does not have a message light, a "stutter tone" can alert the user to new voice mail. The user hears the tone when a message comes in during a call, or when the user picks up the telephone to make a call.

Stuttertone

Some PBX telephone sets, such as those for hotel/motels, include special features for their increasingly telephone/computer-intensive guests. These sets offer two lines, lots of special features, and voice mail.

Attendant Console Services

One of the most overlooked parts of a PBX system is the human operator who provides the first impression of a company to its customers. Despite their vital function, PBX operators are not often appreciated by the businesses they work for or customers they serve. Telephone operators receive obscene calls, bomb threats, and personal threats, and are generally mistreated. In addition, most operators have little or no chance for job enrichment or promotion.

However, PBX operators are often the most vital part of a company's information system; they usually know where everyone is, who has moved where, and what to do in case of an emergency.

In addition, they can provide the following key functions from the PBX operator console:

- Call processing—A PBX operator can connect incoming callers to PBX extensions.

- Company directory assistance—A PBX operator can provide extension numbers and direct-dialing numbers.

- "Meet-me" conference calls—In a meet-me conference, callers dial a predetermined telephone number and security access code, which connects them to a telephone conference call that may include up to six people. In some cases, the conference connections are made automatically; in others, the PBX operator serves as the "conference bridge," greeting incoming callers and connecting them to the conference.

- Night service—When PBX operators go home and turn off the console, incoming calls can be directed to ring throughout the building. From any extension telephone, an employee can dial an access code to answer the incoming call.

- Camp on—A PBX operator can place an incoming call on hold, waiting for a specific extension that has a call in progress. As soon as the first call is completed, the "camped-on" call rings at the extension.

Administration and Management Reports

As we have seen thus far, the PBX administrator plays a very important role, configuring the system and ensuring it is used correctly. The following management features provide detailed information on calls being processed and completed through a PBX system.

CDRs

Most telecommunications managers do not consider themselves telephone police; however, companies do consider unauthorized telephone abuse to be theft of company property. Telephone fraud represents a $1 billion loss to U.S. businesses each year.

To help a PBX administrator prevent this sort of fraud, most PBX systems have the ability to record all calls and sort them by almost any criteria, including date, time, number called, frequently called numbers, extension number, and user name. If necessary, a PBX report can identify a specific extension that called a particular number at a certain time.

Hotel/motel PBXs have the ability to print a Call Detail Report (CDR) instantly, to total the telephone-use fees that must be added to a customer's bill at check-out time. Without this instant reporting, hotels could lose thousands of dollars of revenue.

Test Reports

PBXs, like CO switches, perform a variety of internal tests. The results of these tests are presented as reports, often in Hypertext Markup Language (HTML) format for viewing with an Internet browser. These reports help the administrator monitor the general health of the system, and are useful to service technicians in case of a failure.

Busy-Hour Studies

One of the administrator's key responsibilities is to determine the number and type of trunks a business needs. Special management reports, called "busy-hour studies," provide information that helps an administrator make those decisions.

The "busy hour" is the hour during which a network or office telephone system carries its greatest traffic. For most businesses, the busy hour occurs in mid-morning, as employees organize their work for the day. The general objective of an administrator is to provide enough transmission capacity to carry busy-hour traffic.

In actual practice, it is wasteful and expensive to provide enough capacity to carry 100 percent of the busy-hour traffic. Thus, an administrator must determine how much of this peak traffic is acceptable to block. In other words, the administrator estimates the acceptable percentage of inbound callers who will receive a busy signal, and the percentage of outbound callers who must wait for a free line.

PBX Enhancements

A variety of other systems can be added to a PBX to provide specialized and enhanced services.

Voice Response

Ninety percent of all PBXs shipped today come with voice mail and voice response, also known as Interactive Voice Response (IVR) or Voice Response Unit (VRU). These systems allow callers to use the telephone touchpad to access information ranging from store locations to credit card transactions. Some banks even allow customers to pay their bills by means of IVR.

IVR is a rapidly growing field, which can reduce the staff workload and, when properly implemented, increase the level of customer service.

Voice Recognition

Voice recognition technology allows a computer to understand the human voice. This technology has been around for more than two decades, and it is just now beginning to be widely used. Computer answering services now ask you to speak your instructions, and directory assistance services ask you to speak the name and location of the number you need.

As 10-digit dialing becomes more common in large cities, voice recognition may be more accurate than button pushing for entering telephone numbers. However, one of the greatest potential applications is voice Internet access, providing access to electronic mail (e-mail) and other applications for people without personal computers (PCs).

Call Following

Users want calls to get through to them, wherever they are, whatever the time of day. As staff increasingly work remotely, calls can be forwarded to a sequence of different locations until the called party is found, as shown on the Follow-Me Call Flow Diagram.

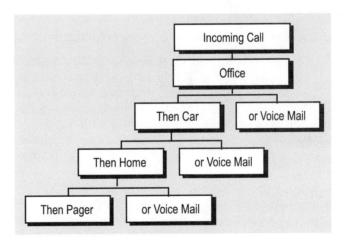

Follow-Me Call Flow

ACD

Customer service centers that receive a high volume of incoming calls use a special kind of PBX called an "Automatic Call Distributor (ACD)." ACDs route incoming calls to agents based on programmed criteria, such as the agent that has been idle the longest. If an agent is not available to take a call, the ACD holds the call in a queue and the caller hears a "please hold" message.

Other Auxiliary Equipment

Other common types of auxiliary equipment include:

- Station Message Detail Reporter (SMDR)—Creates a log of all incoming and outgoing telephone calls

- Uninterruptible power supply (UPS)—Enables a PBX to operate during a power failure

- Direct Station Selector (DSS)—Displays which stations are being used in a telephone system

- Headset—Provides hands-free telephone operation for either analog or digital telephones

PBX Costs and Requirements

In addition to the one-time installation cost, a PBX system usually incurs the following ongoing charges:

- Equipment maintenance and upgrades

- Lease or finance charges

- Trunk usage

- DID termination service charge

- DID numbers in blocks of 10, 20, or 100

- Office space, heating/cooling and electrical power

- Staff salaries and training

Activities

1. A PBX auxiliary function that provides callers the ability to access company information by means of their keypad is known as _____.

   a. IVR

   b. Voice recognition

   c. Call following

   d. ACD

2. _____ is a PBX function that routes incoming calls to agents based on programmed criteria.

   a. IVR

   b. Voice recognition

   c. Call following

   d. ACD

3. A PBX function that allows company staff to effectively work remotely by forwarding calls to them where ever they are located is known as _____.

   a. DSS

   b. Call following

   c. ACD

   d. Camp on

4. Match the PBX functions and features to its description.

ARS

Call tracking

Call forwarding

DID

Hunting

Call pickup

Music on hold

DISA

Call restrictions

   a. Callers hear music or messages while waiting for the destination extension to pick up _____

   b. Controls what types of calls may be placed from an extension _____

   c. Allows users to dial in to the PBX to access inexpensive long-distance capabilities _____

   d. Allows callers to bypass the attendant or operator and ring the destination extension directly _____

   e. A capability programmed into an extension that transfers calls made to one extension automatically to another _____

   f. A feature that allows any one of a defined workgroup of extensions to answer a call destined for any other workgroup member _____

   g. Provides the capability to record call aspects through the use of numeric codes _____

   h. Routes calls to alternate extensions if the original destination is busy _____

   i. Allows control of trunk use based on factors such as time of day or call type _____

5. Explain how a PBX processes a call.

_____

_____

_____

Extended Activities

1. Many vendors provide PBXs for small to very large companies. Some of the larger players are Avaya Communication (formerly Lucent Technologies) and Nortel. Research the products available from these companies, and compare their features and applications.

   _____

   _____

   _____

   _____

2. Another feature of PBXs, commonly used in telemarketing firms, is the autodialer. The autodialer automatically dials telephone numbers in a database, and when the called customer picks up, connects the call to the first available telemarketing representative.

   Listen carefully when the next telemarketer calls your home or business. You may hear a pause before someone answers your "hello." This is the delay between the time you answer the call and the time it takes the autodialer to connect to a representative. A properly programmed autodialer will provide no discernible pause.

   Name an autodialer you are familiar with and its features.

   _____

   _____

   _____

   _____

Lesson 6—PBX Features and Functions

A PBX can improve the operation of many businesses. However, some businesses cannot do without a PBX, because they rely on specific features of PBX systems. This lesson discusses many of the features and functions found with typical PBX systems and discusses how they are typically used.

Objectives

At the end of this lesson you will be able to:

• Describe what a call accounting system is and what it does

• List and describe the primary PBX features

• Give an example of how each PBX feature can be used in a typical business

 **Key Point**

A PBX can do almost anything a CO switch can do.

Call Accounting

Call accounting systems are also called "SMDR or CDR systems." They are computers that track individual telephone calls. Call accounting systems are often dedicated PCs connected to a PBX by means of a serial port. The PC and associated software monitor every telephone call made by means of the PBX, and store information about each call. Call accounting software is used to retrieve the information, sort it, and provide reports about an organization's calling patterns. The Call Accounting Configuration Diagram illustrates this type of system.

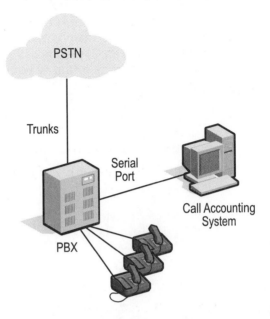

Call Accounting Configuration

Call accounting systems are used for more than simply tracking calls and producing managerial reports. They are often used to track the usage of lines and trunks for traffic engineering purposes.

Authorization Codes

Call accounting systems may also detect fraudulent use of telephone systems. If a company thinks the telephone system is being used inappropriately, authorization codes are issued to users of the system. These codes are used to create reports that detail the telephone calls for individual departments or employees. In addition, authorization codes can allocate, or "bill-back," the cost of telephone service to each department's budget.

Account Codes

bill back to customer

Call accounting reports are essential to some types of businesses. For example, law and accounting firms use detail reports to bill clients for telephone time spent on their behalf. These types of organizations use account codes coupled with call accounting systems. Each customer has a specific account code, so the call accounting system can produce detailed reports of the telephone usage for each account.

An alternative to on-site call accounting hardware and software is a service bureau. Large companies often hire service bureaus to administer call accounting services from a remote location. Service bureaus dial in to the PBX from a remote location and collect the client organization's call data.

Voice Mail Systems

Voice mail systems are answering machines built into a PBX, or stand-alone PCs with voice mail software. A configuration showing a PC-based voice mail system is shown on the PC-Based Voice Mail Diagram.

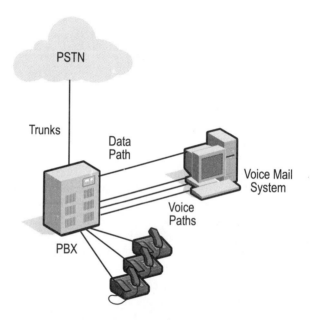

PC-Based Voice Mail

With PC-based voice mail systems, two types of connections are made between the PBX and PC. Voice paths connect an outside caller with the mailbox of the called party.

A data path is used to carry call control information, such as the dialed number or the caller ID (for internal calls or ISDN), and control signaling that enables features such as call notification lights.

Signaling information may be passed between the voice mail system in the PBX over analog or digital voice lines. Other ways of passing signaling information include RS-232-C and packet-switched serial connections between devices.

When an inbound caller receives a busy or no answer condition, the PBX sends the call to a hunt group programmed for the voice mail system. The PBX and its software locate a free line within the hunt group and connect the call to the voice mail system. If, for some reason, the voice mail system fails, the system administrator may reprogram the PBX to route calls to an attendant or disable the voice mail hunt group temporarily.

If the system uses in-band signaling, call information travels across either the same line or over a second analog line. A system that uses a digital link such as Station Message Desk Interface (SMDI) passes call information over this link. The signaling information tells the voice mail system which mailbox to open. The analog connection then passes the mailbox owner's greeting to the caller, and carries the caller's message to the voice mail system where it is recorded on the storage medium.

When the caller hangs up, the PBX signals the voice mail system to release the line. The voice mail system then sends a signal to the PBX to turn on the message-waiting indicator.

Design Factors

When implementing a new voice mail system, you must consider the number of system users, voice messaging ports on the PBX, and automated attendants (described later) that will be needed. In other words, the PBX must have enough voice messaging ports to accommodate the maximum number of simultaneous voice messages that could potentially be placed.

You must also decide how to notify users that voice mail is waiting. In most cases, this will be determined by the features available on existing desk sets. If existing telephones have "message waiting" lights, most users prefer to use them. If lights are not available, and the customer does not want to upgrade the equipment, then the system can deliver a "stutter tone" to alert users to waiting messages. The user hears the tone when a message comes in during a call, or when the user picks up the telephone to make a call.

Unified Messaging

Some voice mail systems also come with unified messaging features. Unified messaging systems provide a single graphical interface that helps users manage voice mail, e-mail, and faxes.

Incoming messages are stored on the voice mail system's hard drive. Notifications are sent, by means of a LAN, to each user's computer. Using the graphical interface, users can read text documents, listen to voice mail (on computer speakers or the telephone), store documents on the local hard drive, or print text messages.

Broadcasting

Voice mail systems also offer message broadcasting, which sends the same message to multiple voice mail boxes.

Voice Mail Security

In Lesson 5, you learned that DISA can be a target for toll fraud when improperly administered. Advanced voice mail features also have the potential to become a security problem if not carefully set up and closely monitored.

In general, voice mail is vulnerable to several types of potential security problems:

- Curiosity—Hackers are often motivated by the excitement of breaching a system. They may not intend to do harm, but may damage the system as they explore it.

- Malice—Intentional damage can be done by disgruntled employees, former employees, or anyone else who dislikes the company. Depending on the size and number of voice mail security holes, this damage can range from rude messages left in mailboxes to severe system disruptions.

- Industrial espionage—Voice mail is often full of confidential messages, sales leads, and other sensitive information that could damage the company or an employee if known by a competitor.

- Illegal business use—Some criminals breach voice mail systems to set up untraceable mailboxes for their own use.

- Toll fraud—Criminals use advanced features, such as call transfer or outcalling, to access outgoing lines and steal long-distance service. This is a popular tool among drug dealers who regularly call South American or Asian countries.

As with DISA, prevention is the best way to protect a voice mail system. The following security guidelines will discourage most hackers. Many of these are already implemented in major voice mail systems:

- Grant system privileges only as needed. Use class of service (CoS) restrictions to customize each user's access to features such as remote access or call transfer.

- Prevent callers from transferring from voice mail to an outgoing line, or restrict outbound transfers to certain numbers.

- Eliminate all unused voice mail boxes. Do not set up boxes before they are needed, and close a box as soon as an employee leaves the company.

- Be serious about passwords. When assigning a new mailbox, create a random password. To make passwords harder to guess, require that they are at least six to eight characters long; set even longer passwords for administrative access. Require users to change their passwords regularly, and emphasize the importance of not writing passwords in obvious places.

- Limit the number of attempts to log in to voice mail. Some systems lock a voice mail box after three unsuccessful password attempts.

- Regularly review reports of system activity for unusual patterns.

- Plan for the worst. Voice mail security should be a key element in your overall communications security plan. This plan should include predetermined procedures to follow in case of a security attack. As you develop your plan, make your telecommunications service provider a full partner in the process. By including your provider in your procedures, you can more quickly shut down a security attack if one occurs.

Automated Attendants

Automated attendants are machines, integrated into PBX systems, that answer the telephone and play a now-familiar recorded message:

> "Thank you for calling our company. If you know your party's extension, please dial it now. Otherwise, stay on the line and an operator will assist you shortly."

Automated attendants can supplement a staff of live operators during very busy times, when the staff may not be able to handle all of the incoming calls. Some businesses use an attendant to answer all incoming calls, allowing a receptionist to perform other tasks when not providing personal service to callers. Automated attendant systems can also allow callers to select options from a voice menu, to automatically route calls to different departments.

CoR

CoR, also called "CoS," allows a telephone administrator to define user rights for a telephone system. Some PBXs allow an administrator to define up to 64 classes of telephone users. Each of those classes can be assigned a different set of call-origination and call-termination restrictions. After classes have been defined, the administrator assigns individual users to groups, as well as voice terminals, voice-terminal groups, data modules, and trunk groups.

A simple example of CoS is a telephone that does not permit direct long-distance calls, such as a lobby courtesy telephone or hospital room telephone. In large organizations, CoS can be used to specify whether voice-terminal users can activate any number of PBX features, or access certain trunks or services. For example, a CoS can allow users to make long-distance calls, but only after they enter an account code to authorize the call and track the toll charges. Other CoS settings can make it impossible for users in certain departments to call each other.

Call Pickup

Call pickup allows someone to remotely answer the ringing telephone of a person who is not available. To use call pickup, simply dial a code number (or press a function key) plus the extension that is ringing, and then answer the call as if it were your own.

Call Park

Call park is a more flexible type of call hold, that allows the call recipient to resume the call from any extension on the system.

Call Forwarding

Call forwarding allows a telephone user to redirect a telephone call to another telephone. For example, telephone calls in an office can be forwarded to an extension in another part of the building.

Call Announcement

When a PBX user transfers a call to another user, call announcement allows the first user to speak to the second user before the second person answers the forwarded call. This feature makes smoother customer service possible, because the first user can explain who the caller is, and what has transpired, before the second user takes over the call.

In contrast, a "blind transfer" means a call is simply forwarded to a second extension. The first user cannot control the call or talk to the newly called party.

Call Waiting

Call waiting alerts a called party that another incoming call is waiting. Without call waiting, the second caller receives a busy signal. With call waiting enabled, the called party hears a short beep or click when a second call comes in. To put the first caller on hold and answer the second call, the called party briefly presses the switch hook once.

DAU

When customers are waiting in a queue to talk to an agent, they will wait more patiently if they are politely encouraged to do so. A digital announcement unit (DAU) plays a variety of recorded messages to callers on hold, according to the call treatment script. For example, a DAU typically plays an initial greeting that asks customer to stay on the line and wait for the first available agent. Subsequent messages can reassure callers that they will soon be served, or invite them to exit the queue by leaving voice mail messages for agents.

Activity

1. Match the following terms with the correct description:

   Also called CoS

   Telephone call redirection

   Machines that answer telephone calls

   Used for telephone call accounting

   Remote answer of a call

   Recorded message playing while caller is on hold

   Resume a call from any extension

   Computers that track telephone calls

   Incoming call alert

   a. Call accounting

   _____

   b. Authorization code

   _____

   c. Automated attendant

   _____

   d. CoR

   _____

   e. Call pickup

   _____

   f. Call park

   _____

g. Call forwarding

_____

h. Call waiting

_____

i. DAU

_____

Extended Activity

1. Go to the Web site **http://www.lucent.com**
   and find information on the following subjects:

   a. Call accounting systems

   b. Voice mail systems

   c. Automated attendants

   d. CoR

   e. DAU

Lesson 7—Computer Data and the Voice Network

The analog network was designed to carry signals that represent the human voice. When computers came along, many years after the voice network was firmly established, methods were developed for sending computer information over the voice network. This lesson reviews the differences between digital and analog signals, and where these two different signal types are used in a typical network.

Objectives

At the end of this lesson you will be able to:

- Describe the differences between analog and digital signals

- Explain the basic function of a modem

 **Key Point**

Digital signals must be converted to go across the analog voice network.

Analog and Digital Signals

Without conversion, digital signals (computer signals) cannot be sent over an analog facility designed to carry voice frequencies. The Analog/Digital Signals Diagram illustrates differences in the ways in which digital and analog signals are formed. Analog signals are waves. Digital signals are a series of pulses with very short rise (leading edge of signal) and fall (trailing edge) times, forming a "squared-off" signal pattern.

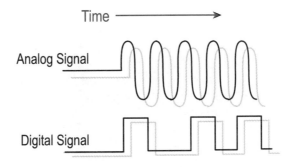

Analog/Digital Signals

These quick transitions cause high-frequency, harmonic signals that are often over 8,000 cycles per second. In a digital data stream, information sent in a series of pulses represents a binary 1 or 0. For example, a rise at a given point might represent a binary 1, and a fall at a given point might represent a binary 0. Because the telephone system is designed to carry the human voice within a frequency range of approximately 300 to 3,400 Hz, it cannot accommodate these high-frequency signals. Any attempt to send such information down an analog facility results in a blurring or distortion of the digital pulse, making it lose its squared-off appearance. When this happens, it is difficult to see where a digital pulse begins and ends. Other factors affecting the integrity of digital transmissions are:

- Loss of signal strength occurs as the distance traveled increases.

- Transmission speed also affects data integrity: the higher the data rate, the more pulses sent. As more pulses are sent, they grow closer together and become more prone to distortion.

- Noise, such as electrical equipment or atmospheric conditions, also affects the digital data stream.

Digital computer signals are converted to analog signals by a modem so the voice network can be used to carry computer data.

Modems

A modem is a device that performs digital-to-analog and analog-to-digital signal conversion. The term modem is a contraction of "modulator-demodulator." Modems are used in pairs, one at each end of the telephone line. Modems attach to a computer by means of an RS-232 cable, or they are contained within the computer itself (internal modems). The RS-232 and Modems Diagram illustrates the use of an external modem.

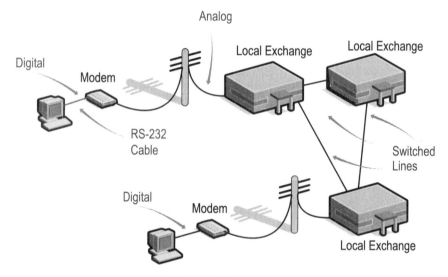

RS-232 and Modems

To transmit a message, a modem accepts digital data from a computer. The modem modulates (impresses) the digital signal onto an analog carrier frequency that can be used on the voice network. If amplitude modulation (AM) is being used, the signal strength, or amplitude, is changed to represent the digital data. The receiving modem demodulates the signal, generating digital data that is transmitted to the terminal or computer. The signal falls within the range of 300 to 3,400 Hz, thus it can be transmitted across the telephone network as if it were a voice conversation.

One modulation technique represents 0s and 1s by switching the audible tone off and on, respectively. However, this method can transmit data at a maximum rate of approximately 1,200 bits per second (bps). More complex encoding methods can increase the data rate significantly.

The modems at either end of a connection must use the same modulation/demodulation technique. A variety of standards have been published to enable modems from different manufacturers to be used together.

Modems do not have to be used to communicate across a tele-communications network. In many cases, information is sent across the network in digital format from end to end, as we will see in later sections.

Activities

1. What does a modem do and why is it necessary?

   _____

   _____

   _____

   _____

2. Discuss what limits the speed at which standard modems can be used for accessing information using the voice network.

   _____

   _____

   _____

   _____

3. Why can't digital signals with a high-frequency component be placed on lines designed to carry analog signals?

   _____

   _____

   _____

   _____

Extended Activity

If possible, review modems found in your school or organization and discuss their characteristics.

_____

_____

_____

_____

Lesson 8—Digitizing the Voice

As the benefits of a digital telecommunications infrastructure became apparent, it was necessary to take the analog voice and convert it to a digital format. This lesson covers digitizing analog voice signals so they are compatible with the digital telecommunications network.

Objectives

At the end of this lesson you will be able to:

- Describe why it is necessary to convert from analog to digital for communication of voice signals across the telecommunications network

- Describe why it is necessary to convert from digital to analog for communication of computer signals across the telecommunications network

 **Key Point**

The analog voice must be converted into digital format.

Analog to Digital

The first part of the Analog-to-Digital Conversion Diagram (A) represents the original analog waveform. Part (B) represents digital pulses that control the sampling rate of the analog waveform. The digital pulses open a "gate" for the duration of their pulse widths, reading the amplitude of the analog waveform for this period of time. The sampled analog waveform appears as pulses (C) that are each correlated to a specific number (D). This number represents one sample of the voice signal. The binary representation of this number (E) is transmitted digitally across a circuit. At the receiving end, the reverse process takes place to convert the digital signal back to the original analog waveform.

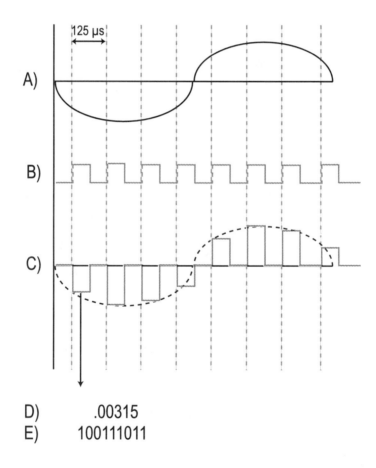

D)	.00315
E)	100111011

Analog-to-Digital Conversion

A typical sampling rate (number of times a byte is generated) is 8,000 times per second, approximately twice the bandwidth required for an analog voice signal. Research has determined that a sampling rate of at least two times the highest frequency component of the original signal results in accurate representation of the original intelligence.

A coder/decoder (codec) is the device that takes the analog voice signal and converts it to digital (binary) format for transmission over a digital circuit. The Analog-to-Digital Conversion Diagram illustrates this concept.

Analog-to-digital conversion is also called "A-to-D conversion" or "ADC." The most common example of this is found in a codec. This device takes the analog voice signal and converts it to digital (binary) format for transmission over a digital path, such as a T1. The output of a codec is combined with other outputs and multiplexed onto a high-speed digital network.

Mixing It Up

A MUX is the piece of computer/telephony equipment that allows multiple signals to travel over the same physical media. There are different types of MUXs, such as time-division MUXs and frequency-division MUXs. The MUX Diagram shows three analog voice signals, converted by codecs, multiplexed onto a serial digital bit stream. The input to a codec is analog, the output is digital. The input to the MUX is multiple (low-speed) digital bit streams. The output of the MUX is a high-speed digital bit stream.

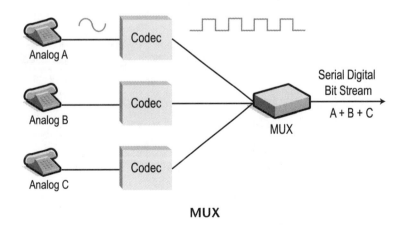

MUX

With the use of codecs and MUXs, analog voice signals can be converted to digital format, combined, and then sent as one digital bit stream through the telecommunications network.

TDM

TDM combines many digital bit streams with relatively low bit rates into a single bit stream with a relatively high bit rate. It is, in essence, a way for many slow communications channels to "time share" a very fast channel. The advantage is that the cost per bit transmitted on a single fast channel is lower than on multiple slower channels.

TDM is accomplished by simply interleaving data from several bit streams. This can be done on a bit basis or byte basis, called "bit interleaving" or "byte interleaving," respectively. The TDM Diagram illustrates this concept. During time interval 1, 8 bits from source channel 1 are transmitted. During successive intervals, bytes from successive source channels are transmitted on the output channel. A complete set of values from each input channel is called a "frame."

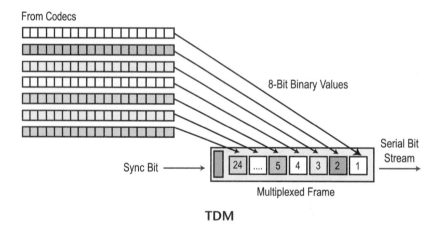

TDM

WDM

Two other types of multiplexing that bear mentioning here in contrast with TDM are wavelength-division multiplexing (WDM) and dense wavelength-division multiplexing (DWDM). WDM and DWDM use multiple light wavelengths to transmit signals over a single optical fiber. Think of a prism that takes a beam of light and refracts it into several wavelengths of separate colors. This is a picture of what WDM is like. Each wavelength carries information at rates as high as 2.5 gigabits per second (Gbps). With optical technology advances, DWDM has seen more and more wavelengths, or channels, squeezed into an optical fiber. Aggregate rates as high as 1 terabit, or one trillion bps, are possible with this technology. Thus, WDM is actually more like FDM in that separate channels within a transmission pipe are each carrying a stream of data. These technologies are utilized in moving Internet Protocol (IP) traffic on the Internet backbone. The terms packet-over-WDM and packet-over-DWDM are used to describe these services.

Activities

1. A codec is required only at the transmitting station.
   True or False

2. How many bps does it take to transmit a voice signal in digital format if the analog signal is sampled 8,000 times per second, and each sample generates one 8-bit byte?

   _____

   _____

3. Why is it necessary to perform ADC of a voice signal?

   _____

   _____

   _____

4. Draw a diagram that shows four analog telephones communicating by means of codecs and MUXs with four other analog telephones. Indicate on the diagram where analog and digital signals are found.

Extended Activities

1. Using the Web, research the following products and discuss in class:

   a. Codecs

   b. MUXs

   c. Channel banks

2. Using the Web, research the details of TDM. How many time-division multiplexed channels are used to form a T1 digital circuit? What is the bandwidth of each channel, and what is the resulting high-speed (aggregate) output bandwidth? Can multiple T1s be combined to form higher-bandwidth multiplexed circuits?

   _____

   _____

   _____

   _____

3. Get in groups of four and have the students "multiplex" their first names. One student from each group will write each name on a sheet of paper. Then one letter from each name, representing a character of data, will be placed one by one on a separate line, representing the output stream of a MUX.

Lesson 9—Integration of Services

This lesson looks at one way to combine data and voice signals for transfer across the telecommunications network. As we continue through this course, we will see other methods to combine voice data and other signal types for transfer across a wide area.

Objectives

At the end of this lesson you will be able to:

- Describe the transfer of both voice and data across a wide area

- Explain how MUXs can transmit both voice and data across a wide area using digital technology

 **Key Point**

Voice and data look the same when they are in binary format.

Ones and Zeros

With the exception of the local loop, the telecommunications infrastructure has become digital. In many metropolitan areas, the local loop is made up of circuits that are digital. When the entire network, from one subscriber to another, is digital, voice and data can be combined and sent across the same physical circuitry.

The Digital Network Diagram illustrates this concept. In this diagram, both voice and data signals are combined by means of a MUX. The MUX in this example is a digital MUX, combining multiple digital signals onto a high-speed digital circuit.

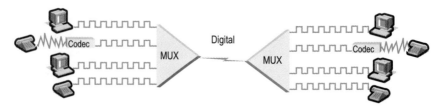

Digital Network

Data Transfer

Consider the data from one computer to another. Information from a computer is binary in nature; it consists of 1s and 0s. Therefore, the output of the computer can be sent to the MUX directly. (In practice, a digital modem is normally used.) The MUX takes the digital information from the computer, combines it with other inputs, and sends it across the network by means of the high-speed line. The high-speed circuit in the Digital Network Diagram is illustrated by a lightning bolt, indicating a communications link, commonly a WAN link.

The output of the MUX is the combination of computer and other data inputs. The output is combined and sent across the communications link to another MUX. On the receiving end, the MUX takes the serial bit stream and "demultiplexes" it to the correct port, in this case another computer.

Voice Conversations

Voice signals can also be fed into the MUX. Notice that the diagram contains two methods for sending digital voice across a wide area. The top telephone has an analog output. This output is fed into a codec that produces a digital signal corresponding to the analog output. The output of the codec goes into the MUX, where it is combined with other signals and sent across the WAN.

Digital telephones provide the conversion inside the telephone itself. A separate box for coding and decoding the analog signal is not required. An ISDN telephone, for example, produces a digital output signal from the telephone. The output of a digital telephone is sent to a MUX, where it is combined with other signals to be sent across the WAN.

Activities

1. Draw a diagram that shows eight low-speed devices, including five data and three analog voice. These devices are connected into individual MUX ports, and multiplexed onto a high-speed line. At the other end of the high-speed line is another MUX that contains similar devices on each port.

2. If each port is capable of sending 64 kilobits per second (Kbps) of digital information, how fast does the high-speed line need to be to accommodate all of the devices?

   _____

3. If a dedicated T1 line (1.5 megabits per second [Mbps]) is being used, what is the percentage of line utilization when all devices are in use?

   _____

Extended Activities

1. Research the early developments of digitizing the voice and integration of services. Include in your research the following topics:

    a. Converting the analog network to a digital network

    b. Using T1 MUXs to combine voice and data services

    c. Early developments of ISDN

Lesson 10—Elements of the Telecommunications Business

The Telecommunications Act of 1996, and the resulting breakup of the Bell System, created several new business entities that now make up the telecommunications system. The Act also redefined the business practices of the telecommunications industry, to ensure a level competitive playing field for all of these new players. In this lesson, we introduce the various types of companies that provide telecommunications services, and explain the rules and pressures that govern the way they do business with each other.

Objectives

At the end of this lesson you will be able to:

- Name and describe the entities created by the Telecommunications Act of 1996

- Name the different kinds of companies competing in the local market

- Explain the main provisions of the Telecommunications Act of 1996

Key Point

The players and rules of the telecommunications business are defined in the Telecommunications Act of 1996.

The Players

Before the breakup of the Bell System, the telecommunications business was a much simpler (if less competitive) place. Now, a wide variety of companies are offering a wider variety of communication services. Each of these companies can be classified as one of the following major types:

- Interexchange carrier (IXC)

- Regional Bell Operating Company (RBOC) or local exchange carrier (LEC)

- Competitive local exchange carrier (CLEC)

- Competitive access provider (CAP)

IXCs

In the AT&T breakup, long-distance companies (AT&T, MCI, and others) were called IXCs because they provided telephone and data services between local access and transport areas (LATAs). Thus, the interstate, or more correctly, the interLATA portion of a call is transported by an IXC and handed off to a LEC to be carried to the final destination. IXCs also provide international telephone and data services. AT&T, which once controlled the entire long-distance market, now accounts for only 60 percent of long-distance service, which is still a formidable amount.

Although IXCs compete for a slice of overall long-distance revenue, they have learned to use competition to their advantage. For example, MCI is AT&T's largest customer; if MCI does not have a circuit to a caller, it passes the call to AT&T for processing.

RBOCs/LECs

The 22 local telephone companies that were split off from AT&T were reorganized into seven RBOCs. These companies also became known as LECs because they provided calling services within a local calling area. These companies make telephone connections to subscribers' homes and businesses, provide telephone services, and collect fees for those services.

Each of the RBOCs, or LECs, provides service to multiple LATAs, and dominates the local market within those LATAs. However, calls that travel between LATAs must be routed through an IXC. In other words, even if a call travels between two LATAs served by the same LEC, that call will be carried by an IXC, not the LEC that serves both LATAs.

Therefore, the terms RBOC and LEC are equivalent. In addition, to distinguish them from other players that are rapidly entering local markets, RBOCs and LECs are also known as incumbent local exchange carriers (ILECs).

CLECs

The Telecommunications Act of 1996 required that the Bell Telephone Companies "unbundle" the resale of components of local calling. This opened up the marketplace to competition, because competitors can resell an array of services formerly provided only by the Bell companies. Resale of local services enables new competitors to avoid the high cost of building their own physical communication system, including installing copper wiring, routing optical fiber, and adding wireless equipment.

These CLECs are telecommunications resellers, or brokers, who sell data services, Internet access, and local toll calling to businesses and residential customers. The bulk of the sales to date have been to business customers in urban areas.

Some CLECs route calls over a mix of their own fiber optic, wireless, and copper facilities, as well as over facilities they lease at a discount from LECs. According to the Telecommunications Resellers Association survey of their members, published on December 1, 1998:

- Fifty-six percent are total resellers of incumbent telephone company services.

- Thirty-eight percent offer a combination of their own fiber optic and wireless facilities, plus resold services.

- Six percent offer facilities-based interconnection of unbundled network elements.

The local market is very enticing to other industries that have not historically been involved in telecommunications. With the expectation that the market will be a $50 billion industry by 2005, everyone wants to get into the act:

- Gas and electric companies are using their fiber optics and rights-of-way to become CLECs. For example, Montana Power is now Touch America.

- Cable television companies can use their installed coaxial cable for voice and data offerings, and not just television.

- Internet service providers (ISPs) are going after domestic and international data Internet traffic, and then targeting voice over IP (VoIP).

- Wireless (cellular) service providers simply bypass LECs for local access.

- IXCs may now enter local markets under the right conditions.

CAPs

Another new player in the industry is the CAP. In major metropolitan areas, CAPs initially provided fiber optic links between customers and IXCs, avoiding the hefty access fees charged by the LECs. Specifically, they only carried traffic between a LEC and an IXC. With fiber optic links in place in major metropolitan areas, some CAPs are now able to expand their offerings and become CLECs.

Regulated Competition

The goal of the framers of the Telecommunications Act of 1996 was to promote uniform local telephone competition. However, the following factors have slowed local competition as mandated by the Act:

- Legal challenges to the Act

- Interconnection disagreements between ILECs and competing local carriers

- Service interruptions when customers change from ILECs to competitors

The Act takes away from each state the ability to approve competition in local telecommunications. It lays down a time frame, and a method, by which competition will be opened to a variety of vendors. It also outlines a procedure for local telephone companies to expand their operations into manufacturing and interLATA service, as well as in-region and out-of-region telecommunications.

An Expanded Role for the FCC

The Act redefines the relationship of the state public utility corporations (PUCs) to the Federal Communications Commission (FCC). Essentially, it is up to the states to approve rates for local calling and resale and interconnection of LEC services to competitors. However, resale rates charged by ILECs cannot be above their own costs.

RBOCs/LECs were immediately allowed to sell long-distance service from outside their regions. They are not required to form a separate subsidiary to sell out-of-region long-distance, electronic publishing, and alarm monitoring services.

Enforcement of provisions and details of implementation of the Act were left, for the most part, to the FCC. Its rulings on wholesale rates, and its right to set rates, were challenged by the state PUCs, LECs, and independent telephone companies. They contended that the 1934 Communications Act granted state utilities commissions the prerogative of setting resale and wholesale discounts in their states. The U.S. Supreme Court ruled in January 1999 that the FCC has jurisdiction on pricing. It also ruled that the Act is constitutional in setting conditions for only RBOCs, but not independent telephone companies, for entry into interregion long distance.

LNP

In a competitive telecommunications arena, customers who wish to change service from the LEC to a CLEC would lose their existing telephone number and be assigned a new one from the CLEC's wire center. This is undesirable for businesses that spend large sums of money to publicize their telephone numbers and do not want to change numbers for any reason.

Therefore, the Telecommunications Act wanted to give both CLECs and LECs the ability to select and protect assigning telephone numbers. Under the Act, both LECs and CLECs agree to provide customers with the ability to change telephone companies without changing telephone numbers; this service is referred to as Local Number Portability (LNP).

Shared Platforms

The Act also requires both LECs and CLECs to use the same technology to provide similar services. For example, a CLEC is not allowed to lock in its customers by giving away proprietary handsets that do not work with the associated LEC's network.

Network Interconnection

To offer competing service, a CLEC must connect its network to that of the LEC. Therefore, the Act states that the LEC cannot unfairly require the CLEC to interconnect at inconvenient places, or make unreasonable demands on the CLEC. This concept, called "co-location," means that the LEC may not require that a CLEC provide interconnection at a specific CO and pay exorbitant fees for that access.

Unbundled Local Loops

The LEC must lease copper wires or fiber optic channels to the CLEC at a "reasonable price." The term "unbundled" means that the LEC does nothing more than provide the physical wire, fiber link, or digital channel. (However, "unbundled" can mean different services or components to different companies. When negotiating for unbundled service, be absolutely sure what you or your customers are getting.)

The Act required LECs to make unbundled local loops available, simply because the LECs owned most of the physical wires. However, today many LECs are leasing unbundled loops from CLECs and other new carriers. Why? Because building or constructing these links is too expensive. If a LEC does not already have cables or wires that go where needed, it is cheaper to lease them from a CLEC.

The high cost of new loops is the reason so many new competing carriers are being created from power/electric companies, railroads (Sprint was originally started by the Southern Pacific railroad), and even city sewers (in Paris and Japan where there is no conduit or other means). These entities are using their existing rights-of-way, underground conduits, and other facilities to provide these links at a lower cost than LECs.

Reciprocal Compensation

Reciprocal compensation simply means that the CLEC and LEC pay each other for calls passing over their wires.

Tariffs

Tariffs are documents a regulated telephone company files with a state PUC or the FCC. A tariff is a public document that details the services, equipment, and pricing offered by a telephone company (a common carrier) to all potential customers. Regulatory authorities do not normally approve tariffs. They accept them, until they are successfully challenged before a hearing of the regulatory body or in court.

The term "common carrier" means that the company must offer its services to everybody at the prices and conditions outlined in its public tariffs. However, tariffs do not carry the weight of law behind them. If you or the telephone company violates them, no one will go to jail.

Tariffs are much different today than in the past. Before the Telecommunications Act of 1996, tariffs were a check and balance to control, in the public interest, a regulated monopoly. There was no reason to sell anything for less than the established tariff because there was no competition.

However, in today's competitive marketplace, many telephone companies violate their own tariffs by charging lower fees than those listed, or bundling services together at a discount. Many users now regard tariffs as a starting point for bargaining, rather than the "last word."

The Sample Tariff Rates per Month Table lists a few sample rates from some of the various ILEC companies. (We will discuss each of these services later in this course.) As you can see, rates for many items are close or identical, while prices vary widely for other items. Therefore, when shopping for telecommunications services, customers should always get proposals in writing and compare features.

Sample Tariff Rates per Month

Company	Direct Inward Dialing	Direct Outward Dialing	Two-Way	Centrex	ISDN-Basic Rate	ISDN-Primary Rate
Bell South	$66	$63	$63		$93	$1,741
Ameritech	$65	$63	$63		$33	$1,580
Bell Atlantic	$72	$66	$66	$27	$58	$1,446
GTE	$60	$60	$60	$26	$95	$1,421
Southwestern Bell	$65	$58	$58	$18	$48	$1,116

Effects of Competition

This new competitive atmosphere has put pressure on telecommunications companies in terms of price, service area, and technology. These pressures have created several effects, as described below.

Legal Struggles

As you saw above, the FCC requires that a LEC lease unbundled copper pairs or fiber optic channels to a CLEC at a "reasonable price," which is the same as the actual cost to the LEC. In other words, the LEC may not mark up the cost of its wiring. This requirement is the major bone of contention for LECs. LECs maintain there should only be a 15 percent discount for an unbundled local loop. An unbundled local loop is generally defined as a channel without management, provisioning, repair, or billing; all those features would be provided by the CLEC. CLECs state that 15 percent makes it unprofitable for them, and the discount should be 30 percent or more. It appears the courts will decide this matter.

In the long-distance market, IXCs currently pay LECs three cents for every call processed through a LEC. However, AT&T and other IXCs believe (or so they say) that it only costs a LEC one cent to process a call. In other words, this $100 billion industry is fighting over pennies per call. However, there are billions of calls, and, therefore, millions of dollars at stake.

Price Pressure

There is also pressure on IXCs to reduce their overall prices. While local rates, in many cases, have more than doubled over the past 10 years, long-distance rates have fallen to almost unbelievably low prices, from more than 50 cents per minute before 1984, to 10 cents or less today. It is also likely that, with Internet telephony and other new services, rates will fall even more in the future, to probably 10 cents per minute for international calls as well.

Today, Sprint offers free calling on Fridays, and MCI offers calls for five cents per minute on Sundays. This trend indicates that by 2005, or shortly thereafter, much of long distance will probably be free.

Slamming

Slamming is the practice of switching a customer's long-distance service from one IXC to another, without the customer's knowledge or permission. The customer does not know the change has been made until a new bill arrives. This is considered fraud and it is illegal; however, some long-distance companies are doing it. In the future, slamming will likely occur for LECs as well.

Niche Companies

CLECs are not the only ones grabbing local business. There are a myriad of companies targeting local small- and medium-sized businesses. These small telecommunications companies focus on a well-defined niche of customers, such as small businesses, home businesses, or rural subscribers, and they retain them by providing world-class customer service.

In the future, there may be a few dominant brand names, such as AT&T, coexisting with hundreds of local brands. This is almost uncannily similar to what is happening in the beer industry: a few large dominant players provide mass-marketed products, while hundreds of brew pubs specialize in local or regional brands.

Activities

1. Define a CLEC.

   _____

2. Explain the original purpose of a tariff, and contrast that with the way tariffs are used today.

   _____

   _____

   _____

   _____

3. List and describe at least three provisions of the Telecommunications Act of 1996.

   _____

   _____

   _____

   _____

4. Explain the term "slamming."

   _____

   _____

5. Define an IXC.

   _____

   _____

Extended Activities

1. In your area, do your cable or electric companies provide alternative telecommunications services? How do these services compare to those provided by your LEC?

   _____

   _____

   _____

   _____

2. Broadband services, such as Digital Subscriber Line (DSL) and cable modem, may be purchased through a LEC or CLEC. Do CLECs in your area provide broadband access? If so, how do their rates compare to those charged by your LEC?

   _____

   _____

   _____

   _____

Summary

This unit reviewed the foundation and structure of telecommunications networks. The telecommunications infrastructure has developed over many years and was originally designed for voice communication. As the need to send data over the voice network developed, different types of services and offerings were introduced to accommodate voice and data communication as well as other types of services. The transfer of information over the telecommunications network can be limited to a short distance, such as through a city, or over longer distances, using various types of technologies and devices.

The process used to organize and manage the telecommunications infrastructure varies from country to country and has undergone many changes in the last few decades. In some cases, the pricing and control of access to networks is tightly regulated. In other cases, it is open to competition and a mixture of rates and services.

Unit 1 Quiz

1. Which of the following refer to the links that connect local exchanges?

   a. Modems

   b. Analog

   c. Trunks

   d. End offices

2. What is the primary connection type between COs?

   a. Analog

   b. Digital

   c. Asymmetric

   d. Asynchronous

3. Which two of the following are ways to classify networks such as LANs and WANs? (Choose two.)

   a. Type of PC technology

   b. Type of host connectivity

   c. Geographic coverage

   d. Type of links connecting the networks

4. What type of networking facilities is provided by a telecommunications company?

   a. Public

   b. Private

   c. Hybrid

   d. Internal

5. What is the primary difference between a LAN, MAN, and WAN?

   a. Number of nodes in a network

   b. Type of nodes in a network

   c. Distance between groups of nodes in a network

   d. Size of the organization where the nodes exist

6. Which two of the following are uses for a modem?
(Choose two.)

   a. Amplify analog signals

   b. Convert digital signals to analog signals

   c. Repeat digital signals

   d. Convert analog signals to digital signals

7. What is the copper cabling that connects many homes and businesses to the first CO?

   a. Local loop

   b. Trunk lines

   c. Digital loop

   d. Leased lines

8. Which term is the name for a carrier that provides interLATA calling services?

   a. IXC

   b. RBOC

   c. CLEC

   d. LEC

9. Which of the following resells the services provided by the incumbent telephone company?

   a. IXC

   b. LEC

   c. RBOC

   d. CLEC

10. Which service, dictated by the Telecommunications Act of 1996, allows customers to move their telephone service from a LEC to a CLEC without having to change their telephone number?

    a. Shared platforms

    b. LNP

    c. Network interconnection

    d. Unbundled local loops

11. Which of the following is the term given to the IXC practice of switching a customer's long-distance service from one carrier to another without the customer's knowledge?

    a. Pushing

    b. Moving

    c. Driving

    d. Slamming

12. Which PBX feature allows a caller to resume a call from any other extension on the system?

    a. Call forwarding

    b. Call waiting

    c. Call answer

    d. Call park

13. Denying an extension the ability to connect direct long-distance calls is an example of which telephone system function?

    a. Class of denial

    b. Automated attendant

    c. CoS

    d. Denial of service

14. Which piece of PBX auxiliary equipment allows an operator to view the status of an extension?

    a. ACD

    b. DSS

    c. UPS

    d. SMDR

15. Which PBX enhancement allows callers to access company information directly from the telephone keypad, without talking to an operator or attendant?

    a. IVR

    b. ACD

    c. Automated attendant

    d. DSS

16. Which of the following is considered telephone system auxiliary equipment?

    a. Headset

    b. UPS

    c. Trunks

    d. Administrative terminal

17. Which three of the following are considered PBX components? (Choose three.)

    a. Trunks

    b. CDRs

    c. Extension lines

    d. Telephones

18. Which PBX enhancement allows a computer to understand a human voice, and respond according to spoken commands?

    a. Interactive Voice Response

    b. Automatic Call Distribution

    c. Direct Inward Dialing

    d. Voice Recognition

19. Which PBX enhancement allows calls to reach the called party, wherever they are located?

    a. Call forwarding

    b. Voice mail

    c. Automatic Call Distributor

    d. Call transfer

20. Which telephone station set feature allows a caller to dial a number with a two or three digit abbreviated access code?

    a. Abbreviated dialing

    b. Call transfer

    c. Speed dialing

    d. Call acceleration

21. Which attendant console capability allows the attendant to set up a meeting between a group of callers?

    a. Call processing

    b. Call servicing

    c. Camp on

    d. Conference calling

22. Which PBX system report helps telecommunications managers to reduce telephone system abuse?

    a. Test reports

    b. Call detail reports

    c. Busy-hour studies

    d. Station detail reports

23. Which statement best describes the busy hour, as the term applies to voice networking?

    a. It is the hour when the telephone administrator is most busy

    b. It is the hour when the company operator takes the most calls

    c. It is the hour when only outbound call volume is the greatest

    d. It is the hour when the telephone system carries its greatest traffic

24. Which PBX features enhance PBX security? (Choose two.)

    a. Call pickup

    b. Call accounting

    c. Automated Attendants

    d. Class of restriction

25. Why is it important to understand the basis for telephone networks for an understanding of computer networks?

    _____

    _____

    _____

    _____

26. What are some of the trends in WANs?

_____

_____

_____

_____

27. Why is digital information transfer preferred over analog signaling?

_____

_____

_____

_____

28. What is a tariff and how does it affect telecommunications services?

_____

_____

_____

29. How are CO networks arranged and why?

_____

_____

_____

_____

Unit 2
WAN Concepts and Components

The telecommunications network provides the transport path for moving information across long distances. There are many types of information, such as voice, data, and video. In addition, there are many methods that can be used to transport information across a wide area network (WAN). This unit looks at basic concepts and components used to move information from source to destination across a telecommunications network.

Lessons

1. Physical and Logical Circuits
2. Connecting to WAN Circuits
3. Connecting to Analog Networks
4. Analog Modems
5. Modem Compatibility
6. Connecting to Digital Networks
7. Microwave Communications
8. Satellite Communications
9. End-to-End Connectivity

Terms

adjacent channel interference—Adjacent channel interference is interference caused when a signal exceeds its assigned frequency band and "spills over" into the band assigned to another signal.

American Standard Code for Information Interchange (ASCII)—ASCII is one of the most widely used codes for representing keyboard characters on a computer system. ASCII uses 7 bits to represent 128 elements. For example, when the character "A" is pressed on the keyboard, the ASCII binary representation is 1000001. The other major encoding system is EBCDIC. See Extended Binary Coded Decimal Interchange Code (EBCDIC).

amplitude modulation (AM)—AM imposes a signal pattern on a carrier wave (consistent electrical signal) by varying the height of the wave or how far from the center it swings.

asynchronous—An asynchronous operation is one in which characters are not transmitted on any strict timetable. The start of each character is indicated by transmitting a start bit. After the final bit of the character is transmitted, a stop bit is sent, indicating the end of the character. The modems must stay synchronized only for the length of time it takes to transmit the character. If their clocks are slightly out of synchronization, data transfer will still be successful.

automatic repeat request or automatic retransmission request (ARQ)—ARQ is a method commonly used by communicating devices to verify data upon receipt. The sender calculates and encodes an error-detection field and sends it with the data. The receiver then recalculates the field, and compares it with that which was received. If they match, the receiver acknowledges receipt (ACK); if the match fails, the receiver negatively acknowledges the data's receipt (NAK), and the sender retransmits. The sender must store the transmitted data until it receives either an ACK or NAK.

bandpass filter—A bandpass filter is an electronic device that accepts, or passes, a particular band of frequencies and blocks all others. Bandpass filtering is the basis of FDM.

baseband—A baseband modem is a modem that does not modulate a signal before transmission, thereby transmitting the signal in its native form. Baseband signaling is the transmission of either digital or analog signals at their original frequencies.

bits per second (bps)—Bps is a measurement of the number of binary bits transmitted per second. Common modem speeds are 28,800 and 56,000 bps (28.8 and 56 Kbps, respectively).

broadband—Two methods are used to transmit signals between nodes: baseband and broadband. A broadband system is one that transmits signals into separate carrier channels simultaneously over cable, similar to television or stereo cable. In the context of LANs, broadband refers to analog transmission of digital signals, and baseband refers to digital transmission of digital signals.

C band—The C band is a portion of the electromagnetic spectrum ranging in frequency from 4 to 6 GHz, used for satellite communications.

carrier—A carrier is a company that provides communications circuits. The digital communication services, designated T1, T2, and so on, are also referred to as carriers.

channel service unit (CSU)—A CSU is a device that connects customer equipment to digital transmission facilities, such as a T1 circuit. The CSU is the device that actually generates the transmission signals on the local loop, that is, the telephone channel. CSUs are normally coupled with DSUs in a device called a "CSU/DSU." See data service unit (DSU).

characters per second (cps)—The acronym cps is typically used to describe the number of characters a printer can print per second.

Consultative Committee for International Telegraphy and Telephony (CCITT)—CCITT is a subcommittee of ITU, responsible for standards used in communications, telecommunications, and networking. CCITT standards include X.25, V.42, and the ISDN I-series recommendations.

convergence technologies—Convergence technologies are protocols and systems that allow different types of media to be transported over the same network. One of the best examples of a convergence technology is ATM, providing for the prioritization and transport of different types of media, such as voice, data, and video.

data circuit-terminating equipment (DCTE)—See data communications equipment (DCE).

data communications equipment (DCE)—DCE devices are OSI model Layer 1 devices that are responsible for properly formatting the electrical signals on a physical link, and performing signal clocking and synchronization.

data service unit (DSU)—A DSU is a device that takes data from a LAN device and creates digital information suitable for public transmission facilities. A DSU is necessary to connect CPE to digital transmission facilities, such as a T1 circuit. It is normally used in conjunction with a CSU in a device called a "CSU/DSU." See channel service unit (CSU).

data terminal equipment or data termination equipment (DTE)—DTE is equipment, often a computer, that executes Layer 2 and higher processes. DTE depends on the services of the DCE to connect to a communications link.

DB-9—A DB-9 connector is the 9-pin, D-shaped connector specified by the EIA/TIA 574 serial communications standard. A DB-9 connector can either use female (receptacle) or male (plug) pin configurations.

DB-25—A DB-25 connector is the 25-pin, D-shaped connector specified by the EIA/TIA RS-232-C serial communications standard. A DB-25 connector can either use female (receptacle) or male (plug) pin configurations.

differential phase-shift keying (DPSK)—DPSK represents digital data by encoding digital values as shifts in the analog signal's phase. The data is represented as a change in the phase, rather than as a specific signal phase.

digital signal level 0 (DS0)—DS0 is a 64-Kbps channel that provides the bandwidth required for one analog voice telephone line. The DS0 signal is the fundamental building block of the North American digital signal hierarchy.

EIA/TIA-562—EIA/TIA-562 specifies an unbalanced, electrical-only serial communications standard similar to RS-232 but providing greater bandwidth (64 Kbps). EIA/TIA-562 can interoperate with RS-232 drivers and receivers in many applications.

EIA/TIA-574—EIA/TIA-574 was developed to alleviate confusion arising between the official RS-232 interface and the popular 9-pin version developed by IBM. This standard specifies the DB-9 interface, and recommends the use of the EIA/TIA-562 standard instead of RS-232 electrical levels. EIA/TIA-574 supplies the minimum number of communications lines for nonsynchronous serial data transfer between DTE and DCE.

Electronic Industries Association/Telecommunications Industry Association (EIA/TIA)—EIA and TIA represent companies providing communications, materials, products, systems, distribution services, and professional services around the world.

Extended Binary Coded Decimal Interchange Code (EBCDIC)—EBCDIC is the IBM standard for binary encoding of characters. It is one of the two most widely used codes to represent characters, such as keyboard characters. (ASCII is the other.) See American Standard Code for Information Interchange (ASCII).

fade—The gradual weakening of a signal over distance, often called "attenuation," is referred to as fade.

flow control—Flow control is a method of controlling the amount of frames or messages sent between two computer systems. Practically every data communication protocol contains some form of flow control to keep the sending computer from sending too many frames or packets to the receiving node.

forward error correction (FEC)—FEC is a technique of error detection and correction in which a transmitting host computer includes some number of redundant bits in a frame's data payload. These redundant bits allow the receiving device to re-create and recover from transmission errors, eliminating the need to retransmit.

frequency modulation (FM)—FM is a method of modifying a signal so that it can carry information. The carrier (original sine wave) has its frequency modified to correspond to the information being carried.

frequency-shift keying (FSK)—FSK is a method of representing a digital signal with analog waveforms. FSK represents a 0 as a specific frequency, and a 1 as another frequency.

gain—Gain is the increase in a signal's power, voltage, or current. Signal amplifiers create gain.

Gallium Arsenide Field Effect Transistor (GaAs-FET)—A GaAs-FET is a field effect transistor composed of gallium arsenide. A FET is a transistor designed to provide an output signal even when supplied with an input signal near zero power.

geostationary—Satellite communications systems transmit signals from earth stations to satellites located in space. Antennas located on earth are pointed at a geostationary satellite (also referred to as geosynchronous) that is located in an orbit of approximately 22,300 miles (35,800 km), and is at a fixed point in the sky.

geosynchronous—See geostationary.

gigahertz (GHz)—One GHz is the measurement for a signal that cycles 1 billion times per second.

Gunn diode—A Gunn diode is a microwave oscillator that operates based on the negative differential resistance properties of gallium arsenide. The Gunn diode is named after John Battiscombe Gunn.

handshaking—Handshaking refers to the initialization process that two or more computers go through before they are able to communicate. It is the first part of each and every data communications protocol, and is used to establish initial setup parameters.

harmonic distortion—A harmonic frequency is a multiple of a lower frequency. For example, 4,000 and 6,000 Hz are both harmonics of 2,000 Hz. Harmonic distortion describes the tendency to amplify and transmit harmonics of an input signal. Amplifier feedback, the shrieking sound caused by a microphone too close to a loudspeaker, is a type of harmonic distortion.

High-Level Data Link Control (HDLC)—HDLC is an ISO communications protocol that represents a wide variety of Data Link Layer protocols, such as SDLC, LAPB, and LAPD. The operation of HDLC consists of the exchange of different types of frames, including information frames, supervisory frames, and unnumbered frames. Two communicating computers exchange commands and responses by means of the three different types of frames.

interference—Interference refers to any energy that interferes with the clear reception of a signal. For example, if one person is speaking, the sound of a second person's voice interferes with the first. See noise.

International Standards Organization (ISO)—ISO is a voluntary organization, chartered by the United Nations, that defines international standards for all fields other than electricity and electronics. (IEC handles that.) ANSI represents the United States in ISO.

International Telecommunication Union-Telecommunications Standardization Sector (ITU-T)—ITU-T is an intergovernmental organization that develops and adopts international telecommunications standards and treaties. ITU was founded in 1865 and became a United Nations agency in 1947.

jitter—Jitter is a signal distortion caused when a carrier signal is not synchronized to its reference timing positions. Jitter can cause transmission errors and loss of synchronization for high-speed synchronous communication links.

Ka band—The Ka band is a portion of the electromagnetic spectrum ranging in frequency from 20 to 30 GHz, used for satellite communications.

Ku band—The Ku band is a portion of the electromagnetic spectrum ranging in frequency from 11 to 14 GHz, used for satellite communications.

meshed—A meshed network is a network that consists of multiple physical paths between endpoints.

modulation—Modulation is the process of modifying the form of a carrier wave (electrical signal) so that it can carry intelligent information on a communications medium.

Modulo—Modulo is the term used to describe the maximum number of states for a counter. For example, in a satellite communications link, modulo 128 indicates that the packet counter can track 128 outbound and inbound packets before the receiver must send an acknowledgment. After the counter reaches its maximum count, it resets to 0.

multipath reflection—Multipath reflection refers to a situation in which a single radio signal is reflected from several obstacles, causing multiple signals to arrive at a receiving antenna. Because the true signal and reflected signals travel different distances, they arrive at different times, causing audio echoes or video "ghosting." This term is also referred to as multipath reception.

noise—Noise refers to any undesired signal or signal distortion. Noise is often caused by electrical interference. See interference.

overreach—When a radio signal is transmitted from a sending antenna to a receiving antenna by means of an intermediate repeater antenna, overreach occurs when the receiving antenna receives the signal from both the sender (directly) and the repeater. This causes signal interference because the signal received from the repeater is slightly delayed by processing.

permanent virtual circuit (PVC)—A PVC is a connection across a frame relay network, or cell-switching network such as ATM. A PVC behaves like a dedicated line between source and destination endpoints. When activated, a PVC will always establish a path between these two endpoints.

phase modulation (PM)—PM is a type of modulation that uses phase changes to encode information onto a carrier. For example, if the wave is traveling up, a phase change sends the wave back down to its negative value (creating two wave "troughs" in a row, instead of a trough and then a crest).

phase-shift keying (PSK)—PSK represents digital data over an analog carrier by varying the signal's phase, or time displacement. PSK can represent more than 1 bit, depending on the number of phase shifts implemented.

PKZip—PKZip is a file compression utility marketed by PKWARE, Inc.

private network—A private network is a network consisting of private lines, switching equipment, and other networking equipment provided for the exclusive use of one customer. In other words, the network and its associated services are not intended for use by the general public.

provisioning—In the context of telecommunications, provisioning is the process of conditioning a telecommunications circuit for use by an organization.

public network—A public network is a network available to the public for transmission of voice, data, and other types of services.

quadrature amplitude modulation (QAM)—QAM is a method of representing digital data with analog waveforms. QAM varies both the phase and amplitude of an analog signal, making it possible to represent four or more digital bits in a single signal.

quantization noise—Quantization noise is the difference between information contained in an analog signal and that contained in its digital form. Also referred to as quantizing distortion, quantization noise occurs when an analog signal is converted to digital, or digital to analog. The more accurate the conversion, the less quantization noise is contained in the signal.

quantized—An analog signal is quantized when it is converted to a digital format.

rain attenuation—Rain attenuation is the weakening of a radio signal caused by water droplets (rain or fog) in the air. This attenuation increases with the density of fog and rain.

RS-232-D—RS-232-D defines RS-232 serial communications using an RJ-45 connector. The pin assignments for RS-232-D are as follows:

Pin 1—DCE Ready, Ring Indicator

Pin 2—Received Line Signal Detector

Pin 3—DTE Ready

Pin 4—Signal Ground

Pin 5—Received Data

Pin 6—Transmitted Data

Pin 7—Clear to Send

Pin 8—Request to Send

sideband—A sideband is a range of frequencies below or above a signal's carrier-wave frequency (AM) or center frequency (FM). The total bandwidth of a signal is the carrier (center) frequency plus its upper and lower sidebands. Single sideband is an inherent property of FM.

sliding window—The term windowing is also referred to as a sliding window. Windowing provides a method for protocols such as TCP to control the flow of data. It also allows multiple packets or frames of data to be acknowledged with a single response.

smart jack—A smart jack is a device a carrier can attach to the end of a T-carrier circuit to enable the carrier to test the line's condition without the need to manipulate the CPE. The smart jack appears as an RJ-48 jack, and can plug directly into the CSU.

switched virtual circuit (SVC)—An SVC is a temporary connection established through a switched network. During data transmission, an SVC behaves like a wire between the sender and receiver. ATM VCs and telephone connections are both examples of SVCs.

synchronous—A synchronous operation is one in which two communicating devices closely synchronize their internal timing circuits (usually by transmitting a burst of bits of a fixed length before the data). To transmit data, a sending device, such as a modem, puts a 1 or a 0 on the line every so often. A receiving device samples the line on the same timetable as the sending device to receive the information accurately. The devices must stay synchronized to communicate without errors.

Synchronous Data Link Control (SDLC)—SDLC is a subset of the HDLC standard. It is a Data Link Layer protocol most often found in SNA networks.

time slice—In TDM, a time slice (or time slot) is a fixed period of transmission time allotted to traffic from one process, application, or user.

transponder—A transponder is a device carried onboard a satellite that receives a weak microwave signal and amplifies, conditions, and retransmits it back to earth.

Universal Asynchronous Receiver/Transmitter (UART)—A UART is a portion of a serial interface that performs parallel to serial conversion; adds start, stop, and parity bits; monitor's the port's status; controls circuit timing; buffers data; and then reverses the process on the receiving end.

V.10—V.10 is an ITU recommendation for serial communications over unbalanced circuits.

V.11—V.11 is an ITU recommendation for serial communications over balanced circuits.

V.35—The CCITT (ITU) V.35 recommendation specifies a balanced, electrical serial modem communications interface that operates up to 48 Kbps. ITU rescinded V.35 in 1988, and specified the V.10 and V.11 standards as its replacement.

V.90—V.90 is the ITU-T standard for PCM modems running at up to 56 Kbps. V.90 allows for downstream (toward the user) data rates of 56 Kbps (limited to 53 Kbps by FCC regulations) and upstream rates of up to 33.6 Kbps.

V.22bis, V.32bis, V.34bis, V.42bis—The V series includes ITU-T standards for sending data, by means of a modem, over the telephone network:

- V.22bis is an older modem standard for transfer rates up to 1,200 bps.

- V.32bis defines full-duplex, dial-up capabilities up to 14.4 Kbps.

- V.34bis is an improved standard that uses compression techniques to achieve speeds up to 33.6 Kbps.

- V.42bis is a group of protocols that provide error correction by allowing the receiving device to request retransmission of corrupted data.

V.FC—V.FC is a modem communications protocol that supports speeds up to 28.8 Kbps.

virtual circuit—A virtual circuit is a communications path that appears to be a single circuit to the sending and receiving devices. A virtual circuit can traverse multiple physical circuits.

wavelength—A signal's wavelength is the distance an electrical or optical wave travels in a single cycle. Wavelength is inversely proportional to frequency; the greater the wavelength, the shorter the frequency.

white noise—The term white noise refers to random electrical noise or static. See noise.

Lesson 1—Physical and Logical Circuits

This unit reviews the physical foundation that makes up virtually all networks in use today. The intent of this lesson is to familiarize you with circuit types used for communication over WAN facilities.

Objectives

At the end of this lesson you will be able to:

- Describe the concept of a virtual circuit

- Describe the difference between a switched virtual circuit (SVC) and permanent virtual circuit (PVC)

- Explain the steps for an SVC information transfer

Key Point   *A virtual circuit has the appearance of a single physical circuit.*

Circuits and Virtual Circuits

A circuit is the physical connection between two communicating devices. A circuit is also referred to as a channel. Physical circuits can be classified into two broad categories:

- Exclusive-use physical circuit

- Shared-use physical circuit

An exclusive-use physical circuit is one in which a computer and attached devices do not share the circuit with any other device. Examples are the physical circuit connecting a monitor to a video card and the circuit connecting a printer to a parallel port. This type of circuit is shown on the Exclusive-Use Physical Circuit Diagram.

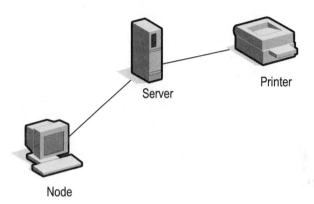

Exclusive-Use Physical Circuit

A shared-use physical circuit is one in which multiple devices share the same physical media. Access to the shared media depends on the media access protocol used, such as Token Ring or Ethernet. The Shared-Use Physical Circuit Diagram demonstrates this arrangement, also referred to as a bus.

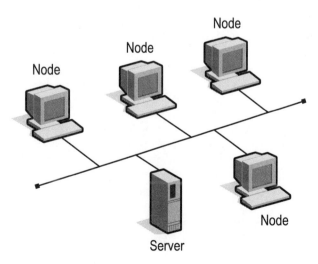

Shared-Use Physical Circuit

A virtual circuit is a communications path that appears to be a single circuit between the source and destination nodes. A virtual circuit is not a physical circuit; it is a logical connection between devices configured over one or more physical circuits.

There are two types of virtual circuits: PVCs and SVCs.

- A PVC behaves like a dedicated connection between source and destination endpoints. A PVC will always establish a predefined path between these two endpoints.

- An SVC is analogous to a public-switched telephone service, in that calls can be made dynamically between a source endpoint and any destination endpoint in a network. The end devices establish a connection on demand and disconnect when communications cease.

PVCs and SVCs

Virtual Circuit

The choice of whether to use a PVC or SVC varies between networks depending on traffic volumes, traffic patterns, degree of connectivity, types of applications, and other parameters. The PVCs and SVCs Table presents some differences between the two types of virtual circuits. Networks can have a mix of PVCs and SVCs.

PVCs and SVCs

PVC	SVC
Statically defined at configuration	Dynamically established when there is information to send
Connection always configured regardless of whether there is information to send	Connection released when there is no more information to send

The primary difference between a PVC and SVC occurs when connections are defined and resources are allocated. PVCs are typically provisioned by a network operator, whether the operator is a carrier (public services) or management information systems (MIS) staff member (private networks). After the PVC is provisioned, the connection is available for use at all times unless there is a change in the service or a service outage. On the other hand, SVCs are established by the end user, not the network operator. Prior to each use, an SVC connection is established to the destination end user. The connection is cleared after each use.

SVC applications are ideal for networks that have the following characteristics:

- Highly meshed connectivity

- Intermittent applications

- Remote site access

Highly meshed connectivity refers to large networks that need any-to-any connectivity, not to be confused with meshed networks that consist of multiple nodes connected by many dedicated physical connections. Multiple virtual circuits can traverse the same physical connections, connecting multiple sites simultaneously. In a networking environment where there is a need to communicate with many locations, SVCs may offer the best solution. The advantages of SVCs are magnified as the number of locations and degree of connectivity requirements increase. Highly meshed networks are becoming more common as more and more companies use intranets. It is conceivable that all end users will have their own World Wide Web (Web) pages within an organization. This will increase the amount of peer-to-peer intracompany traffic. Additionally, a highly meshed network can offer a cost-effective solution for occasional intercompany connections to suppliers, partners, and even customers, provided they all subscribe to the same service.

A network that has highly intermittent applications most often translates to traffic that is unpredictable and short in duration, such as electronic mail (e-mail) traffic. Because SVCs only consume network bandwidth when there is information to send, they are a good solution for short-duration applications.

Initially, some small office and telecommuter locations may not be able to justify the cost of PVCs for all locations to which they need connectivity, because of low traffic volumes and intermittent use. These locations can start with SVCs and gradually migrate to PVCs as traffic volumes increase. A hybrid PVC/SVC solution can be implemented as well. PVCs are often established between locations that require frequent exchange of information, and SVCs are established at locations that only need occasional interaction.

SVC Information Transfer

The transfer of information across an SVC consists of three primary events:

1. Call setup
2. Data transfer
3. Call release (also known as call clearing)

The SVC Sequence Diagram illustrates these steps.

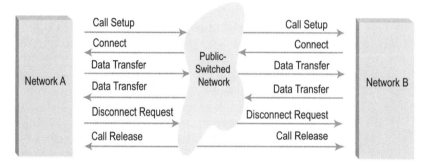

SVC Sequence

When information needs to be sent across an SVC, a setup message is sent to a destination network. After the setup phase is complete and the connection has been established, information can be sent back and forth across the network.

The call release phase consists of a disconnect message sent from the source to the destination. The connection to the network is released at both networks, and a circuit no longer exists between the two networks.

Activities

1. Describe a virtual circuit.

    _____

    _____

    _____

2. For each of the following situations, determine whether the subject behaves more like a logical circuit (PVC or SVC) or a physical circuit (shared or exclusive):

    a. Personal computer (PC) accessing a server across an Ethernet local area network (LAN)

        _____

    b. PC accessing a server across a Token Ring LAN

        _____

    c. Modem connecting a user to the Internet

        _____

    d. Two networks tied together with a T1 circuit

        _____

3. Draw a sequence diagram illustrating the steps/events for an SVC data transfer.

4. Is the diagram below an example of a PVC or an SVC?

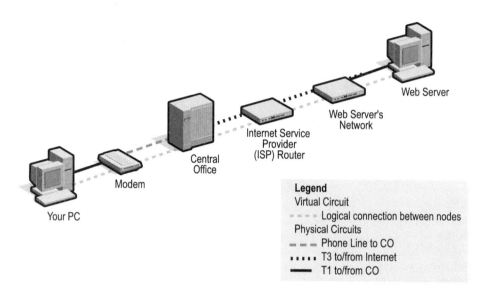

Extended Activities

1. Research how nodes on X.25 packet-switching networks connect, and how they illustrate the concept of an SVC. Summarize your findings.

_____

_____

_____

_____

2. What types of networks use PVCs? How do users of these services benefit over those who use SVCs? How do users of SVCs benefit over users of PVCs?

_____

_____

_____

_____

Lesson 2—Connecting to WAN Circuits

WAN circuits are used to move different types of information across a telecommunications network. This lesson presents the different ways to connect to a WAN.

Objectives

At the end of this lesson you will be able to:

- Describe the layers where data terminal equipment (DTE) and data communications equipment (DCE) function in a WAN

- Explain the concepts of DCE and DTE

 **Key Point**

DCE and DTE are commonly used telecommunications terms.

DCE

Hub
moDem
Switch

Traditional telephony nomenclature for equipment that requests services is DCE. The term data circuit-terminating equipment (DCTE) is also used. DCE can include such items as:

- Modem, if the transmission channel is an analog channel (that is, at least the local loop is an analog channel)

- Digital-encoding device, if the transmission channel is a digital channel

DCE devices are Open Systems Interconnection (OSI) model Layer 1 devices responsible for properly formatting the electrical signals on a physical link, and performing signal clocking and synchronization. DTE is equipment (often a computer) that executes Layer 1, Layer 2, and higher-layer processes; however, it can also be a terminal or other specialized equipment, such as an automated teller machine. Telecommunications terminology lumps all such devices together under the term DTE. The DTE and DCE Diagram illustrates the difference between the two types of equipment.

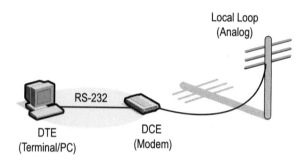

DTE and DCE

DTE-to-DCE Protocols

Router = DTE

Many different standards exist for the DTE/DCE interface. Two important standards are the Electronic Industries Association (EIA) RS-232-D standard and the wideband International Telecommunication Union-Telecommunications Standardization Sector (ITU-T) V.35 standard.

Both standards specify the Physical Layer (mechanical and electrical) properties of the interface and its procedural characteristics. RS-232-D uses a 25-pin connector, called a "DB-25," for the cable that runs between the DTE and DCE (as well as a 9-pin variant, DB-9); V.35 uses a 34-pin V.35 connector. Both the DTE interface and DCE lie at Layer 1 of the OSI model. There are still additional protocols to be considered: those between DTE devices (through DCE), and those between DCE devices themselves.

Layer Upon Layer   In most environments, protocols are grouped into protocols associated with a local area network (LAN), and protocols associated with a WAN. For example, communication might take place between a computer on one LAN with a computer on another LAN using a Layer 3 protocol, such as Internet Protocol (IP). IP packets can be transported across a WAN using a Layer 2 WAN protocol such as frame relay over Layer 1 T1 circuits (discussed later).

As presented in Lesson 1, the type of circuit and connection used between LANs may be either PVC or SVC, depending on the requirements. For example, if we have two LANs we want to connect directly, we might use a PVC as shown on the PVC Diagram. This PVC, implemented using Layer 2 WAN services, may traverse a digital circuit that only executes Physical Layer protocols, such as Dataphone Digital Service (DDS) or T1, and provides only point-to-point connectivity.

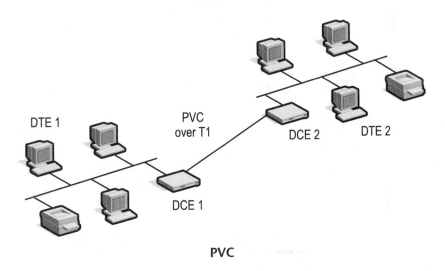

DTE 1   PVC over T1   DCE 2   DTE 2

DCE 1

PVC

On this diagram, information generated by DTE 1 travels through DCE 1, across the PVC to DCE 2. This device then transfers the information across the LAN to the destination DTE (DTE 2).

The SVC Diagram illustrates connectivity between two DTE devices connected by means of an SVC. In this diagram, three, and potentially many more, LANs are connected to a telecommunications service that provides switched connectivity. If DTE 3 were to send data to DTE 4, the DCE devices that attach each of these devices to the network would first establish a connection between themselves. After this virtual circuit is established, the DTE devices could send information to each other. After communication between DTE devices is complete, the virtual circuit is terminated.

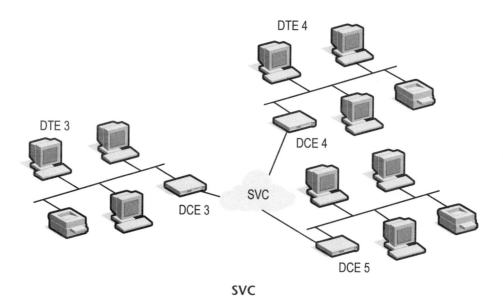

SVC

It should be noted that computers are rarely referred to as DTE; however, in telecommunications terminology, the term is still widely used to group devices that access a WAN. Also note that DCE devices are not necessarily devices that connect to "cabled" networks. These devices can be capable of sending information by other methods, such as microwaves and satellite technology.

Activities

1. List the applicable DTE and DCE interfaces for the following connections:

   a. PC to external modem

   _____

   _____

   b. Terminal connecting to a PVC by means of a digital encoding device

   _____

   _____

   c. Computer connecting to an SVC by means of a modem

   _____

   _____

   d. Terminal connecting to another terminal across a dial-up connection by means of a modem

   _____

   _____

Extended Activity

1. Using the Web, research other Physical Layer standards for DTE-to-DCE connectivity. Include in your research the following standards:

   a. RS-422

   b. RS-423

   c. RS-449

Lesson 3—Connecting to Analog Networks

This lesson reviews key terms and concepts related to connecting computers to the analog network.

Objectives

At the end of this lesson you will be able to:

- Define terminology related to modems

- Describe the basic components of a modem

- Given a link speed, compute the transfer time of different file sizes

 **Key Point**

Modems are needed when sending information across an analog network.

Modem Concepts

When discussing modems, the terms baud, bits per second (bps), bytes, and characters per second (cps) are used. Baud, named after the 19th century French inventor Baudot, originally referred to the speed a telegrapher could send Morse code. It later came to mean the number of times per second a signal changes state. A bit is a single binary piece of data that can be represented by a 0 or 1, thus, it may appear that bps and baud are the same. However, phase shifting and other modulation and data-handling techniques allow more than 1 bit to be transmitted with each baud in high-speed modems; that is, 28,800 bps can be transmitted with a substantially lower baud rate of 3,600 8-bit cps. Therefore, the proper term to use when talking about high-speed modems is bps.

Although a normal byte ("character") contains 8 bits, start and stop bits, which are required for an asynchronous data stream, are added by a sending serial port's Universal Asynchronous Receiver/Transmitter (UART) (pronounced "u-art") and removed by a receiving UART.

The start and stop bits, also known as overhead, reduce the actual throughput. Without the start and stop bits, a throughput of 3,600 cps ([28,800 bps])/([8 bits per character]) could be realized. However, overhead reduces the actual throughput to 2,880 cps ([28,800 bps])/([10 bits per character]). If data compression is enabled, and the data is compressible, the throughput will be greater. This will vary depending on the compressibility of the data, line quality, and a number of other factors. If downloading from the Internet, be aware that the servers we are connected to may be serving many clients simultaneously, and the "time slice" we get may result in data being supplied at a slower rate. With frequent starts and stops, or when connecting to a busy server, we may notice that our 28.8 modem is not getting a chance to perform at its peak; it is waiting more than it is working.

Internal vs. External Modems

An internal modem is a card that plugs into a personal computer's (PC's) bus. These cards contain their own serial port onboard, and use a PC's power supply. External modems are normally self-contained in their own case (or may be rack-mounted in commercial versions), have a separate power supply, and connect to a computer by means of a cable to one of the serial ports on the back of a PC. The Modem Types Diagram illustrates internal and external modems.

External Modem

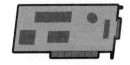
Internal Modem

Modem Types

There are advantages of each type of modem, including:

- Internal modems are typically less expensive because they have no case or power supply. They also require less desk space because they are inside the computer.

- External modems generally incorporate a panel of lights, light-emitting diodes (LEDs), or a liquid crystal display (LCD) to display information about the current session, and aid in problem diagnosis and resolution. External modems can be powered on and off to reset independently from a computer.

UART

Serial devices, such as serial modems, use a UART interface chip to communicate with a PC. External modems connect to a PC using a serial cable hooked to one of the PC's UART-based serial ports; internal modems have a UART-based serial port onboard. Basically, UARTs convert parallel data from a computer into a serial data stream, and vice versa.

RS-232

RS-232 defines the interface between a computer and an external modem. We use the term RS-232 to refer generically to a family of standards developed by EIA, ITU-T, and the International Standards Organization (ISO) to provide computer interfaces to the outside world, especially the telephone network. (Today the official name for the base standard is EIA-232; however, RS-232 is commonly used.) These standards define a serial interface (the computer transmits 1 bit at a time) for data transfer rates such as 19,200 bps. The RS-232 standard defines the meaning of the different signals and their respective pin assignments on a standard 25-pin (DB-25) serial connector, as shown on the RS-232 Cable Connector Pin Placement Diagram.

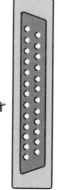

1 (FG) Frame Ground
2 (TD) Transmitted Data
3 (RD) Received Data
4 (RTS) Request to Send
5 (CTS) Clear to Send
6 (DSR) Data Set Ready
7 (SG) Signal Ground
8 (DCD) Data Carrier ~~Signal Detect~~
9 Positive Voltage
10 Negative Voltage
11 Unassigned
12 (SDCD) Secondary DCD
13 (SCTS) Secondary CTS

14 (STD) Secondary Transmitted Data
15 (TC) Transmit Clock
16 (SRD) Secondary RD
17 (RC) Receive Clock
18 Unassigned
19 (SRTS) Secondary RTS
20 (DTR) Data Terminal Ready
21 (SQ) Signal Quality Detector
22 (RI) Ring Indicator
23 (DRS) Data Rate Selector
24 (SCTE) Clock Transmit External
25 (BUSY) Busy

RS-232 Cable Connector Pin Placement

A special case of DTE-to-DTE communications occurs frequently. This is when two DCE devices are physically close together (for example, connecting two computers in the same room). Is it necessary to provide two modems, or can an RS-232 cable simply connect them? In fact, an ordinary cable will not work properly; however, by simply crossing certain wires in a cable, the DTE devices can use the cable by itself. This type of cable is called a "null modem" cable. The Null Modem Diagram illustrates this concept.

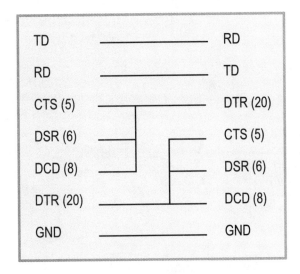

Null Modem

Modem Signals

Although vendors market many different types of modems, all units share common elements: power supply, transmitter, and receiver. The power supply usually takes 120 or 220 volts (V) alternating current (AC) and transforms it into the direct current (DC) voltage required for operation of a modem's internal circuitry; however, an internal modem uses DC voltage provided by the computer's motherboard. The transmitter modulates the digital data into analog form. The receiver demodulates analog signals and changes them into their original digital format, as illustrated on the Modulation Diagram.

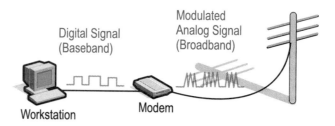

Digital Signal (Baseband)

Modulated Analog Signal (Broadband)

Workstation

Modem

Modulation

Generally, modems are classified as either synchronous or asynchronous. A synchronous modem contains a clock source and phasing circuits, while an asynchronous modem does not. In synchronous transmission, data is sent continuously in regular, clocked intervals. Asynchronous modems do not need clocking sources because each data character is framed by start and stop bits. These modems synchronize on every character; a PC modem is an asynchronous modem.

Activities

1. Start and stop bits are only used for asynchronous transmission. True or False

2. Describe the function of a UART.

   _____

   _____

3. Fill in the chart below showing how long it will take to move certain files across different link speeds. Also indicate the amount of overhead necessary for each.

   For example, to calculate the overhead (2 bits/character) for a 20-kilobyte (KB) (20,000-byte) file, first take the number of bytes in the file and multiple by 10 (8 bits per character plus 2 overhead bits):

   20,000 x 10 = 200,000 total bits transmitted

   Now calculate the number of overhead bits:

   20,000 x 2 = 40,000 total overhead bits

   Divide the overhead bits by the total bits transmitted and multiply by 100 to get the overhead percentage:

   (40,000/200,000) * 100 = 20-percent overhead

   To calculate elapsed time in seconds, take the total bits transmitted and divide by the transmission speed:

   200,000/28,800 = 6.94 seconds

File Size (8-bit characters)	Transmission Speed (Kbps)	Overhead (bits per character)	Overhead (%)	Elapsed Time (seconds)
20 KB	28	2		
20 KB	56	2		
500 KB	28	3		
500 KB	56	3		
1 MB	56	2		
1 MB	128	2	20	
10 MB	56	2		
10 MB	128	2		

Extended Activity

Use a modem eliminator (null modem) cable and Microsoft Windows 95/98/NT Direct Cable Connect feature to connect two computers, such as a laptop and desktop computer. Use Windows Help to assist in the system configurations. Transfer a file between the two computers.

Lesson 4—Analog Modems

Modems are essential components of a data communications network, because they allow communication between digital devices transmitting information over the public or private telephone network, consisting, in part, of analog facilities.

Objectives

At the end of this lesson you will be able to:

- Describe common modem protocols used in today's networks

- Explain the basics of modem protocols and how they are used to communicate information across a telecommunications network

 **Key Point**

Modulation is the process of converting digital information to analog information. Demodulation is the process of converting analog information back to digital.

Modem Protocols

*Slow —
dial anywhere
but slow.*

DCE devices at each end of a communications channel must share the same protocol. A variety of protocols are defined and, in some cases, standardized for communication over analog links (between modems).

Any protocol for communication between modems defines:

- The electrical characteristics of the link that determine the maximum bit rate at which the modems can exchange data

- Whether they will employ compression

- Whether they operate in asynchronous (start-stop) or synchronous mode

- Whether they operate in full- or half-duplex mode

A leased line typically has four wires, although it is possible to lease a two-wire line. A four-wire half-duplex circuit uses one wire pair to transmit in one direction, and the other wire pair to transmit in the other direction; however, transmission does not take place in both directions simultaneously. Four-wire half-duplex is faster than using a single wire pair for both directions, because it is not necessary for the modems to wait for the line to "turn around" each time the direction of data transmission reverses.

Four-wire full-duplex means that data is transmitted in both directions simultaneously, using one wire pair for each direction. In principle, full-duplex allows data to flow in both directions simultaneously. As a practical matter, the primary advantage to full-duplex transmission is that, while messages flow in one direction, "acknowledgments" of previously transmitted messages can flow back to the sender in the opposite direction simultaneously.

It is also possible to implement full-duplex operation on a single pair of wires by using different carrier frequencies in either direction, in a manner similar to frequency-division multiplexers (MUXs).

Modulation

Because portions of the public telephone network may carry analog signals, digital signals must be converted to analog form by a process called "modulation." Modulation modifies the form of a carrier wave (electrical signal) so it can carry intelligent information on some sort of communications medium. Digital computer signals (baseband) are converted to analog signals for transmission over analog facilities, such as the local loop. The opposite process, converting analog signals back into the original digital state, is referred to as demodulation. There are three basic types of modulation, as illustrated on the Modulation Techniques Diagram:

- Frequency modulation (FM)

- Amplitude modulation (AM)

- Phase modulation (PM)

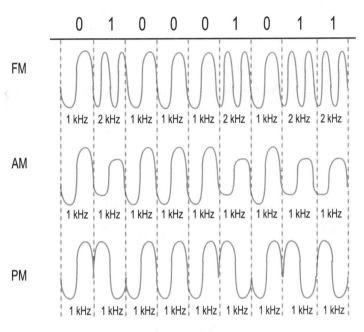

Modulation Techniques

FM *Frequency Modulation*

Pitch

FM is a method of modulating a signal's frequencies so that different frequencies represent different types of intelligence. The most common FM is frequency-shift keying (FSK), a two-level technique used on AT&T 103 and 113 Series modems. FSK modulation represents changes in the binary bit pattern by alterations in the frequency of an audio tone. This line is assumed to be in a steady binary 1 or "mark" state when it is idle, represented by one frequency of tone. When the data bit value 0 is sent, the modem changes to another tone frequency, causing a unique—almost musical—effect during the sending of data. FSK modulation works well for relatively low speeds; however, as the speed of the digital signal increases, the time allocated to shift frequencies is reduced. Both the production and detection of audible changes become more difficult.

AM ~Amplification~ ~Modulation~

AM is a signal modulation technique that changes the sound level, or amplitude, of a signal to represent different types of intelligence. As the simplest modulation technique, AM generates a single carrier frequency signal. If the resultant wave is of high amplitude, it denotes a binary 1; if it is of low amplitude, it denotes a binary 0. AM is highly susceptible to line interference. Quadrature amplitude modulation (QAM) is a combination of AM and PM. This method uses two signals at the same frequency; however, they are 90 degrees out of phase with each other so that the highest amplitude point on waveform A occurs 90 degrees after the same point on waveform B. These signals are combined, or summed, into one signal for transmission. This is known as 16-QAM and is illustrated on the QAM 16-Point Constellation Diagram. This diagram illustrates the relationship between the phase variations (lines) and amplitude values (dots).

~Cable/QAM~
~AM/PM~

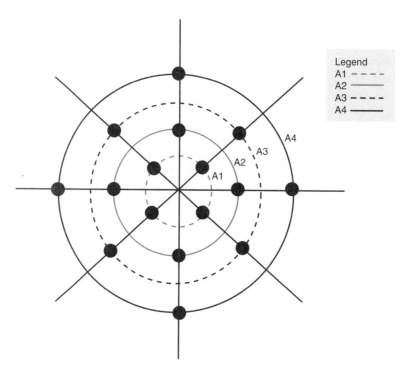

QAM 16-Point Constellation

The transmitting circuit can apply four possible levels of amplitude (A1, A2, A3, and A4) to represent different combinations of 4 bits at four separate angles on the transmitted waveform. In this example, the transmitter sets the amplitude at the waveforms' 45-, 135-, 225-, and 315-degree positions. Because each of these four positions can be set to any of the four amplitudes, this combination of four possible amplitudes at four sampling points results in 16 possible different conditions, each representing 4 bits of information. The output results in a 4:1 ratio of bits to baud, effectively quadrupling the circuit's throughput.

It is also possible to represent 32 different conditions (32-QAM), generating twice as much information, by either sampling at 22.5-degree intervals, or setting eight possible amplitudes per sample angle.

PM *Phased Modulation*

PM is a modulation technique where a change in signal phase can represent a specific intelligence type. Phase-shift keying (PSK), a type of PM, uses changes in the phase of a signal, or its timing relationship to a fixed reference, to indicate a change in the bit pattern. Bits are represented by two phase changes; dibits are represented by four phase changes. A reference oscillator determines the phase angle change of the incoming signal, which, in turn, determines which bit or dibit (two bits) is being transmitted. Differential phase-shift keying (DPSK) compares the phase angle of the incoming signal to the previously received dibit. A change in phase is interpreted as a specific two-digit binary number, depending on the angular difference between the waveforms. This method does not require a separate reference wave, thereby reducing the amount of circuitry in the modem. PSK is used in many medium-speed modems, and is combined with AM in high-speed applications to form QAM, the technique for 9,600 bps and higher.

Modem Operations

Modems are often capable of operating at several different speeds. Users can adjust operation speeds by means of software commands or changes in components, wires, or switch settings. A modem's fallback rate refers to its capability to detect poor line conditions and lower transmission speeds to prevent errors. For example, a modem operating at 28.8 Kbps may fall back to 9.6 or 4.8 Kbps when line conditions deteriorate.

The V.32bis standard includes a provision for an optional fall-forward feature. This allows a modem to actively poll the line, determine when conditions improve, and then reset itself to the highest rate conditions warrant. This can be a very valuable feature, because a small line impairment at the beginning of a lengthy file transfer could turn a 30-minute telephone call into an expensive 3-hour data transfer. With fall forward, a modem might only be at the lower speed for a few minutes.

Limited-distance modems can often provide high data rates over private lines for a local area. As the data rate increases, the distance over which transmission is effective decreases, sometimes dramatically.

Under ideal telephone line conditions, 28.8-Kbps modems transmit data at 28,800 bps. By using data compression, the modems can achieve throughputs of twice or more that rate on compressible files.

The 28.8-Kbps modem "standards" are V.FC and V.34. The V.FC protocol is an interim protocol developed by Rockwell and introduced ahead of the V.34 standard. V.34 is a more robust protocol, and already most new 28.8-Kbps modems meet the V.34 standard (or both V.34 and V.FC for backward compatibility).

The 28.8-Kbps modems use nearly the full bandwidth of the present day telephone system. Actually they use more than the "rated" bandwidth; that is, 28.8 Kbps is pushing the speed limit of the current analog telephone system. A couple of high-end modems have been developed with an extension of the 1994 V.34 standard that support speeds up to 33.6 Kbps (AT&T and USR Courier). However, many users of these modems will not be able to achieve connections at these rates because of telephone line conditions.

Because binary numbers used in QAM and DPSK can only represent discrete points on the continuous source analog waveform, the digits sent across the local loop and reconstructed at the other end can only approximate the original analog waveform. The difference between the original waveform and the reconstructed quantized waveform is called "quantization noise," and it limits modem speed.

If quantization noise limits the analog communications channel to 35 Kbps, then how do we accomplish connection speeds approaching 56 Kbps on a V.90 modem? The V.90 standard specifies that there may only be one analog-to-digital conversion in the path between your carrier and your modem. Because quantization noise affects only analog-to-digital conversion, not digital-to-analog, and V.90 circuits are digital up to the central office's (CO's) end of the analog local loop, V.90 can eliminate the effects of quantization noise on the downstream path; this is the key to V.90. Additionally, because the standard requires that the original digital signal present only 256 discrete signal levels to the CO's digital-to-analog converter, and these levels are easily recovered from the received analog waveform by the receiver's analog-to-digital converter, no information is lost in the analog-to-digital conversion processes. However, the upstream data is limited to approximately 35 Kbps by quantization noise.

Here is how the process works:

1. The server connects, in effect, digitally to the telephone company trunk.

2. The server signaling is such that the encoding process uses only the 256 pulse code modulation (PCM) codes used in the digital portion of the telephone network. In other words, there is no quantization noise associated with converting analog-type signals to discrete valued PCM codes.

3. These PCM codes are converted to corresponding discrete analog voltages and sent to the analog modem by means of an analog loop circuit, with no information loss.

4. The client receiver reconstructs the discrete network PCM codes from the analog signals it received, decoding what the transmitter sent.

Data is sent from the V.90 digital modem over the local loop as binary numbers. If the above-listed conditions exist, rates nearing 56 Kbps can be achieved across the local loop. The V.92 standard proposes to increase the upstream data rate to 48 Kbps, while maintaining downstream rates of approximately 53 Kbps.

ADSL = Asymetric DSL — faster ↑ + ↓
faster down than up.

Activities

1. PAM is a combination of AM and PM. True or False

2. List and describe the modem protocol considerations.

   _____

   _____

   _____

   _____

   _____

3. Describe half-duplex and full-duplex and their relationship to two-wire and four-wire lines.

   _____

   _____

   _____

   _____

4. Briefly describe 16-QAM.

   _____

   _____

5. Fill in the chart below showing how long it will take to move certain files across different link speeds and at different compression rates. Disregard overhead.

   There are several ways to calculate the results of compression applied to a file. For example, if a file is 30 percent compressed, that means 70 percent of the original size is being transmitted (100 - 30 = 70). If a 20-KB file is 30 percent compressed, the elapsed time is calculated by:

   20,000 x 8 = 160,000 total bits to be transmitted

   160,000 x 0.70 = 112,000 bits as a result of 30-percent compression

   112,000/56,000 = 2 seconds elapsed time

Another way to calculate the elapsed time is to apply the formula:

$$Et = \{[Fs-(Fs \times Pc)] \times Bc\}/Ts$$

Where   Et = Elapsed time in seconds

Fs = File size in bytes

Pc = Percent compression

Bc = Bits per character

Ts = Transmission speed in bps

File Size (8-bit Characters)	Transmission Speed (Kbps)	Percent Compression	Elapsed Time (seconds)
20 KB	56	0	
20 KB	56	30	
500 KB	128	20	
500 KB	128	40	
1 MB	256	30	
1 MB	256	50	
10 MB	256	30	
10 MB	256	70	

Extended Activities

1. Go to the Web site **http://www.3com.com/technology** and read the white paper entitled "3Com V.90 Technology." Be prepared to discuss in class.

2. Go to **http://www.nwfusion.com** and search for the terms V.90 and V.92. How do the standards differ in their implementations? How does V.92 improve upon V.90? Why are Internet service providers (ISPs) and telecommunications carriers concerned over this new modem standard? Summarize your findings.

_____

_____

_____

_____

_____

_____

Lesson 5—Modem Compatibility

To communicate, modems must be synchronized. This synchronization occurs so that each individual bit that travels down a communications circuit can be received correctly. This lesson covers synchronization and other important operation characteristics of modems.

Objectives

At the end of this lesson you will be able to:

- Distinguish between asynchronous and synchronous communication

- Explain why bit timing is important

 **Key Point**

WANs use both synchronous and asynchronous communication.

Timing is Everything

To ensure an orderly data flow across a communications facility, a time relationship, known as synchronization, must exist among the bits that make up the messages. The two basic forms of synchronization are asynchronous and synchronous. PC-to-PC transmissions by means of modems usually occur in asynchronous mode. Synchronous mode accommodates communications from PCs or terminals to mainframes.

Asynchronous operation means that characters are not transmitted on any strict timetable, as illustrated on the Asynchronous and Synchronous Transmission Diagram. The start of each character is indicated by transmitting a start bit. After the final bit of the character is transmitted, a stop bit is sent, indicating the end of the character. Typically another bit is added to each character referred to as a parity bit. A parity bit is used as a crude form of error checking in asynchronous networks. With even parity, the parity bit plus the number of 1s in the character equal an even number. With odd parity, the parity bit plus the number of 1s in the character is an odd number. The receiving circuit counts the bits and checks the parity bit, and uses this information to detect transmission errors. The modems must stay synchronized only for the length of time it takes to transmit the 8 bits. If their clocks are slightly out of synchronization, data transfer will still be successful.

Asynchronous

PPP.
point to point protocol

Synchronous
RoB/Bit Signalling
TDM

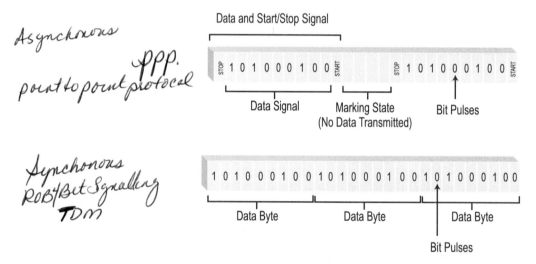

Asynchronous and Synchronous Transmission

Synchronous operation is the opposite: the modems must first closely synchronize their internal timing circuits, usually by transmitting a burst of bits of a fixed length just before the data. To transmit data, the sending modem puts a 1 or a 0 on the line every so often. The receiving modem samples the line on the same timetable and transmits the condition of the line (1 or 0) to the DTE. The modems must remain synchronized to communicate.

Data Compression and Error Control

Data compression is a technique that eliminates repetitious characters and encodes recurring character groups. This dramatically improves data transfer rates. The Consultative Committee for International Telegraphy Telephony's (CCITT's) V.42bis, offered on most high-speed modems, provides 4:1 compression. Thus, a 14.4-Kbps modem with V.42bis has a maximum throughput rate of 57.6 Kbps. Files already reduced by compression programs such as PKZip, will not be further compressed by these protocols. Moreover, the 4:1 compression rate is only theoretical. For example, V.42bis usually yields between 2:1 and 3:1 compression, depending on the type of data and telephone line conditions.

One of the main problems of data transmission is the varying quality of analog voice-grade telephone lines. In addition to the usual limitations of analog lines, many errors can enter the bit stream from transient noise, harmonic distortion, phase jitter, and other signal disruptions. Current solutions to these problems include expensive line conditioning and/or selection of modems that perform sophisticated line-equalization functions. Forward error correction (FEC) techniques enable a processor to put a bit stream through a series of complex algorithms before transmission occurs, resulting in a rearranged bit sequence with extra bits added to the original block of data. At the receiving end of the communications circuit, another processor decodes the bit stream. The bits inserted at the transmitting end determine whether the block was received correctly, and correct any blocks received incorrectly. These adjustments all occur without retransmission of any part of the original data.

To accommodate growth in the use of microcomputer dial-up links, error-correction protocols have been introduced to ensure file transfer data integrity. Online information services, e-mail facilities, and packet networks all require different protocols. Furthermore, PC-to-host links have their own protocol specifications. No single protocol meets all communication needs, and users have several options. Some facilities have circumvented the protocol compatibility issue by implementing error-correcting modems that allow a host to communicate with various American Standard Code for Information Interchange (ASCII)-based systems without disturbing the host software or communications port.

Modem Compatibility

"Handshaking" refers to the initialization process that two or more computers go through before they are able to communicate. It is the first part of each and every data communications protocol. Control signals are exchanged between communicating devices that establish the connection. Standards govern the signals required to set up, transmit, and terminate calls. For a handshake to occur, modems must be compatible. Mixing modems from different suppliers in one network is a common practice because data communications networks are frequently implemented in stages, with ongoing equipment procurements over long periods of time. When organizational changes occur, suppliers that first provided network modems may no longer be doing so. In addition, in organizations without central network management, several individuals may be purchasing equipment for one integrated network. Because most equipment in a network is replaced as it begins to age or malfunction, users can easily switch suppliers. Data communications involves both geographic and corporate distance, which can lead to a division of responsibility and different restrictions on the communications facilities.

AT&T Compatibility

Just as IBM traditionally set the standards for mainframe communications and equipment, AT&T has set the standards for communications by means of modems. Although this situation is changing, many older AT&T modems (often referred to as Bell System modems) are still well known, widely used, and frequently duplicated by other vendors. Modems compatible with a particular AT&T modem specification are likely to be compatible with one another, even if manufactured by different vendors. Manufacturers of AT&T-compatible modems tend to embellish original AT&T specifications with convenience features to distinguish their products from those of competitors.

Compatibility between modems depends significantly on the exactness with which their modulation techniques conform to the AT&T specification. A vendor that has benefited from refining an AT&T standard may alter a specification to such a degree that the unit is incompatible with the original AT&T product. For the most part, manufacturers claiming AT&T compatibility need not be regarded with suspicion.

**CCITT
Compatibility**

Many dial-up and private-line modems conform to CCITT standards, such as the older standard V.32bis for 14.4-Kbps transmission. CCITT V Series modem specifications call for newer, faster modems to be backward compatible with their earlier counterparts.

Because signaling conventions and equipment differ from continent to continent, compatibility problems can arise when modems designed primarily for European facilities are used on North American networks. For example, a V.22bis modem made for U.S. operation can generally initiate a call to a European-based V.22bis modem because it will tolerate minor differences in facilities encountered while establishing the call. The same call cannot be completed if the European modem is the originator.

**Hayes
Compatibility**

Another type of compatibility, indigenous to microcomputer modems, involves the Hayes AT (short for ATtention) command structure. Primarily, Hayes compatibility relates to modem commands, modem responses, and the ability to provide settings that are compatible with various communications programs. Hayes-compatible products have speakers for audibly following calls in progress, front-panel status lights on external units, and auto dial, auto answer, manual dial, and manual answer features for asynchronous operation.

Activities

1. What are start and stop bits used for in communication?

   _____

   _____

2. What type of communication needs a clock?

   _____

   _____

3. If the following bytes were being transmitted and the parity was odd, what would the parity bit be set to in each (0 or 1)? (Note: Normally parity is used with 7-bit codes.)

   a. 11001011

   _____

   b. 10101010

   _____

   c. 00011010

   _____

   d. 11111111

   _____

4. What is FEC?

   _____

   _____

   _____

5. Which is more efficient, synchronous or asynchronous transmission? Explain.

   _____

   _____

   _____

6. Fill in the following chart:

In these calculations, instead of compression being expressed as a percentage, it is shown as a ratio. Calculate the ratio as a percentage and plug the value in as illustrated previously. For example, a compression ratio of 3:1 means for every 3 bytes, 1 byte is output. A percentage is calculated by:

$$100 - (1/3) = 0.667 \text{ or } 66.7\text{-percent compression}$$

Apply the formula:

$$Et = \{[Fs-(Fs \times Pc)] \times Bc\}/Ts$$

Where Et = Elapsed time in seconds

Fs = File size in bytes

Pc = Percent compression

Bc = Bits per character

Ts = Transmission speed in bps

File Size (8-bit characters)	Transmission Speed (Kbps)	Compression Ratio	Elapsed Time (seconds)
20 KB	56	3:1	
20 KB	56	2:1	
500 KB	128	2:1	
500 KB	128	3:1	
1 MB	256	3:1	
1 MB	256	2:1	
10 MB	256	2:1	
10 MB	256	3:1	

Extended Activity

Transfer a file between two PCs, or a PC and laptop, using a modem eliminator (null modem) cable and Windows 95/98 dial-up networking capabilities. Determine the transfer rate of the file transfer. Next, compress the file and send it again. Compare the two results.

_____

_____

_____

_____

Lesson 6—Connecting to Digital Networks

When connecting to an analog network, modems are used to convert digital pulses to analog waveforms. However, a WAN may be made up of physical circuits that can transport digital information. This lesson looks at methods used to connect to digital networks.

Objectives

At the end of this lesson you will be able to:

- Explain when a channel service unit (CSU) and data service unit (DSU) are used for WAN connectivity

- Name at least one digital service provided by telecommunications carriers

Key Point

Data may travel from source to destination across a WAN in digital format.

DTE/CSU Interface

CPE
Customer
premise
Equipment

The local loop for digital service always terminates at a CSU in a subscriber's building, as illustrated on the CSU/DSU Diagram.

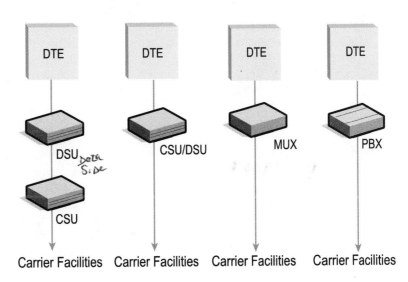

CSU/DSU

143

The CSU is the device that actually generates transmission signals on the local loop, that is, the telephone channel. A DTE connects to a CSU in several ways, including:

- Through a DSU—When digital services were first made available to subscribers, telephone companies would never allow subscriber equipment to attach directly to a local loop, therefore, a CSU was provided by the telephone company. The DSU was a separate device provided by a subscriber. Today, CSUs and DSUs are combined in a single device CSU/DSU typically owned by a subscriber.

- Through a MUX.

- Through a channel bank that is part of a private branch exchange (PBX)—A CSU will often be built into a PBX.

It should be noted that for many data networking devices, the CSU/DSU functionality is included as part of the actual device and not a separate component. An example is a router with a WAN port for connecting to a T1 circuit.

Smart Jack

A carrier can terminate a T1's local loop through a smart jack. A smart jack allows the carrier to perform T1 circuit integrity checks independent of the customer-owned CSU/DSU equipment. The smart jack appears as an RJ-48 connector, and is commonly plugged in to the customer premises equipment (CPE). The carrier activates the smart jack by sending a signal down the T1's transmit side, causing the smart jack to electrically disconnect from the CSU/DSU and loop back the T1 circuit to the carrier. The carrier can then test the circuit without dispatching a technician or looping back the CSU/DSU.

Subrate Facilities

Anything less than 1 channel/DS0

Any facility that operates at a data rate less than digital signal level 0 (DS0) (64 Kbps) is referred to as a subrate facility. AT&T's DDS and British Telcom's KiloStream are examples of subrate facilities. The first digital telecommunications facilities made available to subscribers were based on DS0 in North America and equivalent services in other parts of the world, and were therefore subrate facilities. Other subrate facilities are very similar.

DDS

DDS provides a subscriber with access to a digital network spanning the United States. The subscriber uses all or some portion of a DS0 channel. The following DDS services are offered:

- 2,400 bps leased

- 4,800 bps leased

- 9,600 bps leased

- 19.2 Kbps leased

- 56.0 Kbps leased

- 56.0 Kbps switched

A subscriber must connect to a DDS facility through a CSU/DSU. The local loop operates at the bit rate of the service the subscriber has selected. However, from the end office onward, the telephone company multiplexes it with other DDS lines and voice channels on T-carriers. This includes multiplexing multiple DDS lines onto a single 64-Kbps DS0 channel.

DDS II operates at the same speeds and in the same manner as DDS, but also provides a diagnostic channel for each primary subrate channel. A subscriber can, with newer CSU/DSU equipment, take advantage of the diagnostic channel for nondisruptive testing and network management purposes.

Multiple subrate facilities can be multiplexed into a single DS0 by a subscriber. This is called "subrate multiplexing."

Activities

1. Contrast using a modem with using a CSU/DSU. When should you use one over the other?

   _____

   _____

   _____

   _____

2. What digital service(s) are provided by telecommunications carriers?

   _____

   _____

3. Determine the number of DS0s (64-Kbps circuits) it will take to accommodate each of the following combined individual subrate services. For each column, list the number of circuits required.

Transfer Rates	Number of 64 Kbps Circuits (Clear Channel)	Number of 56-Kbps Circuits	Total Bit Stream Speed
3-19.2 Kbps, 1-56 Kbps			
4-19.2 Kbps 1-33.6 Kbps			
3-33.6 Kbps 2-14.4 Kbps			
4-19.2 Kbps 7-56 Kbps 2-14.4 Kbps			

Extended Activities

1. Using the Web, research current developments in the following types of products:

   a. CSU

   b. DSU

   c. DDS and DDS II

   d. PBX

2. Research digital communications services available in your country. The following Universal Resource Locator (URL) provides links to many international telecommunications agencies:

   http://www.fcc.gov/mmb/asd/bickel/foreign. html

Lesson 7—Microwave Communications

Microwave communications are used to communicate between networks in a variety of ways. Microwave may be used to communicate voice or data traffic over short, line-of-site distances, or over longer distances with the use of microwave repeaters. This lesson reviews basic principles of microwave systems.

Objectives

At the end of this lesson you will be able to:

- Describe how microwave communications are used in networking

- List advantages and disadvantages of microwave networks

 **Key Point**

Microwave circuits use RF signals to communicate bits between two points.

Fundamentals of Microwave Communications

Microwave communications is one of the most widely used transmission methods in the United States. Microwave systems normally use FM. Operating characteristics involve generating a radio frequency (RF) signal that is, in turn, modulated, amplified, and passed to a transmitting antenna system. The resultant signal passes through the air to a receiving antenna where it is sampled, amplified, and demodulated. In general, microwave characteristics are similar to low-frequency radio, except microwave is considerably more efficient at both an engineering and cost level than lower-frequency radio transmission.

For example, the wavelength for a very high frequency (VHF) channel with a frequency of 50 megahertz (MHz) is approximately 20 feet (6 meters). To obtain maximum signal efficiency, a receiving antenna is normally set to one-half the signal's wavelength. This would mean the receiving antenna for this 50-MHz signal would have to be approximately 10 feet long. On the other hand, a 4-gigahertz (GHz) microwave signal sustains a wavelength of just 3 inches, which reduces not only required antenna size, but capital outlay as well.

Microwave systems operate over line-of-sight paths. This means that for a signal to pass from transmitter to receiver, each antenna system must be able to "see" the other. At first, this approach may appear restrictive; however, at the higher frequencies used in microwave transmission, radio waves exhibit quite similar qualities to those of light waves. (For example, they can be focused.) As a result, over short distances, users can readily manipulate signal orientation to maintain line-of-sight through use of intermediate antennas or passive reflectors. Over longer distances, a series of secondary transmission/receiving systems, or relays, must be used. These components provide additional gain and directional control for line-of-sight maintenance, as well as obstacle avoidance. The Microwave Repeater Diagram illustrates this type of microwave system.

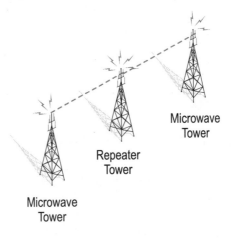

Microwave
Tower

Repeater
Tower

Microwave
Tower

Microwave Repeater

Microwave systems have their disadvantages. Microwave signals have a fundamental tendency to fade. Typically this results from signal-based interference or environmental effects, such as multipath reflection or heavy rain. Signal interference may be in the form of overreach, where a signal feeds past a repeater to a receiving antenna at the next station, and is typically controlled through definition of a zigzag signal path or use of alternate frequencies between receiving stations. Another type of signal-based anomaly occasionally occurs due to adjacent channel interference, where a channel can overpower an adjacent channel or cross the guardband between channels. This has been largely eliminated by advancements in bandpass filtering.

On the environmental side, multipath anomalies occur when a main wave, traveling line-of-sight between antennas, is reflected over a secondary path due to effects fostered by climatic changes, such as heavy ground fog. The Multipath Anomaly Diagram illustrates this concept. Because the secondary wave traces a longer distance to the antenna than the main wave, it arrives slightly out of phase. This creates a condition that results in reduced signal level. Rain attenuation typically occurs as a result of signal power absorption at frequencies greater than approximately 10 GHz.

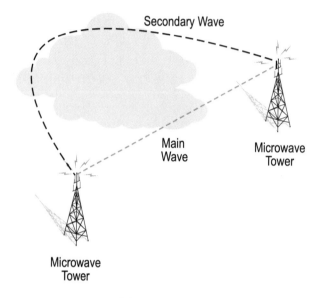

Multipath Anomaly

Microwave Components

Components and methods required to initiate a microwave network are readily available. Typically, they fall into one of four categories:

- MUXs

- Modems

- Transmitters/receivers

- Antenna equipment

MUXs

There are two types of MUXs used in microwave systems: time-division MUXs and frequency-division MUXs.

Both AM and FM are used with microwave systems; however, the majority of today's microwave systems use FM technology. This is due to single sideband's increased bandwidth efficiency over longer distances.

Modems

The primary advantage of using microwave technology over analog systems, such as a dial-up connection, is the inherent noise reduction capabilities of the microwave system's digital inputs and outputs. This results in improved signal integrity as a signal passes from transmitter to repeater to receiver, over long distances. This noise reduction capability allows a microwave system to accurately re-create the 1s and 0s of the original signal intelligence, and regenerate and propagate the original signal accurately over multiple hops. This commonly results in signal quality comparable to that of a T1 network.

Transmitters/ Receivers

The RF output of microwave transmitters varies by the solid-state devices that create the output waveforms. The two most common devices are the Gunn diode and Gallium Arsenide Field Effect Transistor (GaAs-FET).

Gunn diodes provide excellent frequency response and low output noise levels, and typically perform best in the 2 to 23 GHz bands. Use of GaAs-FETs appear to be the trend, particularly in light of convergence technology that will demand continual operation at higher frequency levels.

A microwave receiver, on the other hand, is nearly a mirror image of a transmitter. An antenna receives a signal and passes it on to a receiver or repeater as required.

Antenna Equipment

There are two types of antennas used in microwave systems: parabolic and horn. This increases efficiency by concentrating signal strength in a narrow beam. Antenna efficiency is expressed in terms of "gain." The antenna itself is a passive component, meaning it does not alter the received intelligence in any way. Signal gain is proportional to antenna diameter; therefore, the antenna system does have a direct effect on system performance. The larger the antenna, the higher the amplitude of the received signal.

Activities

1. What are the advantages and disadvantages of microwave systems?

   _____

   _____

   _____

   _____

   _____

2. How does the fact that microwave technology is "line of sight" impact the decision of whether to use microwaves?

   _____

   _____

3. How might microwave technology be beneficial in a rural area?

   _____

   _____

4. How might microwave technology be beneficial in a city?

   _____

   _____

5. What is the primary advantage of using microwave technology instead of dial-up connection?

   _____

   _____

Extended Activities

1. Using the Web, research current developments in microwave technology. In your research, answer the following questions:

   a. How are microwaves used to transmit data in a metropolitan area network (MAN)?

   _____

   _____

   b. How are microwaves used to communicate information between two buildings in the same office complex?

   _____

   _____

   c. At what speeds do microwaves operate?

   _____

   _____

   d. What microwave alternatives are available in your area?

   _____

   _____

2. Review international microwave communications applications and standards at the following Web sites:

   a. European community:
      http://www.etsi.org

   b. Australia:
      http://www.aca.gov.au/authority

   c. Japan:
      http://www.joho.soumu.go.jp/

   d. Other locations:
      http://www.fcc.gov/mmb/asd/bickel/foreign.html

Lesson 8—Satellite Communications

Satellite systems are frequently used for communicating information across wide areas, especially from one nation to another.

Objectives

At the end of this lesson you will be able to:

- List functions of satellite systems

- Name components found in satellite systems

Key Point

Satellites are primarily used in the television, data communications, and scientific industries.

Linking to a Satellite

A satellite is a communication transmission device that receives a signal from a ground station, amplifies it, and broadcasts it to all earth stations capable of seeing the satellite and receiving its transmissions. A satellite transmission begins at a single earth station, passes through the satellite, and ends at one or more earth stations. The satellite itself is an active relay, much like relays used in terrestrial microwave communications. The Satellite Signal Path Diagram illustrates the path a signal takes through a satellite.

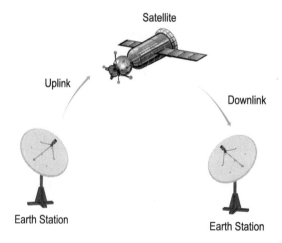

Satellite Signal Path

The four basic functions of a satellite are:

- Receiving a signal from an earth station
- Changing the frequency of the received signal (uplink)
- Amplifying the received signal
- Retransmitting the signal to one or more earth stations (downlink)

Satellite Equipment

Satellite equipment is similar in function to microwave equipment. Common components found in satellite systems are:

- MUXs
- Modems
- Transmitters/receivers
- Antenna equipment

Satellite Frequency Ranges

There are three frequency ranges used in satellite transmission:

- (1) C band—Uplink frequencies in C band are in the 6-GHz range. Downlink frequencies are in the 4-GHz range. *Large Dishes in back yard Full.*
- (2) Ku band—Uplink frequencies in Ku band are in the 14-GHz range. Downlink frequencies are in the 11-GHz range.
- (3) Ka band—Uplink frequencies in Ka band are in the 30-GHz range. Downlink frequencies are in the 20-GHz range. Because *Small dishes* the frequency range for Ka band is higher than C or Ku bands, the wavelength is shorter. Therefore, antennas used for these types of systems are smaller and less expensive.

higher frequency smaller the wave Smaller the dishes

The satellite uplink and downlink frequencies differ to prevent the relatively high-powered transmit signal from interfering with the lower-power received signal. When a signal from the earth station travels the distance between the earth and the satellite (22,238 statute miles), it weakens considerably. If the stronger transmitted signal shared the same frequency as the received signal, it would overwhelm the weaker signal and destroy the carried intelligence.

Satellite Characteristics

Communications satellites have unique attributes that distinguish them from other communications technologies. Some attributes provide advantages that make satellites practical and attractive for certain profitable applications. Advantages of satellites include the following:

- High bandwidth—Satellite signals are at very high frequencies, capable of carrying large amounts of data.

- Low error rates—Bit errors in a digital satellite signal occur almost completely at random. Therefore, statistical systems for error detection and correction, such as FEC, can be applied efficiently and reliably.

Some disadvantages of satellites, making them impractical or unusable for other applications, include the following:

- Signal delay—The large distance from the ground to a satellite in geosynchronous orbit means that any roundtrip (up and down) transmission over a satellite link has an inherent propagation delay of roughly 250 milliseconds (msec) (quarter of a second). This delay creates a noticeable effect in voice communication, and makes the use of satellite links extremely inefficient with data communications protocols that have not been adapted for use over a satellite circuit.

- Earth station size—The combination of Federal Communications Commission (FCC)-mandated, 2-degree orbital spacing of satellites, and the low power of satellite signals in some frequency bands, further combined with the large distances signals must span, produces an extremely weak signal at a receiving earth station. Until new, higher-powered satellites are in place, these factors will tend to result in large earth station antenna diameters, limiting the ease of installation.

- Security—All satellite signals are broadcast, and therefore not secure unless they are encrypted. Any receiving station within sight of a satellite can receive any signal transmitted over the satellite, if the receiving station is tuned to the proper frequency.

- Interference—Satellite signals operating at Ku- or Ka-band frequencies are very susceptible to interference from bad weather, especially rain or fog. Bad weather interference can provide sporadic, unpredictable performance in the K bands from a few minutes to a few hours. Satellite networks operating at C band are susceptible to interference from terrestrial microwave signals. Terrestrial interference in C band limits the deployment of earth stations in major metropolitan areas, where users are more heavily concentrated.

These advantages and limitations of satellite systems heavily influence decisions regarding the use and types of satellite systems selected for private networks. Users with satellite-compatible network requirements (for example, networks with geographically dispersed locations and large bandwidth requirements within the network) may be interested in the economic advantages of satellite over terrestrial networks.

Satellites and Orbits

Communications satellites currently in commercial use occupy geosynchronous orbits in which the period of orbit is equal to that of a point on the earth's surface. Thus, a satellite appears to remain fixed over a position on the earth. This occurs at a distance of 22,300 statute miles (35,800 kilometers [km]) from the surface of the earth on a plane passing through the equator. The velocity of a satellite is 6,879 miles per hour (mph).

The distance to synchronous orbit results in the first major restriction of satellite communications. Radio signals transmitted over satellite links travel at the speed of light (186,000 miles per second or 300,000 km per second). At that speed, a signal takes approximately 125 msec (1/8 second) to reach a satellite from earth, and the same amount of time to return to earth. This 250-msec signal propagation delay, which is inherent in using a satellite channel, is several times the delay for a signal transmitted over any terrestrial link.

Bandwidth

Satellites offer a very large bandwidth, as great as, or greater than, most other transmission media. Consider that a single color television channel occupies 6 MHz. Each transponder (device that receives and retransmits a signal) on most current communications satellites offers a bandwidth of 36 MHz. A typical communications satellite carries 12 or 24 transponders, for a total bandwidth of 432 or 864 MHz, respectively. Most satellite carriers accommodate only one television channel per 36-MHz transponder. This is because the 6-MHz television signal is at video baseband. The television transmitter frequency modulates the signal between 6 and 27 MHz, requiring most of the transponder's available bandwidth.

Satellite Protocols

The special properties of satellite circuits have major effects on the efficiency, and even practicality, of certain data communications protocols. The two most important factors are a satellite channel's inherent 250-msec propagation delay and the relatively high level of noise on satellite channels. Of the two factors, the propagation delay is the more important.

"Sliding window" protocols, such as X.25, permit multiple data blocks to be outstanding and unacknowledged without stopping a sender from transmitting. Protocols that do not permit sliding windows require an acknowledgment for each frame sent and wait for the acknowledgment before transmitting the next frame. The best protocols for satellite transmission are bit-serial protocols, such as High-Level Data Link Control (HDLC) and IBM's Synchronous Data Link Control (SDLC). In these protocols, the unit of transmission is a frame of variable, but usually large, length. Each frame requires acknowledgment of its correct reception from a receiving station; however, the transmitting station can continue sending frames up to the limits of a counter contained in each frame.

This counter, which is incremented with transmission of each frame, defines a frame window, or modulo. It represents the number of frames a station can transmit before it must wait for an acknowledgment from the receiving station. The maximum number of such frames is the window size minus one, and most forms of sliding window protocols use a window size of eight. With a 3-bit window (modulo 8, 000-111), a station can transmit seven unacknowledged frames. The modulo must be set so that the transmitter fills the uplink channel while the receiving earth station sends its acknowledgment for the previous set of frames. If the modulo is set so that the transmitter sends its frames in less than twice the link's roundtrip delay (0.48 second), then the transmitter will be "flow controlled" by the receiver, and the effective data rate of the communications path will be reduced.

For satellite transmission, the most practical window is 7 bits long (modulo 128). With this window, a station can transmit 127 frames before requiring an acknowledgment. As the modulo size increases, the amount of time that actual transmissions can occupy a satellite channel increases in proportion to the constant propagation delay. In other words, use of the channel becomes more efficient as the frame window grows larger.

The propagation delay has the same effect on higher-level protocols, such as the packet protocol specified by X.25. Such protocols have a packet window analogous to a lower-level protocol's frame window. In the case of packet-level protocols, the delay effects are similar yet multiplied, because a frame can contain a number of high-level packets.

All current data communications protocols handle errors in transmission through the retransmission of damaged frames. The general name for this technique is automatic repeat request (ARQ). With ARQ, a sending station stores each frame it transmits until it receives positive acknowledgment of that frame from a receiving station. If the sending station receives no such acknowledgment by the end of a predetermined period of time, it retransmits the frame automatically. Some protocols require that only the unacknowledged frame be retransmitted, and others require that the unacknowledged frame and any frames transmitted between that frame and the end of the "time-out" period be retransmitted. Still other protocols require retransmission of an entire block of frames if the block contains a frame unacknowledged by a receiver.

Because of satellite propagation delay, the error windows of some protocols time out before any acknowledgment can return to an originating station. Such protocols cannot be used over satellite channels. For any ARQ protocol, the time required for acknowledgment must be sufficiently long to accommodate the entire, two-way propagation delay over a satellite channel.

The inherent noisiness of satellite channels compounds the problem of delay for ARQ protocols, because each transmission adds at least one additional two-way propagation delay during which the circuit must remain unused. If only ARQ techniques were used to handle errors, satellite circuits would degrade prohibitively. An additional level of error protection is needed to reduce the number of retransmissions. The noisiness of the satellite channels can require several retransmissions to achieve successful data transfer.

Fortunately, noise encountered on satellite channels is purely random "white" noise. (On terrestrial cable and microwave channels, most noise is caused by transient events of long duration relative to the bit times used. Thus, if 1 bit is damaged, several bits around it are likely to have been damaged by the same "line hit.") On a satellite channel, the probability of error for each bit is totally independent of the probability for any other bit. This randomness makes satellite errors especially easy to correct by purely statistical means.

Most satellite data transmission schemes use some statistical technique for FEC. FEC adds another level of encoding to the data between the PSK level and the frame or character encoding required by the protocol. This extra encoding adds redundant information to the data stream, from which the original pattern of bits transmitted can be extracted by a receiver without retransmission. This occurs even if the original pattern has been altered by noise. With FEC, bit error rates of 1 in 10^7 are possible; that is, there is a probability of 1 in 10 million that a given bit will be received in error. Such techniques, used as a matter of course for satellite transmission, turn an inherently noisy medium into one of the cleanest media for data transmission.

Satellite Use

Satellites are used for a wide variety of purposes. They are primarily used in the television, telephony, data communications, and scientific industries. With respect to data communications, satellites may be used as the primary method for communicating between computers, or as an alternative, backup facility.

Activities

1. List the components found in satellite systems.

   _____

   _____

   _____

2. List the frequency ranges used in satellite systems.

   _____

   _____

   _____

3. List and briefly describe the advantages and disadvantages of using satellites.

   _____

   _____

   _____

   _____

   _____

   _____

4. What is a geosynchronous orbit?

   _____

   _____

5. Why is a larger window size (modulo 128) beneficial when communicating by means of satellite?

   _____

   _____

6. Why don't satellite protocols use ARQ?

   _____

   _____

7. List the four functions of a satellite system.

_____

_____

_____

_____

Extended Activities

1. Go to the following Web sites and review the procedures for learning about satellites:

   a. **http://quest.arc.nasa.gov/smore/teachers/microgravity/index.html**

   b. **www.afrlhorizons.com/Briefs/Mar02/IF0110.html**

2. Discuss how satellites are used for the following applications (use the Web for research):

   _____

   _____

   _____

   _____

   b. Television

   _____

   _____

   _____

   _____

   c. Weather analysis

   _____

   _____

   _____

   _____

d. Radio

_____

_____

_____

_____

e. Data communication

_____

_____

_____

_____

f. Voice communication

_____

_____

_____

_____

g. Espionage

_____

_____

_____

_____

3. Research international satellite communications applications and standards at:

http://www.fcc.gov/mmb/asd/bickel/foreign.html

Lesson 9—End-to-End Connectivity

There are many technical aspects of WANs that have been discussed in this unit. These include the different types of circuits and various ways to use telecommunications devices to connect to the circuits. This lesson looks at how an organization might use many of these concepts in a single network.

Objectives

At the end of this lesson you will be able to:

*   Integrate telecommunications concepts presented in this unit

*   List the various types of connectivity used in WANs

 **Key Point**

The service used by an organization is driven by the application.

WAN Applications

There are as many ways to connect networks as there are applications that need connectivity. Organizations use many different technologies and services for various applications. The Application Connectivity Diagram demonstrates common applications and typical WAN connectivity that fulfill requirements of a specific application.

Application   Circuit/Connectivity

Connectivity to
Overseas Office

Satellite Dish

Connectivity Avoiding
Right-of-Way Issues

Microwave   Microwave
Tower   Tower

Access to the Internet   Packet-Switching
                                     Network

Access to
the Organization's LAN

Modem Bank

Access from
Internal Telephone
Network to CO

PBX

Application Connectivity

For example, if we need to communicate with offices located a substantial distance apart, such as overseas offices, a satellite link may be the best alternative. Although there is inherent transit delay with satellites, they are widely used for data communication over long distances. Satellites may be used as a PVC or on an as-needed basis.

Microwaves are frequently used in a metropolitan area network (MAN) environment, especially where right of way is a problem. For example, it can be very expensive to bury cables under roads or across viaducts over railroad tracks. Microwaves are typically point-to-point PVCs.

Most organizations provide access to the Internet. A PVC may be used to connect to an Internet service provider (ISP) that provides access to the backbone of the Internet. Information travels along this fixed route between the organization and ISP. At the ISP, the information is taken and sent to the Internet backbone, where it is routed to its destination.

Modems may be used by an organization to allow outside access to internal resources. Modem pools are devices that allow simultaneous access by multiple individuals traveling or working from home. SVCs are set up each time someone dials in to a network.

Another common need is to connect a device, such as a PBX, to a CO for efficient use of telephone company connections. A PBX provides connectivity to telephones in other locations. A dedicated circuit or leased line is normally used to connect a PBX to a local telephone company, or to another remote PBX.

As we can see, there are various types of connectivity that exist, each depending on the application needs of an organization. Some applications work best with a permanent circuit, others need the flexibility of a switched circuit.

Activities

1. List types of connectivity used to connect homes and businesses to various applications.

    _____

    _____

    _____

    _____

2. Using at least two WAN applications discussed in this lesson, draw a diagram that incorporates the select solutions into a network.

Extended Activities

1. Using the Web, find information on the following types of products:

    a. PBXs

    b. Modem banks

    c. Satellite dishes used for data communications

    d. Microwaves used for data communications

Summary

This unit covered various methods used to connect to a WAN. We began by looking at the difference between physical and logical circuit connections. We also looked at the different types of physical interfaces for connecting DTE devices to DCE devices.

Modems are used to convert digital information to analog information at one end of many networks, and back to digital on the other end. Modems provide this conversion because digital computers must transmit information across the predominantly analog local loop. Digital modems can be used as well, if the communications path between endpoints supports digital information.

Microwave and satellite technology is also used to move information across a wide area. Both types of devices have their strengths and weaknesses. Typically, microwaves are used to move information in a MAN, especially where right of way is an issue. Satellites are used for communication across extremely wide areas and applications that can tolerate long propagation delays inherent in satellite technology.

Unit 2 Quiz

1. For which two of the following processes is a modem used? (Choose two.)

    a. Amplify analog signals

    b. Convert digital signals to analog signals

    c. Repeat digital signals

    d. Convert analog signals to digital signals

2. Which of the following is an example of a modem specification?

    a. T1

    b. T3

    c. EIA-232-D

    d. V.90

3. Which of the following best describes the function of a codec?

    a. Converts analog signals to digital signals

    b. Converts digital signals to electrical signals

    c. Amplifies digital signals on the local loop

    d. Converts voice signals to digital signals

4. Which of the following is not an example of modulation?

    a. FM

    b. AM

    c. Analog modulation

    d. PM

5. Microwave communications is best suited for which connectivity application?

    a. Connectivity to an overseas office

    b. Access to a LAN

    c. Resolve right-of-way issues

    d. Access from internal telephone network to CO

6. Which of the following is a disadvantage of using satellite communications for voice transmission?

   a. Propagation delays between sending and receiving equipment

   b. Low bandwidths

   c. High error rates

   d. Unpredictable equipment behavior

7. What products and services do telecommunications carriers offer?

   _____

   _____

   _____

   _____

   _____

8. What are DSUs and CSUs? What are they used for?

   _____

   _____

   _____

9. What is a modem? Name the two interfaces.

   _____

   _____

   _____

   _____

   _____

10. Name two different modulation techniques used in a modem.

   _____

   _____

11. What limits the speed of modems?

_____

_____

_____

_____

12. What drives the need for greater bandwidth in telecommunications services?

_____

_____

_____

13. Why has T1 remained a popular choice when evaluating WAN connectivity options?

_____

_____

_____

14. What does the acronym codec stand for? What is its function and how is that function performed?

_____

_____

_____

_____

15. What is the difference between synchronous and asynchronous communications techniques?

_____

_____

_____

16. What does it mean to be Hayes-compatible?

_____

_____

_____

_____

17. Satellite communications consists of four basic functions. What are they?

_____

_____

_____

_____

Unit 3
Physical Layer WAN Protocols

This unit looks at the most widely used choices for connecting networks in a point-to-point fashion. Point-to-point connectivity is primarily concerned with Physical Layer protocols. These protocols deal with physical media and the transfer of information across physical media. The point-to-point protocols presented in this unit will be discussed in future units as well, as we look at higher-layer protocols, such as Integrated Services Digital Network (ISDN) and frame relay, and how they use the underlying Physical Layers.

Lessons

1. Summary of Data Rates
2. Dial-Up and Leased Lines
3. SW56
4. VSAT
5. T-Carriers and E-Carriers
6. ADSL
7. Cable Modems
8. SONET

Terms

ABAM—ABAM is a designation for 22-gauge, 110-ohm, plastic-insulated, twisted pair Western Electric cable normally used in COs.

add/drop multiplexer (ADM)—An ADM is a MUX that extracts and inserts lower-rate signals from a higher-rate, multiplexed signal without having to demultiplex the higher-rate signal. An OADM is an optical ADM.

Alternate Mark Inversion (AMI)—AMI is a T1 line-coding format in which successive 1 bits, or marks, are alternately inverted. A 0 bit is represented as zero amplitude.

American National Standards Institute (ANSI) standard T1.403-1989—This ANSI standard defines the use of the ESF T-carrier frame format with digital channel banks.

Asymmetric Digital Subscriber Line (ADSL)—ADSL is a relatively new technology used to deliver high-speed digital communications across the local loop.

Asymmetric Digital Subscriber Line (ADSL) Lite—Also known as G.lite, ADSL Lite is a simplified version of ADSL that requires no splitters installed on the customer premises, and can deliver downstream speeds up to 1.5 Mbps.

AT&T Accunet T1.5—AT&T Accunet T1.5 service is one of several AT&T digital services. Accunet T1.5 provides for the transmission of 1.544-Mbps digital signals over terrestrial channels, and uses one of two types of framed DS1 signal formats: D4 or ESF.

AT&T Publication 43801—AT&T Publication 43801 specifically defines Digital Channel Bank's use and operation. It is one of many AT&T documents designed to specify a carrier technology's operation.

attenuation—The weakening of a signal over distance is referred to as attenuation.

automatic protection switching (APS)—APS is a SONET architecture designed to allow SONET to perform network management and error detection from any point in the signal's path.

Binary Eight Zero Substitution (B8ZS)—B8ZS is a T1 channel encoding method that inserts two consecutive 1s, called a "BPV," into a signal whenever eight consecutive 0s are transmitted. This represents a timing mark to the receiver, maintaining synchronization between the sender and receiver. This allows the circuit to provide the entire 64 Kbps of available data bandwidth to each DS0 channel.

bipolar violation (BPV)—In T1 coding formats, a BPV occurs when two consecutive 1 bits have the same polarity.

bit stuffing—Also known as Zero Bit Insertion, bit stuffing allows binary data to be transmitted on a synchronous transmission line. Within each frame are special bit sequences that identify addresses, flags, and so forth. If the information (data) portion of the frame also contains one of these special sequences, a 0 is inserted by the transmitting station and removed by the receiving station.

broadband digital cross-connect—A broadband digital cross-connect interfaces SONET and DS3 signals. It accesses STS-1 signals, and switches at this level. It is the equivalent of a DS3 digital cross-connect, but for SONET.

Broadband-Integrated Services Digital Network (B-ISDN)—ISDN line rates come in three basic varieties: basic, primary, and broadband. Basic or "narrow" ISDN consists of two bearer (B) channels and one data (D) channel. Each B channel can carry one PCM voice conversation or data at a transmission rate of 64 Kbps. The ISDN-PRI consists of twenty-three 64-Kbps B channels for carrying voice, data, and video, and one D channel for carrying signaling information; it is similar to T1 signaling. B-ISDN, also called "wide ISDN," has multiple channels above the primary rate. In addition to B and D channels, there are a number of additional channels defined, including the A, C, and H series of channels.

crosstalk—Crosstalk is interference experienced on a communications circuit imposed by adjacent circuits. Crosstalk is affected by cable placement, shielding, and transmission techniques.

digital access cross-connect switch (DACS)—A DACS is a telephone company device that establishes semipermanent (not switched) paths for voice or data channels. All physical wires are attached to the DACS once, then electronic connections between them are made by entering software instructions. Depending on the manufacturer, a DACS may also be called a "DCS."

digital cross-connect (DSX)—A DSX is a cross-connect frame that allows technicians to manually cross-connect T1s with patch cords and plugs. See digital access cross-connect switch (DACS).

E and M signaling—E (ear) and M (mouth) signaling is a telephony signaling arrangement where separate circuit leads, the E and M leads, are used for circuit supervision and signaling. The near end applies -48 V DC to the M lead, which applies a ground to the far end E lead. The M lead indicates the near end's desire to activate the circuit, and the far end's E lead indicates this to the receiver.

E1—E1 carrier standards are the European standards that are similar to the North American T-carrier standards. E1 is similar to T1; however, it specifies a 2.048-Mbps data rate and supports 30 communications channels.

echo cancellation—Echo cancellation is a technique that allows for the isolation and filtering of unwanted signals caused by echoes from the main transmitted signal. An echo canceller puts a signal on the signal's return path that is equal but opposite to the echo signal. This serves to cancel out the echo signal.

Extended Superframe (ESF)—Extended superframe is a method of arranging T1 channel samples in groups of 24 frames. Each frame is 193 bits long, consisting of 24 eight-bit samples plus one framing bit.

Facility Data Link (FDL)—FDL is the enhanced link diagnostics, network reporting and control, and other circuit monitoring functions enabled by ESF. FDL is allowed 4 Kbps of the ESF T1 signaling channel.

fast-packet switching—Fast-packet switching is a packet-switching technology that operates at the Physical and Data Link Layers of the OSI protocol stack. Because fast-packet switching is located at these lower layers (only a small amount of processing is needed) and is associated with small packet sizes, it operates at very high speeds.

Fiber Distributed Data Interface (FDDI)—FDDI is a LAN standard specifying a 100-Mbps token-passing network using fiber optic cable.

foreign exchange (FX)—An FX is a trunk service that lets businesses in one city operate in another city by allowing customers to call a local number. The number is connected, by means of a private line, to a telephone number in a distant city.

foreign exchange office (FXO)—The FXO is the CO providing the FX service.

foreign exchange subscriber (FXS)—The FXS is the subscriber side of an FX service.

fount—Fount is another term for Customer-Controlled Reconfiguration of a digital access cross-connect.

frequency shift—Frequency shift is an FM method of transmitting a binary bit stream over an analog carrier wave. A binary 0 is represented by a lower frequency, while a 1 is represented by a higher frequency.

hybrid fiber coax (HFC)—HFC is a network design method, common in the cable television industry, that combines optical fiber and coaxial cable into a single network. Fiber optic cables run from a central site to neighborhood hubs. From those hubs, coaxial cable serves individual homes.

impedance—In an AC circuit, impedance is the circuit's total resistance to current flow. The lower the impedance, the better quality the circuit. Impedance in telecommunications circuits varies by frequency.

Java—Java is an interpreted, platform-independent, high-level programming language developed by Sun Microsystems. Java is a powerful language with many features that make it attractive for the Web.

keep alive bits—Keep alive bits, also known as fill bits or stuff bits, are sent across a communications link to maintain synchronization between end devices when no data is traveling across the link. Without keep alive bits, the circuit's receiver will time out and drop or error out the circuit.

line overhead (LOH)—The SONET LOH is that portion of the SONET frame that controls reliable payload transport between network elements.

line terminating equipment (LTE)—SONET LTE are devices that operate at the SONET line layer, such as ADMs. PTE performs the functions of LTE.

local exchange carrier (LEC)—LECs is another term for the local telephone company.

low-pass filter—A low-pass filter is a device designed to pass only signals below a certain point, and cut off those frequencies above the highest passable frequency.

network interface (NI)—An NI is the interconnection point between a subscriber's equipment and the carrier's network, located on the subscriber's premises.

network interface unit (NIU)—An NIU is an electronic device that acts as the demarcation point between the carrier's network and CPE. An NIU can include protective devices that disconnect the circuit in the case of a lightning strike, and can conduct an automatic loopback to test the line's integrity.

operation, administration, maintenance, and provisioning (OAM&P)—The specific functions of managing a system or network, such as those that provide alarm indications, management messages, and configuration interfaces.

optical carrier (OC)—OC is the term used to specify the speed of fiber optic networks conforming to the SONET standard. OC designates the optical characteristics of SONET technologies.

path overhead (POH)—The SONET POH is that portion of the SPE that carries the OAM&P information for end-to-end network management.

path terminating equipment (PTE)—SONET PTE consists of network elements that originate and terminate transported services.

plain old telephone service (POTS)—POTS is a term used to describe basic analog telephone service provided by a LEC or CLEC.

public-switched telephone network (PSTN)—PSTN is the worldwide voice telephone network accessible to anyone with a telephone.

Rate-Adaptive Digital Subscriber Line (RADSL)—RADSL is a transmission technology that allows for adaptive, high-speed data transfer over existing twisted pair telephone lines. RADSL uses intelligent DSL modems that sense the local loop's performance characteristics and dynamically adjusts the transmission speed accordingly. RADSL supports downstream transmissions up to 7 Mbps, and bidirectional transmissions up to 640 Kbps.

Robbed bit signaling—Robbed bit signaling is technique used on certain T1 circuits, such as emulated tie trunks, where bits are robbed from the T1 frames to indicate signaling, such as off-hook, on-hook, ringing, and so forth. These robbed bits leave only seven bits per channel for carrying digitized voice or data.

section overhead (SOH)—The SONET SOH is that portion of the SONET frame dedicated to the transport of status, messages, and alarm indications for SONET link maintenance.

section terminating equipment (STE)—SONET STE are those devices that operate at the SONET section layer, such as SONET regenerators. PTE and LTE perform STE functions, as well.

Superframe (SF)—A superframe is a method of arranging T1 channel samples in groups of 12 frames. Each frame is 193 bits long, consisting of 24 eight-bit samples plus one framing bit.

Switched Multimegabit Data Service (SMDS)—SMDS is a high-speed cell-switched data communications service offered by telephone companies that enables organizations to connect geographically separate LANs into a single WAN or MAN.

switched services—Switched services refer to transmission provided over a network of nondedicated lines. A switched connection is a temporary transmission path created when needed, and then released. Basic telephone service is an example of a switched service.

Synchronous Digital Hierarchy (SDH)—SDH is an international standard for synchronous data transmission over fiber optic cables, equivalent to the North American SONET standard. SDH defines a standard rate of transmission at 155.52 Mbps, which is referred to as STS-3 at the SONET electrical level and as STM-1 for SDH. STM-1 is equivalent to SONET's OC level 3.

Synchronous Optical Network (SONET)—SONET is the standard for connecting fiber optic transmission systems. SONET was proposed by Bellcore in the mid-1980s and is now an ANSI standard.

synchronous payload envelope (SPE)—The SONET SPE is the portion of the SONET frame that carries the payload data.

Synchronous Transport Signal Level 1 (STS-1)—STS-1 is the building block of SONET bandwidth at 51.84 Mbps. STS designates the electrical characteristics of the SONET standard. The STS-1 rate was chosen for its ability to transport the entire bandwidth of a DS3 (T3) signal, which is approximately 45 Mbps.

T1—In 1962, the Bell System installed the first "T-carrier" system for multiplexing digitized voice signals. The T-carrier family of systems, which now includes T1, T1C, T1D, T2, T3, and T4 (and their European counterparts E1, E2, and so on), replaced FDM systems, providing much better transmission quality.

TIA/EIA-568—The TIA/EIA-568 standard addresses telecommunications wiring within a commercial building.

tie line, tie trunk—A tie line (tie trunk) is a dedicated circuit that links two points without having to dial a telephone number. Many tie lines provide seamless background connections between business telephone systems.

very high-bit-rate Digital Subscriber Line (VDSL)—VDSL is a version of ADSL service that delivers up to 52 Mbps downstream, and 1.5 to 2.3 Mbps upstream.

very small aperture terminal (VSAT)—A VSAT is a small-diameter (approximately 1.5 to 3 meter) satellite antenna, used for satellite point-to-multipoint communications.

virtual tributary (VT)—A VT is a lower-level channel that has been multiplexed to become part of a higher-capacity channel. For example, 28 T1 (DS1) channels can be multiplexed to form 1 T3 (DS3) channel; each of the T1 channels is considered a tributary of the T3.

wideband digital cross-connect—A wideband digital cross-connect is similar in function to a broadband digital cross-connect, except it switches at the VT (or DS1) level.

Lesson 1—Summary of Data Rates

This lesson summarizes the most popular Physical Layer protocols that exist for providing connectivity to wide area network (WAN) and metropolitan area network (MAN) networking environments. We begin this lesson by looking at low-speed technologies, such as dial-up and leased lines, and we progress to higher-speed technologies, such as T3 and OC-3. We will look at applications that might use each of the options, and the associated performance that each application may require.

Objectives

At the end of this lesson you will be able to:

- Name the low- and high-speed options for Physical Layer MAN/WAN connectivity

- Determine which technology is most appropriate for a given business application

 **Key Point**

WAN Physical Layer protocols vary widely in speed and cost.

Point-to-Point Links

Point-to-point links establish a physical connection between local and remote stations. These links come in a variety of data rates, and as speed and capability increase, cost increases as well. Because a point-to-point link provides dedicated bandwidth for the life of the circuit, the cost of moving data this way is usually much higher than with switched services. In addition, when constructing a MAN or WAN using point-to-point links, we must buy these dedicated facilities for each line of communication we want to establish. This means the number of links increases rapidly with the number of nodes: 3 links for 3 nodes, 10 links for 5 nodes, and so on. Switched services let us establish the necessary number of dedicated links as virtual circuits over a shared communications service. Switched services such as Asynchronous Transfer Mode (ATM) and frame relay are primary alternatives when connecting remote networks.

Local exchange carriers (LECs) offer traditional telecommunications services that use existing telephone company voice network facilities and the copper local loop between a customer and central office (CO). The bottom rung of the point-to-point ladder is the analog connection, using modems to carry data over leased or switched lines. Leased lines are full-time connections between two specified locations; switched lines are regular telephone lines (often called "plain old telephone service [POTS]"). Modems became extremely popular in the first half of the 1990s; however, they have reached their maximum speed due to the dictates of physical law. The fastest modems today, using the V.90 standard, operate near 56 kilobits per second (Kbps). This rate, although theoretically attainable, is often impractical given the signal-to-noise ratio on unconditioned voice-grade telephone circuits.

Dataphone Digital Service (DDS) is also called "digital data service." Connections are made to DDS using a special box called a "channel service unit/data service unit (CSU/DSU)." A CSU/DSU replaces the functions of a modem in an analog scenario. DDS provides speeds ranging from 2.4 to 56 Kbps. DDS lines are full-time leased connections between two specified locations and support a fixed bandwidth. They are usually used to construct private digital networks.

Next on the point-to-point ladder, after DDS, is Switched-56 (SW56) service, which enables dial-up digital connections to any other SW56 subscriber in the country. SW56 service uses a CSU/DSU just as a leased-line DDS; however, it includes a dialing pad for entering the telephone number of the remote SW56 system.

And finally, at the top of the point-to-point ladder are the truly high-speed digital services, including:

- Fractional T1 (FT1)

- T1

- T3

- Synchronous Optical Network (SONET)

Various Data Rates and Associated Applications

The Physical Layer Technologies Table presents key Physical Layer technologies most often used for connection to a WAN. Associated data rates, physical media, and applications are also listed. Technology choices are based on need and economics. Each of these is discussed in detail in the lessons that follow.

Physical Layer Technologies

Technology	Data Rate	Physical Media	Application
Dial-up	14.4 to 56 Kbps	Low-grade twisted pair	Home office connectivity to office and Internet
DDS leased line	56 Kbps	Low-grade twisted pair	Small business low-speed access Office-to-office connectivity Internet connectivity
SW56	56 Kbps	Low-grade twisted pair	Small business low-speed access Office-to-office connectivity Internet connectivity Link backup
FT1	64 to 768 Kbps	Low-grade twisted pair	Small to medium business Moderate-level speed Internet access
Satellite (DirectPC)	400 Kbps downstream, 33.6 Kbps upstream	Airwaves	Small business with moderate-level speed Internet access
T1	1.544 Mbps	Low-grade twisted pair Optical fiber Microwave	Medium business Internet access Point-to-point LAN connectivity
E1	64 Kbps to 2.048 Mbps	Low-grade twisted pair Optical fiber Microwave	Medium business Internet access Point-to-point LAN connectivity
ADSL	128 Kbps to 8 Mbps	Low-grade twisted pair	Medium business High-speed home Internet access
Cable modem	512 Kbps to 52 Mbps	Coaxial cable	Medium business High-speed home Internet access

1.544 full T1
1536   T1-RBS   Raw bit
1.472   T1 PRI w/out D-channel
    (64k x 23 channels)

Physical Layer Technologies (Continued)

Technology	Data Rate	Physical Media	Application
E3	34.368 Mbps	Twisted pair Fiber optic cable Microwave	Large business Internet access ISP backbone access
T3	45 Mbps	Twisted pair Fiber optic cable Microwave	Large business internet access ISP backbone access
OC-1	51.48 Mbps	Fiber optic cable	Backbone, campus Internet to ISP
OC-3	155.52 Mbps	Fiber optic cable	Large company backbone Internet backbone connectivity
OC-24	1.24 Gbps	Fiber optic cable	Large company backbone Internet backbone connectivity

Bandwidth

Bandwidth is the difference between the highest and lowest frequencies that can be transmitted across a transmission line or through a network. It is measured in hertz (Hz) for analog networks, and bits per second (bps) for digital networks.

Different types of applications require different bandwidths for effective use, as shown on the Application Speed Table.

Application Speed

Application	Speed
PC communications	300 bps to 56 Kbps
Digital audio	1 to 2 Mbps
Compressed video	2 to 10 Mbps
Document imaging	10 to 100 Mbps
Full-motion video	1 to 2 Gbps

The greater the range of frequencies a medium can handle, the greater its information-carrying capacity. For example, most analog modems transmit data within a 300- to 3,400-Hz frequency range in the middle of a bandwidth.

Although signal characteristics are usually optimal in the middle of a bandwidth, transmission limited to the middle of the band restricts the amount of bandwidth available for data. To compensate for this factor, conventional modems use sophisticated, multiple-bit encoding algorithms to squeeze as much data as possible over one carrier in each direction. A disadvantage of this solution, however, is an increase in the amount of data lost during line hits or other error-inducing conditions on the transmission medium. One goal of much of modem design work is to minimize data losses while transferring larger amounts of data.

Activities

1. What are the low- and high-speed options for WAN connectivity?

    _____

2. Name the four high-speed digital services.

    _____

    _____

    _____

    _____

3. Characterize dial-up, T1, ADSL, and SONET in terms of business applications.

    _____

    _____

    _____

    _____

    _____

    _____

    _____

Extended Activities

1. For each of the technologies listed below, name router products that support each of the physical interfaces:

   a. SW56

   _____

   b. T1

   _____

   c. ADSL

   _____

   d. OC-1

   _____

   e. OC-3

   _____

Lesson 2—Dial-Up and Leased Lines

Standard telephone lines can be used for transmission of digital and analog information. This lesson looks at the predominant means of transmitting information across standard telephone lines: dial-up and leased-line technologies.

Objectives

At the end of this lesson you will be able to:

- Describe the characteristics of dial-up connectivity

- List the advantages and disadvantages of dial-up versus leased-line technologies

 **Key Point**

Dial-up connectivity uses the switched network provided by the telephone company.

Dial-Up Connections

A dial-up line is a circuit that exists between two nodes and uses the switched telephone network to communicate, as illustrated on the Switched Line Diagram. Dial-up lines provide the following characteristics:

- 2.4-to-56-Kbps transfer rates

- Any-to-any connectivity (one at a time)

- Compatible modems at each end

- Call initialization required before transmission

- Inexpensive

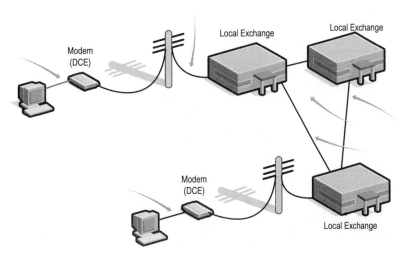

Switched Line

Leased Lines

Leased lines are set up on a permanent basis by a LEC or long-distance carrier. The most popular type of leased line is the T1. T1 equipment is readily available to carry both voice and data traffic at increments of 56 or 64 Kbps. Leased lines are most appropriately used when traffic requirements are steady and uninterrupted service is important.

Advantages of leased lines over dial-up lines are:

• Information security

• Constant quality of service (QoS)

• Circuit control

Disadvantages of leased lines over dial-up lines are:

• Expense

• Dedicated line between sites or nodes

• Equipment needs and costs that increase with the number of required connections

DDS

Digital Data Services *(handwritten)*

1900 *(handwritten)*
2400 *(handwritten)*

Digital signaling offers much more bandwidth than analog signaling, and at higher reliability. By eliminating the conversion of digital data to an audio signal and back again, a digital signaling system eliminates many of the problems modems must deal with: audio noise, phase and frequency shift, clock synchronization, variable line quality, and signal attenuation. The electronics for attaching data terminal equipment (DTE) devices to a digital link are also much less complex, which in the end, results in much less expense for equivalent bandwidth.

DDS links are leased, permanent connections, running at fixed rates of 2.4, 4.8, 9.6, 19.2, or 56 Kbps. A CSU/DSU device at each end provides the interface between a two-wire DDS line and traditional computer interfaces, such as RS-232. A typical local area network (LAN) interconnection uses two DDS-compatible bridges and external CSU/DSUs, as shown on the DDS Connectivity Diagram.

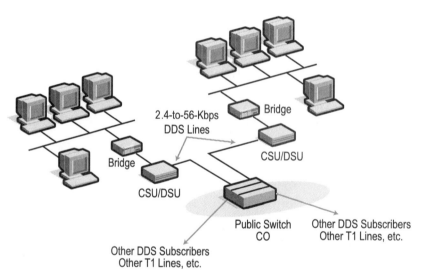

DDS Connectivity

Inside the CO, a DDS line is merged into the regular flow of traffic on T1 and T3 carrier facilities, which route it to its destination. The DDS route is established when the service is purchased, and bandwidth on the necessary trunk carriers is carved out at that time. The rates for this consists of a fixed monthly fee for DDS, plus mileage charges based on the interoffice distance traversed over telephone company trunks. The requested data rate determines the fixed monthly fee.

DDS has physical limitations primarily related to the distance between a CSU/DSU and the serving CO. DDS works reliably when the route distance between a subscriber and CO is less than 30,000 feet (local loop cable length). An office only 1 or 2 miles from a CO may nevertheless have 20,000 feet or more of intervening cable, due to the circuitous routes local loops often take in metropolitan areas. Most telephone companies use a designated line when providing DDS; telephone company engineers trace the shortest possible route over existing copper facilities to get from the CO to a subscriber's location. Telephone company field technicians then visit cable vaults along the route to make the necessary physical connections establishing the designated route.

Activities

1. Compare and contrast characteristics of leased lines versus dial-up circuits.

   _____

   _____

   _____

   _____

2. On the diagram below, list the analog and digital parts of the circuit.

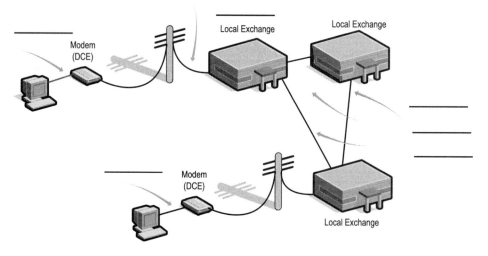

3. List the advantages of leased lines over dial-up lines.

   _____

   _____

   _____

4. List the disadvantages of leased lines over dial-up lines.

   _____

   _____

   _____

Extended Activity

Using the Web, visit at least three carrier services sites that offer DDS. List the features you found for this service.

_____

_____

_____

_____

_____

Lesson 3—SW56

SW56 is used in a variety of ways in computer networks. In some cases, it provides primary connectivity between networks; however, it is more typically found as a backup for primary routers. This lesson covers the function and use of SW56 technology.

Objectives

At the end of this lesson you will be able to:

- Describe how SW56 is used in networking

- Explain the basic principles of SW56

 **Key Point**

SW56 is primarily used for low-speed access and link redundancy.

SW56 Service

SW56 is another service provided by a telephone company. The SW56 Configuration Diagram illustrates this service. SW56 is a digital service that requires a CSU/DSU combination to attach a router or bridge to a telephone line.

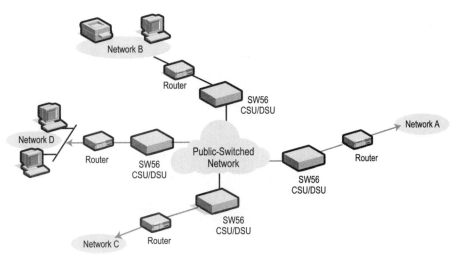

SW56 Configuration

When a full-time connection is unnecessary, we can save money by using switched digital service, generally referred to as SW56. As its name implies, SW56 is only available at the fixed rate of 56 Kbps. An SW56 link is similar to a DDS setup. A DTE connects to the digital service by means of a CSU/DSU. An SW56 CSU/DSU includes a dialing pad for entering the telephone number of the destination SW56 station.

SW56 Operation

SW56 uses the same telephone numbers as a local telephone system, and use charges are the same as those for business voice calls. SW56 can be used for long-distance links, because an SW56 call is carried over the long-distance digital network similar to a digitized voice call. We can choose a long-distance company to service our SW56 calls just as we do for voice calls. With the advent of competing switched digital services, such as frame relay, the cost of SW56 is falling to less than one hundred dollars per month in most areas.

SW56 also has applications in video and voice. Many teleconferencing coder-decoders (codecs) combine two or more SW56 lines to obtain 112- to 384-Kbps bandwidth for sound or video. Other codecs are available for transmitting high-fidelity audio (384 Kbps is sufficient for compact disc [CD]-quality sound transmission), and voice teleconferencing systems. SW56 lines are inexpensive enough that some networks use them to provide a primitive bandwidth-on-demand capability for long-distance WANs.

The SW56 Connectivity Diagram illustrates a network in which two offices need to bridge their two LANs. Most often, interoffice LAN traffic is light, and a single SW56 connection is adequate. There are peak traffic periods, however, where greater bandwidths are required. A LAN bridge feature called "dynamic bandwidth adjustment" solves this problem. Each bridge connects to multiple digital lines, in this case, four SW56 lines. As traffic conditions warrant, one of the LANs dials additional digital calls to the other bridge, combining the bandwidth of all calls in 56-Kbps increments, as needed. With four SW56 lines, bandwidths of 56, 112, 168, and 224 Kbps are possible. The calling bridge is configured to maintain the call for a certain length of time after traffic volume drops, to avoid repeated calls when the average traffic volume is high but not continuous. Bandwidth-on-demand bridges and routers frequently have integrated CSU/DSU devices.

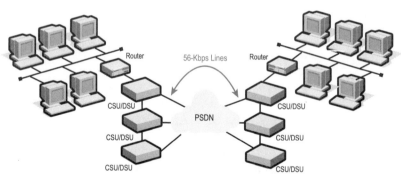

SW56 Connectivity

Activity

List applications that would use SW56 technology today.

_____

_____

_____

_____

Extended Activities

1. Using the Web, find information on at least three products that have SW56 connectivity. Describe each product and how the SW56 port is used for WAN connectivity.

    _____

    _____

    _____

    _____

    _____

    _____

2. Find out whether your local provider provides SW56 connectivity.

    _____

    _____

    _____

Lesson 4—VSAT

Very small aperture terminals (VSATs), also known as micro earth stations or personal earth stations, represent a technological innovation in the field of satellite communications that allows for reliable transmission of data by means of satellite.

Objectives

At the end of this lesson you will be able to:

- Discuss the best applications for VSAT technology
- List the advantages and disadvantages of VSAT technology

 **Key Point**

VSAT technology provides relatively high-speed connectivity for many applications.

VSAT Use

VSATs use small-diameter antennas of typically 0.9 to 1.8 meters (m). With its great reliability, versatility, and flexibility, VSAT technology offers a cost-effective alternative to other communication options.

Since the late 1970s, when VSATs were first successfully demonstrated as receive-only terminals, great advances have taken place. In receive-only configurations, a data signal is broadcast from a central hub to all terminals in the network. These terminals are not equipped to transmit signals. Both C-band (4/6 gigahertz [GHz]) and Ku-band (11/14 GHz) are used in one-way VSAT networks. Decreasing Ku-band equipment costs and crowding of the C-band by terrestrial microwave radio systems have increased the popularity of Ku-band systems in recent years.

Today the two-way or interactive configuration, capable of handling both voice and data, is more popular. Interactive networks offer a fast solution of providing reliable data communications in environments of embryonic telecommunications infrastructures. These networks are being used extensively in developing countries throughout the world and in eastern Europe, as illustrated on the VSAT Application Diagram.

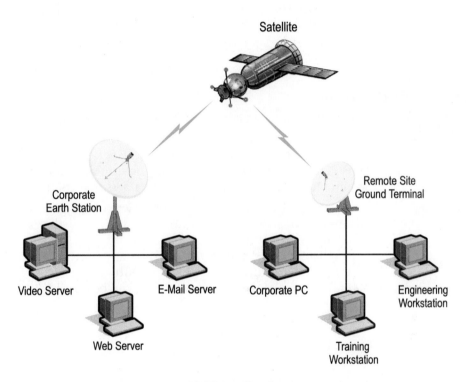

VSAT Application

Advantages of VSAT include:

- Small (0.9 to 1.8 m) receiving antenna

- Versatile and flexible connectivity to almost any location

- Fast connections up to and including E1 (2.048 megabits per second [Mbps])

A major disadvantage of VSAT services is cost for some part-time, low-bandwidth applications, such as Internet access. In these applications, terrestrial solutions are generally less expensive; however, when a remote or isolated location needs connectivity quickly, VSAT solutions are a good choice.

Satellite Applications

A better-known VSAT service, satellite-based Internet access systems, represents a major platform for broadband delivery as we enter the next century. Systems, such as Hughes Network Systems' DirecPC, transmit data from a geosynchronous communications satellite to a dish antenna attached to a personal computer (PC).

Two-way satellite broadband platforms will likely offer substantial advantages over wireline technologies, including the lack of in-ground capital investment, flexible and high-speed bandwidths, high reliability, and the ability to reach any location with almost no setup time. Although satellites currently download data in the 400-Kbps range, downloads of 10 Mbps will be possible in the next several years.

Activities

1. What is driving the need for higher and higher bandwidths for the home and business users?

   _____

   _____

   _____

   _____

2. How will satellite and VSAT technology play a role in Internet connectivity?

   _____

   _____

   _____

   _____

3. Why are two-way platforms critical to VSAT technologies?

   _____

   _____

   _____

   _____

4. List the advantages and disadvantages of VSAT technology.

   _____

   _____

   _____

   _____

Extended Activity

Go to the following Web sites and review VSAT use:

http://www.hughes.com and
http://www.spacenet.com/tools/satellite_basics/

Summarize your findings.

_____

_____

_____

_____

Lesson 5—T-Carriers and E-Carriers

T-carriers and E-carriers have existed in the telecommunications industry for quite some time. They are still widely used technologies for connectivity of business voice and data communication.

Objectives

At the end of this lesson you will be able to:

* Describe the differences between T1, FT1, and T3 systems

* List applications that use T1, FT1, and T3 technologies

 **Key Point**

T-carriers are a primary means of point-to-point network connectivity.

T1, FT1, and T3

With the exception of an analog voice signal originating at a microphone of a telephone handset and audio tones that must be reproduced at a speaker in a handset at the other end, a telephone network is binary in nature. Switches are essentially binary, rotary telephones. They generate a series of pulses to represent numbers. Control signals, such as a dial tone, busy signal, and ring, are binary. Because of the binary nature of telephony, conversion of the analog network to digital was a natural and logical course. In fact, the conversion was essentially complete in the United States for a network then serving 180 million telephones less than 20 years after the basic technology became available; however, electromechanical switches are still in use in some rural areas.

N1

When solid-state electronics became available in the late 1950s, voice digitization became feasible. The advantages of voice digitization, with a signal having only two possible values (0 and 1), include:

- Voice digitization is less susceptible to interference, and it is easier to distinguish noise from a signal.

- It can be reproduced exactly when it passes through switching, multiplexing, or transmission equipment.

- It is easier to mix a voice signal with other binary information, such as signals between switches.

Digital signals also enabled a better method of multiplexing, called "time-division multiplexing (TDM)." In 1962, the Bell System installed the first "T-carrier" system for multiplexing digitized voice signals. Frequency-division multiplexing (FDM) had previously been developed to multiplex analog voice signals. The T-carrier family of systems, which now includes T1, T1C, T1D, T2, T3, and T4 (and their European counterparts E1, E2, and so on) replaced the FDM systems, providing much better transmission quality.

Note that T1 and its successors were designed to multiplex voice communications. Therefore, T1 was designed such that each channel carries a digitized representation of an analog signal that has a bandwidth of 4,000 Hz. A T-carrier channel, or digital signal level 0 (DS0), requires 64 Kbps to digitize a 4,000-Hz voice signal. As mentioned earlier, the most accurate digital representation of an analog signal occurs when the signal is sampled at twice its bandwidth. When a DS0 is sampled, 8 bits represent each sampled amplitude. Eight bits times 8,000 samples per second equals 64,000 bps.

T-carrier rates are shown in the T-Carrier Rates Table. FT1 is a service offered by a telephone company that provides users of telecommunications services optional data rates from 64 Kbps to 1.544 Mbps in DS0 increments. The service is referred to as "fractional" T1 because a user can specify the desired rate, which is a fraction of the normal T1 rate (1.544 Mbps). FT1 is a low-cost alternative to purchasing a full T1, and it only uses a portion of the bandwidth.

T-Carrier Rates

Standard	Line Type	Number of Voice Circuits	Bit Rate
North America			
DS0	—	1	64 Kbps
DS1	T1	24	1.544 Mbps
DS1C	T1C/D	48	3.152 Mbps
DS2	T2	96	6.312 Mbps
DS3	T3	672	44.736 Mbps
DS4	T4	4,032	274.176 Mbps
Europe			
E1	M1	30	2.048 Mbps
E2	M2	120	8.448 Mbps
E3	M3	480	34.368 Mbps
E4	M4	1,920	139.264 Mbps
E5	M5	7,680	565.148 Mbps
Japan			
1	F-1	24	1.544 Mbps
2	F-6M	96	6.312 Mbps
3	F-32M	480	34.064 Mbps
4	F-100M	1,440	97.728 Mbps
5	F-400M	5,760	397.20 Mbps
6	F-4.6G	23,040	1,588.80 Mbps

28 T1s in a T3. [handwritten annotation]

T1

T1 circuits are dedicated services connecting networks or LANs over extended distances. The Sample T1 Configuration Diagram presents a typical configuration. This diagram illustrates how a T1 or T3 circuit could be used to connect two networks. The T1 multiplexers (MUXs) and T1 line provide connectivity for voice traffic, as well as data traffic, across the same physical circuit. The flexibility offered by T1s can be advantageous in certain circumstances. For example, if two networks are connected by a T1 and data transmission rates are slow, it may be possible to move some of the channels from voice to data.

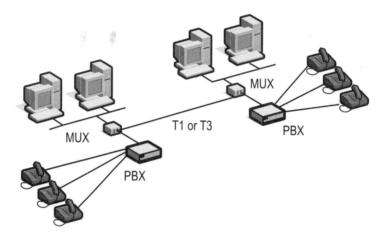

Sample T1 Configuration

When locations are connected with point-to-point T1 lines and users of the network experience blocked calls (busy lines), the designer has several options for remedying the situation. Analog lines may be added between the locations. Other options include adding a T1 or FT1 line.

As with a DDS circuit, we lease a T1 circuit between two locations. Unlike a DDS circuit; however, we have the ability to partition the bandwidth into multiple 64-Kbps channels, taking responsibility for establishing calls and performing other traffic management tasks away from the CO. The DS0 Network Diagram demonstrates this by showing a typical four-office telephone network built using individual DS0 lines. The DS0 line design requires preallocating a number of lines, called "tie lines," between offices; these carry "inside," interoffice calls. Another group of DS0 lines must be allotted to each office to access the public-switched telephone network (PSTN) for "outside" calls. As traffic patterns change, lines must be moved or added between offices, a time-consuming and inconvenient task.

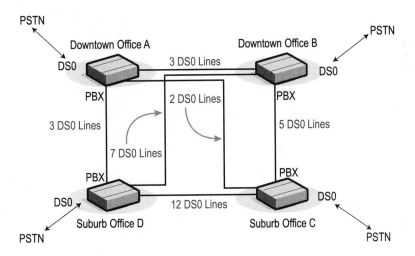

DS0 Network

The T1 Network Diagram demonstrates a way to consolidate inter-office communications into a single backbone consisting of four T1 lines capable of meeting changing traffic demands on the fly. Because T1 service includes the ability to switch DS0s within the local CO's network, any DS0 in one office can be switched to any DS0 in another office or to the PSTN. Data use of a T1 takes advantage of these abilities by means of the T1 MUX, a network terminating device that plays a role similar to that of an SW56 CSU/DSU. The difference is that the T1 MUX handles 24 DS0 channels instead of just 1 channel. A T1 MUX splices up to twenty-four 64-Kbps DS0 channels into a single T1 1.544-Mbps bit pipe.

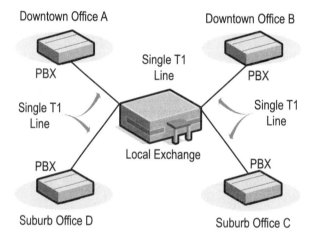

T1 Network

T1 and T3 circuits are useful WAN options because they offer adaptable bandwidth at essentially fixed costs within a metropolitan area. T1- and T3-capable routers and bridges typically support one or more T1 or T3 circuits, and automatically make connections with other routers or bridges in a network. The T1 WAN Diagram illustrates a typical T1-based WAN. As network designers, we program the router or bridge to specify the adjacent routers or bridges for each digital circuit. We can also specify bandwidth-on-demand parameters to change bandwidth in DS0 increments, similar to the technique used with SW56 lines.

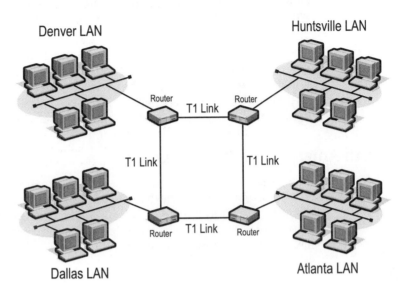

T1 WAN

FT1

Leasing a T1 line means paying for the entire 1.544-Mbps bandwidth 24 hours a day, whether it is used or not. FT1 lets us lease any 64-Kbps submultiple of a T1 line. We might, for example, lease only six channels to obtain six 64-Kbps channels or an aggregate bandwidth of 384 Kbps. FT1 is useful whenever the cost of a dedicated T1 is prohibitive. FT1 is not as efficient or flexible as switched services because we are paying to have a fraction of leased bandwidth available on a 24-hour basis. However, FT1 has an intrinsic feature not available with full T1 circuits: multiplexing DS0 channels outside our own enterprise T1 network.

Because we are not leasing an entire T1 circuit, we cannot dictate the location of the other end of the circuit. After all, we will be sharing the T1 with other customers. The remote end of an FT1 circuit is at a telephone company-managed digital access cross-connect switch (DACS). Everyone leasing an FT1 has the far end of the circuit embedded in the DACS, where the telephone company has established its own network of T1 interconnects. Any two companies sharing the same DACS can switch among each other's DS0 channels, provided the telephone company has configured the two companies as interoperating organizations. This interoperability can be an advantage when a large central organization (for example, government agency) needs to interoperate with many smaller organizations (for example, contractors).

Due to the one-end nature of FT1, a separate FT1 circuit must be leased for each node in a network. Contrast this with T1 circuits, where we need only lease one circuit between each pair of nodes. For this reason, as the size of the fraction increases, FT1 eventually becomes more expensive than T1. Typically, this occurs at approximately 75 percent of the full T1 bandwidth.

T3 and North American Digital Hierarchy

The North American Digital Hierarchy is created using a series of MUXs, as shown on the North American Digital Hierarchy Diagram. DS1 signals are fed into DS2 MUXs, that are then combined with other DS2 MUXs and multiplexed to DS3 levels and so forth. DS3 (or T3) is another service offering. The T3 rate is 44.736 Mbps.

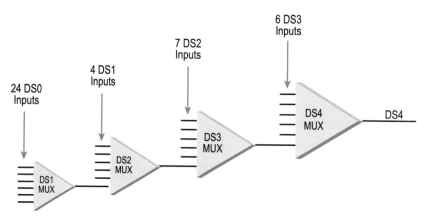

North American Digital Hierarchy

Signal Shapes and Codes

A digital cross-connect (DSX) consists of equipment frames (patch panels) where cabling between system components is connected. Each digital signal is defined for, and handled by, its own cross-connect. Thus, for example, DSX-1 is used to interconnect equipment operating with DS1 signals.

The shape of a DS1 pulse is defined at the DSX-1 cross-connect. AT&T Publication 43801, Digital Channel Banks and Objectives, describes the requirement of this pulse to drive from 0 to 655 feet of 22-gauge ABAM cable between the channel bank and the DSX-1. The maximum reframe time is defined at 50 milliseconds (msec). The DS1 pulse is a slightly relaxed version the DSX-1 pulse mask. The Comparison of DSX-1 Signals and DS1 Signals Table shows the specification (less template) of the DSX-1 signal and how it compares to the DS1 signal specification.

Comparison of DSX-1 Signals and DS1 Signals

Functions	DSX-1	DS1
Line rate	1.544 MHz +/- 200 Hz	1.544 MHz +/- 75 Hz
Cable length at DSX point	ABAM/655 ft.	6,000 ft.
Pulse amplitude	2.4 to 3.6 V	2.7 to 3.3 V
Receive attenuation	<10 dB	15 to 22.5 dB
Line build out	Yes	0.0, 7.5, 15 dB
Max successive 0s	15 (or B8ZS)	15 (or B8ZS)

The American National Standards Institute (ANSI) standard T1.403-1989 specifies Extended Superframe (ESF) use with channel banks. Fundamentally, the signals and templates (signal shapes) are the same. Modern integrated circuit (IC) manufacturers have ensured that their products meet all of the specifications. When we are communicating to the CO or the carrier, we are using DS1; when we are regenerating the signal after the demarcation point, we are using DSX-1.

Note that the DS1 signal template is bipolar. This means that a plus voltage, zero voltage, and minus voltage are important to the coding of the signal. This bipolar coding used in T1 framing is called "Alternate Mark Inversion (AMI)." This means if a "1" or mark is coded as a positive voltage, the very next "1" must be a minus voltage or the result will be a bipolar violation (BPV).

The Two AMI Sequences Diagram shows a valid AMI sequence and a sequence with a BPV.

Two AMI Sequences

Notice that in the Comparison of DSX-1 Signals and DS1 Signals Table there is reference to the "maximum successive zeros." One of the requirements of the coding sequence, and thus the signal shape of the DS1, is that a 1 bit is sent to maintain the timing synchronization. For example, a signal that was sending all 0s would be a constant zero voltage line. Eventually the timing of the system would be lost.

The standard requires that no more than 15 0s can be sent before a 1 is transmitted. In telephone applications, this was accomplished with bit 7. Bit 8 is sometimes used for signaling—called Robbed Bit Signaling—and thus cannot be universally used. The human ear would never detect these slight variances in the lower-order bits. When sending data, however, using bit 7 and bit 8 for purposes other than faithfully representing the data being presented for transport yields disastrous consequences. Thus, a mechanism had to be developed for data-only applications.

The easiest approach, and a technique still in use in DDS applications, is to make every bit 8 a 1 and to use only the lower 7 bits for data. This 7/8 mode (7 data bits out of 8 bits transmitted) yields 56 Kbps instead of the standard DS0 rate of 64 Kbps. This technique also disallowed the use of signaling bits.

The Binary Eight Zero Substitution (B8ZS) line coding standard improves upon this technique. B8ZS intentionally inserts BPVs in the data stream to be decoded as a signal.

[Handwritten margin notes:]

Q

4 Kinds of BPV

1. high, normal, high
2. high, high
3. low, normal, low
4. low low

Should Alternate between high & low — AMI

With B8ZS coding, each block of 8 consecutive 0s is replaced with a B8ZS code word. If the bit pulse preceding the inserted code is transmitted as a positive pulse (+), the inserted code is 000+-0-+ (BPVs in bit positions 4 and 7). If the bit pulse preceding the inserted code is transmitted as a negative pulse (-), the inserted code is 000-+0+-(again, BPVs in bit positions 4 and 7).

The B8ZS Diagram shows how B8ZS works.

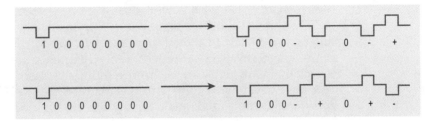

B8ZS Diagram

B8ZS — lnks w/ PRI

This is the standard for Clear Channel Capability, as referenced in AT&T Publication 62411, Appendix B. It is part of the ANSI T1.403-1989 standard as well. B8ZS coding supports a full 64 Kbps per channel, making this the line coding choice for ISDN-Primary Rate Interface (PRI) circuits over T1 carriers.

T1 Signaling

Bridge = switch

SD2 = HDLC

T1 circuits can use one of two methods of transporting call signaling; Channel Associated Signaling (CAS) or Common Channel Signaling (CCS). When a T1 circuit is used to emulate tie trunks, it must pass signaling information between the connected endpoints. This is performed using CAS, also known as a Robbed Bit Signaling.

Robbed Bit Signaling "robs" bits from the T1 data stream to represent call states, such as on-hook, off-hook, ringing, and so forth. A codec samples a T1 channel 8000 times a second, and represents each sample with eight binary bits. T1s organize these samples into frames of 24 samples each, one sample per channel, so that one frame equals 24–8 bit samples, or 192 bits. Depending on the T1 framing pattern used, the signaling bits are robbed from the 6th and 12th frames (Superframe framing) or the 6th, 12th, 18th, and 24th frames (Extended Superframe framing). Because the signaling bits are taken from each channel's eight sample bits, only seven bits remain for transporting voice or data. Hence, robbed bit signaling only allows for 56 Kbps bandwidth per channel.

Common Channel Signaling (CCS) dedicates one full T1 channel to call signaling. This frees the full bandwidth (64 Kbps) of the remaining channels for user information; this is the signaling method used to support ISDN-PRI services. This dedicated signaling channel provides a path for transporting advanced call signaling information such as that available on the SS7 network.

Cabling

ABAM cable is called out in the DSX-1 specification and is a physical cable that was manufactured by AT&T. It uses unshielded twisted pair (UTP) with a wire size of 22 American Wire Gauge (AWG). Some authorities suggest it is pulp-insulated, while others suggest it is plastic-insulated. In any event, ABAM cabling, per se, is no longer available. Modern cable manufacturers, however, especially those active in Electronic Industries Association (EIA)-568, have developed cables with specific categories or levels. Category/Level 2 cable is adequate for the T1 data rate and has the following characteristics:

- 24 AWG

- Two pairs

- 100-ohms impedance at 0.772 megahertz (MHz)

- 7-decibel (dB) attenuation/1,000 feet at 0.772 MHz

- 41-dB crosstalk at 1,000 feet

Several manufacturers make this cable type. A summary of the category/level types per RS-568 is listed in the New Cable Types (Proposed EIA-568) Table.

New Cable Types (Proposed EIA-568)

Level	Service Type	Speed
1	POTS	N/A
	RS-232/RS-562	19.2 to 115.2 Kbps
	T1, FT1	64 Kbps increments
	ISDN-BRI	144 Kbps
	RS-422	Up to 1.0 Mbps
2	IEEE 802.3 1BaseT	1.0 Mbps
	IBM System 3x/AS400	1.0 Mbps

New Cable Types (Proposed EIA-568)

Level	Service Type	Speed
	T1	1.544 Mbps
	ISDN-PRI	1.544
	IBM 370	2.36 Mbps
	IEEE 802.5	4.0 Mbps
3	Wang	4.3 Mbps
	IEEE 802.5 10BaseT	10.0 Mbps
	IEEE 802.5 Token Ring	16.0 Mbps
4	IEEE 802.5 Token Ring	16.0 Mbps
	New Arcnet	20.0 Mbps
5	X3T9.5 TPDDI	100.0 Mbps

OC1 = 5.184 mbps
OC3 = 1.55 mbps
CAS = out of band
CCS =

RBS — In band

/TAS

B = Bearer
PayloAD,
D. Delta Ctrl

NFAS

Connectors

The discussion of connectors sometimes becomes confusing because there is a difference between "de facto" standards, things used in products, and specifications. AT&T specifies that the network interface (NI) should be a subminiature 15-pin female connector with the following pinout:

1	Send data (tip)
2	Reserved for network
3	Receive data (tip)
4	Reserved for network
5	Not defined
6	Not defined
7	Not defined
8	Not defined
9	Send data (ring)
10	No connect
11	Receive data (ring)
12	No connect
13	No connect
14	No connect
15	No connect

AT&T Publication 62411 further states that "in such cases where ISDN standards need to be met, an 8 pin mini-modular connector is recommended" with the following pinout:

1	Transmit (ring)
2	Not used
3	Not used
4	Receive (ring)
5	Receive (tip)
6	Not used
7	Not used
8	Transmit (tip)

To complicate the matter, the ANSI T1.403-1989 specification calls for "one of four Universal Service Ordering Code (USOC) connectors (RJ-48C, RJ-48X, RJ-48M, and RJ-48H)" with pin assignments as follows:

1	Receive (ring)
2	Received (tip)
3	Not used
4	Transmit (ring)
5	Transmit (tip)
6	Not used
7	Not used
8	Not used

The ANSI pinout and connectors are considered the "de facto" standard for currently available hardware.

| **Applications** | Where can we use these DS1/DSX-1/T1 signals? There are several applications and specific equipment that can be applied: |

- DACS

- D4 channel bank

- Private branch exchange (PBX)

- CSU

- Subrate Data MUX (SRDM)

- FT1

The most important issue is that there can be T1 networks that are customer-owned and T1 networks that use the AT&T Accunet T1.5 system. The applications will be the same; however, the constraints on the equipment are more stringent using the AT&T connection.

DACS

There are three DACS compatibility levels. The first is DS1, which operates at the full T1 rate. The second level is "bundled" or 1/4 T1 level. This allows the customer to utilize Customer-Controlled Reconfiguration or "fount" at the CO. The third level is at the 64-Kbps or DS0 level. Here, DTE channels A and B create a single T1 signal sent to the CO. The CO splits these into two T1 trunks: one carrying channel A and the other carrying channel B. The CO device that performs this function is a DACS. A DACS may also be configured to provide trunk failover capabilities, thus if one of the trunks goes down, the data will reroute to a standby trunk. In the past, almost all DACS were owned by the telecommunications companies; today, many communications users are using DACS functionality on their own networks.

D4 Channel Bank

A T1 signal must somehow be split into the 24 separate and distinct voice channels. This is performed while the signal is still in digital form. The codecs must then convert each channel's digital signal into analog signals for use on the subscriber loops. Most channel banks are owned and operated at the COs; however, since deregulation in the 1980s, more users own T1s as telephone carriers continue to reduce the cost of the local loop (the wires from the CO to the customer premises).

PBX

The intended use of T1 was to combine as many voice telephone lines as possible using a digitizing technique (Pulse Code Modulation [PCM]). Tie lines between PBXs account for many private T1 network applications, supported through two- and four-wire ear and mouth (E and M) signaling techniques through the T1 MUX. A two-wire foreign exchange (FX) subscriber (FXS) function (dedicated line to a distant CO) and two-wire FX office (FXO) function (the CO version) can also be supported by the T1 trunk. In the latter mode, the T1 line acts as an extension cord. The primary way in which customers use this function is through the T1 MUX.

CSU

A DS1 from the telephone company to the customer must be given the proper termination, line protection, and message handling capability. In the past, the CO supplied this equipment; however, today it is usually customer premises equipment (CPE). The CSU output is the DSX-1 signal. The most common CSU is found in a T1 MUX; however, CSUs can also stand alone.

A DSU takes unipolar data from the terminal and converts it to a bipolar DS1 signal. In many ways, it also acts as a CSU. A CSU should perform the following functions:

- Regeneration
- Loopback
- Keep alive

Regeneration is part of the DSU functionality. Loopback is commanded from the carrier in one of two ways:

- Using an inline data pattern with D4 SF formatting
- Using the Facility Data Link (FDL) with ESF formatting

If the FDL is already being used in the DSU, it would be rather straightforward to incorporate the appropriate responses to the carrier loopback command structure. An "SF CSU," which is still commonly used with D4 channel banks, can also be used.

Circuit Costs

Lower T1 circuit costs are enabling more and more companies to carry bandwidth-intensive applications, including video conferencing and other image-transfer programs. Users looking to increase bandwidth from a simple, lower-bandwidth, voice-grade digital circuit capacity to a T1 can experience only a slight increase in cost. This downward trend in pricing is countered by the introduction of new services. For short-term data networking needs, carriers are offering a variety of reliable, high-quality switched digital services. High-speed, packet-switched services are applying similar pressures. Frame relay, for example, is being used for high-speed (56 Kbps to 1.5 Mbps), bursty data transmission needs.

Activities

1. What are the advantages and disadvantages of an FT1 over a T1 connection?

    _____

    _____

    _____

    _____

2. If one 64-Kbps DS0 channel costs $50 per month, and a full T1 costs $520 per month, what multiple of DS0s would be the breakeven point using FT1, versus the additional cost of a full T1?

    _____

    _____

3. If a T3 costs $4,200 per month, at what multiple of T1s (from the previous problem) would the T1s cost more than a T3?

    _____

    _____

4. List some applications for T1, FT1, and T3 carriers.

    _____

    _____

    _____

Extended Activity

Using the Web, find information on at least three products that use T1 connectivity for data communications. List the products and associated features.

_____

_____

_____

_____

_____

_____

Lesson 6—ADSL

Asymmetric Digital Subscriber Line (ADSL) is intended for the last leg into a customer's premises: the local loop. As its name implies, ADSL transmits an asymmetric data stream, with much more going downstream to a subscriber and much less coming back.

Objectives

At the end of this lesson you will be able to:

- Explain why ADSL is asymmetric
- Describe the advantages of ADSL over other local loop access methods

 **Key Point**

ADSL provides for more bandwidth downstream toward a subscriber.

Fundamentals of ADSL (Asymmetric DSL)

The reason ADSL is asymmetric has less to do with transmission technology than with the cable plant itself. Twisted pair telephone wires are bundled together in large cables. Fifty wire pairs to a cable is a typical configuration toward a subscriber. However, cables coming out of a CO may have hundreds or even thousands of pairs bundled together. An individual line from a CO to a subscriber is spliced together from many cable sections as they fan out from the CO. (Bellcore claims the average U.S. subscriber line has 22 splices.) Alexander Graham Bell invented twisted pair wiring to minimize the interference of signals from one cable to another caused by radiation or capacitive coupling; however, the process is not perfect.

All of this interference, bundling, and splicing limits the local loop to approximately 1.1 MHz of bandwidth; ADSL distributes this bandwidth asymmetrically. In other words, ADSL provides more downstream (to the user) bandwidth than upstream (from the user) bandwidth. The majority of target applications for digital subscriber services are asymmetric. Video-on-demand (VOD), home shopping, Internet access, remote LAN access, multimedia access, and specialized PC services all feature high data rate demands downstream to a subscriber, but relatively low data rate demands upstream. For example, Motion Picture Experts Group (MPEG) movies with simulated videocassette recorder (VCR) controls require 1.5 or 3.0 Mbps downstream; however, they work just fine with no more than 64 Kbps (or 16 Kbps upstream). Internet Protocol (IP) protocols for Internet or LAN access push upstream rates higher; however, a 10 to 1 ratio of downstream to upstream rates does not compromise performance in most cases.

ADSL has a range of downstream speeds depending on distance, as presented in the ADSL Data Rates Table.

ADSL Data Rates

Data Rate (Mbps)	Wire Gauge (AWG)	Distance (feet)	Wire Size (mm)	Distance (km)
1.5 or 2	24	18,000	0.5	5.5
1.5 or 2	26	15,000	0.4	4.6
6.1	24	12,000	0.5	3.7
6.1	26	9,000	0.4	2.7

Upstream speeds range from 16 to 640 Kbps. Individual products today incorporate a variety of speed arrangements, from a minimum set of 1.544/2.048 Mbps downstream and 16 Kbps upstream to a maximum set of 8 Mbps downstream and 640 Kbps upstream. All of these arrangements operate in a frequency band above POTS, leaving POTS independent and undisturbed, even if a premise's ADSL modem fails. The ADSL Connectivity Diagram illustrates typical connectivity for this type of subscriber line.

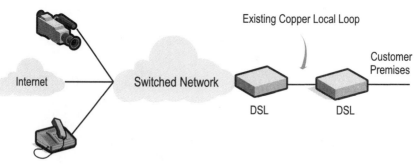

ADSL Connectivity

As ADSL transmits digitally compressed video, among other things, it includes error-correction capabilities intended to reduce the effect of impulse noise on video signals. Error correction introduces approximately 20 msec of delay, which is too much for LAN and IP-based data communications applications. Therefore, ADSL must know what kind of signals it is passing, to know whether to apply error control. (This problem occurs for any wire-line transmission technology over twisted pair or coaxial cable.) ADSL is used for circuit-switched and packet-switched services (such as an IP router), as well as for ATM-switched data. ADSL must connect to PCs and television set top boxes at the same time. Collectively, these application conditions create a complicated protocol and installation environment for ADSL modems, resulting in modems with functions well beyond simple data transmission and reception.

The ADSL Configuration Diagram provides an overview of an ADSL network. An ADSL circuit connects an ADSL modem on each end of a twisted pair telephone line. It creates three information channels:

- High-speed downstream channel that connects to an ATM network
- Medium-speed duplex channel
- POTS channel, which is split off from the digital system by filters, thus guaranteeing uninterrupted POTS, even if ADSL fails

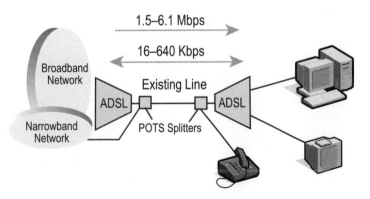

ADSL Configuration

ADSL uses analog signals, but spreads them out over a range of frequencies 100 or more times greater than dial-up modems. The spectrum is sliced into dozens of narrow bands, as if 100 modems were sending signals over one wire simultaneously.

ADSL is considered the most viable version of Digital Subscriber Line (DSL), because it works over long distances. Downstream data rates depend on several factors: the length of the copper line, its wire gauge, presence of bridged taps, and cross-coupled interference. Line attenuation increases with line length and frequency, and decreases with wire diameter.

Because many applications planned for ADSL involve a real-time signal, link- and network-level error control protocols cannot be used. Therefore, ADSL modems incorporate forward error correction (FEC).

To create transparent multiple channels at various data rates, ADSL modems divide the available bandwidth by either FDM or echo cancellation, as illustrated on the ADSL Bandwidth Diagram.

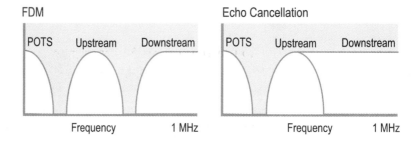

ADSL Bandwidth

FDM assigns one band for upstream data and another band for downstream data. TDM further divides the downstream path into one or more high-speed channels and one or more low-speed channels. The upstream path is also multiplexed. Echo cancellation, on the other hand, assigns the upstream band to overlap the downstream band, and separates the two by local echo cancellation.

An ADSL modem multiplexes downstream channels, upstream channels, and maintenance channels together in blocks, attaching an error code to each block. A receiver corrects errors occurring in the transmission, up to the limits of the code and block length. Technical and practical problems must be overcome to enable widespread deployment of ADSL, including adoption of standards and readiness of the local loop.

Local loops have significant numbers of antiquated coils (for example, loading coils originally installed to mute noise during voice calls). The coils act as low-pass filters that cut off all frequencies above 4 kilohertz (kHz). Therefore, any loading coil on the loop between the local distribution node and a subscriber's home must be removed before ADSL can be connected.

In addition, there are problems throughout the telephone system, including overlong loops that attenuate signals, nonterminated wire pairs, and crosstalk between wires. The aforementioned 22 splices in the typical U.S. telephone line enable line noise and crosstalk, which reduces effective data rates.

DSLs and Internet Access

The local loop or "last mile" of the communications network deals with the Physical and Data Link Layers of the Open Systems Interconnection (OSI) model. Communications providers, such as cable companies, telephone companies, and satellite transmission companies, are currently investing billions of dollars in creating broadband infrastructure in the local loop. This section provides an overview of these developments.

Why High-Speed Local Loop Is "Hot"

There are four major reasons for the current brisk pace of development and deployment of high-speed Internet local access solutions:

- Increasing popularity of the Internet—Connecting to the Internet is now the number one reason people buy a computer. Given a "taste" of bandwidth, both businesses and consumers are increasing the demand for advanced World Wide Web (Web) technologies, such as full-motion video and enhanced interactivity, which require even more bandwidth.

- Pressure from software and hardware providers—These providers see high-speed local access to the Internet as crucial to their continued growth. Microsoft, particularly, believes that faster access will make it possible to enhance the Internet with more television-like graphics and video, which would increase the market for PCs loaded with Microsoft software. That is, even if all the issues with high-level Internet congestion and server overload were resolved, the speed over the last mile would remain the limiting factor. Microsoft's recent $1 billion investment in cable companies served as a "wake-up call" to telephone companies, as well.

- Accelerated development of Internet applications—Advances in browser interfaces and "universal" programming languages (for example, Java) are speeding Internet applications development. Advanced software products for home/work integration (for example, telecommuting and extranets) are gaining more attention. The media and advertising industries are pushing applications involving two-way communication with consumers to collect marketing data and facilitate impulse shopping.

- Intensifying competition—There is significant competition to provide broadband connection to the home. Telephone and cable companies are squaring off against each other to provide service to the growing number of "Netizens" (Internet subscribers).

Options for Local High-Speed Internet Access

The Internet Access Solutions Table summarizes mass-market solutions for Internet access currently used or being tested in some areas of the United States.

Internet Access Solutions

Variables	56-Kbps Modem	ISDN	ADSL Lite	RADSL	ADSL	Cable Modem	FT1	T1
Speed to user	56 Kbps	128 Kbps	1.5 Mbps	7 Mbps	8 Mbps	30 Mbps	56/64 Kbps	1.544 Mbps
Speed from user	33.6 Kbps	128 Kbps	128 Kbps	1 Mbps	1 Mbps	3 Mbps	56/64 Kbps	1.544 Mbps
Cost per month*	$20	$60–$100	$40–$100	$40–$200	$40–$200	$30–$60	$150 + $0.65/mi	$200 + $13.5/mi

* Monthly costs are estimates and include ISP-equivalent services (e.g., content and browser).

The 56-Kbps modem is the fastest dial-up solution available to consumers today. It is an inconvenient, "narrow band" solution, provided here for comparison with the broadband solutions.

ISDN is an end-to-end switched digital network that integrates enhanced voice and image features with high-speed data and text transfer. Built on top of standard UTP telephone wire, ISDN provides two rates of service: basic and primary. The relevant version for the mass market is ISDN-Basic Rate Interface (ISDN-BRI), which provides three channels over one pair of twisted copper wires: two 64-Kbps bearer (B) channels and one 16-Kbps data (D) channel for signaling or packetized data. The two B channels can be bonded together to provide a total speed of 128 Kbps.

Although available since the early 1990s, ISDN has not caught on because of availability and price issues. (LECs have been reluctant to cannibalize their T1 business.) Estimated 1997 penetration was only approximately 5 percent of total telephone lines. (ADSL and Rate-Adaptive Digital Subscriber Line [RADSL] can deliver ISDN, although it takes away from the bandwidth for data.)

Cable modem is a technology for providing broadband Internet access over a cable television provider's hybrid fiber coax (HFC) network. It is a broadcast technology analogous to an Ethernet LAN. Bandwidth is shared and packets move around in a store-and-forward scheme. The cable modem located in each subscriber's home filters out information not addressed to that particular subscriber. The remaining information is delivered to the subscriber's computer, by means of a virtual point-to-point connection.

Cable modem downstream speeds have the potential to reach 36 Mbps, although most PCs cannot handle that speed. End-user connections are limited to 10 Mbps, the maximum speed through any 10BaseT Ethernet PC connection.

xDSL is the modem technology that converts existing twisted pair telephone lines into access paths for multimedia and high-speed data communication, while simultaneously providing POTS. Developed in the 1980s to deliver VOD over telephone lines, xDSL has the potential to deliver data at 160 times the speed of a 56-Kbps modem. The speed of a particular xDSL installation depends on the variant of the xDSL protocol, thickness of the copper wire, and distance from the telephone company's CO. Various types of DSL technologies include:

- ADSL provides downstream transmission rates of 1.544 Mbps across up to 18,000 feet of twisted copper pair wire, 6.312 Mbps up to 12,000 feet, and 8.448 Mbps up to 9,000 feet (all 24-gauge wire). ADSL is asymmetric in that downstream data rates (to the user's desktop) are faster than upstream data rates (from the user's desktop). Asymmetric solutions are attractive because they match Internet user patterns. A typical Internet surfing scenario involves few keystrokes to download a 100-kilobyte (KB) Graphics Interchange Format (GIF) file.

- RADSL is a variation of ADSL that overcomes varying conditions and lengths of copper cable. RADSL has the same maximum data rates as ADSL, but both downstream and upstream rates are adjusted to line conditions at the time of transmission, which depend on line length and interference (crosstalk).

- Early in 1998, Compaq, Microsoft, and several regional Bell operating companies (RBOCs) formalized their support for ADSL and announced a plan to develop ADSL Lite, a slightly slower version of ADSL that does not require installation of a splitter, which separates off POTS. Initiation of ADSL Lite requires only plugging in an ADSL modem and contacting an Internet service provider (ISP).

- Very high-bit-rate Digital Subscriber Line (VDSL) promises downstream rates of approximately 13 Mbps across up to 4,500 feet of twisted pair copper wire, 26 Mbps up to 3,000 feet, and 52 Mbps up to 1,000 feet (all 24-gauge wire).

Activities

1. List the advantages and disadvantages of the following technologies:

    a. 56-Kbps modem

        _____

        _____

        _____

        _____

    b. ISDN

        _____

        _____

        _____

        _____

    c. ADSL Lite

        _____

        _____

        _____

        _____

    d. RADSL

        _____

        _____

        _____

        _____

    e. ADSL

        _____

        _____

        _____

        _____

f. Cable modem

_____

_____

_____

_____

2. Why is ADSL asymmetric?

_____

_____

_____

Extended Activity

Visit the ADSL Forum Web site at **http://www.adsl.com** and research the latest developments in ADSL.

Lesson 7—Cable Modems

Cable modems are another technology aimed at the local loop. They offer much more than basic video services, providing Internet connectivity and other home and small business applications.

Objectives

At the end of this lesson you will be able to:

* Describe the basics of cable modem technology

* Compare the services of cable modems and ADSL

 **Key Point**

Cable modems provide video, telephone, and data services to a subscriber.

Cable Modem Technology

The Internet by Means of Cable Modem Diagram provides an overview of cable modem access over an HFC network. HFC networks are composed of a fiber feeder from a cable head end to a neighborhood optical node serving several hundred homes. A signal travels from the node to each home over coaxial cable. A network interface unit (NIU) inside the home includes a cable modem and other electronics, and perhaps a power supply.

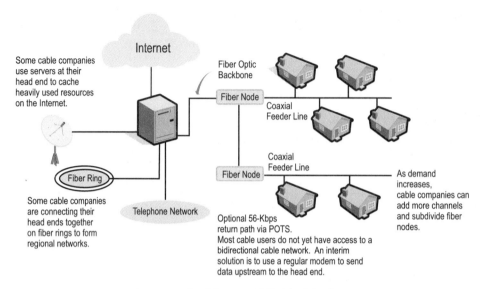

Internet by Means of Cable Modem

A cable modem is a complex device incorporating a tuner, which separates data signals from broadcast streams (video) from telephony; parts from network adapters, bridges, and routers; network management software agents, which enable a cable company to monitor operations; and encryption devices. Each cable modem has an Ethernet port. As a result of this configuration, up to three cable wires can be provided from the NIU: a coaxial wire delivering broadcast video to a television, an Ethernet wire connecting to a PC, and a twisted pair of wires connecting to a telephone.

The most common cable modems create a downstream data stream out of one of the 6-MHz television channels that occupy the spectrum between 50 and 750 MHz. Common cable modems create an upstream channel carved out of the currently unused band between 5 and 42 MHz. The current HFC cable network uses a 750-MHz spectrum, equivalent to 110 downstream channels of 6-MHz bandwidth (a Federal Communications Commission [FCC] limit) each. Spectrum bandwidth from 5 to 42 MHz is reserved for upstream signaling and telephony. Using 64-quadrature amplitude modulation (QAM), downstream transmission can occur at rates as high as 30 Mbps.

The downstream channel is continuous; however, it is divided into cells or packets, with each packet addressed to a particular subscriber. The downstream portion of the spectrum supports a mix of analog video, digital broadcast, interactive video, telephone, and data services. Downstream transmission does not disturb transmission of television signals to the television set. Upstream transmission rates vary by modem vendor. To avoid collisions, systems are being designed to place each upstream packet onto the network with control signals embedded in the downstream information stream.

There are two types of cable modems: two-way cable modems and telephone return cable modems. Telephone return cable modems allow subscribers of cable networks that have not been upgraded for two-way communication to obtain the benefits of high speed on the downstream link. The majority of cable modems in use today are telephone return modems.

A cable modem provides the equalization to compensate for signal distortion, address filtering, transmitting and receiving functions, automatic power adjustments, adjustments in amplitude (to compensate for temperature changes), signal modulation, and compensation for delays caused by variable distances from the head end. Transmission Control Protocol (TCP)/IP software is required in a computer.

Cable providers must overcome several technical and practical problems to enable widespread deployment of cable modems. These include technical standards for CPE and readiness of the cable plant for two-way traffic. In addition, on the upstream path, analog noise problems are significant and difficult to resolve.

ADSL or Cable Modem? The Subscriber's Perspective

From the end-user's perspective, both ADSL and cable modem offer a continuous connection, thus making the Internet as immediately accessible as a compact disc read-only memory (CD-ROM) drive. Both currently require a visit by an installer. The choice of ADSL or cable modem depends upon the user's preferences regarding shared bandwidth, price, and choice of host (ISP or corporate LAN):

- Shared bandwidth—ADSL involves a dedicated connection, while cable modem requires users to share access in a traditional Ethernet broadcast network. With multiple cable modem users online, downstream speeds can fall as low as 64 Kbps, substantially below the advertised 10 Mbps. Cable companies intend to install more head end equipment as higher numbers of subscribers slow down access. A more troubling aspect of the shared cable modem network is lack of security. A marginally skilled "hacker" could dig his or her way into a neighbor's computer files.

- Price—This variable appears to be a very important consideration for subscribers. A recent Yankee Group survey found that two-thirds of Internet users want faster access, but only 10 percent are willing to pay a service fee of $40 per month, which includes Internet access. Example monthly fees are listed in the Sample ADSL Access Rates Table.

Sample ADSL Access Rates

Downstream Speed	Average Monthly Fee ($)
256 Kbps	40
512 Kbps	65
768 Kbps	80
1 Mbps	120
4 Mbps	480
7 Mbps	840

- Choice of host—A telephone company's ADSL service is based on a hub and spoke model, in which the hub can be either a corporate LAN or an ISP. In the case of Qwest Communications, the hub location must buy a "megacentral" connection at a speed of 1.5 to 45 Mbps. This allows each "megabits" user to sign up with an ISP of his or her choice. In contrast, the leading cable modem services currently link only to their proprietary content offering, which includes Internet access. A subscriber does not have a choice of ISP.

Activities

1. Discuss the advantages and disadvantages of cable modems.

    _____

    _____

    _____

    _____

2. Contrast and compare cable modems and ADSL services.

    _____

    _____

    _____

    _____

3. What is an HFC network?

    _____

    _____

    _____

Extended Activities

1. Research the latest developments in cable modem technologies. Summarize your findings.

    _____

    _____

    _____

    _____

2. Research the latest developments in ADSL technologies. Summarize your findings.

_____

_____

_____

_____

_____

Lesson 8—SONET

Fiber optics has been used for some time in public long-distance networks. (Recall Sprint's television advertisements where the sound of a pin dropping was heard over a long-distance line.) Links in the first generation of fiber optics were entirely proprietary in nature, including architectures, equipment, protocols, formats for multiplex frames, and so on. SONET standardizes optical transmission.

Objectives

At the end of this lesson you will be able to:

- Describe the purpose of SONET development and deployment

- Explain the protocols that make up SONET architecture

- List devices used in a SONET-based network

 **Key Point**

> *SONET uses the term OC as the data rate descriptor.*

SONET Standard

Standardization of optical carrier (OC) services has obvious advantages to telephone companies, making it possible for them to select equipment from multiple vendors and interface with other telephone companies "in the glass," that is, without converting back to copper. SONET allows synchronous signals as low as DS0 to be switched without being demultiplexed.

The SONET standard defines a signal hierarchy similar to that which we saw for T-carriers, but extending to much higher bandwidths, as presented in the SONET Bandwidth Table. The basic building block is the Synchronous Transport Signal level 1 (STS-1) 51.84-Mbps signal, chosen to accommodate a DS3 signal. The hierarchy is defined past STS-48, that is, 48 STS-1 channels for a total of 2,488.32 Mbps, capable of carrying 32,256 voice circuits. The STS designation refers to the interface for electrical signals. The optical signal standards are correspondingly designated OC-1, OC-2, and so forth. Current OC rates are as high as OC-768 (40 gigabits per second [Gbps]).

SONET Bandwidth

STS and OC	SDH	Rate (Mbps)	Number of DS1s	Number of DS3s
1		51.84	28	1
3	1	155.52	84	3
9		466.56	252	9
12	4	622.08	336	12
18		933.12	504	18
24	8	1,244.16	572	24
36	12	1,866.24	1,008	36
48	16	2,488.32	1,344	48

SONET began as a U.S. standard, and was later incorporated into the international standard Synchronous Digital Hierarchy (SDH). SDH has been standardized by the International Telecommunication Union-Telecommunications Standardization Sector (ITU-T). SONET/SDH meets the worldwide need for standardization. The difference between the two standards is shown in the above table. SONET uses the term OC or STS as the data rate descriptor. SDH uses Synchronous Transport Mode (STM).

SONET Advantages

SONET has important advantages for those who use switched networks for communications:

- The SONET standards provide a low-level platform upon which other standards, such as those described in this section, can be based.

- SONET makes it possible for subscribers to purchase equipment that interfaces "in the glass" with switched public networks. For example, SONET interfaces are available to Switched Multimegabit Data Service (SMDS) and ISDN.

- Even the earlier offerings, OC-1 to OC-3, make new applications combining data, voice, and video images both technically and economically feasible.

- SONET provides direct, transparent interfaces to Layer 2 WAN protocols, such as ISDN. For example, SONET appears to ISDN interfaces as a continuation of the ISDN network, which is based on copper cable.

The SONET standard includes extensive network operation and management facilities. A significant portion of the SONET bandwidth is allocated for out-of-band control signaling for this purpose. This management system has its own OSI-compliant communications architecture. Ultimately, subscribers will be able to interface directly to this capability, running the SONET "stack" on their own computers.

SONET Protocol Architecture

The SONET and OSI Model Diagram shows how SONET architecture relates to the OSI model. Keep in mind that SONET is a Physical Layer standard; it deals with the transmission of bits of data and the electrical and optical forms of these bits. The SONET Physical Layer is divided into four layers: path, line, section, and photonic.

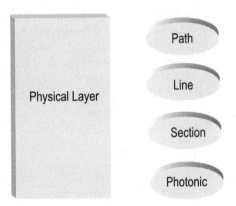

SONET and OSI Model

Subloyers of Layer 1

Unit 3

Path Layer

(4)

The path layer is the logical connection for end-to-end management and delivery of data. This layer is responsible for establishing a complete path over the SONET network between end network interface devices called "service adapters." The service adapters map DS3, ISDN, Fiber Distributed Data Interface (FDDI), or other protocols onto the SONET network. The SONET path layer's function is similar in concept to a Network Layer protocol's responsibility to establish an end-to-end path between internetworked nodes.

The path layer is the entry and exit point for services in SONET. Through a portion of reserved bandwidth called the "path overhead (POH)," the path layer has responsibility for the following functions occurring between network elements:

- Map and transport of services
- Equipment status
- Connectivity
- Error monitoring
- User-defined functions

Path terminating equipment (PTE) consists of network elements that originate and terminate transported services. PTE, such as SONET DXS systems, read, interpret, and modify the POH. Services positioned, or mapped, into the STS-1 path layer are called the "payload." The payload can be placed anywhere within the portion of the SONET frame that carries the mapped services, called the "synchronous payload envelope (SPE)." The POH resides within the payload. The payload and POH compose the SPE, which is discussed in more detail later.

Line Layer

(3)

The line layer is responsible for reliable transport of the path layer payload and POH across the transmission medium (usually fiber optic cable). The line layer multiplexes and synchronizes STS-1s into STS-3s, STS-3s into STS-9s, and so on. Network elements operating at the line layer are called "line terminating equipment (LTE)." The line layer provides the following LTE-to-LTE functions for the path layer payload and POH:

- Synchronization
- Payload location

242

- Multiplexing

- Error monitoring

- Automatic protection switching (APS)

These functions are performed with a portion of bandwidth in the STS called the "line overhead (LOH)," which is read, interpreted, and modified by any equipment that terminates this layer. Examples of LTE are SONET fiber optic MUXs, including ADMs. PTE also performs the functions of LTE, just as a router functions at both the Network and Data Link Layers.

Section Layer

The section layer provides functionality similar to the Data Link Layer of the OSI model. The section layer is responsible for transporting the STS-N across fiber optic cable, building STS-N frames, and moving them from the source to the destination. Network elements at this layer are called "section terminating equipment (STE)." Using a reserved portion of the STS-1 called the "section overhead (SOH)," the section layer performs the following STE-to-STE functions:

- STS identification

- Framing

- Error monitoring

- User-defined functions

SOH is read, interpreted, and modified by all equipment that terminates this layer. Just as a router must support the lower layers, PTE and LTE perform STE functions. SONET regenerators, used to extend SONET optical transmission distances, are examples of STE network elements.

Photonic Layer

The photonic layer is responsible for transmission of bits across optical fiber. This layer converts electrical input signals to optical signals and vice versa. A transceiver is the device used to convert electrical signals to optical signals. Optical equipment communicates at this layer, and there is no overhead. The primary function of this layer is to scramble and then convert electrical STS-N frames to light pulses for transmission as OC-N across optical fiber. Scrambling ensures ones density for synchronization and extends the operating life of the laser transmitters. Parameters monitored at this level include optical pulse shaping, power levels, and wavelength.

SONET Multiplexing

SONET uses the STS-1 bit rate (51.84 Mbps) as the basic building block. Higher transmission speeds are multiples of the STS-1 rate. The SONET STS-3 Multiplexing Diagram demonstrates the basic multiplexing structure of SONET. Any type of service, ranging from DS0 to high data rate switched services, such as Broadband ISDN (B-ISDN), can be accepted at the SONET path layer by the service adapters. An adapter maps the signal into the payload envelope of the STS-1. New services and signals can be transported by adding new service adapters at the edge of the SONET network. In this example, three STS-1s are multiplexed into an STS-3 at the line layer and converted into an OC-3 signal at the section layer.

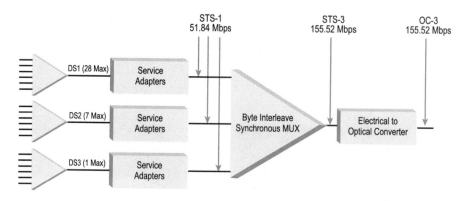

SONET STS-3 Multiplexing

Each input is eventually converted to a base format of a synchronous STS-1 signal (51.84 Mbps) or higher. Lower-speed inputs, such as DS1s, are first bit or byte multiplexed into virtual tributaries (VTs), which group these lower-speed circuits together to form STS-1s. Then, as illustrated on the SONET Synchronous Multiplexing Diagram, these synchronous STS-1s are multiplexed together in either a single- or two-stage process to form an electrical STS-N signal.

Logically
= to a sub
rate sonet

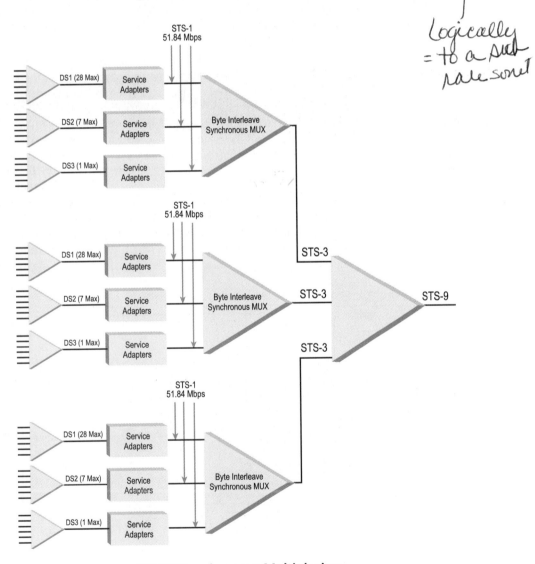

SONET Synchronous Multiplexing

STS multiplexing is performed at the byte interleave synchronous MUX. Bytes are interleaved together in a format such that low-speed signals are visible. Then a conversion takes place to convert the electrical signal to optical form, the OC-N signal.

Multiple STS-1 frames can be multiplexed together to form higher-speed signals.

SONET Frame Format

28 TIs - 1 T3

The SONET frame format is shown on the SONET Frame Format Diagram. It can be divided into two parts: the transport overhead and SPE. The SPE can also be divided into two parts: STS POH and payload. The payload is the user data being transported and routed over the SONET network. After the payload is multiplexed into the payload envelope, it can be transported and switched through SONET without the need for interpretation at intermediate nodes. Thus, SONET is said to be service-independent or transparent. The STS-1 payload has the capacity to transport up to:

- 28 DS1s *(T3 s)*
- 14 DS1Cs
- 7 DS2s
- 1 DS3
- 21 E1s

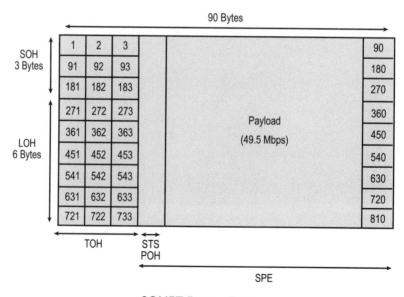

SONET Frame Format

A frame is transmitted byte-by-byte beginning with byte 1, going from left to right until byte 810 is transmitted. The entire frame is transmitted in 125 microseconds (µs) .

Each of the sections in the frame corresponds to specific "headers" in the SONET frame. The LOH and SOH are typically combined and represented as the transport overhead (TOH). The POH is carried as a portion of the payload. The Sample SONET Configuration Diagram shows the section, line, and path portions of a SONET network. Overhead is added for each of these portions to allow for simpler multiplexing and lower circuit maintenance. Path level overhead is carried from end to end. Repeaters are referred to as regenerators.

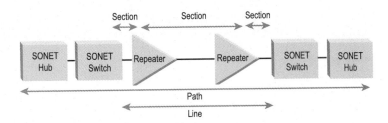

Sample SONET Configuration

SONET also defines sub-STS-1 levels called VTs. VTs map sub-STS-1 services, such as DS1 and DS2, into STS-1 frames. There are four VT speeds defined as listed in the VTs Table. Tributaries can be viewed as inputs to a SONET-based system.

VTs

Type	Transports	VT Rate (Mbps)
VT1.5	1 DS1	1.728
VT2	1 CEPT1	2.304
VT3	1 DS1C	3.456
VT6	1 DS2	6.912

Within an STS-1 frame, each VT occupies a number column as illustrated on the STS-1 Framing Diagram. Within the STS-1, many VT groups can be mixed together to form an STS-1 payload.

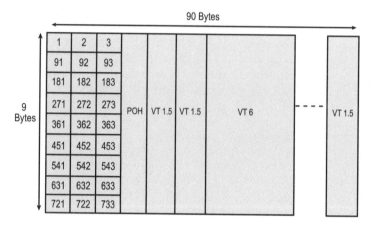

STS-1 Framing

Clocking is a key aspect of digital communications. Clocking ensures that the sender and receiver recognize when bits appear in the data stream. SONET VTs also require clock signals for data stream synchronization. Synchronous and asynchronous multiplexing techniques are two methods in which DS1 signals can be combined into higher-bit-rate data streams; SONET uses synchronous multiplexing. To better appreciate SONET's synchronous multiplexing system, first consider asynchronous multiplexing.

Asynchronous multiplexing multiplexes DS1s together into DS2s and then into DS3s. Because clock references vary between individual circuits, multiplexing techniques must allow for these variations. Asynchronous multiplexing accomplishes this by using a method called "bit stuffing," which adds bits to the data stream to fill in the "gaps" between clock rates; bit stuffing is discussed in more detail in Unit 4. In order to access the individual DSx signals, the receiver must first demultiplex the combined signals, removing the added bits as well. SONET's synchronous multiplexing techniques combine DSx VTs into STS-1 SPEs. SONET uses a set clock reference of 1.7288 Mbps per VT1.5 (DS1). This set reference value allows the STS-1 to carry each VT within the SPE so that each VT is visible to each PTE without the need for the receiver to demultiplex the STS-1 payload. The result is faster access to the DSx signals than that of asynchronous multiplexing techniques. An individual VT containing a DS1 can be extracted without demultiplexing the entire STS-1.

SONET Network Elements

There are several components that may be used in a SONET-based network. Some of the more common components are:

- ADM   *add Drop Multiplier.*
- Broadband DCS   *Digital Cross Connect*
- Wideband DCS
- Terminating multiplexer (TMUX)
- Regenerator   *(Optical Repeater*

An ADM/demultiplexer (deMUX) can multiplex various inputs into an OC-N signal. It can be used at terminal sites or intermediate network locations to insert or remove DSx or OC-N signals into an existing OC-N signal. It is configured as a hub as shown on the ADM Diagram. At an add/drop site, only those signals that need to be accessed are dropped or inserted. The remaining traffic continues straight through without interruption, and does not require special equipment or extra processing. An ADM is considered LTE.

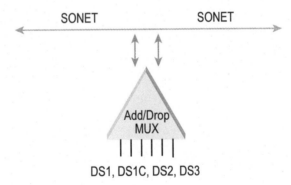

ADM — Add-Drop Multipler

A broadband DCS switches STS-1s within various OC rates. The SONET Broadband DCS Diagram depicts this component. One major difference between a cross-connect and ADM is that a cross-connect provides the capacity to interconnect a much larger number of STS-1s than an ADM.

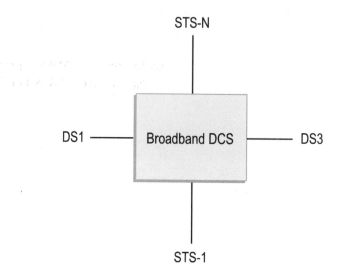

SONET Broadband DCS

The wideband DCS is similar to the broadband DCS, except that it switches at VT levels, as illustrated on the SONET Wideband DCS Diagram.

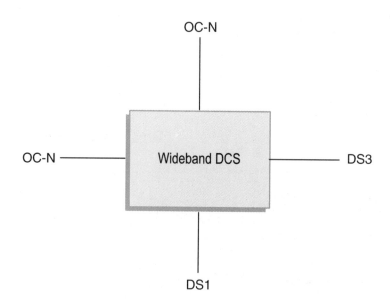

SONET Wideband DCS

The wideband DCS accepts DS3s and DS1s. Only the required VTs are accessed and switched, leaving the OC-N signals intact, allowing for more granular multiplexing/demultiplexing than that allowed by a broadband DCS. The wideband DCS is PTE.

TMUXs are devices used to access a SONET network, as illustrated on the SONET TMUX Diagram. The TMUX is PTE, and is used as an entry-level access point to the edge of the SONET network.

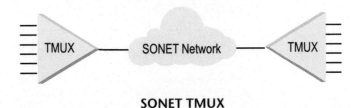

SONET TMUX

The SONET regenerator increases the optical signal level of the OC-N when long distances between devices dictate its use. The regenerator replaces the SOH in the received STS-N frames, but leaves the LOH, POH, and payload intact. Thus, a regenerator is STE. The SONET Regenerator Diagram illustrates this concept.

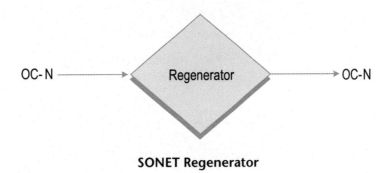

SONET Regenerator

Activities

1. Why was 51.84 Mbps chosen as the fundamental rate for SONET?

   _____

   _____

2. What is the difference between SDH and OC?

   _____

   _____

3. Considering the SONET STS-N data rates, why would ATM normally operate at 155 and 622 Mbps?

   _____

   _____

4. At which OSI layer would you classify SONET?

   _____

   _____

5. List and briefly describe the four protocol layers of the SONET architecture.

   _____

   _____

   _____

   _____

   _____

   _____

Extended Activities

1. What technologies can SONET support? Is it possible to carry voice conversations over SONET? How would a voice network interface with a SONET network? How would you interface an IP network to SONET? What devices would you use?

_____

_____

_____

_____

_____

_____

_____

2. Research the Physical Layer protocols used for the Internet backbone. Summarize your findings.

_____

_____

_____

_____

Summary

This unit covered many of the Physical Layer protocols used to move information across a WAN. When making decisions regarding WAN technologies, it is often a trade-off between availability, price, and performance. When selecting a WAN technology to fit a given telecommunications need, the carrier used will determine the choices available for WAN connectivity. The technologies presented in this unit represent many of the commonly offered point-to-point technologies used in WANs.

Depending on the services provided by the telecommunications carrier, the selected service is often a trade-off between the cost of the service and the bandwidth provided by the carrier. Usually the higher the bandwidth, the more expensive the service. For example, it is less expensive to use modems and a dial-up network than a T1 service; however, the bandwidth that a T1 provides can be 50 times greater than a dial-up solution (30 Kbps versus 1.5 Mbps).

These technologies are used in both point-to-point and switched services. As we will see in the next unit, Data Link Layer protocols use these Physical Layer protocols to move information across a single link. For example, it is common to see ATM running over SONET, or frame relay running over T1. Understanding each layer and the choices in technologies will greatly benefit the computer networking professional.

Unit 3 Quiz

1. Which of the following describes the functions of a VSAT?

    a. Provides connectivity to a satellite

    b. Provides connectivity to microwave systems

    c. Provides connectivity to a PBX

    d. Provides connectivity to the local loop

2. FT1 consists of multiples of which type of channel?

    a. 64-Kbps channels

    b. 58-Kbps channels

    c. T1 channels

    d. T3 channels

3. DDS uses which of the following?

    a. Satellite communications

    b. CSU/DSU

    c. Analog modems

    d. Codecs

4. Which of the following best describes a DTE?

    a. End device or node in a network

    b. Communicating device maintained by a telephone company

    c. High-speed switch

    d. CSU/DSU

5. A T1 line type is equivalent to the _____ standard.

    a. DS0

    b. ISDN-BRI

    c. DS1

    d. E1

6. What is the reason the transmission rate of data traveling across a T1 channel could be 56 Kbps?

    a. A portion of a T1 channel is used for in-band signaling for voice communications.

    b. A total of 56 Kbps is the highest theoretical rate for data communications across a T1.

    c. T1 only transmits information at 56-Kbps rates.

    d. It is the most efficient means of using the T1 channel.

7. Which of the following is a fiber optic technology?

    a. T3

    b. T1

    c. SONET

    d. Ethernet

8. Which of the following is the purpose of a MUX?

    a. Map low-speed input signals to a high-speed output signal

    b. Map high-speed input signals to a low-speed output signal

    c. Convert analog signals to digital signals

    d. Convert digital signals to analog signals

    e. None of the above

9. Which of the following are the building blocks for SONET?

    a. STS-1

    b. 51.84 Mbps

    c. 48 Kbps

    d. 64 Kbps

    e. Both a and b

10. What is the primary difference between an STS signal and OC signal?

    a. STS is digital, OC is analog.

    b. STS is low speed, OC is high speed.

    c. STS is electrical, OC is optical.

    d. STS is binary, OC is optical.

11. The STS payload can transport which of the following?

    a. 28 DS1s

    b. 1 DS3

    c. 28 T1s

    d. 1 T3

    e. All of the above

12. Which three of the following are CSU functions?
    (Choose three.)

    a. Impedance matching

    b. Regeneration

    c. Keep alives

    d. Loopback

13. The use of a coding signal consisting of a positive voltage, zero voltage, and negative voltage is called which of the following?

    a. B8XS

    b. AMI

    c. DXI

    d. ESF

14. Which two of the following are examples of a BPV?
    (Choose two.)

    a. Six 0s, followed by a 1 bit (0000001)

    b. One 0, followed by two consecutive 1s. The first 1 bit measures 5 volts, while the second measures -5 volts (011)

    c. Three 0s, followed by one 1 bit at 5 volts, another 0, and then a 1 bit at 5 volts (000101)

    d. One 1 bit at -5 volts, followed by three 0s, followed by one 1 bit at -5 volts (10001)

15. What occurs on a T1 link when two one-bits appear consecutively with the same polarity?

    a. AMI

    b. BPV

    c. B8ZS

    d. DSX

16. What happens to a T1 link if a consecutive stream of 0 bits traverses it without a 1 bit inserted at some point?

  a. The receiver automatically transmits the last frame received

  b. The circuit will lose timing and fail

  c. The receiver will add 1's as needed

  d. The circuit's available bandwidth will increase

Unit 4
Data Link Layer WAN Protocols

This unit covers the protocols used to move information across point-to-point networks. These protocols are associated with the Data Link Layer of the Open Systems Interconnection (OSI) model. Other protocols, such as frame relay and Asynchronous Transfer Mode (ATM), which are covered in the next unit, are used to move information across switched networks. We will examine the most predominantly used protocols in today's wide area network (WAN) environments.

Lessons

1. A Layer Above
2. HDLC
3. SLIP and PPP
4. End-to-End Connectivity

Terms

Compressed Serial Line Interface Protocol (CSLIP)—CSLIP is an Internet protocol that reduces the overhead TCP communications imposes on data traffic. For example, in a simple character-based terminal communication, TCP and IP headers can add almost 4,000 percent overhead, considering an ASCII character is 1 byte long, and each character can be carried in a single packet. Each packet carries 20 bytes of TCP header information, and another 20 bytes of IP information. CSLIP reduces the TCP header portion to 3 to 5 bytes, reducing overhead to approximately 300 percent.

frame relay—Frame relay is a wide-area data transmission technology that normally operates at speeds of 56 Kbps to 1.5 Mbps. A frame relay is essentially an electronic switch. Physically, it is a device that connects to three or more high-speed links and routes data traffic between them.

High-Level Data Link Control (HDLC)—HDLC is a Data Link Layer transmission protocol used for data communications. The HDLC protocol embeds information in a data frame that allows devices to control data flow and correct errors.

High-Level Data Link Control (HDLC) information frame—An HDLC information frame is an HDLC frame that carries data between two computers. See High-Level Data Link Control (HDLC), HDLC supervisory frame, and HDLC unnumbered frame.

High-Level Data Link Control (HDLC) supervisory frame—An HDLC supervisory frame is an HDLC frame that two computers exchange to control the flow of data between them. For example, by inserting the appropriate codes in the supervisory frame, a computer can acknowledge the receipt of data, or request a retransmission. See High-Level Data Link Control (HDLC), HDLC information frame, and HDLC unnumbered frame.

High-Level Data Link Control (HDLC) unnumbered frame—An HDLC unnumbered frame is a frame that exchanges control information between two communicating computers. For example, by inserting the appropriate codes in the supervisory frame, a computer can change operating modes or request a disconnect. See High-Level Data Link Control (HDLC), HDLC information frame, and HDLC supervisory frame.

Internet service provider (ISP)—An ISP is an organization Internet users must go through to access the Internet backbone.

Link Access Procedure Balanced (LAPB)—LAPB is a Data Link Layer protocol implemented from the HDLC standard. Primarily used in X.25 networks, LAPB provides an error-free link between two connected devices.

Link Access Procedure for D Channel (LAPD)—LAPD (or LAP-D) is part of the ISDN layered protocol. It is very similar to LAPB, and operates at the Data Link Layer as well. LAPD defines the protocol used on the ISDN D (signaling) channel to set up calls and other signaling functions.

Link Control Protocol (LCP)—LCP is a transmission protocol used by PPP to set up and test a serial connection.

Network Control Protocol (NCP)—NCP is a protocol that allows PPP to simultaneously support multiple Layer 3 protocols over a single connection.

Point-to-Point Protocol (PPP)—PPP is a protocol that allows a computer to use TCP/IP by means of a point-to-point link. PPP is based on the HDLC standard that deals with LAN and WAN links, and operates at the Data Link Layer of the OSI model.

request for comment (RFC)—RFC documents are working notes of the Internet research and development community. A document in this series can be on essentially any topic related to computer communication, from a meeting report to the specification of a standard.

Serial Line Internet Protocol (SLIP)—SLIP is not an official Internet standard, but a de facto standard included in many implementations of TCP/IP. It was originally developed to provide remote connectivity to UNIX TCP/IP hosts.

Synchronous Data Link Control (SDLC)—SDLC is widely used as a data link protocol by IBM SNA mainframe-based systems. SDLC works in a master/slave mode, where one node controls how other nodes access the network.

X.25—X.25 has been a long-time standard for packet switching. The X.25 interface lies at OSI Layer 3, rather than Layer 1. X.25 defines a protocol stack as having three layers.

zero bit insertion—Bit stuffing allows binary data to be transmitted on a synchronous transmission line. Within each frame are special bit sequences that identify addresses, flags, and so forth. If the information (data) portion of the frame also contains one of these special sequences, a 0 is inserted by the transmitting station and removed by the receiving station.

Lesson 1—A Layer Above

Thus far in this course we have seen different concepts and components used to access a WAN. We have also looked at Physical Layer protocols, protocols designed to move bits across a physical media. The main concern at the Physical Layer is moving analog and digital information across a cable or through the air.

Now we move up the protocol stack to the Data Link Layer, where the sequence of Physical Layer bits provides meaning to the devices on each end of a link.

Objectives

At the end of this lesson you will be able to:

- Describe basic protocol functions at the Data Link Layer

- Describe the differences between circuit-switched and packet-switched networks

 **Key Point**

Data Link Layer headers are used to move WAN frames across a link.

Data Link Layer Protocols

The protocols at the OSI Data Link Layer are the ones used to get information "into the box," so it can, in turn, be delivered to the processes at the higher layers. In that regard, these protocols are normally less complex than those above them. Whereas we may find many fields in a Transmission Control Protocol (TCP) message because of the various services offered by the Transport Layer, the function of Data Link Layer protocols is essentially limited to local, group, and broadcast address recognition. The Data Link Layer may also provide basic error handling and recovery mechanisms, such as frame retransmission. In addition, both connection-oriented and connectionless modes of operation are available.

WAN technologies and their corresponding protocols are used where geographically dispersed networks and subnetworks need to be logically and physically interconnected. Originally, WAN network speeds were low compared to local area network (LAN) speeds; however, improved carrier technologies are raising transfer rates substantially. Whereas 9600- and 19200-baud WANs were commonplace in earlier days, physical layer services such as T1 (1.544 megabits per second [Mbps]) and T3 (45 Mbps) are often used in today's WANs.

Reliable WAN Networks

In addition to higher-speed carriers, newer, more efficient protocols are being used in WANs. For example, frame relay, a Layer 2 protocol, is replacing X.25's three-layered protocol stack to take advantage of the extreme reliability of the newer carrier technologies. Frame relay is often found riding on T1 (or E1, which is the European standard) carriers, and is being used more frequently as the protocol between network routers.

Wide-area networking is generally grouped into two categories:

- Packet switched—Information packets carrying full addressing and data are sent over paths established between end nodes. The path each packet takes may vary as the packet travels to the destination device.

- Circuit switched—After a circuit is established, similar to a telephone call, no further connection protocols are necessary. The session then takes place with very little addressing overhead. A certain amount of addressing is still required, because multiple stations can exist in a multipoint network.

Packet-switched networks are referred to as connectionless, because no connection is established. As in Internet Protocol (IP) networks, packets of information are passed from node to node, with a packet possibly traversing many nodes before it arrives at its destination. Many packets can be moving between the same nodes simultaneously. The Packet-Switched Network Diagram illustrates this type of network configuration.

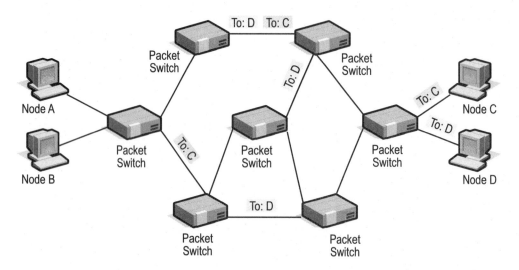

Packet-Switched Network

Note that packet-switched networks still need Data Link Layer and Physical Layer protocols to move information between devices connected to a link. The underlying protocols may be connection-less or connection-oriented, depending on the protocol.

Circuit-switched networks establish a physical connection between two nodes, and packets are passed between nodes by "switching" them through intermediate points, either other nodes or a host computer. Circuit-switched networks are analogous to the voice telephone system, and such connections are often referred to as virtual circuits. A virtual circuit establishes a single route for data that does not vary for the life of the connection. Therefore, they are connection-oriented. Frame relay and ATM networks are examples of circuit-switched networks. The Circuit-Switched Network Diagram illustrates this type of network configuration.

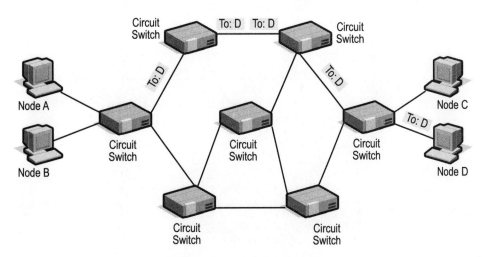

Circuit-Switched Network

In the early days of data communication, all networks were circuit-switched, and many still are. For networks that cover wide areas, the emphasis has shifted to packet switching, simply because it permits interconnection of many more nodes into a single network. With packet switching, fewer communication channels are required (because channels are shared by many users), and interconnection of networks is much easier to accomplish. The Internet is a good example of a large packet-switching network.

Activities

1. What is the basic function of Data Link Layer protocols?

   _____

   _____

2. Describe the difference between packet-switched and circuit-switched networks.

   _____

   _____

   _____

   _____

   _____

Extended Activities

1. Find out how your organization connects to the Internet, and what Physical Layer and Data Link Layer protocols are used on the LAN and WAN sides.

2. Determine whether these protocols are connectionless or connection-oriented.

Lesson 2—HDLC

High-Level Data Link Control (HDLC) is one of the most common Data Link Layer protocols used in wide-area networking. HDLC and its subsets provide the mechanism for moving information across a physical link.

Objectives

At the end of this lesson you will be able to:

- Describe basic HDLC communication across a WAN link
- Describe HDLC commands and frame format

 **Key Point**

HDLC provides the intelligence for transmitting a series of bits across a physical link.

HDLC was built on top of SDLC.
↑
1ST

HDLC Operation

Layer 2

One of the most common Data Link Layer protocols is HDLC. Two other protocols that are subsets of this protocol suite are Synchronous Data Link Control (SDLC), which is used in IBM Systems Network Architecture (SNA) remote environments, and Link Access Procedure for D Channel (LAPD), which is used in X.25 WAN environments. There are three types of link stations defined in HDLC. The HDLC unbalanced configuration defines a primary and secondary station, as presented on the HDLC Unbalanced Configuration Diagram. The third is a combined station, as presented on the HDLC Balanced Configuration Diagram.

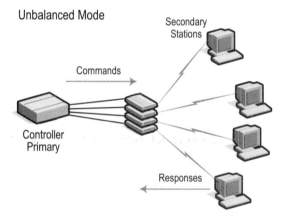

HDLC Unbalanced Configuration

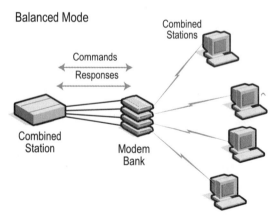

HDLC Balanced Configuration

HDLC

The station types in these configurations are as follows:

(1) • Primary station—Sends commands and accepts responses (referred to as the "master" node). This configuration is often seen in IBM hosts. A primary station is further described as a polling environment.

(2) • Secondary station—Accepts commands and sends responses (referred to as the "slave" node). This configuration appears in secondary stations communicating over remote lines to an IBM mainframe primary station.

(3) • Combined station—Sends or accepts commands and responses. This type of link station is found in balanced configurations where communication is on a peer-to-peer basis, such as Link Access Procedure Balanced (LAPB) of the X.25 protocol suite. The HDLC Balanced Configuration Diagram illustrates this type of setup.

HDLC Protocol

The HDLC Frame Format Diagram shows the fields in an HDLC frame. These frames are used to communicate across a given physical link between two communicating devices, similar to an Ethernet frame over a 10BaseT segment.

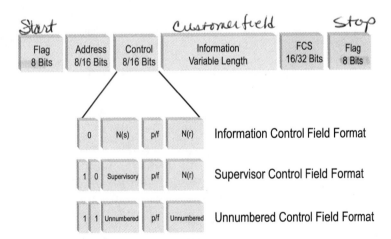

HDLC Frame Format

The fields in an HDLC frame include:

- Flag (1 byte [octet])—The Flag field is used for synchronization of the bit stream. Each frame starts off with this flag, which is a hexadecimal 7E. Only the flag byte will have 6 bits set in a row. If a character that has 6 or more consecutive bits needs to be transmitted, a technique called "zero bit insertion," or "bit stuffing," is used to ensure the data character is not mistaken for a flag character. This 0 bit is stripped off at the receiver before forwarding the frame to the higher layers. The protocol replaces the fifth consecutive 1 with a 0, changing the character's form.

- Address (1 or 2 bytes)—The Address field contains the address of the secondary station (if unbalanced).

- Control (1 or 2 bytes)—The Control field denotes the type of frame (supervisory or information), and contains counters to keep track of transmitted and received frames for acknowledgment and flow control. The Control field format is as follows:

  - Frame ID (1 or 2 bits).

  - 0—Information transfer (I) frame (data transfer between stations).

  - 10—Supervisory (S) frame (polling, data acknowledgment, and control).

  - 11—Unnumbered (U) frame (polling, testing, station initialization, and control).

  - Supervisory, unnumbered, or send sequence number (NS) (2 or 3 bits)—Varies by the frame type in length and purpose.

  - Poll/final (P/F) (1 bit)—Indicates poll from primary station or final frame from secondary.

  - Receive sequence number (NR) (3 bits)—Used by information and supervisory frames to acknowledge the number of successfully received frames. For unnumbered frames, this is a portion of the Unnumbered Modifier Function that determines the unnumbered frame's purpose.

- Information ("I" field) (variable)—The Information field contains the data, if any. For most HDLC stations, this field is usually no larger than 256 or 512 bytes, although there are some implementations that transmit larger frames.

The HDLC trailer includes:

- Frame check sequence (FCS) (2 bytes)—The FCS field contains a checksum to ensure data integrity.

- Flag (1 byte)—The Flag field is used to signal the end of a frame, and possibly the start of the next frame. This character takes the form of hexadecimal 7E, similar to the flag byte.

The various commands used in HDLC are listed in the HDLC Commands Table.

HDLC Commands

Field Type	Field ID	Function
Information	I	Exchange User Data (Data from the Network Layer)
Supervisory	RR	Receiver Ready—Positive Acknowledgment
Supervisory	RNR	Receiver Not Ready—Positive Acknowledgment
Supervisory	REJ	Reject—Negative Acknowledgment, Go Back N Frames
Supervisory	SREJ	Selective Reject—Negative Acknowledgment, Selective Repeat
Unnumbered	DISC	Disconnect—Terminate Connection
Unnumbered	DM	Disconnect Mode—Secondary Disconnect
Unnumbered	FRMR	Frame Reject
Unnumbered	RSET	Reset
Unnumbered	SABM	Set Asynchronous Balanced Mode
Unnumbered	SARM	Set Asynchronous Response Mode
Unnumbered	SIM	Set Initialization Mode
Unnumbered	SNRM	Set Normal Response Mode

HDLC Commands (Continued)

Field Type	Field ID	Function
Unnumbered	TEST	Test
Unnumbered	UA	Unnumbered Acknowledgment
Unnumbered	RIM	Request Initialization Mode
Unnumbered	RD	Request Disconnect
Unnumbered	UI	Unnumbered Information
Unnumbered	UP	Unnumbered Poll
Unnumbered	XID	Exchange Identification

As illustrated on the Unbalanced Transfer Sequence Diagram, a typical SDLC session (unbalanced) uses the following command and response sequence to connect and transfer information:

1. The primary station sets the normal response mode (SNRM) command with an unnumbered frame.

2. The secondary station sends an unnumbered acknowledgment (UA) frame.

3. The primary station sends a supervisory frame initializing the receiver ready (RR) function and sets the P/F bit to 1, polling the secondary station for information.

4. The secondary station sends its information frames, incrementing the Control field send sequence number (NS) bits as it sends each frame. The primary responds with information frames (to the requestor).

5. The primary acknowledges the last frame by sending a supervisory frame with the NR bits set to the number of received frames. It then sends an unnumbered disconnect (DISC) command frame.

6. The secondary station responds with UA, sometimes followed with an unnumbered disconnect mode (DM) frame.

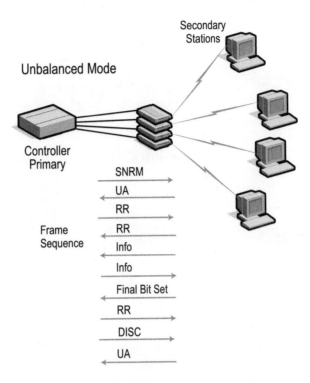

Unbalanced Transfer Sequence

Activities

1. Contrast HDLC unbalanced and balanced configurations.

   _____

   _____

   _____

   _____

2. List the three HDLC frame formats.

   _____

   _____

3. What supervisory command would be sent to indicate a station does not wish to have information sent to it?

   _____

Extended Activity

1. Find three Web sites that have information on each of the following protocols. Summarize your findings.

   a. HDLC

   b. SDLC

   c. LAPB

   d. LAPD

   _____

   _____

   _____

   _____

Lesson 3—SLIP and PPP

Serial Line Internet Protocol (SLIP) and Point-to-Point Protocol (PPP) are used to transfer IP information across a serial link. These two protocols are widely used to connect a home or business user to the Internet by means of an Internet service provider (ISP).

carries / protocol
static

Objectives

At the end of this lesson you will be able to:

* Describe the difference between SLIP and PPP

* Explain the basic concepts of SLIP and PPP

> 🔑 **Key Point**
>
> *SLIP and PPP are used to move IP packets across a serial link.*

SLIP

Layer 2

SLIP dates back to the early 1980s when it was originally implemented in Berkeley Software Distribution (BSD) 4.2 UNIX. It is a simple encapsulation of an IP datagram asynchronously transmitted over serial lines using an RS-232 interface. A typical connection is shown on the SLIP Access Diagram. A home or small business user attached to the Internet typically uses a modem to access Internet services by means of an ISP. At the user's computer, the IP packet is placed in a SLIP (or PPP) frame and sent to the modem. The modem transmits the information across the telephone network to the ISP modem. The ISP's modem is attached to a router that decapsulates the SLIP frame, takes the original IP packet generated by the user, and encapsulates this packet in a WAN protocol frame to route it across the Internet to the proper destination.

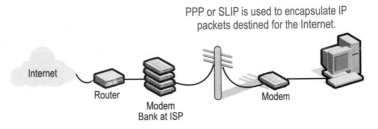

PPP or SLIP is used to encapsulate IP packets destined for the Internet.

Internet   Router   Modem Bank at ISP   Modem

SLIP Access

The SLIP Diagram illustrates how the IP packet (datagram) is inserted into the SLIP frame, which consists of two hexadecimal "C0" characters.

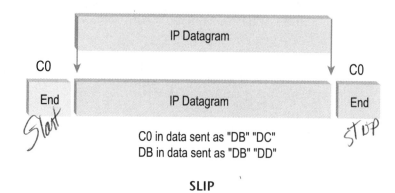

SLIP

The only control character used is a hexadecimal "C0." This is a special character used to delimit the endpoints of a SLIP frame. What happens if "C0" is the actual data? Hiding this character in the data is accomplished by using the SLIP escape character "DB." If a "C0" appears in the data, it is transmitted as a two-character sequence of "DB" "DC." If the SLIP escape character itself appears in the data, it is represented by a "DB" "DD" sequence.

There are a few drawbacks of SLIP. Each end must know the other end's IP address, because there is no way of exchanging this information in the protocol. Because there is no "type" field that could be used to direct the data to one of several protocol stacks, if it is being used to transfer IP datagrams, it can only be used to direct information to that particular Network Layer stack. Finally, there is no checksum to allow for error detection on noisy telephone lines, which means the higher layers are responsible for error detection and recovery.

CSLIP

Because SLIP is usually run over relatively slow-speed serial lines and often used for applications such as Telnet, a compressed version called "compressed SLIP (CSLIP)" was specified (Request for Comment [RFC] 1144). Telnet is an interactive application and can be very inefficient when sending just a few bytes at a time. A typical TCP/IP connection sends source and destination addresses and various indicators and flags in every packet header. After two hosts establish a Telnet session, there is no need to resend this information. For example, to send just three characters in a TCP/IP session requires 43 bytes to be transferred. (Each header, IP, and TCP is 20 bytes.) By using CSLIP, the 40 bytes of header overhead can be reduced to between 3 and 5 bytes. Information such as IP addresses, TCP fragmentation indicators, and type of service (ToS) flags need not be sent, as illustrated on the CSLIP Diagram.

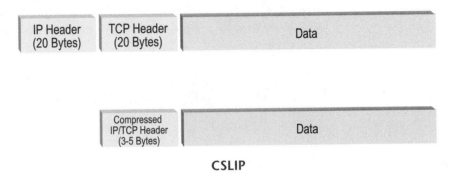

CSLIP

PPP

(Layer 2)

PPP is used by higher-layer protocols, such as TCP/IP, to provide simple WAN connectivity between users. It replaces SLIP and solves some of the inefficiencies found in SLIP. PPP supports either asynchronous (character-oriented) or synchronous (bit-oriented) transmission links.

A frame has information embedded within it so it can be directed to the proper destination above the Data Link Layer. The format of a PPP frame is similar to the HDLC frame layout presented earlier. There are three formats of a PPP frame depending on whether it is carrying data or control information. The PPP Information Frame Diagram presents the fields in a PPP frame header.

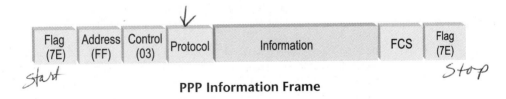

start *Stop*

PPP Information Frame

The fields in a PPP frame header include:

- Flag (1 byte)—A Flag field is used for synchronizing the bit stream "7E."

- Address (1 byte)—The Address field is always "FF."

- Control (1 byte)—The Control field is set to "03."

- Protocol (2 bytes)—The Protocol field contains addressing for the higher layers. This field is similar, but not identical, to the Ethernet Type field (Ethertype). Some common addresses are:

  0021H—TCP/IP

  0023H—OSI

  0027H—Digital Equipment Corporation (DEC)

  002BH—Novell

- Information (variable)—The Information field contains data that may be preceded by Network Layer headers, such as IP.

- FCS (2 bytes)—The FCS field is used to ensure data integrity.

- Flag (1 byte)—The Flag field signals the end of the frame, and possibly the start of the next frame.

A Link Control Protocol (LCP) can be used to specify certain data link options, such as which characters are going to be control characters on an asynchronous link. It can also be used to negotiate not having to send a flag or address byte, and reduce the size of the Protocol field from 2 bytes to 1 byte for more efficient line use. The PPP Link Control Frame Diagram presents an LCP frame header.

PPP Link Control Frame

As in HDLC frames, PPP frames require special consideration regarding sending a flag byte as data.

On a synchronous link, this is taken care of by the hardware using a technique called "zero bit insertion" or "bit stuffing." If a flag character appears as data on an asynchronous link, it is sent as a 2-byte sequence of "7D" "5E." "7D," the American Standard Code for Information Interchange (ASCII) escape character is sent first, followed by the data character with its sixth bit complemented. A "7E" flag character with its sixth bit complemented is equal to a "5E." The escape character itself would be sent as "7D" "5D." In addition, ASCII control characters (any value lower than a "20") would be sent the same way. For example, a BEL character, which could be used to cause the speaker on a personal computer (PC) to sound a "beep," is a hexadecimal 07. It would be sent as a 2-byte sequence "7D" "27." (Again, the sixth bit is complemented.)

The third format of a PPP frame is used to negotiate items such as using header compression. The PPP Network Control Frame Diagram presents a Network Control Protocol (NCP) frame used for this purpose. This protocol can also be used to dynamically negotiate the IP addresses for each end of the link, such as when you connect to your ISP over a dial-up connection, and enables PPP to support multiple Layer 3 protocols over the same connection.

Flag (7E)	Address (FF)	Control (03)	Protocol (8021)	Network Control Data	FCS	Flag (7E)

PPP Network Control Frame

Activities

1. Match the feature with the supporting protocol:

    a. PPP

    b. CSLIP

    c. SLIP

    Reduces the TCP header size _____

    Dynamically negotiates IP addresses _____

    Can only carry one type of higher-layer protocol at a time
    _____

    Frame similar to HDLC frame _____

    Provides no checksum _____

    Supports either asynchronous or synchronous links _____

2. List the properties of PPP that provide a more robust service than SLIP.

    _____

    _____

    _____

Extended Activity

Download and review RFC 1144 from the Internet. Summarize your findings.

_____

_____

_____

_____

_____

_____

Lesson 4—End-to-End Connectivity

The purpose of this lesson is to demonstrate how the concepts presented in this unit are commonly used in wide-area networking.

Objectives

At the end of this lesson you will be able to:

- Understand how Data Link Layer and Physical Layer protocols work together

Key Point

Many Data Link Layer and Physical Layer protocols are necessary to move information across a WAN.

Connecting to the Internet

To show how many different Physical Layer and Data Link Layer protocols are used in a network and demonstrate how both connection-oriented and connectionless protocols are used in a network, consider the Internet Connectivity Diagram.

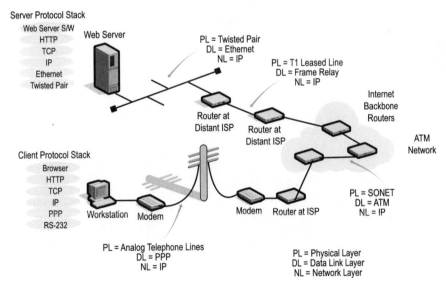

Internet Connectivity

If a user was accessing a remote World Wide Web (Web) site, the protocols shown on this diagram might be used. At the client workstation, IP packets are sent by means of the Internet to a remote Web server. To move this information from source (client) to destination (server), many different protocols may be used. Note that at the Network Layer and layers above it, the protocol stack stays virtually the same. At the lower layers, each link may require different Physical Layer and Data Link Layer protocols, as shown on the diagram.

The workstation first transmits the IP packet across an analog telephone line. To do this, the IP packet is placed in a PPP frame and transmitted to a router at the ISP. The router takes the IP packet and encapsulates it inside another Data Link Layer protocol, such as ATM. In this example, ATM is using fiber optic technology (Synchronous Optical Network [SONET]) at the Physical Layer to move information across the fiber optic link.

Information (IP packets) is routed across the Internet backbone until it arrives at the distant ISP where the Web server attaches to the Internet. In this example, the destination network attaches to the Internet using frame relay at the Data Link Layer and T1 at the Physical Layer. The IP packet moves across the frame relay link until it arrives at a router attached to the LAN where the Web server resides.

The Internet Connectivity Diagram illustrates an Ethernet network using twisted pair. The router takes the IP packet, puts it inside of an Ethernet frame, and sends it to the Web server. At the Web server, the IP packet, TCP message, and Hypertext Transfer Protocol (HTTP) Web page request are processed, and a reply is generated.

Activity

Draw a diagram showing Internet connectivity from your home PC to an ISP. Show the PC protocol stack and use PPP as the protocol to the ISP modem.

Extended Activity

1. Look up additional information on the subjects covered in this lesson. Find information from RFCs and vendor white papers that further describe the technical details of these protocols, including:

   a. PPP

   _____

   _____

   b. SLIP

   _____

   _____

   c. CSLIP

   _____

   _____

Summary

Information moves across a WAN using different types of Physical Layer and Data Link Layer protocols. This unit reviewed some of the common protocols used in WANs. HDLC and HDLC subsets, such as SDLC, LAPB, and LAPD, are used to move information from one physical device to another using services of the Physical Layer. PPP is another protocol based on HDLC.

Some Data Link Layer protocols are connection-oriented, and others are connectionless. For example, Ethernet is a connection-less LAN protocol, and frame relay is a connection-oriented WAN protocol. Connectionless and connection-oriented protocols are found in different parts of a network, and a single request for a Web page may go across a network that consists of both.

Unit 4 Quiz

1. What is the primary difference between a packet-switched network and circuit-switched network?

   a. A circuit-switched network is point-to-point.

   b. A packet-switched network deals with packets, and a circuit-switched network deals with circuits.

   c. The route a packet travels over a packet-switched network is always the same, whereas the route a packet travels in a circuit-switched network is never the same.

   d. The route a packet travels over a packet-switched network can be different, whereas the route a packet travels over a circuit-switched network is always the same for the length of the session.

2. What is the purpose of a Physical Layer protocol?

   a. Transmit messages to the correct process

   b. Transmit packets to the end node

   c. Transmit frames to the next node

   d. Transmit bits across a physical link

3. What is the purpose of a Data Link Layer protocol?

   a. Transmit messages to the correct process

   b. Transmit packets to the end node

   c. Transmit frames to the next node

   d. Transmit bits across a physical link

4. The Physical Layer remains the same as information moves from source to destination in a network. True or False

5. The Data Link Layer remains the same as information moves from source to destination in a network. True or False

6. SDLC is a subset of the HDLC suite of protocols. True or False

7. An escape character is used to hide control characters in a communications bit stream. True or False

8. SLIP provides more features than PPP. True or False

9. The term connectionless only applies to Layers 2 and 3 of the OSI model. True or False

Unit 5
Higher-Layer WAN Protocols

Wide area network (WAN) communications systems are typically based on public, connection-oriented services. Connectionless services, such as the Internet Protocol (IP), are those that do not establish a set path for a communications session to take place.

Many data networks are like this; data packets travel from one point to another by means of whatever path is available at any particular time. Packets are assembled at the other end of the connection to reformulate the original message. Data packets can take varying routes through the network and arrive at different times; however, this does not mean other applications, such as voice transmission, can tolerate such time lags. As the core backbone speeds of carrier networks increase, these delays are less of an issue.

The trend in WAN networking for network-to-network transfer of information is connection-oriented services at the Data Link Layer, and connectionless services at the Network Layer. This unit reviews connection-oriented switched services commonly used to move information across a wide area. These services include Integrated Services Digital Network (ISDN), frame relay, and X.25.

Lessons

1. ISDN Concepts

2. ISDN Protocols

3. ISDN Implementation

4. Frame Relay Concepts

5. Frame Relay Protocols

6. Frame Relay Implementation

7. X.25

Although we refer to this unit as Higher-Layer WAN Protocols, these protocols are essentially Data Link Layer protocols. However, these protocols go beyond simple link connectivity by providing connection services across an entire WAN, normally across multiple links. It is for this reason that we refer to them as higher-layer protocols.

Terms

backward explicit congestion notification (BECN)—BECN is a frame relay framing bit that the frame relay device sets in transmitted frames traveling away from frames that have experienced congestion.

Integrated Services Digital Network-Basic Rate Interface (ISDN-BRI)—ISDN-BRI provides two "bearer" channels (B channels) of 64 Kbps each, plus one control channel (D channel) of 16 Kbps. See Primary Rate ISDN.

bursty—A network traffic pattern in which a lot of data is transmitted in short bursts at random intervals is referred to as "bursty."

committed burst size (CBS)—CBS is the number of bits a circuit can transfer over a period of time.

committed information rate (CIR)—CIR is the guaranteed average data rate for a frame relay service.

common channel signaling (CCS)—Digital telecommunications systems require a method to set up and maintain calls. CCS, which dedicates a separate communications channel to control signaling, is becoming the predominant method of carrying signaling information between devices, thus eliminating problems associated with control signaling within the voice channel.

customer premises equipment (CPE)—CPE, which also stands for customer-provided equipment, refers to telephone equipment that resides at a customer site.

data link connection identifier (DLCI)—A DLCI is part of a frame relay frame. It is a 10-bit address that identifies the virtual circuit the frame belongs to. The DLCI identifies the logical channel between a user and network, and has no network-wide significance.

Dial-on-Demand Routing (DDR)—DDR is a technique used with circuit-switched links that allows the router to initiate a connection only when information is present at the router interface. The router drops the connection after transmission ends.

discard eligibility (DE) bit—The DE bit is a bit set in a frame relay frame that indicates the frame may be dropped to free bandwidth for higher-priority frames in times of network congestion.

dumb terminal—A terminal that totally depends on a host computer for processing capabilities is referred to as a "dumb" terminal. Dumb terminals typically do not have a processor, hard drive, or floppy drives; they have only a keyboard, monitor, and method of communicating to a host (usually through some type of controller).

excess burst size (EBS)—EBS is the maximum amount of uncommitted data (in bits) in excess of the CBS that a frame relay network can attempt to deliver during a time interval. This data is generally delivered with a lower probability and is treated as discard eligible.

excess information rate (EIR)—The frame relay EIR is a data rate over and above the CIR. The data exceeding the CIR is given best effort delivery by the carrier and is considered discard eligible.

forward explicit congestion notification (FECN)—FECN is a frame relay framing bit that the frame relay device sets in transmitted frames to indicate to the receiving devices that congestion has occurred in the frame's path from the source to the destination.

frame relay access device (FRAD)—A FRAD is a frame relay network device required for connecting to a network, such as a switch or router.

Integrated Digital Network (IDN)—A network that integrates both digital transmission and digital switching into a single digital network, such as ISDN.

Integrated Services Digital Network (ISDN)—ISDN is a digital multiplexing technology that can transmit voice, data, and other forms of communication simultaneously over a single local loop. It provides the following services:

- Access to the telephone network from a local loop.

- Access to communications channels of varying capacities suitable for various uses (for example, voice, data, and video). Access is possible from a single local loop connection to the network. The ISDN provider takes care of multiplexing the various channels for long-distance transmission.

- "On demand" establishment of any kind of communications link, with tariffs based on use.

Integrated Services Digital Network-Basic Rate Interface (ISDN-BRI)—ISDN-BRI provides two "bearer" channels (B channels) of 64 Kbps each, plus one control channel (D channel) of 16 Kbps. See Integrated Services Digital Network-Primary Rate Interface (ISDN-PRI).

Integrated Services Digital Network-Primary Rate Interface (ISDN-PRI)—ISDN-PRI is also called "T1 service." It offers 23 "bearer" channels (B channels) of 64 Kbps each, plus 1 control channel (D channel) of 64 Kbps. See Integrated Services Digital Network-Basic Rate Interface (ISDN-BRI).

Interactive Terminal Interface (ITI)—ITI is an informal telecommunications term for the combined ITU-T X.3, X.28, and X.29 recommendations.

International Telecommunication Union (ITU)—ITU Telecommunications Standardization Sector (ITU-T) is a sector of ITU, which sets network standards for public telecommunications.

ITU-T I.430—ITU-T I.430 is the ITU Layer 1 specification for the ISDN-BRI S/T interface. Each BRI frame is 48 bits long and repeated 4,000 times per second for a total line bit rate of 192 Kbps.

ITU-T I.431—ITU-T I.431 is the ITU Layer 1 specification for the ISDN-PRI operating at 1.544 Mbps (North America) or 2.048 Mbps (Europe).

ITU I.451—ITU I.451 is the ISDN specification for the UNI basic call control at the Network Layer. See ITU Q.931.

ITU Q.920—ITU Q.920 is the ISDN specification for the general aspects of UNI at the Data Link Layer. See ITU Q.921.

ITU Q.921—ITU Q.921 is the ISDN specification for UNI at the Data Link Layer. See ITU Q.920.

ITU Q.930—ITU Q.930 is the ISDN specification for the general aspects of UNI at the Network Layer. See ITU Q.931.

ITU Q.931—ITU Q.931 is the ISDN specification for the UNI Network Layer basic call control. See ITU Q.930.

local significance—Local significance means that an address only identifies a point-to-point link, not an entire end-to-end connection. Frame relay DLCI and ATM VCI have local significance.

network termination type 1 (NT1)—An ISDN NT1 multiplexes TE1 and TE2/TA devices at the OSI model Physical Layer and interfaces the local loop.

network termination type 2 (NT2)—An ISDN NT2 usually resides at the carrier's facility as a PBX or switch. The NT2 provides Layer 2 and 3 services.

network termination type 12 (NT12)—An ISDN NT12 is a device that performs both the NT1 and NT2 functions.

Network-to-Network Interface (NNI)—NNI describes the connection between two public frame relay services. Providers use NNI to monitor the frame relay network's status. An NNI is also an ATM network interface.

packet assembler/disassembler (PAD)—A PAD is an X.25 network device that takes characters from a terminal or host and frames them into packets for transport across the network. The receiver then removes the characters from the packets for transmission to the destination terminal or host.

Packet Layer Protocol (PLP)—PLP is an OSI model Layer 3 protocol that manages connections between DCE and DTE anywhere in an X.25 network. PLP accepts data from a Transport Layer process, breaks the data into packets, assigns the packets a Network Layer address, and takes responsibility for error-free delivery of the packets to their destination. PLP establishes virtual circuits and routes packets across the circuits. PLP also handles packet multiplexing.

protocol data unit (PDU)—A PDU is a datagram created by a particular layer of an open system reference model. A PDU is used to provide peer-to-peer communications between local and remote processes.

Signaling System 7 (SS7)—SS7 is a telecommunications protocol defined by ITU as a way to offload PSTN data traffic congestion onto a wireless or wireline digital broadband network. SS7 is characterized by high-speed packet switching and out-of-band signaling. Out-of-band signaling does not take place over the same path as the data transfer (or conversation); a separate digital channel is created, called a "signaling link" where messages are exchanged between network elements. SS7 architecture is set up so that any node can exchange signaling with any other SS7-capable node, not just between directly connected switches.

spoofing—Spoofing means that a router responds to a local host in lieu of sending information across a WAN link to a remote host. The local host thinks the response came from the remote host/network, when it really came from the router.

statistical time-division multiplexing (STDM)—STDM is a more flexible method of TDM. TDM allocates a fixed number of time slots to each channel, regardless of whether the channel has data to send. In contrast, a statistical MUX analyzes transmission patterns to predict gaps in a channel's traffic that can be temporarily filled with part of the traffic from another channel.

terminal adapter (TA)—A TA is a hardware interface between a non-ISDN TE2 and an ISDN network.

terminal equipment type 1 (TE1)—A TE1 is an ISDN device providing a four-wire, twisted pair, native ISDN digital interface.

terminal equipment type 2 (TE2)—A TE2 is a device connected to an ISDN network, but which does not understand ISDN protocols. A TE2 requires a TA to connect to an ISDN network.

User-Network Interface (UNI)—UNI specifies the procedures and protocols between user equipment (FRAD) and the frame relay network. UNI also defines the interface between an ATM network device and the ATM network.

V.24—ITU-T V.24 defines interface characteristics for serial data interchange between DTE and DCE, similar to RS-232-C.

X.3—X.3 is the ITU recommendation that describes the operation of the X.25 PAD in a public packet-switched network. X.3 defines the parameters that govern PAD control over asynchronous terminal operation.

X.21—ITU X.21 defines the interface between DTE and DCE in synchronous operations across a public data network. X.21 is only used for link establishment and connection control functions.

X.21bis—X.21bis is the CCITT recommendation that specifies the V.series modem serial interface.

X.28—ITU X.28 defines the terminal-to-PAD interface for DTE accessing a public-switched network's PAD facility.

X.29—ITU X.29 specifies the procedures for handshaking and user data transfer between a PAD and a packet mode DTE or another PAD.

X.75—X.75 is an international standard and ITU-T recommendation for linking X.25 networks. X.75 defines the connection between public networks and the terminal and transit control procedures to be used when transferring data between public networks.

X.121—ITU X.121 is the recommendation for packet mode data device numbering systems. X.25 uses the X.121 protocol.

Lesson 1—ISDN Concepts

Having discussed Physical Layer WAN protocols and Data Link Layer protocols, we turn our attention to protocols that move information across switched networks. We will discuss ISDN first, because it is widely implemented and provides a framework for understanding other WAN products that provide integration of multiple services.

Objectives

At the end of this lesson you will be able to:

- Describe ISDN services

- Identify the differences between ISDN-Basic Rate Interface (ISDN-BRI) and ISDN-Primary Rate Interface (ISDN-PRI) services

 **Key Point**

ISDN provides transport of multiple user services.

IDNs

As analog transmission and switching components were rendered obsolete by superior digital technologies, a new set of protocols was needed to benefit from the full potential of the digital systems. ISDN provides a framework for the development of these components and protocols.

We have already seen how telephone companies have largely completed conversion of their voice networks from analog to digital. We have also seen how they have made the resulting integrated digital network (IDN) directly accessible for data communications by first offering Dataphone Digital Service (DDS), and later, T-carrier service in North America and equivalent services elsewhere. We have also seen limitations of the services offered. ISDN represents a logical migration of voice-oriented IDN toward a network that serves multiple purposes: voice, data, video, fax, and all other forms of electronic communication, regardless of the source. The ISDN Network Diagram illustrates the services ISDN can transport.

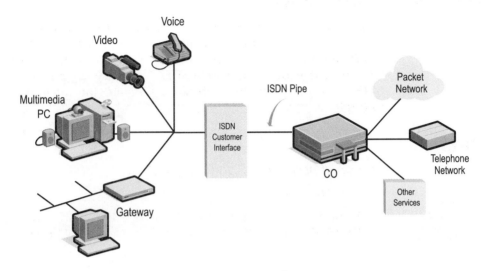

ISDN Network

ISDN can be characterized in two ways:

- As a bundle of services offered for transmission of voice, data, and other forms of communication by means of the switched telephone networks of the world

- As a set of protocols that defines a standard interface to the network, making it possible for many vendors to supply both hardware and software to take advantage of the services offered

ISDN Services

We subscribe to ISDN in the same way we subscribe to voice services. Of course, the end office must offer ISDN. The process of making ISDN available is a gradual one, and only some end offices currently offer this technology.

Public-switched networks have begun to adopt common channel signaling (CCS) through the Signaling System 7 (SS7) signaling protocol. SS7 is an international high-speed, packet-switching protocol used on telecommunications backbones that provides redundant data and signaling paths between nodes. ISDN takes advantage of this capability. All signaling for ISDN is out-of-band, that is, CCS.

ISDN provides access to digital channels. Three types of channels are available for subscriber use, as listed in the ISDN Access Table.

ISDN Access

Channel	Rate (Kbps)	Applications
D	16	Control signaling
B	64	Data Voice Fax Slow-scan video
H0 H1 H2	384 1,536 1,920	Backbone networks Full-motion video Multiplexing

- D channels—These channels operate at 16 kilobits per second (Kbps). They are provided for CCS; however, they can also be used for data. Each D channel is associated with one or more channels of another type. The channel can be used, for example, to tell a telephone company which ISDN subscriber the other channels are to be connected to. CCS eliminates the problem of distinguishing control signals from data. By using a single channel for signaling for several data channels, bandwidth is saved. A D channel can also be used for transmitting certain types of data that require low bit rates.

- B channels—These channels operate at 64 Kbps and are used to carry circuit-switched data, voice, fax, slow-scan video, and so on. Slow-scan video refers to video applications that do not require smooth motion of pictures, such as transmitting the slides of a presentation.

- H channels—These channels operate at 384 (H0), 1,536 (H1), or 1,920 (H2) Kbps, and are used for applications requiring high bandwidth, such as backbone networks and full-motion video. They can also be multiplexed by a subscriber in the same manner as T-carrier channels.

These access speeds are often referred to as narrowband ISDN. Broadband ISDN (B-ISDN) is ISDN at speeds of 154 megabits per second (Mbps) and higher. Note that the basic building block for ISDN channels is digital signal level 0 (DS0): B channel = 1 x DS0,

H0 channel = 6 x DS0, H1= 24 x DS0, and H2 = 30 x DS0. The D channel is used for control, and typically does not carry data.

Two basic services are offered; the choice depends on our needs. Of course, we might require more than one kind of service, just as we might require more than one telephone line. The basic services include:

- Basic rate service—Also known as BRI, this service provides one D channel and two B channels, and is sometimes referred to as "two B plus D" or "2B+D." Although this service can provide 144 Kbps of usable capacity, the D channel is normally reserved for signaling.

- Primary rate service—Also know as PRI, this service is structured around the bandwidths of T1 (1.544 Mbps) for North America and Japan and E1 elsewhere (2.048 Mbps). It includes an optional D channel and a number of B and H channels, in combinations that do not exceed the allowable bandwidth when necessary overhead is included. Primary rate service (1.544 Mbps) is also known as 23B+1D.

The recommended starting point for justification of ISDN-PRI service is between 11 and 25 lines. After selecting the required services, connections for the channels are set up in several ways:

- Semipermanent—Set up by prior arrangement, this is the ISDN equivalent of a leased line.

- Circuit-switched—This is similar to using a modem on today's switched public network to establish a connection to another user. An important difference is that a D channel is used to transmit the control information necessary to establish and terminate a call.

- Packet-switched—This is X.25 packet switching. Software is available that allows ISDN networks to appear as if they were X.25 networks, performing packet switching at the Network Layer.

ISDN also provides a number of services not previously available to data communications users. Many of these are similar to services provided to users of the voice network. For example, ISDN can provide a subscriber with numbers for incoming calls, block incoming calls, transfer a call to another ISDN subscriber, and connect to multiple ISDN subscribers (like a conference call).

Activities

1. Describe basic rate and primary rate services.

   _____

   _____

   _____

   _____

2. Discuss the capabilities of ISDN and whether you think ISDN will be available for a long time as a service.

   _____

   _____

   _____

   _____

3. Discuss the concept of "integrated services," and what this means today versus when ISDN was originally developed.

   _____

   _____

   _____

   _____

4. List and describe the three types of channels used by ISDN.

   _____

   _____

   _____

Extended Activities

1. Go to the following World Wide Web (Web) sites and research ISDN information:

    a. ISDN Tutorial:
    http://public.pacbell.net/ISDN/connect.html

    b. ISDN Information and Web Links:
    http://webopedia.internet.com/TERM/I/ISDN.html

2. Research whether ISDN is offered in your area, and the rate charged for the service.

Lesson 2—ISDN Protocols

This lesson covers the protocol layers used to get information across an ISDN network. A set of standards was developed to describe the protocols and functions used to move information across a switched ISDN network.

Objectives

At the end of this lesson you will be able to:

- Name the protocol layers of ISDN

- Explain the functions of each layer of the ISDN protocol stack

- Describe the different methods that devices use to interface to an ISDN network

 **Key Point**

ISDN protocols allow for the transport of multiple types of services.

Fundamentals of ISDN Protocols

ISDN is defined by a set of standards written by the International Telecommunication Union-Telecommunications Standardization Sector (ITU-T). The ISDN Protocols Diagram lists these standards. The standards are called the "I-series of recommendations." There are 75 standards documents in six sections. These sections include general ISDN structure, service capabilities, overall network aspects and functions, ISDN user-network interfaces, internet-work interfaces, and maintenance principles. It is far beyond the scope of this course to describe these standards in detail; however, we will look at key features of the ISDN user-network interface and some of the important communications protocols that have been adopted.

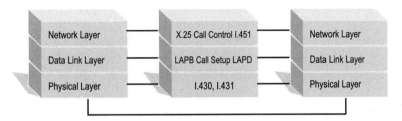

ISDN Protocols

Because ISDN uses CCS (on the D channel), there are two sets of protocols: one for CCS and one for data (channels B and H, respectively), as the ISDN Protocols Diagram illustrates. These layers and associated protocols are as follows:

- Physical Layer—ITU-T I.430 (B channels) and ITU-T I.431 (H channels) define the physical interfaces, such as cabling and electrical signals, to the ISDN devices.

- Data Link Layer—Link Access Procedure for D Channel (LAPD) (D channel) and Link Access Procedure Balanced (LAPB) (data channel over packet-switched network), based on High-Level Data Link Control (HDLC), specify the ISDN frame formats.

- Network Layer—ITU-T I.451 is used for SS7 switching and X.25 is used for packet-switched data to establish logical connections between devices.

ITU-T groups ISDN protocols in the following manner:

- E-series—The E-series protocols define the public-switched telephone network (PSTN) standards for ISDN. An example is E.164, the ITU-T standard for international telecommunications numbering.

- I-series—The I-series protocols address concepts, terminology, and general methods. I.430 applies to ISDN-BRI Physical Layer specifications, and I.431 applies to ISDN-PRI Physical Layer specifications.

- Q-series—The Q-series protocols address how switching and signaling operate. Q.920 and Q.921 describe the User-Network Interface (UNI) at the Data Link Layer, and Q.930 and Q.931 describe the ISDN Layer 3 signaling standard. Q.931 is also known as I.451.

Physical Attachment to ISDN

Physical Layer standards describe the protocol used at the Physical Layer (Open Systems Interconnection [OSI] Layer 1) to connect to ISDN. They define the multiplexed frame format for basic and primary service interfaces. Additionally, physical layer protocols define the cable connecting the data terminal equipment (DTE) to the ISDN. The cable has eight wires, and terminates with an RJ-45 connector.

Data Link Layer Call Setup, LAPD

LAPD defines the protocol used on the D channel to interface with a telephone company's SS7 network for setting up calls and other signaling functions. The LAPD frame format is shown on the LAPD Frame Format Diagram. This is the Data Link Layer frame format of ISDN. LAPD is a derivative of LAPB, the Data Link Layer protocol used by X.25.

Flag—1 byte, start of frame, and end of previous frame
Address—2 bytes, logical address
Control—1 or 2 bytes, identifies frame as supervisory,
information, or unnumbered
Information—Variable
FCS—2 bytes, Frame Check Sequence for error correction
Flag—1 byte, end of frame

LAPD Frame Format

Network Layer Call Control, I.451

I.451 defines a high-level protocol for controlling switching and other signaling to SS7.

Network Layer Packet-Switching, X.25

ISDN defines X.25 as the protocol used at the Network Layer for packet switching.

ISDN CPE

ISDN defines a set of terms to describe the various pieces of equipment found on a subscriber's (customer's) premises, also known as customer premises equipment (CPE). By defining this equipment, the terms further define the interface to ISDN. The ISDN Attachment Diagram presents the various terms used.

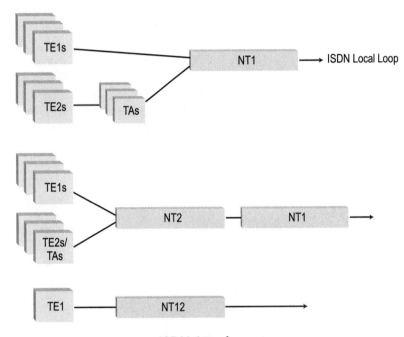

ISDN Attachment

The following terms describe the ISDN CPE:

- Terminal equipment type 1 (TE1)—This refers to DTEs that are ISDN-capable and support the I.430 ISDN framing protocol. TE1 ranges from computers to telephones.

- Terminal equipment type 2 (TE2)—If a DTE does not provide a built-in ISDN interface (it is not a TE1), it is a TE2 and requires a terminal adapter (TA) to attach to ISDN. An analog device is an example of a TE2.

- TA—TAs are used to attach a non-ISDN device (TE2) to a network termination type 1 or 2 (NT1 or NT2, respectively).

- NT1—This device multiplexes ISDN native devices (TE1) and non-ISDN devices (TE2/TA) at the Physical Layer and interfaces the local loop to the central office (CO).

- NT2—This is an intelligent device operating at the Network Layer (OSI Layer 3). NT2 attaches to the ISDN local loop through an NT1. It can perform switching and multiplexing of TE1s/TE2s across multiple B channels in a PRI line.

- NT12—This type of network termination device combines the functions of NT1 and NT2 in a single cabinet.

The Typical ISDN Connectivity Diagram shows how a TA is used to connect a telephone and a personal computer (PC) to an ISDN network. If a voice conversation is not active, the PC can transmit information at the full 128-Kbps bandwidth. After a telephone call is initiated, the 128-Kbps bandwidth is shared between the data and voice transfer.

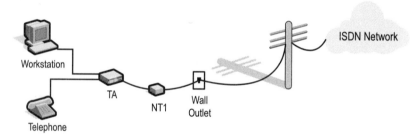

Typical ISDN Connectivity

ISDN Reference Points

BRI and PRI are two of the many interfaces referred to in the ISDN specification. As "user-to-network" interfaces, BRI and PRI refer to the point at which a user's data enters the ISDN network. These interface points connect the CPE, such as the NT1 network terminator, to the ISDN local loop. In Europe and other parts of the world, the NT1 is located at the CO, and is not considered CPE.

ISDN standards define several other interface reference points, which are conceptual and usually physical connections between network entities. These access points provide a convenient way to discuss points on an ISDN network or identify locations and methods for users to access an ISDN. These reference points are presented on the ISDN Reference Points Diagram, and include:

- V—Reference point between the carrier's end of the local loop and exchange switching equipment

- U—Reference point between NT1 devices and the CO (In North America, "U" is the local loop.)

- T—Reference point between NT1 and NT2 equipment (if separate devices)

- S—Reference point between an NT2 and TE1, or between an NT2 and a TA

- R—Reference point between a non-ISDN device and TA

[handwritten left margin:] ISDN Reference Pts. V, U, T, S, R

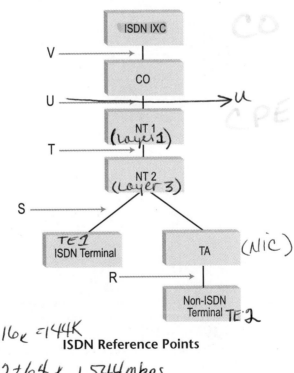

ISDN Reference Points

[handwritten annotations on diagram: CO, CPE, →U, (Layer 1) near NT 1, (Layer 3) near NT 2, TE1, (NIC) near TA, TE 2 near Non-ISDN Terminal]

[handwritten bottom:]
ISDN:
BRI 2B + 1D = 128$_K$ + 16$_K$ = 144K
     64K   16K
PRI 23B + 1D - 1.472 + 64 x 1.544 mbps
     64K   64K

Activities

1. Name the protocol layers of ISDN.

    _____

    _____

    _____

    _____

2. What is the function of LAPD at Layer 2?

    _____

    _____

    _____

    _____

3. Describe the following ISDN CPE:
    a. TE1, TE2

        _____

        _____

    b. TA

        _____

        _____

    c. NT1

        _____

        _____

    d. NT2

        _____

        _____

    e. NT12

        _____

        _____

4. Discuss how the ISDN Attachment Diagram and CPE relate to the ISDN Reference Points Diagram.

_____

_____

_____

_____

Extended Activities

1. Using the Web, research current products for each CPE listed in this lesson. Describe the function of each of these products.

_____

_____

_____

_____

_____

_____

2. Find out from a local service provider (telephone company) what it would take to have ISDN services provided for your home or organization.

_____

_____

_____

_____

Lesson 3—ISDN Implementation

ISDN can be used in a variety of ways. This lesson reviews several ways ISDN is used for networking different types of services.

Objectives

At the end of this lesson you will be able to:

- Describe how PCs and telephones can connect to an ISDN network

- Explain how ISDN might be used to provide remote networking connectivity and redundancy

 **Key Point**

ISDN can be used as a primary or alternate route in a computer network.

ISDN Applications

Digital signal quality, reliability, flexibility, and fast call setup make ISDN an excellent technology for data networking applications, such as:

- Basic network connectivity

- Internetworking of remote offices

- Dial-on-demand remote networking

- Network redundancy and overflow

Basic Network Connectivity

ISDN is often used for basic home and small business connectivity, typically connecting local area network (LAN)-based computers and telephone lines to another network by means of the public-switched network. This is shown on the ISDN Basic Connectivity Diagram.

ISDN Basic Connectivity

Internetworking of Remote Offices

In this configuration, a user calls in to a remote access server from home or another location using ISDN-BRI to connect to host computers on the enterprise network. A remote access server (RAS) makes the remote user appear as a locally connected client on the LAN, with all attendant services and privileges. The Remote Office Connectivity Diagram illustrates this concept.

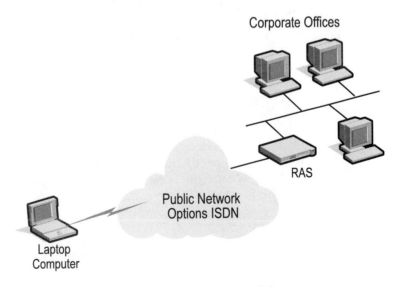

Remote Office Connectivity

The transfer rate of a 5-megabyte (MB) file using analog telephone lines, Switched 56 (SW56) services, and ISDN are listed in the Transfer Rates Table.

Transfer Rates

Transfer Method	Transfer Rate (Kbps)	Elapsed Time (minutes)
Modem	28.8	23.15
SW56	56	11.9
ISDN	128	5.21

Remote office internetworking opens new avenues of communication for corporate employees who travel extensively, work at home, or require after-hour access to the office. At the central site, the internetworking device receives incoming data calls from various locations through pools of dial-in lines, provides security authentication and validation of callers by means of login procedures, and routes calls over the corporate network.

In addition, a growing number of small- to medium-sized remote offices are now connecting to corporate backbones to access centralized information or exchange electronic mail (e-mail) messages. The small number of users at these remote sites does not usually warrant a dedicated leased line to the central site. Users at remote offices might have a local LAN for sharing common resources, such as printers, fax machines, and application servers. Smaller remote offices might provide dial-up access to corporate network resources just for individual users. In either case, exchanging e-mail messages or retrieving information from central computers requires at least a temporary WAN connection. ISDN and other switched services are well suited for remote configurations, because they provide a telephone circuit only when information needs to be transferred. Some internetworking devices have the intelligence to schedule these connections when telephone rates are more economical, for added cost savings.

Dial-on-Demand Remote Networking

Remote users that need access to a corporate LAN might reach it more economically through network links provided by a local LAN site. For example, to save long-distance access charges, business travelers can dial in to a local branch office LAN and allow the network to route the traffic to the final destination, which might be in another state or country. Depending on the traffic pattern between the local and remote LANs, the WAN connection can be a leased line or dial-up (ISDN-BRI) link. When connecting over a dial-up connection, the local LAN initiates the connection on demand and aggregates multiple circuits to offer the appropriate level of service. This is called "Dial-on-Demand Routing (DDR)."

Because of ISDN's fast call-setup capability, the DDR connection appears to the client as a direct connection to the remote LAN. The connection between LANs remains active as long as WAN traffic is present; the local LAN router disconnects the WAN link when there is no more WAN traffic to pass. This DDR capability operates transparently to the client application, saving ISDN link charges.

When the WAN link is inactive, a local router process called "spoofing" causes the client application to see a logical link to the remote LAN. The router sends "keep-alive messages" to the client application to convince it that the link with the remote LAN still exists. When the client once again must pass traffic to the remote LAN, the local LAN router automatically reestablishes a dial-up session with the remote LAN, and passes the data traffic over the resumed WAN connection.

Network Redundancy and Overflow

Mission-critical applications have strong reliability and availability requirements that make fault tolerance an important criterion in network design. Redundancy is usually the preferred way to achieve fault tolerance. For example, many companies use a leased line as the primary WAN connection to ensure constant availability of a data path, while leasing another line to serve as a backup. This is an expensive solution because the backup line is needed only when the primary line malfunctions, yet companies pay a monthly charge for the redundant line regardless of whether it is used. A dial-on-demand connection, such as an ISDN-BRI line, is a more affordable solution for backup to a primary leased line. As shown on the Network Redundancy Diagram, a DDR line is automatically activated by the network routers when a failure occurs on the primary line (a T1, for example), with no apparent degradation of network service. If the primary line is a high-speed pipe running at T1 or E1 rates, several lower-speed dial-up circuits can be aggregated to achieve comparable high-bandwidth capacity.

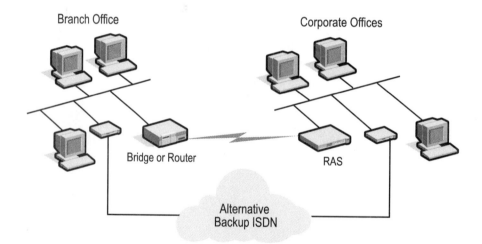

Network Redundancy

ISDN can also be used to carry the overflow of data connections when the data load increases. When a primary line reaches maximum capacity, a bridge or router can detect the bandwidth bottleneck, dial one or more ISDN circuits in real time, and route overflow traffic through the B channels.

Activities

1. Fill in the table with the computed transfer rates. Use the following formulas:

    Multiply the file size in bytes by 8 bits per byte to determine the number of bits transferred:

    2 MB x 8 bits = 16 Mb

    Divide the file size in bits by the transfer rate to calculate the estimated transfer time (in seconds):

    16 Mb / 28,000 bps = 571.4 seconds

File Size (MB)	Transfer Method	Estimated Transfer Time (seconds)
2	1 ISDN channel (64 Kbps)	
2	2 ISDN channels (128 Kbps)	
2	28.8-Kbps modem	
2	56-Kbps circuit	
2	Full T1 (1.544 Mbps)	

2. Draw a diagram showing three PCs and two telephones connecting to an ISDN network.

3. Draw a diagram illustrating remote network connectivity as well as network redundancy.

Extended Activity

Using the Web, research products that contain ISDN interfaces for WAN connectivity. Find at least three different types of routers that use ISDN. Draw a diagram that shows how one of these products would be used to connect two LANs.

Lesson 4—Frame Relay Concepts

Frame relay is an adaptation of the ISDN interface for the purpose of providing frame relay services across a WAN. The standard defines an interface between an enterprise network and packet-switching network. The term frame is used because frame relay builds data frames and can asynchronously multiplex these frames from multiple virtual circuits (endpoints) into a single high-speed data stream. The term relay is used because each frame relay device forwards the frames as they move through the network without examining the frame's payload or demultiplexing the data stream. Most local and long-distance carriers offer frame relay.

Objectives

At the end of this lesson you will be able to:

- Describe the basic operation of frame relay

- Explain how frame relay uses virtual circuits to move information across a network

Key Point

Frame relay was originally designed to move data across a WAN.

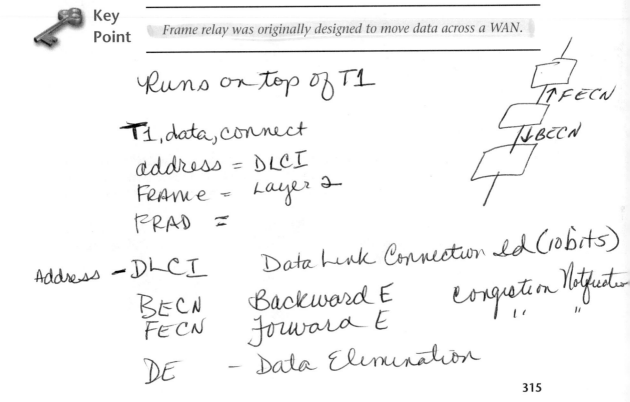

Runs on top of T1

T1, data, connect
address = DLCI
FRAME = Layer 2
FRAD =

Address — DLCI   Data Link Connection Id (10 bits)
    BECN   Backward E   congestion Notifier
    FECN   Forward E   " "
    DE   — Data Elimination

↑ FECN
↓ BECN

What Is Frame Relay?

A frame relay network is a switched network that moves frame relay frames from one network to another network. Logically, a frame relay is an electronic switch or switches running frame relay software. Physically, it is a device that connects to three or more high-speed links, and routes data traffic between them. The Frame Relay Diagram illustrates the operation. Virtual circuits have been established as shown on the frame relay network portion of the diagram: virtual circuit 1 (VC1) from multiplexer (MUX) A to MUX C, virtual circuit 2 (VC2) from MUX A to MUX D, and virtual circuit 3 (VC3) from MUX A to MUX E. All three circuits flow through Frame Relay B.

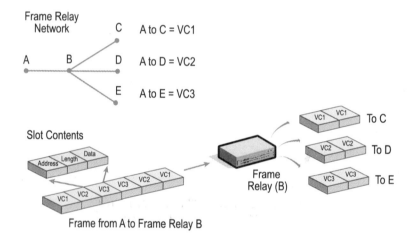

Frame Relay

Data for all three circuits flows into MUX A. The MUX places data from all three virtual circuits into frames, storing an address and length with the data. (This diagram was simplified by showing all data the same length.)

The frames are transmitted from MUX A to MUX B. MUX B must demultiplex the frames and forward them to the appropriate network: MUXs C, D, and E.

Another view of a similar network is shown on the Frame Relay Network Diagram. Here routers feed a frame relay network. VC1 could be a path from router 1 to router C. VC2 could be a path from router 1 to router D, and VC3 could be a path from router 2 to router E.

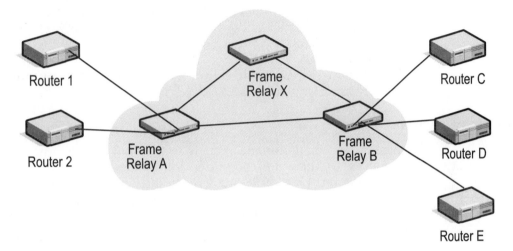

Frame Relay Network

Frame relay has several characteristics, including:

- As defined by ITU-T, frame relay can be T1 or E1 bandwidth. It is ITU-T's intention that frame relay fall under cell relay (Asynchronous Transfer Mode [ATM] is discussed in a subsequent lesson), with respect to satisfying user bandwidth requirements. However, current frame relay service providers are promising T3 bandwidth, thus frame relay will overlap with cell relay at its high end.

- Frame relay was originally intended for data communications, rather than voice, video, or other time-sensitive information.

- Only connection-oriented service is provided. Unlike other ISDN packet services, the network does not offer a complete connection mode data link service. Although frame relay is connection-oriented, it does not provide for end-to-end error detection and correction; a frame either makes it across the network or it does not. The frame's Address field and cyclic redundancy check (CRC) are local to each interface and are changed by the network as each frame moves through the network devices.

- Frame relay discards frames with errors without providing notification to the sender or receiver; it assumes the physical links are reliable. Error recovery is left up to higher-layer protocols, such as Transmission Control Protocol (TCP).

- Frame relay, a Data Link Layer protocol suite, is faster than X.25, a Network Layer suite. Whereas X.25 provides error correction and recovery, windowing, and other higher-layer services, frame relay only delivers frames to the next frame relay device.

Frame relay's variable length frames are not well suited for voice or video, which require a steady data stream.

Frame Relay Terms

There are several important terms to understand regarding frame relay. Two of these are committed information rate (CIR) and committed burst size (CBS). CIR is the guaranteed average data rate for a particular service, and CBS is the number of bits that can be transferred during some time interval.

CIR and CBS are important terms to consider when purchasing frame relay service. The result of the formula t = CBS/CIR provides the guaranteed number of bits over a period of time (t) that a particular service will transfer. For example, a CIR of 256 Kbps and a CBS of 512 kilobits (Kb) means that the network will move 512 Kb in any given 2-second period (2s = 512 Kb/256 Kbps); this is the guaranteed rate for periods of congestion.

Under light loads, the network's actual throughput will be greater than the CBS; this is referred to as excess burst size (EBS). The excess information rate (EIR) corresponds to the EBS and is the excess data rate a provider allows over a given time period. Other important terms in a frame relay environment are:

- Frame relay access device (FRAD)—A FRAD is a device that provides access to a frame relay network. In a LAN, this is typically a router.

- *Uses to Network Interface* UNI—A UNI specifies the signaling and management functions between a frame relay network device and end user's device.

- Network-to-Network Interface (NNI)—An NNI specifies the signaling and management functions between two frame relay networks.

Activities

1. Which of the following is a device that provides access to a frame relay network?

   a. ECS

   b. FRAD

   c. NNI

   d. UNI

2. What is the CIR?

   a. Guaranteed average data rate for a service

   b. Number of bits that can be transferred over a period of time

   c. Throughput that can be realized during periods of low network usage

   d. Signaling and management functions between two frame relay devices

3. Frame relay is well suited to voice and video applications. True or False

4. CIR is the actual frame relay network throughput realized at times of low usage. True or False

5. CBS defines the number of bits that can be transferred during some time interval. True or False

6. Describe the basic operation of a frame relay network.

   _____

   _____

   _____

   _____

   _____

Extended Activity

Locate a white paper on frame relay from a networking hardware vendor. Write a summary of the paper.

_____

_____

_____

_____

_____

_____

_____

_____

_____

Lesson 5—Frame Relay Protocols

This lesson evaluates frame relay from a technical perspective, focusing on how the available bandwidth is allocated and how virtual circuits are created in a frame relay network. This lesson also reviews the protocol details of frame relay.

Objectives

At the end of this lesson you will be able to:

- Describe how frame relay uses virtual circuits to move data across a network

- Draw a frame relay frame encapsulating higher layers

- Describe the protocol header used by frame relay

 **Key Point**

Frame relay frames contain network addresses.

Permanent and Virtual Circuits

In frame relay networks, applications share available bandwidth. However, frame relay can give active applications full access to the network's bandwidth when no other applications are sending or receiving information. Because frame relay switches have the intelligence and capability to obtain and interpret network status and take corrective action, frame relay can reroute traffic when problems occur. Typical private lines do not have this capability.

Frame relay carries network traffic over virtual circuits; these circuits are mapped from end-to-end through one or more NNIs. More than one virtual circuit may be mapped over an NNI, and each virtual circuit takes its turn accessing the bandwidth available at the NNI ports.

The amount of time each virtual circuit has on the port depends on the circuit's CIR. The telecommunications carrier assigns each circuit a CIR as it provisions (creates) the circuit. Depending on the circuit provisioning, a circuit can take advantage of periods of low network usage across the NNI by bursting above its CIR.

To illustrate how a frame relay circuit can adjust to increased bandwidth requirements, compare time-division multiplexing (TDM) to frame relay, as shown on the Frame Relay Bursting and Performance Diagram. In TDM, a larger file is given more time to move over the network. In frame relay, a larger file is given more bandwidth over the network, using the same period of time as a smaller file. This again depends on how the carrier provisions the circuits.

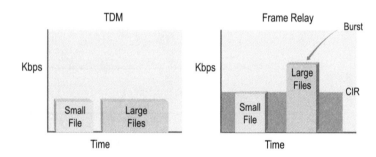

Frame Relay Bursting and Performance

Frame Relay Frame

The frame relay frame is based on the HDLC LAPD frame format. It consists of a leading and trailing flag, the variable-length Information field, the locally significant Frame Check Sequence (FCS) field, and the frame relay Header field. The frame relay Header field is key to the operation of the frame relay virtual circuit.

Within this 2-byte frame relay Header is the 10-bit data link connection identifier (DLCI), used to designate the connection's virtual circuit addresses. These 10 bits allow for over 1,000 virtual circuit addresses for each NNI physical interface. The remaining header bits are used for congestion and circuit control, and are listed on the Frame Relay Frame Format Diagram.

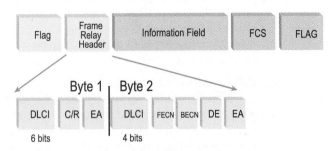

DLCI: Data Link Connection Identifier
C/R: Command/Response Field Bit
EA: Address Extension Bit (allows 3- or 4-byte header)
FECN: Forward Explicit Congestion Notification
BECN: Backward Explicit Congestion Notification
DE: Discard Eligibility Indicator

Frame Relay Frame Format

A frame relay frame consists of:

- Flag—A flag, 7E, indicates the start and end of each frame.

- DLCI—A DLCI is used to identify the virtual circuit for a frame. Frame relay devices derive this 10-bit address from the first 6 bits of the first octet, and the first 4 bits from the second octet of the frame relay header. The DLCI identifies the logical channel between a user and network, and has no network-wide significance.

- Command/response (C/R)—The C/R bit is not used.

- Extended address (EA) bits—EA bits are used to extend an address from 10 to 12 bits. EA bits are not typically used.

- Forward explicit congestion notification (FECN) bit—The FECN bit is set to notify a user that congestion was experienced as the frame traversed the network. It is set by the network and not the user.

- Backward explicit congestion notification (BECN) bit—The BECN bit is set to indicate that congestion may be experienced by traffic sent in the opposite direction.

- Discard eligibility (DE) bit—A DTE on the frame relay network, such as a router, may set the DE bit to indicate to frame relay devices that this frame is of less importance relative to other frames without the DE bit set, and might be discarded in congestion situations.

- Information field—This field contains user data. The maximum recommended payload is 1,600 bytes; the minimum payload is 1 byte. Frame relay devices in the network disregard the content in the information portion of the frame. Supervisory (control) information is passed by means of a separate DLCI and is considered "out-of-band" signaling.

- FCS field—The FCS field is used to check that the frame has been received without errors. At the end of each frame, an FCS is submitted by the access device to ensure bit integrity. Frames that have errors are discarded. Unlike X.25, frame relay endpoint devices recognize that frames have been dropped and recovered by reinitiating transmission.

LAPD's Information field (I field) is variable in length. Although the theoretical maximum integrity of an FCS is 4,096 bytes, the actual maximum integrity is vendor-specific. Frame relay standards ensure the "minimum maximum" value supported by all networks is 1,600 bytes. The I field contains data passed between devices over a frame relay network. User data may contain various types of protocols (protocol data units [PDUs]), which are used by access devices. According to Internet Engineering Task Force (IETF) Request for Comment (RFC) 1490, an industry-standard mechanism for specifying which protocol is in the I field, the I field may also include "multiprotocol encapsulation." With or without multiprotocol encapsulation, protocol information sent in the I field is transparent to a frame relay network.

Frame relay uses bits in the header to indicate network congestion. The network may send congestion condition notifiers to access devices through FECN and BECN bits. Access devices are responsible for restricting data flow under such congested conditions. To manage congestion and fairness, frames may be tagged for discard with a DE bit. Frame relay specifications provide a method for flow control; however, they do not guarantee implementation of those standards on devices. This is a vendor-specific issue that is often a key difference in the performance of vendors' products, but it does not generally interfere with basic frame relay interoperability.

Network and access devices may pass special management frames with unique DLCI addresses, called "Local Management Interface (LMI) frames." These frames provide a signaling standard between a CPE router and the frame switch, monitor a link's status, and reflect whether the link is active or inactive. LMI frames also pass information regarding the current status of permanent virtual circuits. Frame relay's original specification did not provide for this kind of status. Since then, American National Standards Institute (ANSI) and Consultative Committee for International Telegraphy and Telephony (CCITT) specifications developed and incorporated a method for LMI, now known "officially" as Data Link Control Management Interface (DLCMI). *(control) mgmt)*

The frame relay protocol is straightforward; frame relay network devices are only responsible for moving frames from the source to the destination. If invalid frames are received by a frame relay device, they are discarded without sending notification to a sending or receiving station. No sequencing of frames is supported. No control information is sent in the frame Information field, only user data. Frame relay devices do not acknowledge frames at the receiving end of the network.

BECN and FECN are used in frame relay networks to indicate congestion. The Frame Relay BECN/FECN Diagram shows how the messages would be transmitted if congestion was occurring at Device C. Device C detects congestion in the direction of Device E. Device C sets the FECN bit on frames destined for Device E; Device E knows to redirect or drop frames as necessary to avoid congestion. Device C also sets the BECN bit on frames destined for Device A, informing it of congestion between Devices C and E. Device A takes necessary action to avoid this congestion between Devices C and E.

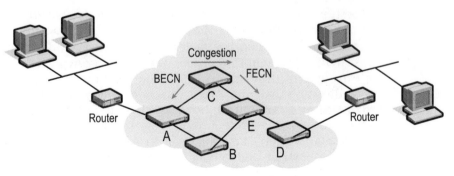

Frame Relay BECN/FECN

Frame Relay Addressing

A frame relay connection is a type of virtual circuit, referred to as a data link connection (DLC). In the majority of frame relay equipment, and therefore services, DLCs are permanent virtual circuits (PVCs), predefined by both sides of the connection. Switched virtual circuits (SVCs) are also defined in the frame relay specifications and are gaining in use. The original service offerings for frame relay were PVC-based, a trend that has continued to the present day. PVCs efficiently serve the needs of most existing data applications. There is, however, growing vendor support and implementation for SVC capabilities, to meet emerging applications and stimulate intercorporate communication.

Each DLC, whether a PVC or SVC, has an identifying DLCI. A DLCI changes as the frame travels from segment to segment, similar to the physical address changes that occur in a routed Ethernet LAN. In an Ethernet LAN, each node has a physical address. These addresses are included in the Ethernet frame, and the source and destination addresses remain constant as long as the packet the frame carries stays on the LAN. However, when using TCP/IP and addressing a device across a router, the Data Link Layer Medium Access Control (MAC) address changes as the packet moves from network to network. The sender addresses the frame to the router MAC address, the router addresses its frame to the next router, and so on.

Similarly, frame relay devices (NNI or UNI) change the DLCI (frame source and destination addresses) as the frame moves from device to device. This is called "local significance," and the DLCI only pertains to the local segment of the frame relay network. The initial DLCI that the sending FRAD uses to address the frame to the next frame relay device may not be the same DLCI that the final frame relay device uses to pass the frame to the FRAD at the destination network. Therefore, we need to know both the local and remote DLCIs for any link we are provisioning across a frame relay network. Routing tables in each intervening frame relay switch, whether in the carrier's network or a private network, take care of directing frames to the proper destination, alternately reading and assigning DLCI values in the control portion of the frames, as appropriate.

A DLCI is the portion of the frame that identifies the logical chan-nel between an end device and network. Because the DLCI only identifies the connection to the network, it is up to the network devices to map the two communicating DLCIs. The Frame Relay Addressing Diagram illustrates this scenario.

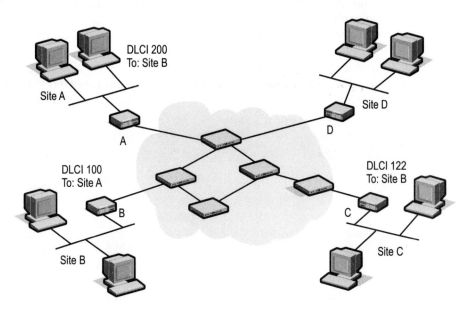

Frame Relay Addressing

In this diagram, DLCI 200 is routed by the frame relay network from Site A to Site B, where each device alters the DLCI to match the local link. The frame finally appears at Router B as DLCI 100. All data sent from Site B to Site A is addressed to DLCI 100, and appears on DLCI 200 at Site A. Improper configuration of DLCIs is a com-mon mistake. Frame relay is designed to carry both Data Link Layer frames from other topologies as well as Network Layer packets.

Interconnecting LANs Using Frame Relay

Frame relay was designed to handle various types of LAN traffic. It is ideal for sending LAN traffic over a wide area because of its speed and flexibility. Devices that attach LANs to a frame relay network encapsulate the data frame or packet inside the frame relay frame and send it over the network. This is shown on the Frame Relay Encapsulation Diagram.

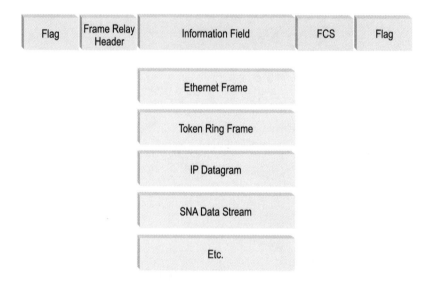

| Flag | Frame Relay Header | Information Field | FCS | Flag |

Ethernet Frame

Token Ring Frame

IP Datagram

SNA Data Stream

Etc.

Frame Relay Encapsulation

At the other end of the network, information is removed from the frame relay frame and sent to the final destination.

Activities

1. Describe frame relay addressing.

   _____

   _____

   _____

2. Describe the function of the BECN and FECN indicators.

   _____

   _____

   _____

   _____

3. Draw a protocol stack and corresponding frame relay frame that consists of encapsulating a TCP/IP packet.

4. Discuss where you might see the above information in a computer network.

   _____

   _____

   _____

   _____

Extended Activity

Go to the Frame Relay Forum Web site at **http://www.frforum.com** and review the latest information on frame relay. Review the frame relay overview provided by the Frame Relay Forum. Summarize your findings.

_____

_____

_____

_____

_____

_____

_____

Lesson 6—Frame Relay Implementation

Most organizations are adopting neither a pure public nor pure private network architecture, but a combination of the two—a hybrid network design. This has become a standard architecture in the industry among large organizations. This is why it is important to evaluate PSTN services side by side with private line services when designing and implementing a WAN.

Objectives

At the end of this lesson you will be able to:

- Describe how frame relay is typically implemented in an enterprise network

- Explain the difference between public, private, and hybrid frame relay networks

- Evaluate the advantages and disadvantages of frame relay versus private line networking

 **Key Point**

Enterprise networks implement frame relay in a variety of ways.

Frame Relay Implementation Options

Frame relay, as with many of the technologies discussed in this course, may be implemented in several forms. Conceptually, there are three ways to implement a frame relay network:

- As a private network solution

- Using public facilities

- As a hybrid solution, using both private and public facilities

Private Frame Relay

A private frame relay network can be constructed without the use of public facilities. In this example, illustrated on the Private Frame Relay Network Diagram, the network is implemented using frame relay by connecting several sites using frame relay equipment owned and operated by a customer.

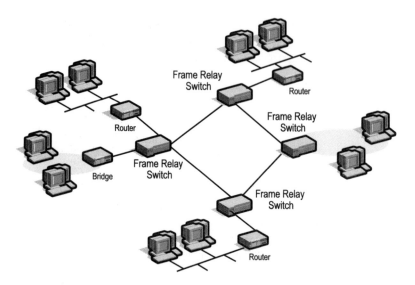

Private Frame Relay Network

Public Frame Relay

Another implementation of frame relay technology is through the use of public facilities. In this example, the frame switches and frame relay backbone are owned and operated by a telecommunications service provider. A customer does not have insight into the switches and switch configurations or paths the information takes from source network to destination network. The customer does not have to manage the network either. Virtual circuits are provisioned for each specific site and can be used only by that end user. The cloud in the Public Frame Relay Network Diagram illustrates this concept.

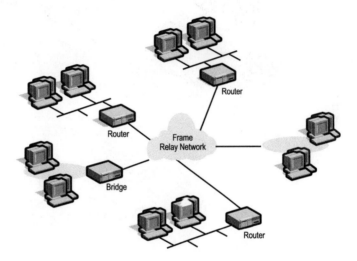

Public Frame Relay Network

Hybrid Frame Relay

Private and public facilities and equipment can be combined to form a hybrid frame relay network. The decision to use public, private, or a mixture of the two is made based on each business application. It may also be necessary to combine public and private facilities or other technologies if service is not available in a particular area that needs connectivity to the overall network. The Hybrid Frame Relay Network Diagram illustrates the concept of a hybrid frame relay network.

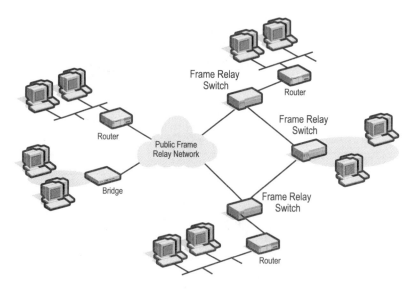

Hybrid Frame Relay Network

End-User Access to Frame Relay Networks

End-user devices can access frame relay networks in a wide variety of ways. Typically, PCs and workstations use frame relay networks, as do many voice and video applications. End-user devices include:

- PCs
- Workstations
- Controllers
- Private branch exchange (PBX) equipment

End-user devices are connected to CPE, such as bridges and routers, that have frame relay capabilities. The CPE devices take information from the network and place the information into frame relay frames. The frame relay frames are passed to the frame relay switch by means of the UNI. The UNI connection is between the CPE and frame relay network. There are many connection possibilities, as shown on the End-User Connectivity Diagram. Frame relay switches within the frame relay network provide the connectivity between endpoints over an NNI.

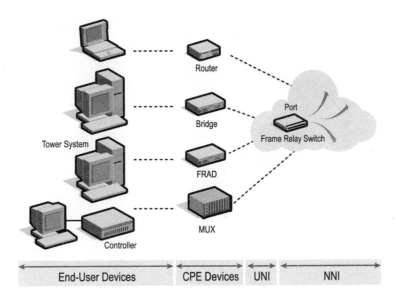

End-User Connectivity

Frame Relay vs. Private Line Networking

Private, point-to-point lines, such as T1, are widely used in computer networks to connect sites. Private lines use TDM for communication of traffic across a WAN. This section differentiates between a native point-to-point T1 service, and a frame relay service using various Physical Layer services, including T1.

The emphasis in wide-area networking is shifting away from dedicated networks toward switched alternatives. The reason is because the higher quality of the public-switched network makes switched alternatives highly reliable and efficient. The latest generation of public network services, including frame relay and ATM services, is continuing this trend.

One of the reasons there is a growing demand for frame relay is the decrease in complexity of a frame relay network versus a T1 network. As the number of endpoints grows, frame relay makes more and more sense. This is illustrated on the T1 vs. Frame Relay Network Diagram.

Frame Relay Network

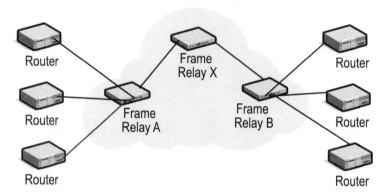

T1 Mesh Network

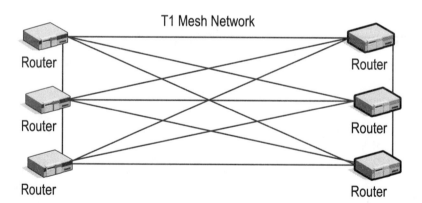

T1 vs. Frame Relay Network

It should be noted that typical frame relay implementations use T1 as the Physical Layer service. In other words, frame relay rides on top of a T1-based point-to-point service. The distinction being made in this section is between a point-to-point T1 service and a frame relay service using various Physical Layer services.

Frame Relay Services

Frame relay services today can deliver data at very high rates. Source and destination points communicate from their locations to the frame relay cloud over leased-line connections, which generally are full T1 or fractional T1 (FT1) connections.

To transmit data to its proper destination, frame relay frames incorporate addressing information, which the network uses to ensure proper data routing through the service provider's switches. This addressing essentially lets users establish virtual circuits to communicate over the same access links.

Part of what makes frame relay so attractive to network managers is its use of a public data network, or cloud, that enables an organization to minimize line, equipment, and management costs associated with maintaining its own complex mesh-topology WAN. Such savings are possible because most of the burden of designing and maintaining a frame relay data network falls on the service provider, companies such as AT&T, MCI, and Sprint.

There are many advantages to this arrangement. For one, it relieves a network manager of the burden of managing the overall infrastructure. It also reduces the amount of effort necessary to make needed changes.

If a network manager needs to increase the bandwidth or number of access points to the cloud, for example, he or she will most likely only need to make a few telephone calls to the provider, and then make slight adjustments to the central-site router. If additional speed is needed for new applications, in many cases, added bandwidth can be provided on demand.

Public Frame Relay Services

The first public frame relay service was introduced in the United States in 1991. There are currently a large number of service providers in the frame relay market. Services provided are illustrated on the Frame Relay Public Services Diagram, and include:

- Basic frame relay transmission
- Multiple access alternatives
- Customer network management
- Internet access

- International connectivity
- Managed network services
- Frame relay to ATM internetworking

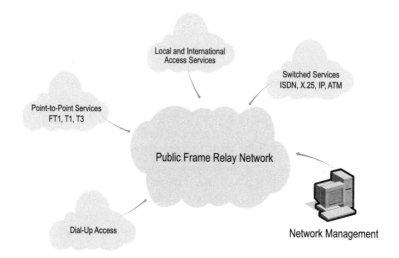

Local and International
Access Services

Switched Services
ISDN, X.25, IP, ATM

Point-to-Point Services
FT1, T1, T3

Public Frame Relay Network

Dial-Up Access

Network Management

Frame Relay Public Services

There are many ways to access a frame relay network, as noted above. Analog dial-up access using modems is a suitable choice for mobile workers, telecommuters, and occasional network users. Switched access options, such as ISDN and SW56 are also available.

Bandwidth on Demand

The capability to provide bandwidth on demand is what makes frame relay so well suited to bursty data traffic. Being able to provide added bandwidth is the result of frame relay's use of statistical multiplexing, which does not require that a link be up and dedicated at all times. Rather, frame relay uses bandwidth only when there is data requiring transmission.

Other more traditional WAN transports use TDM, whereby each data transmission requires dedicated bandwidth across a WAN. A disadvantage of this method is that even "data silence," periods when the network is passing no data, requires the link to be up and dedicated.

Unlike a leased line, frame relay can be set up with two connection speeds: CIR and EIR. CIR is the guaranteed average bandwidth available, determined by our estimate of normal traffic. If network traffic increases past the CIR, the cloud will attempt to open additional circuits and complete the transmission.

Conditional Bursting

Bursting above the CIR is available only when the network is not congested, usually during nonpeak periods. This capability is especially useful for branch offices located in different time zones. Because of the different zones, each branch office would reach its peak and burst at intervals. When the network is not congested, we can actually burst data in some cases at capacities up to two times the CIR.

The multiplexing and addressing scheme used by frame relay allows a large central site to be connected to the cloud (and hence multiple remote sites), with a single router port and high-speed connection to that cloud. Because the circuits are not dedicated on a conversation-by-conversation basis to any specific remote site, many remote-to-central site transmissions can take place simultaneously.

If we have multiple sites in several geographically distant locations, or our organization plans to add multiple sites across the country in a relatively short period of time, odds are that frame relay may save us from putting a significant crimp in our telecommunications budget.

Frame relay is a very cost-effective inter-local access and transport area (interLATA) technology. Frame relay may not be financially attractive (or even possible) for multiple sites in the same LATA, that is, several sites in the same metropolitan area.

Key to determining the cost effectiveness of frame relay is the expense of running a 56-Kbps or T1 (1.544 Mbps) dedicated leased circuit from each office to a frame relay service provider. If all sites are in the same area, it would be cheaper to run dedicated lines to each of them, rather than use frame relay.

Carrier Choice

Although frame relay is a relatively mature technology today, there are still some moving targets that an organization may want to clarify prior to executing an agreement with a specific carrier.

The first issue deals with the CIR. When we subscribe to a frame relay service, we select a CIR for our network connection. The CIR is a data-transport indicator of the average bandwidth provided by the carrier over a given period of time. We select the CIR, depending on the carrier, to match the expected performance across our WAN connection. Typical CIRs range between 56 Kbps and 1.5 Mbps.

Unfortunately, the selected CIR is not always guaranteed. The business success of carriers hinges on building networks as demand requires. A general rule of thumb seems to be that a carrier will add links to its network when the network becomes 70 to 80 percent subscribed. Thus, congestion is really just a delicate term for an oversubscribed network.

With any prospective frame relay provider, we must explore the critical issue of how its network handles "congestion control," which differs widely among carriers. In a nutshell, when some networks get too congested, they discard data frames. Because frame relay performs little to no error detection and correction, the responsibility for retransmission resides with the user's network hardware if frames get tossed out.

We may also want to inquire as to what management reports and vehicles are available, as well as whether up-to-the-minute statistics on utilization percentages, traffic patterns, and frame discard/error rates are available.

After we have selected and signed on with a carrier, we must purchase access to a local exchange carrier's (LEC's) frame relay network. This means that to use the frame relay network, we need to connect an appropriately high-speed pipe from our organization's site to the frame relay network.

Frame Relay Network Requirements

The hardware and software configuration required to connect to a frame relay network is not complex. Each site needs a router with a WAN-connection port (or ports) appropriate to its network protocol, software/firmware for the router that supports frame relay, and a channel service unit/data service unit (CSU/DSU) network interface.

Configuration of the router involves the simple input of the appropriate DLCI information furnished by the frame relay service provider in the configuration tables. Assuming all the various connections—LAN, router to telephone company, and telephone company to frame—are physically correct and activated, the frame relay network connection should be established.

Activities

1. Describe a public, private, and hybrid frame relay network.

   _____

   _____

   _____

   _____

   _____

   _____

2. List the advantages and disadvantages of frame relay versus private line networks.

   _____

   _____

   _____

   _____

   _____

3. Five locations are geographically dispersed across the country. Routers are in place at each location to provide LAN interconnect service across the country. Each router is connected to many LANs within a region, such as different buildings across a city. We will assume the traffic is intermittent, but has high peak rates. Users have point-to-point leased lines of different capacities across the nation, dependent upon the traffic pattern.

   The non-frame relay network, as depicted on the Initial Network Diagram, consists of 5 routers and 14 CSU/DSUs, 4 leased lines rated at 56 Kbps, 2 leased lines rated at 1.544 Mbps (T1), and 1 leased line rated at 256 Kbps (FT1). There are 14 router ports which are incremental costs to the routers. In addition, most router manufacturers tie router performance to the amount of memory purchased with the router.

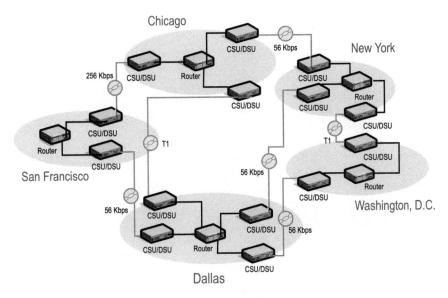

Initial Network

If you look closely at the diagram for the initial network, you should note the following:

- Seven leased lines are being used of varying capacity and distance.

- Fourteen CSU/DSUs are being used.

- Fourteen router ports are being used.

Determine what equipment and services are needed to implement frame relay service. Draw a diagram to reflect these changes.

Extended Activities

1. Review the following Web sites and note the information provided on frame relay. List the products that have frame relay support, and state what each would be used for in wide-area networking.

   a. http://www.nortel.com

   b. http://www.adtran.com

   c. http://www.3com.com

   d. http://www.discountdata.com

   _____

   _____

   _____

   _____

   _____

   _____

   _____

Lesson 7—X.25 (Layer 3)

X.25 was the first <u>connection-oriented</u> Network Layer protocol. It is still commonly used to switch packet traffic over a wide area.

An X.25 network, whether public or private, is typically built largely upon the leased-line facilities of the public telephone network. It uses a Network Layer address (telephone number) so that switches can route traffic by means of multiple paths.

X.25 is quickly being replaced by faster technologies. However, understanding the X.25 protocol and services will help you understand faster and more efficient protocols, such as frame relay and ISDN, which were built upon the foundation of X.25.

Objectives

At the end of this lesson you will be able to:

- Describe how X.25 is used to transport data over a wide area

- Explain the difference between packet switching, frame switching, frame relay, and cell relay

- Name the X.25 protocol layers and describe their functions

- Explain what a packet assembler/disassembler (PAD) is used for

Key Point

Today's fast packet-switched networks are based on X.25.

X.25 Services

X.25 is connection-oriented, and offers two types of service:

Packet

circuit acts like a switch

- PVCs—This is the X.25 equivalent of a leased line, statically defined and always available as long as a network is up. Unlike leased lines, however, more than one virtual circuit can share a physical link.

- Virtual connections—This is the X.25 equivalent of a dial-up connection. A network establishes a connection on a virtual circuit, transfers packets until the application is finished, and then releases the connection.

345

Addressing   ITU-T recommendation X.121 defines a system of assigning addresses to devices on an X.25 packet network. The X.121 system is similar to the numbering plan used for voice telephone networks. Every X.25 user, anywhere in the world, is uniquely identified by a Network Layer address that includes codes for world zone, country, network, and individual user. Thus, an X.25 communication can take place between any two X.25 users, as long as they are both on the same network, or interconnected networks.

X.25 Protocols

The X.25 interface lies at OSI Layer 3, because X.25 provides error-free service to the Transport Layer. However, as we will see later, the overhead associated with the necessary error checking is proving to be unacceptable in today's highly reliable digital networks.

X.25 defines its own three-layer protocol stack, as illustrated on the X.25 Protocol Layers Diagram. The X.25 standard predates OSI. (The first version of X.25 was issued in 1976.) OSI has adopted X.25 Layer 3 as a connection-oriented Network Layer protocol.

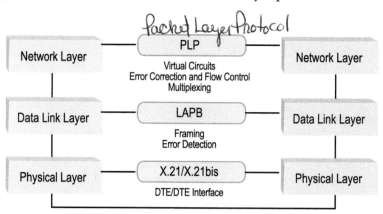

X.25 Protocol Layers

The X.25 standard does not itself fully define all three layers of the stack, but rather refers to other standards. X.75, for example, is a standard that defines the interface between two distinct X.25 networks and is nearly identical to X.25. X.25 consists of these protocols:

- Layer 3—Packet Layer Protocol (PLP)
- Layer 2—LAPB
- Layer 1—X.21 and X.21bis

PLP

PLP operates at the OSI Network Layer. PLP manages connections between data communications equipment (DCE) and DTE anywhere in a network. It accepts data from a Transport Layer process, breaks the data into packets, assigns the packets a Network Layer address, and takes responsibility for error-free delivery of the packets to their destination. PLP establishes virtual circuits and routes packets across the circuits. Because many virtual circuits can share a link, PLP also handles multiplexing of packets.

LAPB

LAPB operates at OSI Layer 2, and provides full-duplex point-to-point delivery of error-free frames across a link. These frames deliver packets to and from processes operating at Layer 3.

LAPB is a subset of the International Standards Organization (ISO) HDLC standard. It is "balanced" because the LAPB standard excludes portions of the HDLC standard having to do with multidrop, "unbalanced" operation.

X.21 and X.21bis

X.21 operates at the OSI Physical Layer. It defines a DTE/DCE interface along the lines of the RS-232 (V.24) standard, except that X.21 was designed for interfacing to a digital network, such as ISDN. Because digital networks were not generally available when X.25 was developed, X.21bis (essentially RS-232) was defined as an interim standard.

PADs

Packet Assembler Dissembler

For an application to transmit data across an X.25 network, the application's network node must have an X.21 or X.21bis interface, and execute processes that provide the LAPB and X.25 PLP services to the Transport Layer. When X.25 was developed, many devices, such as word processors or "dumb" terminals, did not have these components.

To allow these devices to connect to public X.25 networks, ITU-T developed a set of standards to provide access for terminals and DTE that cannot execute the layers of X.25. The standards, informally called the "Interactive Terminal Interface (ITI) standards," are X.3, X.28, and X.29.

The ITI standards collectively define a "black box" or PAD. A PAD accepts a stream of bytes from an asynchronous DTE (such as a PC), "assembles" those bytes into X.25 packets, and transmits the packets on the X.25 network. The PAD performs the reverse operations for data sent back to the DTE. The PAD Diagram illustrates the concept of a PAD.

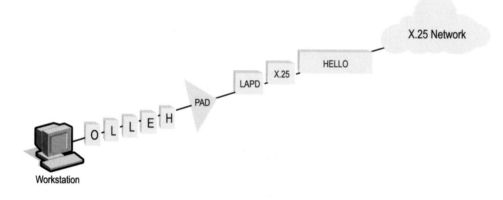

PAD

To the DTE, the PAD looks like a modem. This means that no special software or hardware must be added to the DTE beyond that needed for ordinary asynchronous communications. It is also possible to attach the DTE to the PAD with a point-to-point link using modems. A single PAD can serve several DTE devices, performing a concentrator function by placing data from more than one DTE into a packet when possible.

PLP

PLP uses two basic types of packets, shown on the PLP Formats Diagram:

- Data packets   (1)
- Control packets (0)

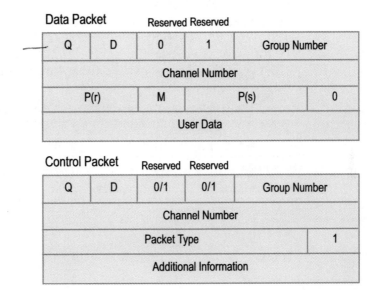

PLP Formats

The fields for both of these types of packets are listed below:

- Q bit—Distinguishes between control and user data information. When the bit is set to 1, the packet contains user data; a bit set to 0 indicates a control packet.

- D bit—Indicates end-to-end acknowledgment of packets.

- Reserved—The 2 bits following D and Q are currently not used.

- Group Number—Contains the logical channel group number.

- Channel Number—Identifies the logical channel number. Together, the channel number and group number form the packet address.

- P(r)—Contains the sequence number of the next packet to transmit.

- M bit—"More data" bit. When set, it means additional related packets are on the way.

- P(s)—Contains the value of the packet sent.

- Packet Type—Identifies the command or instruction contained in a control packet. The PLP Control Packet Types Table illustrates the different packet types that can be used in the X.25/LAPB protocols.

PLP Control Packet Types

Call Setup and Clearing									
DCE to DTE	DTE to DCE	Control Field Value							
Incoming Call	Call Request	0	0	0	0	1	0	1	1
Call Connected	Call Accepted	0	0	0	0	1	1	1	1
Clear Indication	Clear Request	0	0	0	1	0	0	1	1
DCE Clear Confirmation	DTE Clear Confirmation	0	0	0	1	0	0	1	1
Data and Interrupt									
DCE to DTE	DTE to DCE	Control Field Value							
DCE Data	DTE Data	X	X	X	X	X	X	X	1
DCE Interrupt	DTE Interrupt	0	0	1	0	0	0	1	1
Confirmation	Confirmation	0	0	0	1	0	0	1	1
Flow Control and Reset									
DCE to DTE	DTE to DCE	Control Field Value							
DCE RR (Mod 8)	DTE RR (Mod 8)	X	X	X	0	0	0	0	1
DCE RR (Mod 128)	DTE RR (Mod 128)	0	0	0	0	0	0	0	1
DCE RNR (Mod 8)	DTE RR (Mod 8)	X	X	X	0	0	1	0	1
DCE RR (Mod 128)	DTE RR (Mod 128)	0	0	0	0	0	1	0	1
Reset Indication	Reset Indication	0	0	0	1	1	0	1	1
DCE Reset Indication	DTE Restart Confirmation	0	0	0	1	1	1	1	1
Restart									
DCE to DTE	DTE to DCE	Control Field Value							
Restart Indication	Restart Request	1	1	1	1	1	0	1	1
DCE Restart Confirmation	DTE Restart Confirmation	1	1	1	1	1	1	1	1

Control packets are used to establish, conduct, and end an X.25 session. The X.25 Packet Sequence Diagram shows a typical packet-exchange sequence required to set up an X.25 connection and transmit data.

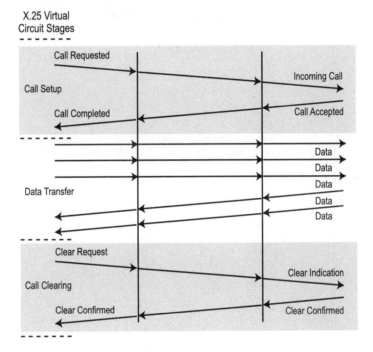

X.25 Packet Sequence

Overhead and Performance Limitations

Today's X.25 networks are being replaced by faster packet/cell networks, such as frame relay and ATM. This is happening because of the following limitations of X.25:

- Low throughput—X.25 networks support DS0 bandwidth at best.

- High overhead—Because X.25 PLP is responsible for error-free delivery of packets, each X.25 node in a virtual circuit, plus the Transport Layer process in the receiving node, must acknowledge each packet received. In addition to every "real" data packet that traverses the network, several acknowledgment packets must also make the trip. The result: effective throughput is far lower than the rated capacity of the physical links composing the network.

- Redundant functions—X.25's overhead was justified when the public telephone networks were slower and largely analog, as they were when X.25 was first introduced in 1976. However, today's digital networks, which are increasingly based on optical fiber, are much more reliable and have sufficient bandwidth, and thus congestion is not likely to occur. As a result, flow control at Layer 3 is not required, and error recovery can simply be left to the higher layers that must perform it in any event.

Activity

Given the following diagram, describe the movement of information from Client A to Client B and back. In your discussion, describe what protocols are used at each device and across the WAN.

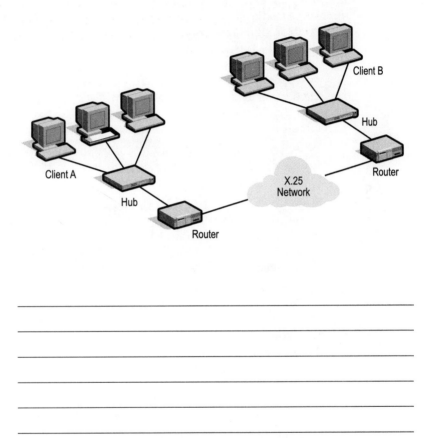

_____

_____

_____

_____

_____

_____

Extended Activity

Given the X.25 Packet Sequence Diagram presented in this lesson, draw X.25 packets as they traverse across a WAN. Assume IP packets are being transported by the X.25 packets. Show which X.25 packets would be carrying IP information and which would be control packets.

Summary

ISDN represents the first digital switched network that is not oriented toward voice communications. Instead, it is designed to serve multiple purposes: voice, data, video, fax, and all other forms of electronic communication. ISDN is both a set of services and bundle of protocols. Services include 16-Kbps D channels for control signaling and other uses that do not require high data rates; 64-Kbps B channels for voice, data, and slow-scan video; and H channels with data rates up to 1,920 Kbps for full-motion video, data network backbones, and so on. ISDN-BRI provides one D channel and two B channels. ISDN-PRI provides B and H channels that add up to T1/E1. Permanent circuits such as leased lines, circuit-switched service, and packet-switched service are provided.

ISDN protocols split the architecture into two parallel parts, one for data and one for control signals, each with its own set of protocols at Layers 2 and 3.

Frame relay is currently offered by most companies and has replaced X.25 as the packet-switching protocol of choice. It operates at Layer 2 rather than Layer 3. It is faster and has less overhead than X.25, and provides T1 data rates rather than X.25's DS0 rate. Frame relay can provide connection-oriented service for data only.

X.25, which provides WAN services up to OSI model Layer 3, is the basis for frame relay. X.25 is still widely used in some international communities. X.25 is important to understand, because it was the first connectionless Network Layer protocol. It uses a telephone number as a destination address, so that switches can route traffic by means of multiple paths. Although still used to switch packet traffic over a wide area, X.25 is quickly being replaced by protocols that offer faster throughput and lower overhead.

Unit 5 Quiz

1. Which two of the following are ISDN Data Link Layer proto-cols? (Choose two.)

   a. HDLC

   b. LAPD

   c. LAPB

   d. SDLC

2. Which of the following is not an ISDN channel?

   a. A

   b. B

   c. D

   d. H

3. What is the speed of ISDN-BRI?

   a. 64 Kbps

   b. 144 Kbps

   c. 1.544 Mbps

   d. 45 Mbps

4. What is the speed of ISDN-PRI?

   a. 64 Kbps

   b. 144 Kbps

   c. 1.544 Mbps

   d. 45 Mbps

5. Which of the following is a characteristic of ISDN (compared to DDS)?

   a. Flexibility of services such as voice and data over the local loop

   b. Higher-speed service offerings

   c. Uses 64 Kbps as a basic building block

   d. All of the above

6. Which of the following is a key concept of ISDN?

   a. Integration of multiple protocols

   b. Integration of multiple services across a single physical link

   c. Integration of computer equipment

   d. Integration of networking components

7. Which of the following will ISDN support?

   a. Video

   b. Voice

   c. Data

   d. All of the above

8. Most of the information carried by ISDN is associated with which channel?

   a. A

   b. B

   c. C

   d. D

9. Which of the following refers to the combination of multiple ISDN channels?

   a. D channel

   b. H channel

   c. X channel

   d. Virtual circuit

10. What is most likely the effective rate of ISDN-BRI?

   a. 64 Kbps

   b. 128 Kbps

   c. 144 Kbps

   d. 1.544 Mbps

11. Which of the following is a reason frame relay is simpler and more efficient than X.25?

    a. It operates at the Data Link Layer instead of the packet layer.

    b. It uses digital circuits to transmit data.

    c. It is a newer technology than X.25.

    d. Frame relay is not simpler than X.25.

12. Which of the following identifies a virtual circuit in a frame relay network?

    a. DLCI

    b. FECN

    c. BECN

    d. CBS

13. Which of the following best characterizes CIR, as referred to in frame relay networks?

    a. Guaranteed average data rate

    b. Guaranteed maximum data rate

    c. Number of bits that can be transmitted in a given time interval

    d. Number of bytes that can be transmitted in a given time interval

14. What is indicated if the DE bit is set?

    a. Frame may be discarded when used with SONET.

    b. Frame may be discarded when used with T1.

    c. Frame may be sent to lower-speed links.

    d. Frame may be discarded when congestion occurs.

15. Frame relay was adapted from which of the following protocols?

    a. T1

    b. T3

    c. ISDN

    d. ATM

16. Which of the following best describes frame relay?

   a. Connectionless, frame-oriented service

   b. Connection-oriented Physical Layer service

   c. Connectionless packet delivery service

   d. Connection-oriented switched service

17. Which of the following are typical frame relay speeds?

   a. 28.8 to 56 Kbps

   b. 56 to 128 Kbps

   c. 56 Kbps to 1.544 Mbps

   d. 1.544 Mbps to 2.4 Gbps

18. Why is frame relay more efficient than X.25?

   a. Fewer layers are used to transfer information.

   b. More layers are used to transfer information.

   c. Frame relay is not more efficient than X.25.

   d. The packet types are different at the Network Layer.

19. Which of the following factors might influence the use of a frame relay network over a T1 mesh network?

   a. Number of endpoints (networks) that need to be connected

   b. Types of computers being used

   c. Type of router being used to connect the network

   d. Physical circuit being used

20. Which of the following might a FRAD refer to?

   a. Device used for sending voice technology over a frame relay network

   b. Router used to connect a LAN to another LAN using frame relay

   c. Switch that interfaces ATM to frame relay

   d. Frame relay application

21. Which of the following technologies is considered the lowest in the protocol stack?

    a. Packet switching

    b. X.25 packet switching

    c. Frame relay

    d. SONET

Unit 6
WAN Solutions

Cell-switching technologies play a major role in moving information across carrier-owned wide area networks (WANs), as well as in private local area networks (LANs), metropolitan area networks (MANs), and WANs.

Asynchronous Transfer Mode (ATM) backbones quickly switch fixed-size cells across multiple links. ATM's connection-oriented nature makes it a reliable service for carrying delay-sensitive applications, such as voice, video, or multimedia. ATM can support bursty LAN data traffic as well.

Switched Multimegabit Data Service (SMDS) is a MAN-only data service available through local exchange carriers (LECs). It is based on the Institute of Electrical and Electronics Engineers (IEEE) 802.6 Distributed Queue Dual Bus (DQDB) protocols, and is designed to provide connections between LANs in a citywide region within a single local access and transport area (LATA). Although SMDS has lost market share to ATM, which is designed to support WAN connectivity, some LECs still offer SMDS services.

Lessons

Terms

base station (BS)—A BS is the 802.16 network component that operates as the central network connection point and provides connection management for a number of subscriber stations. A single BS can service several hundred subscriber stations.

Certificate Authority—A CA is an organization that creates digital certificates for individuals and Web servers after verifying the identity of those persons or sites. A CA signs each digital certificate with its own digital signature, thus vouching for the identity and trustworthiness of the owners of the certificates.

collapsed backbone—When a network's backbone, connecting all the network segments, is contained within a hub, switch, or router, it is considered a collapsed backbone. In an Ethernet network, the bus is collapsed within a hub, and the network devices connect to the bus using UTP cable.

connection identifier (CID)—CID is a 16-bit code used to identify service flows on an 802.16 network.

Cyclic Redundancy Check (CRC)—CRC is the mathematical process used to check the accuracy of the data being transmitted across a network. Before transmitting a block of data, the sending station performs a calculation on the data block and appends the resulting value to the end of the block. The receiving station takes the data and the CRC value, and performs the same calculation to check the accuracy of the data.

Data Exchange Interface (DXI)—A DXI defines the interaction between network devices and an SMDS CSU/DSU. A DXI is also considered the interface between DTE and an ATM CSU/DSU.

Demand Assigned Multiple Access (DAMA)—DAMA is a method of controlling access to the radio channel and involves time slots that are assigned to the subscribers as needed, rather than dedicated to specific devices. In this manner, the channel can dynamically adapt to changing user bandwidth requirements.

digital certificate—A digital certificate is a unique electronic file used to authenticate a user, program, provider, service, or transaction. The certificate usually consists of a file containing a copy of the user's or service's public encryption key, along with the signature of a trusted person verifying that the key does, indeed, belong to the user or service claimed. A Certificate Authority (CA) creates a certificate, and the certificate is encrypted in a way that makes it impossible to forge.

Distributed Queue Dual Bus (DQDB)—DQDB is the IEEE 802.6 standard for MANs. See Switched Multimegabit Data Service (SMDS).

Dynamic Host Configuration Protocol (DHCP)—DHCP provides configuration parameters to Internet hosts. DHCP consists of two components: a protocol for delivering host-specific configuration parameters from a DHCP server to a host and a mechanism for allocation of network addresses to hosts. DHCP is built on a client/server model, in which designated DHCP server hosts allocate network addresses and deliver configuration parameters to dynamically configured hosts.

Ethertype—Ethertype is the type field in an Ethernet frame header used to designate the layer 3 protocol the frame transports.

Forward Error Correction (FEC)—FEC is an error detection and correction technique that sends redundant bits along with the data payload. The receiver uses this redundant information to recreate lost or corrupted data without requesting retransmission.

Frequency Division Duplexing (FDD)—FDD is a radio transmission technique that supports full duplex stations by allowing them to transmit and receive on separate frequencies.

High-Speed Serial Interface (HSSI)—HSSI is a serial data communications interface designed to support data rates up to 52 Mbps.

IEEE 802.1p—IEEE 802.1p is the IEEE extension to the 802.1D MAC bridges standard. It allows for the prioritization of MAC layer frames on the network. The 802.1p standard uses a portion of the 802.1Q VLAN tag to represent one of eight possible priority values, each mapped to one of eight traffic classes.

IEEE 802.1Q—IEEE 802.1Q is a vendor-neutral standard for VLAN implementation. The standard specifies a 2-byte VLAN tag that includes a 12-bit VLAN identifier, which is used by the network switches or bridges to decide to which network segment they should forward each frame. The last switch to handle the tagged frame before passing it to the destination node strips the header from the frame.

IEEE 802.11—The IEEE 802.11 standard is the IEEE standard that specifies medium access and Physical Layer specifications for 1 Mbps and 2 Mbps wireless connectivity between fixed, portable, and moving stations within a local area.

IEEE 802.11a—The IEEE 802.11a standard is an extension to 802.11 for wireless LANs at speeds up to 54 Mbps in the 5GHz band.

IEEE 802.11b—The IEEE 802.11b standard is the "High Rate" amendment ratified by the IEEE in September 1999, which added two higher speeds (5.5 and 11 Mbps) to 802.11. The original 802.11 standard defines the basic architecture, features, and services of 802.11b. The 802.11b specification affects only the Physical Layer, adding higher data rates and more robust connectivity. At this writing, the 802.11b standard is the dominant technology used in WLANs (wireless LANs). 802.11b is also referred to as 802.11 High Rate or Wi-Fi.

IEEE 802.11g—The IEEE 802.1g standard is a draft wireless network standard designed to provide the bandwidth of 802.11a networks while maintaining backward compatibility with 802.11b networks. The 802.11g standard operates in the 2.4-GHz Industrial Scientific Medical (ISM) band.

IEEE 802.16—The IEEE 802.16 standard is the IEEE Wireless-MAN™ standard for wireless WAN and MAN connectivity. The 802.16 standard operates in the 10to 66-GHz licensed and nonlicensed frequency range.

initialization vector (IV)—An IV is a randomly generated code used to start an encryption algorithm and ensure that no two coded strings created with the same key and algorithm begin with the same series of characters.

Institute of Electrical and Electronics Engineers (IEEE) 802.6—This IEEE standard is for MAN protocols. DQDB, the protocol upon which SMDS is based, is defined by IEEE 802.6.

Logical Link Control (LLC)—LLC is a Data Link Layer protocol used to control the flow of information across a physical link. LLC is often used in Ethernet networks that use the IEEE frame type, which does not include a type field. LLC provides a "steering" mechanism to move information from a Data Link Layer protocol, such as Ethernet, to the correct Network Layer protocol, such as IP.

Modified Final Judgment (MFJ)—The MFJ is the agreement reached between the U.S. Department of Justice and AT&T on January 8, 1984, that settled a 1974 antitrust case of the U.S. versus AT&T. The MFJ created the seven RBOCs, divesting AT&T of its local exchange business. The RBOCs were restricted from providing long-distance service. AT&T retained long-distance service and its manufacturing business.

network interface card (NIC)—A NIC is an expansion board inserted into a computer to enable the computer to be connected to a network.

omni-directional antenna—An omni-directional antenna is a common wireless network antenna type, which propagates radio signal in a 360 degree pattern around the antenna pole.

Packet Transfer Mode (PTM)—PTM is a method of information transfer by means of packet transmission and packet switching that permits dynamic sharing of network resources among many connections. Ethernet, FDDI, and frame relay are examples of PTM.

payload header suppression (PHS)—PHS is a technique used to mask redundant cell, frame, or packet header information when one or more of the same type of higher layer data PDUs are transported as the payload of an 802.16 MAC PDU.

payload header suppression identifier (PHSI)—A PHSI is a mask used by 802.16 nodes to identify which redundant payload cell, frame, or packet header information is suppressed within a service flow.

Physical Layer Convergence Protocol (PLCP)—PLCP is the SMDS SIP Level 1 sublayer that adapts a transmission facility to handle DQDB functions. The PLCP sublayer defines how the SMDS 53-byte cell is mapped to the specific transmission system described at the lower sublayer.

public key encryption—Public-key encryption is a cryptographic system that uses two mathematically related keys. One key is used to encrypt a message, and the other to decrypt it. People who need to receive encrypted messages distribute their public keys, but keep their private keys secret.

Quadrature Amplitude Modulation (QAM)—QAM is a signal modulation technique that combines Amplitude Shift Keying (ASK) with PSK. ASK turns the signal off and on to represent digital data. By combining these techniques a single carrier can represent a number of digital bit combinations. For example, 64-QAM represents a total of 64 sets of unique binary bit patterns (000000-111111), or states, with a combination of phase shifts and amplitude changes.

Quadrature Phase Shift Keying (QPSK)—QPSK is a phase shift keying (PSK) technique that uses four phases. PSK is a signal modulation technique that changes a radio signal's phase to represent digital data.

Queued Arbitrated (QA) functionality—QA is an SMDS time slot type that supports asynchronous data traffic. Data is carried on a best effort basis.

queued packet synchronous exchange (QPSX)—QPSX is the predecessor to DQDB, a protocol for communications over MANs.

sectorized antenna—A sectorized radio antenna is divided into two or more parts to allow it to simultaneously support several radio cells. The antenna divides a 360-degree omni-directional signal into equal parts, making each part better able to focus the signal on a more restricted coverage area. Signal gain with an omni-directional antenna is greater than with an omni-directional antenna.

security association (SA)—An SA is created by 802.16 network devices (before a secure connection is established) wishing to communicate by exchanging security information. Such information includes digital certificates for identification and the encryption method and encryption keys to be used.

service flow—Service flow is a specific category of higher layer network data carried across an 802.16 wireless link. Each service flow is identified by a Connection ID (CID). An SS can support up to 64,000 service flows in each direction.

service flow identifier (SFID)—An SFID is a 32-bit identifier assigned to each service flow by the BS, in part to identify the QoS the flow receives on the link. When a service flow is admitted and when it is active, the BS associates the SFID with a corresponding CID.

simple and efficient adaptation layer (SEAL)—SEAL, also known as AAL 5, is used as a simplified adaptation layer for local, high-speed LAN implementations. SEAL is intended for connectionless or connection-oriented variable-bit-rate services.

Subscriber Network Interface (SNI)—SNI is an SMDS term describing CPE access to an SMDS network over a dedicated circuit.

subscriber station (SS)—An SS is the 802.16 network component that provides user connectivity to the 802.16 network. An SS can simultaneously service many different user connections.

Switched Multimegabit Data Service (SMDS)—SMDS is a connectionless service used to connect LANs, MANs, and WANs at rates up to 45 Mbps. SMDS is cell-oriented and uses the same format as the ITU-T B-ISDN standards. The internal SMDS protocols are SIP-1, SIP-2, and SIP-3. They are a subset of the IEEE 802.6 standard for MANs, also known as DQDB.

Switched Multimegabit Data Service (SMDS) Interface Protocol (SIP)—SIP is used for communications between CPE and SMDS carrier equipment. SIP consists of three levels: SIP Level 3 operates at the top of the OSI model Layer 2 MAC sublayer; SIP Level 2 operates at the lower portion of the MAC sublayer; and SIP Level 1 corresponds to the OSI model Physical Layer.

Synchronous Transfer Mode (STM)—STM is a B-ISDN transport-level technique that uses TDM and switching across a UNI. Data communications occurs with an associated clock.

Synchronous Transport Signal level 3, concatenated (STS-3c)—STS-3c is cell mapping that occurs in the ATM TC sublayer that aligns, by row, every ATM cell within the SONET frame payload capacity. In STS-3c mapping, the entire payload of an STS-3c frame is filled with ATM cells yielding a transfer capacity of 149.760 Mbps. Although the SONET STS-3c frame payload is 2,349 bytes, and an ATM cell is 53 bytes, an integer number of ATM cells will not fit into an STS-3c frame.

Synchronous Transport Signal level 12, concatenated (STS-12c)—STS-12c is cell mapping that occurs in the ATM TC sublayer that aligns, by row, every ATM cell within the SONET frame payload capacity. In STS-12c mapping, the entire payload of an STS-12c frame is filled with ATM cells yielding a transfer capacity of 622.08 Mbps.

Time Division Multiple Access (TDMA)—TDMA is a technique used to divide up a transmission channel into frames and time slots. The technique allows multiple subscribers shared access to the channel. A series of time slots are assigned to a frame, and the sender and receiver reference a shared time slot map to determine where in the data stream frames begin and end.

Traffic Encryption Key (TEK)—TEK is a component of the 802.16 network data encryption function used to indicate the encryption pattern the BS and SS use to secure the MAC PDU contents.

Trivial File Transfer Protocol (TFTP)—TFTP is the TCP/IP protocol for file transfer with minimal capability and overhead. TFTP depends on the unreliable, connectionless, datagram delivery service, UDP.

type of service (tos) bits—ToS bits are the set of eight bits in an Internet Protocol (IP) packet header used to designate the type of service a packet is provided across a network. QoS services used for delay-sensitive, bandwidth-intensive services, such as video and Voice over IP (VoIP) modify these bits to suit their needs. Network devices all along the packet's route must recognize these bit settings, and provide the appropriate network services.

virtual channel identifier (VCI)—A VCI is a value in an ATM cell header that uniquely identifies one ATM VC. Each VC is one data transmission from a source node to a destination node.

virtual path identifier (VPI)—A VPI is a value in an ATM cell header that identifies a group of ATM VCs moving from the same source to the same destination.

wireless hotspot—A wireless hotspot is a public place, such as a coffee shop, airport lounge, or hotel lobby that provides wireless network connectivity for paying customers or the general public to use.

Lesson 1—ATM Concepts

ATM is an emerging technology that can transmit voice, video, and data across LANs, MANs, and WANs. It is an international standard defined by the American National Standards Institute (ANSI) and International Telecommunication Union-Telecommunications Standardization Sector (ITU-T). It implements a high-speed, connection-oriented, cell-switching, and multiplexing technology designed to provide users with virtually unlimited bandwidth.

Many people in the telecommunications industry believe ATM will revolutionize the way networks are designed and managed, because it combines the best features of two common transmission methods. Its connection-oriented nature makes ATM a reliable service for delay-sensitive applications, such as voice, video, and multimedia. Its flexible and efficient packet switching provides quick transfer of other forms of data.

In a relatively short period of time, ATM has gained a worldwide reputation as the ultimate means of solving end-to-end networking problems. The popularity of ATM has grown such that virtually every LAN hub and router vendor and service provider is racing to develop ATM-based products. ATM has found widespread acceptance as the technology of choice in the public-switched telephone network (PSTN) and on the Internet backbone. ATM, combined with Synchronous Optical Network (SONET) at the Physical Layer, is being extensively used for high-bandwidth information transfer.

Objectives

At the end of this lesson you will be able to:

- Explain how an ATM network transfers information from source to destination

- Explain the basic characteristics of the ATM protocol

- Describe the functions of the fields of an ATM protocol header

- Describe the key features of ATM, and explain how they allow ATM to transport a variety of data types

Key Point

ATM combines the strengths of STM and PTM.

369

The Need for ATM

In the mid-1980s, telecommunications researchers began to investigate technologies that would serve as the basis for the next generation of high-speed voice, video, and data networks. The result of this research was development of the Broadband-Integrated Services Digital Network (B-ISDN) standards.

B-ISDN was designed to support subscriber services that require both constant and variable bit rates. These services include data, voice, video, imaging, and multimedia applications. The ultimate goal of B-ISDN is to replace the current public network infrastructure and become the universal network of the future. ATM is the foundation on which B-ISDN is to be built.

ATM Protocols

ATM protocols are responsible for moving information across a network. ATM moves information across LANs, MANs, and WANs. This unit reviews the protocols and transfer modes used in ATM-based networks.

Transfer Modes

A transfer mode specifies a method of transmitting, multiplexing, and switching data in a network. Three transfer modes were considered as possible candidates for B-ISDN:

- Synchronous Transfer Mode (STM)
- Packet Transfer Mode (PTM)
- ATM

STM

"Synchronous" means that data communication is organized by a microprocessor clock; a receiving node can detect the beginning and end of a signal because signals start and stop at particular times. Networks that use STM divide each transmission frame into a series of time slots, and then allocate particular time slots to each user. For example, on the STM Diagram, Time Slot 2 is dedicated to the same user in each and every frame.

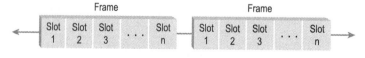

STM

STM is ideal for transmission of voice and video, because it provides a constant-bit-rate service. Voice and video require predictable and guaranteed network access, or the quality of the transmission degrades rapidly.

In contrast, data transmissions are typically bursty; a user is idle for relatively long periods of time between short periods of intense data-transfer activity. For example, in a typical client/server transaction, the client request consumes very little bandwidth. However, when the server responds, a large amount of data is typically transmitted from the server back to the client. The server's response may actually consume the entire bandwidth of the network.

STM is inefficient for data communications because the same time slot in each frame is reserved for a particular user, regardless of whether the user has data to transmit. When a user is idle, the time slot is wasted, because STM does not reassign unused time slots to other users.

Examples of STM technologies include standard T1 circuits, E1 circuits, and Synchronous Digital Hierarchy (SDH) circuits provided by telecommunications carriers.

PTM

In a network technology based on PTM, data is broken into variable-size units of data (packets, datagrams, or frames). Each unit contains both user data and a header that provides information for routing, flow control, and error correction. Instead of establishing a dedicated physical connection between the source and destination station, the network relays packets from one node to another, often in multiple parallel paths, until they reach their final destination. PTM is implemented through technologies such as Ethernet, Token Ring, Fiber Distributed Data Interface (FDDI), X.25, and frame relay. The PTM Diagram illustrates this concept.

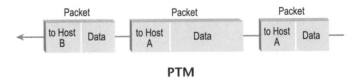

PTM

PTM is excellent for bursty data applications because a station only consumes bandwidth when it needs to transmit data. When a station is idle, its share of network bandwidth can be used by other stations. The resulting variable transmission rates and delay, within reasonable limits, are not critical issues for data communications.

However, PTM does not provide the guaranteed network access required by constant-bit-rate applications, such as voice and video. Voice and video tolerate very little delay in transmission; however, they can handle some loss or inaccurate information.

ATM

Thus far, we have seen that STM is excellent for voice and video applications, but it is inefficient for data applications. On the other hand, PTM is excellent for data applications, but cannot provide the guaranteed bandwidth and low delay required for voice and video.

ATM offers the best of both worlds. It combines the strengths of STM (constant transmission delay and guaranteed capacity) and PTM (flexibility and ability to handle intermittent traffic) in a single transfer mode that meets the needs of voice, video, and data applications.

In computing, the term "asynchronous" usually means that data transmission is coordinated through start and stop signals, without the use of a common clock. However, ATM networks use "asynchronous" to describe how network bandwidth is assigned to user applications. ATM assigns network access to users based on demand, which means that locations in the synchronous data stream are assigned to users in a random, or asynchronous, pattern. The ATM Diagram illustrates this concept.

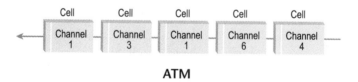

ATM

53|48

Fixed-Length Data Cells

ATM organizes transmission by formatting data into fixed-size units called "cells." Each cell contains 53 bytes that are divided into a 48-byte payload (data) field and a 5-byte header. The fixed length makes it simpler and faster for an ATM switch to process cells. ATM's cell-switching approach also makes efficient use of network bandwidth for bursty data transfers, by allocating cells to applications only as needed. The ATM Cell Diagram illustrates the basic format of an ATM cell.

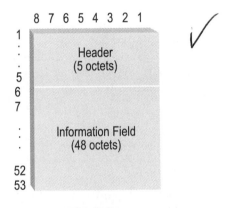

ATM Cell

Connection-Oriented Transmission

In an ATM network, a pair of source and destination nodes establishes a virtual connection before the source begins transmitting data. All cells transmitted between a pair of source and destination nodes follow the same virtual connection or virtual path (VP) (through a network of ATM switches) during the transmission. A later transmission between the same source and destination may follow a different VP; however, the path will not change for the duration of the transmission. This approach improves overall transfer speed by making it simpler and faster to switch cells through intermediate nodes.

The ultimate goal of ATM is to provide extremely high-speed communications that allow voice, video, and data applications to run across a single integrated network. By combining connection-oriented transmission with the use of small, fixed-length cells, ATM solves many of the problems encountered when these applications share the same network:

- The connection-oriented nature of ATM provides minimal delays for voice and video applications.

- The use of fixed-length cells simplifies switch design by allowing the switch logic to be implemented in silicon, in other words, in the switch firmware instead of in software. This greatly reduces the processing time required for each cell, increases switch throughput, and reduces the cost of the switching technology.

- Small video cells are not delayed by large data cells because all cells are the same size. This means it is relatively easy to predict the amount of network delay between any two points. In addition, the variation in delay is significantly decreased, because time-sensitive applications, such as voice and video, can share the same transmission facilities with data applications.

- The use of fixed-length cells rather than time slots overcomes the major weakness of STM, which is wasted bandwidth. An ATM station only consumes bandwidth when it has data to transmit.

Connection-Oriented Mode

In a connectionless network, a predefined end-to-end connection between source and destination nodes is not required for data transmission. As a result, data flow across the network occurs along the best available path, rather than over a predefined path. A connectionless service is sometimes referred to as a datagram service. The Internet Protocol (IP) is an example of a connectionless service.

ATM operates in a connection-oriented mode. A connection-oriented service requires that a virtual connection be established between source and destination nodes before data can be transmitted. The ATM and Virtual Circuits Diagram illustrates the relationship between these two concepts. As previously mentioned, all switched virtual channel (SVC) connections involve three phases:

- Connection establishment

- Data transfer

- Connection termination

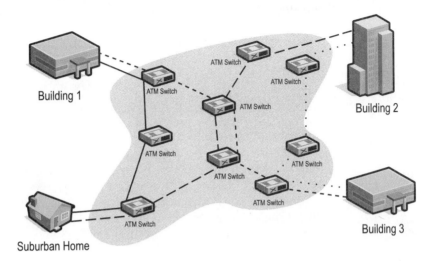

ATM and Virtual Circuits

Connection-oriented networks trade greater complexity required in end nodes to support signaling and connection setup, in return for much greater simplicity in intermediate (switching) nodes. A connection-oriented network has several advantages over a connectionless network when attempting to support real-time, high-speed applications.

A connection-oriented network enables a network to guarantee a minimum level of service. If a network does not have sufficient resources to accept a connection request, the network simply refuses to establish the connection. This guarantees the network will have sufficient resources to support all active connections, and that queue overflows will not occur.

A logical connection between users means the signals travel over the same logical path for the duration of the connection, and switching delay is virtually eliminated. This is important because both voice and video applications are extremely sensitive to variations in transmission delay.

The devices at each end of a virtual channel may operate at different speeds, because an end-to-end physical connection is not established. This allows data to be transmitted at one speed by the source node, while it is received at a different speed by the destination node.

Use of the connection is relatively high while the connection is established. When there is no more data to be transmitted, the connection is terminated, and the previously allocated network resources may now be used by another connection.

Fixed-Length Cells

Connectionless technologies format the data to be transmitted into variable-length packets. ATM uses a fixed-length, 53-byte cell consisting of a 5-byte header and 48-byte Information field. The use of fixed-length cells simplifies switch design by enabling a switch to be implemented in silicon. For example, the switching logic is implemented in hardware devices without the need for an operating system (OS), as in routers. This greatly reduces the processing time required for each cell, increases switch throughput, and reduces the cost of the switching technology.

Header Details

Each ATM cell contains a 5-byte header and 48-byte Information field. The ATM header contains six fields. These are illustrated on the ATM Header Diagram.

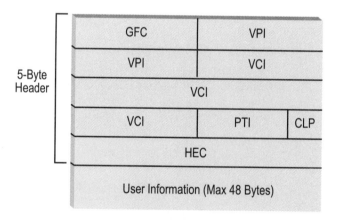

ATM Header

The six fields of the ATM header include:

- Generic Flow Control (GFC)—GFC is 4 bits long and is reserved for future flow control use between a user and network.

- Virtual Pathway Identifier (VPI)—The VPI is 1 byte long and identifies the virtual pathway to which a cell belongs. The VPI has local significance, and each ATM device may change the VPI as the cell traverses the network to its destination.

- Virtual Channel Identifier (VCI)—The VCI identifies the virtual channel (VC) to which a cell belongs. The VCI is a 2-byte field. As with the VPI, the VCI also has local significance, and may change as the cell traverses the network. The VPI/VCI pair tells the ATM switch how to switch a cell.

- Payload Type Indicator (PTI)—The PTI is 3 bits long. It indicates whether the payload contains user, control, or management data. The PTI field also indicates whether the cell has encountered congestion as it traverses the ATM network.

- Cell Loss Priority (CLP)—This single bit is set to 1 to indicate a cell with a low priority; the default is 0, to indicate a regular priority cell. In the event of network congestion, an ATM switch discards low-priority cells (CLP = 1) before discarding cells with a regular priority (CLP = 0). The CLP function is important because it allows certain types of traffic to take priority in a congested network. (

- Header Error Control (HEC)—These 8 bits provide a cyclic redundancy check (CRC) to detect errors in the cell header. Its main function is to validate the VPI and VCI fields to protect against the delivery of cells to the wrong User Network Interface (UNI). Although this field is transmitted as part of the cell header, it is computed and used by the Physical Layer, not the ATM layer.

FCS for ATM FRAM

B-ISDN and ATM

ATM is a subset of the overall B-ISDN standard. The B-ISDN protocol stack is presented on the B-ISDN Protocol Stack Diagram. The three primary layers we will discuss are the bottom three layers. In general, these layers correspond to the Physical and Data Link Layers of the Open Systems Interconnection (OSI) model, and include:

- ATM adaptation layer (AAL)
- ATM layer
- Physical layer

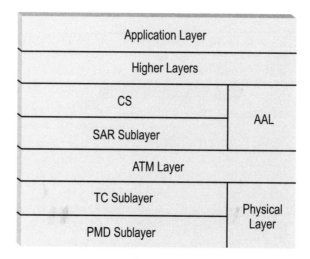

B-ISDN Protocol Stack

These three layers are all contained in one protocol header.

AAL

AAL is an end-to-end process used only by the two communicating end nodes to insert and remove data from the ATM layer. AAL maps higher-layer services, such as Transmission Control Protocol (TCP/IP) or video services, to the ATM layer for transport across the network. AAL provides five different processes, AAL 1 through AAL 5, as presented on the AAL Structure Diagram.

SAR Structure for AAL 1

CSI: Convergence Sublayer Indication
SN: Sequence Number
SNP: Sequence Number Protection
SDU: Service Data Unit

SAR Structure for AAL 2

SN: Sequence Number
IT: Information Type
LI: Length Indicator
CRC: Cyclic Redundancy Check

SAR Structure for AALs 3 and 4

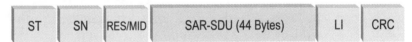

ST: Segment Type
RES: Reserved
MID: Multiplexing Identifier

SAR Structure For AAL 5

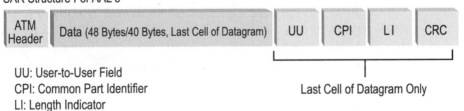

UU: User-to-User Field
CPI: Common Part Identifier
LI: Length Indicator
CRC: Cyclic Redundancy Check

Last Cell of Datagram Only

AAL Structure

The most popular data communications protocols, such as IP, NetWare, and AppleTalk, make use of packets that are variable in length. These packets are almost always larger than can be carried in the Payload field of a single ATM cell. For most ATM devices to exchange data, they must make use of an adaptation layer protocol that segments higher-layer protocol packets into cells for transmission across the network, and reassembles cells received from the network into the original data packet.

AAL 1, constant bit rate (CBR), is designed for CBR data that requires synchronization between sender and receiver. This service is used by voice, video, and similar traffic. AAL 1 adds 4 bytes of overhead for encoded timing information to address the close coordination needs of CBR traffic. Typical protocols used by AAL 1 are Digital Signal level 0 (DS0), DS1, and DS3, allowing an ATM network to emulate voice or DS-type services.

AAL 2 addresses the needs of variable bit rate (VBR) services. The additional overhead needs for AAL 2 are not yet defined.

AALs 3 and 4 are designed for connection-oriented and connectionless data services, respectively. AALs 3 and 4 traffic includes X.25, frame relay, and ISDN D channel signaling.

AAL 5, simple and efficient adaptation layer (SEAL), is used for VBR data transmitted between two users over a preestablished ATM connection. SEAL assumes higher-layer processes will handle error recovery. It is the only AAL process that does not add any overhead to the user information sent to the lower levels. Each AAL process is performed at the convergence sublayer (CS).

The purpose of the two AAL sublayers (CS and segmentation and reassembly [SAR] sublayer) is to convert the user data into 48-byte data for transmission in an ATM cell. The unit of data produced at this layer is a protocol data unit (PDU).

CS

The CS is service-dependent. Services provided by the CS include handling cell delay variation, providing source clock recovery, monitoring lost and misinserted cells and possible corrective action, monitoring user information for bit errors, and reporting on the status of end-to-end performance. In addition to these services, CS is also responsible for dividing data from the next higher layer into logical packet data units (CS-PDUs) that are usable by the SAR sublayer. The processes associated with AAL, and its sublayers CS and SAR, are illustrated on the AAL Process Diagram.

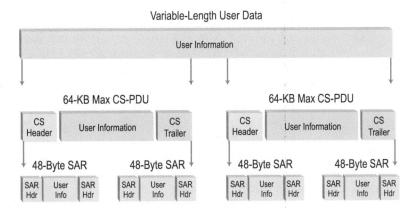

AAL Process

SAR Sublayer

The SAR sublayer is responsible for segmentation of higher-layer information into 48-byte fields suitable for the payload of ATM cells, and the inverse operation, reassembly of cell payload information for the next higher layer. In AAL processes AAL 1 through AAL 4, the SAR sublayer adds data to the PDU sent to the ATM layer. The SAR-PDUs are presented on the AAL Process Diagram.

ATM Layer

The ATM layer is responsible for data transmission between adjacent nodes and transporting data between AAL and the physical layer. During data transport between AAL and the physical layers, the ATM layer adds (or removes) 5 bytes of header information to the SAR-PDU, making a complete ATM cell. In addition to transporting data, the ATM layer is responsible for multiplexing and demultiplexing cells into a single cell stream on the physical layer. The ATM Layers and Routing Diagram illustrates the relationship between these two concepts.

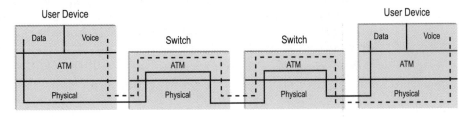

ATM Layers and Routing

The major function of the 5-byte ATM header is to identify the virtual connection to which the cell belongs. The traditional functions of packet headers, such as sequence numbers for error correction and flow control and checksums, are eliminated. This implies that an ATM switch can process a cell very quickly, which eliminates queuing delays while increasing switch throughput.

Each ATM cell contains a small 48-byte Information field. The use of this small field reduces the number of internal buffers a switch must support, while reducing the queuing delay for the switch's buffers. This enables an ATM switch to process cells very quickly, which reduces latency and increases throughput. The switch does not have to allow for varying frame sizes.

Unlike an X.25 network, ATM does not support error correction or flow control on a link-by-link basis. This means that if a physical link introduces a bit error, or is temporarily overloaded resulting in the loss of a cell, no corrective action is taken. An ATM network does not support a facility that allows the node at one end of a point-to-point physical link to request the retransmission of lost or corrupted cells from the node at the other end of the physical link.

There are two reasons it is unnecessary for an ATM network to support these functions:

- The introduction of fiber-based digital transmission facilities has created a relatively error-free transmission environment. Fewer transmission errors mean there is a reduced need for a network to perform error correction.

- Workstations run higher-level protocols, such as TCP, that perform error correction and retransmission. Because the ATM network can concentrate on just switching cells and not worry about error correction, cell throughput at each switching node is substantially increased.

Physical Layer

The physical layer defines how cells are transported over a network. This includes physical interfaces, media, and information rates. The physical layer also defines how cells are converted to a line signal, depending on the media type. ATM is media-independent because it is not tied to any particular physical layer.

The physical layer consists of two sublayers: the transmission convergence (TC) sublayer and the physical medium-dependent (PMD) sublayer.

TC Sublayer

The TC sublayer converts between ATM cells and the bit stream clocked to the physical medium. On transmission, TC basically maps the cells into the time-division multiplexing (TDM) frame format (or the appropriate underlying physical transport protocol). On reception, TC must delineate the individual cells in the received bit stream, either from the TDM frame directly, or by means of the HEC in the ATM cell header.

The HEC code is capable of correcting any single-bit error in the header. It is also capable of detecting many patterns of multiple-bit errors. The TC sublayer generates HEC on transmission, and uses it to determine whether the received header has any errors. If errors are detected in the header, the received cell is discarded. Because the header tells the ATM layer what to do with the cell, it is very important that the header is free of any errors. Otherwise, the cell might be delivered to a wrong user, or an undesired function in the ATM layer may inadvertently be invoked.

The TC sublayer also uses HEC to locate cells mapped into a TDM payload. The HEC will only match data in the 5-byte header, not in the payload. Thus, the HEC can be used to find cells in a received bit stream. After several cell headers have been located through the use of HEC, TC knows to expect the next cell 53 bytes later. This process is referred to as HEC-based cell delineation.

The TC sublayer also performs cell rate decoupling (or speed matching function). Physical media that have synchronous cell time slots (for example, DS3, SONET, SDH, shielded twisted pair [STP], and Fibre Channel-based method) require this function; asynchronous media, such as FDDI, do not. There are special codings in the ATM cell header that indicate whether a cell is unassigned or idle; all other cells are assigned. The transmitting switch multiplexes multiple VPI/VCI cell streams, queuing them if an ATM slot is not immediately available. If the queue is empty when the time arrives to fill the next synchronous cell time slot, the TC sublayer inserts an unassigned or idle cell to maintain a constant bit stream. The receiver extracts unassigned or idle cells and distributes the other, assigned cells to their destinations.

PMD Sublayer

This lowest layer on the B-ISDN protocol stack is the only fully medium-dependent layer. The physical medium is responsible for correct transmission and reception of bits on the medium. This sublayer must guarantee proper bit timing reconstruction at the receiver. Therefore, it is the responsibility of the transmitting peer entity to provide for insertion of the required bit timing information and line coding.

Activities

1. Which field of the ATM cell header identifies the virtual pathway to which a cell belongs?

   a. VPI

   b. VCI

   c. GFC

   d. VIP

2. What does the ATM cell consist of?

   a. 48-byte header and 5-byte Information field

   b. 5-byte header and variable-size Information field

   c. 48-byte Information field and 5-byte header

   d. 48-byte Information field and variable header

3. Which of the following is a benefit of using a connection-oriented network?

   a. It enables a network to guarantee a maximum level of service.

   b. All connections are established, regardless of the level of available network resources.

   c. Devices at each end of the network may operate at different speeds.

   d. Information can travel many different paths for the duration of the connection.

4. The ATM protocol stack consists of three layers that map to the OSI model _____ and _____ layers.

   a. Network, Transport

   b. Physical, Data Link

   c. Data Link, Network

   d. Physical, Application

5. AAL _____ is also known as the SEAL.

   a. 1

   b. 2

   c. 3

   d. 5

6. Which two WAN protocols use cell-switching technology? (Choose two.)

   a. Frame relay

   b. ATM

   c. ISDN

   d. SMDS

7. Describe the three switching technology transfer modes.

   _____

   _____

   _____

8. Describe the services provided by the AAL, ATM layer, and ATM physical layer.

   _____

   _____

   _____

   _____

   _____

   _____

9. How do the features of ATM address multimedia transport?

   _____

   _____

   _____

   _____

Extended Activity

Visit the 3Com Web site at **http://www.3com.com/atm/** and review the white papers provided regarding ATM technology. Review the products mentioned in the text.

Lesson 2—ATM Implementation

ATM is used in a variety of ways to route information by means of cells across LANs, MANs, and WANs. This lesson describes how ATM devices route multimedia information across a network.

Objectives

At the end of this lesson you will be able to:

- Describe how ATM uses virtual paths (VPs) and VCs

- Explain how multimedia communications take place with ATM

- Recognize how ATM devices can be used to switch multiple types of services

- Explain the sample network configuration

 **Key Point**

ATM provides services for transfer of time-sensitive information.

VPs and VCs

Similar to traditional LAN packets, the header of each ATM cell contains addressing information. However, rather than a specific destination address, each header in a cell contains two fields, VPI and VCI, that specify the virtual connection over which the cell should be forwarded. Together, VPI and VCI fields define a routing field that provides an ATM switch with the information it needs to route each cell. The VCs and VPs Diagram illustrates the virtual connection.

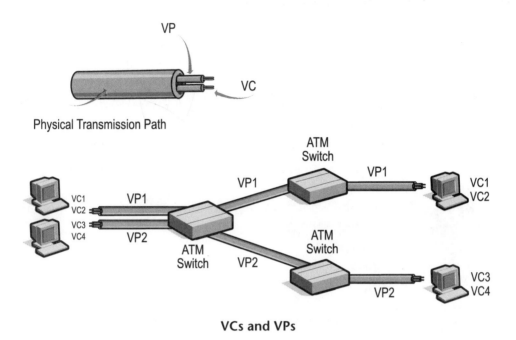

VCs and VPs

(VC)

A VC is a communications circuit that transports ATM cells between two or more endpoints. The endpoints of a VC may be a user-to-user connection, user-to-network connection, or network-to-network connection. The point at which an ATM cell is passed to or from a higher layer is considered the endpoint of a VC.

(VP)

When multiple VCs on the same transmission path are headed for the same destination, they can be grouped into a VP. A VP is a collection of VCs. Think of a VP as performing the same functions as a trunk line in a telephone network; the VP enables a number of VCs to be bundled together for transport between two ATM devices.

ATM in Action

An ATM switch takes a user's data, voice, and video, and chops them into fixed-length cells. The cells are then multiplexed into a single bit stream that is transmitted across a physical medium.

The ATM Use Example Diagram illustrates the role ATM plays in this real-life example, where John is sitting at his workstation. John's workstation has an ATM interface card, sound board with microphone, and video camera. The workstation is connected to a local ATM switch. This switch is attached to a public ATM-based WAN service, to which John's publisher is also connected.

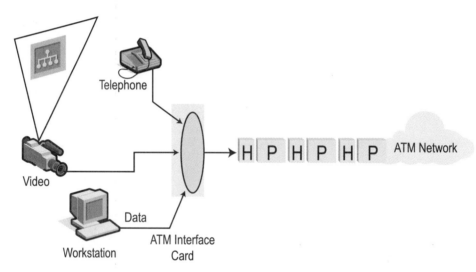

ATM Use Example

John places a multimedia call to the publisher, begins transmitting the data for his manuscript, and begins a conversation with the publisher, in essence, providing text, voice, and video traffic simultaneously, in real time. All the while, John and the publisher are able to see each other's faces. The publisher is reviewing the manuscript at his workstation while having an interactive dialog with John. Let us examine this scenario in detail.

Video and voice are very time-sensitive; the information cannot be delayed for more than a blink of an eye, and the delay cannot have significant variations. Disruption in the video image of John's face, or distortion of his voice, destroys the interactive, near real-life quality of this multimedia application. Data can be sent in either connection-oriented or connectionless mode. In either case, the data is not nearly as delay-sensitive as voice or video traffic. Data traffic is very sensitive to loss. Therefore, ATM must discriminate between voice, video, and data traffic, giving voice and video traffic priority and guaranteed, bounded delay, simultaneously ensuring that data traffic has very low loss.

In the example, a VP is established between John and the publisher, over which three virtual channels are defined for text data, voice, and video. The ATM VC Diagram shows how all three types of traffic are combined over a single ATM (VP), with VCs assigned to the text data (VCI=1), voice (VCI=2), and video (VCI=3).

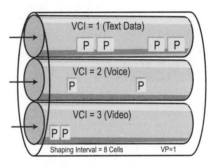

ATM VC

The workstation contains an ATM interface card, where the chopper "slices and dices" the data streams into 48-byte data segments, as shown on the ATM VC Diagram. In the next step, the payload is addressed by prefixing it with the VPI, VCI, and remaining fields of the 5-byte header. The result is a stream of 53-byte ATM cells from each source: voice, video, and text data. These cells are generated independently from each source, such that there may be contention for cell slot times on the interface connected to the workstation. Text, voice, and video are each assigned a virtual channel connection (VCC): VCI=1 for text data, VCI=2 for voice, and VCI=3 for video, all on VPI=0. This example is greatly simplified, because there would normally be many more than just three active VCI values on a single VPI.

Returning to the ATM VC Diagram, this is how John's terminal sends the combined voice, video, and text data. A gatekeeper in his terminal, a device that allocates time slots in the bit stream based on cell priority, shapes the transmitted data in intervals of eight cells (approximately 80 microseconds [μs] at the DS3 rate), normally allowing one voice cell, then five video cells, and finally the remaining—two text data cells—to be transmitted. This corresponds to approximately 4 megabits per second (Mbps) for high-fidelity audio, 24 Mbps for video, and 9 Mbps for text data. All data sources (text, voice, and video) contend for the bandwidth of each shaping interval, with voice, video, and text data being sent in the above proportion. Cells are retained in the buffer by the gatekeeper in case all cell slot times are full in the shaping interval. In practice, a much larger shaping interval is used to provide greater granularity in bandwidth allocation.

ATM Communication

Once a VC is established, ATM cells are transferred between source and destination. Because ATM is not a Network Layer protocol, no routing of cells takes place. At every point in the network, ATM devices process each cell independently of other cells. It is not necessary to combine or acknowledge cells. An ATM switch simply looks to see whether the header is error-free, checks the address, and sends the cell onward. This makes ATM a very efficient protocol. Because all cells during a single call travel the same path, cells arrive at the destination in an orderly fashion, as presented on the ATM Cell Transmission and Format Diagram.

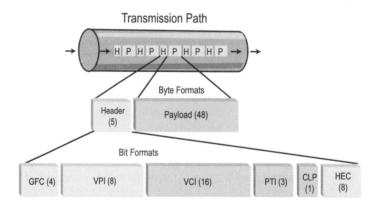

ATM Cell Transmission and Format

In addition to cell processing, an ATM network device must multiplex and demultiplex cells onto a Physical Layer transport protocol, such as T3 or SONET.

ATM Over SONET

An example of a TC sublayer that ATM interfaces with is SONET. ATM is based on either SONET Synchronous Transport Signal level 3, concatenated (STS-3c) (155.520 Mbps) or STS-12c (622.08 Mbps). Concatenated means that the contents of the frames are treated as a continuous bit stream as they cross frame boundaries. The ATM Over SONET Diagram shows how a 53-byte cell maps into a SONET STS-3c frame.

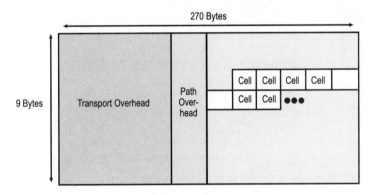

ATM Over SONET

A SONET STS-3c frame, including the header and payload, contains 2,430 bytes arranged in 270, 9-byte columns. The Payload field contains 261, 9-byte columns, for a payload capacity of 2,349 bytes. An STS-3c frame can carry up to 44 ATM cells, padding the remaining STS-3c frame space as needed. The 53-byte cells are mapped into the synchronous payload envelope (SPE) as 53-byte blocks in horizontal format, unlike virtual tributaries (VTs).

ATM LAN/WAN Solutions

When ATM products are implemented as LAN or WAN solutions, they are normally used to speed up the backbone of a network, and provide transport of different types of services. Older, legacy data services, as well as newer, multimedia services need to be combined into one infrastructure. Various ATM devices combine this traffic over an ATM network backbone.

ATM Devices

ATM products should be able to combine voice and video with data traffic from local workgroups, through switches and across high-speed ATM WANs. ATM products should offer support for the latest ATM standards (nonproprietary), and provide transport for private, public, and hybrid network solutions.

ATM products must interface data, voice, and video networks without requiring expensive upgrades to existing equipment, and without compromising the services those networks provide to their end users. ATM products must offer native interfaces to a variety of existing networks including:

- Local ATM
- Ethernet
- Frame relay
- Private branch exchange (PBX) equipment
- T1/EI multiplexers (MUXs)

The Sample Network Diagram shows how devices are combined to form a private enterprise WAN. This WAN could just as easily be attached to public carrier services.

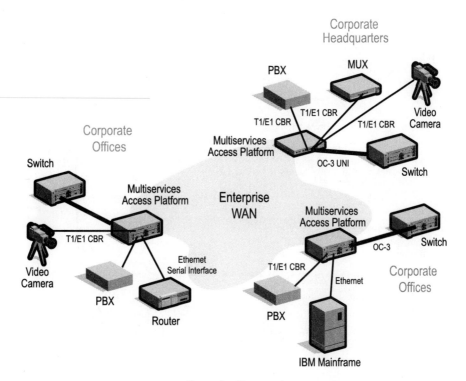

Sample Network

Note that legacy services are supported, because IBM mainframe hosts can attach to an access device by means of Ethernet. Voice traffic by means of a PBX can also be attached to this device that has Optical Carrier (OC)-3 WAN and campus interfaces to other buildings and networks. Access devices also provide transport of video services through T1 and E1 interfaces.

Activities

1. Describe how ATM uses VPs and VCs.

   _____

   _____

   _____

   _____

2. Draw networks using ATM in the following configurations:
   a. ATM as a backbone
   b. ATM over a wide area
   c. ATM to the desktop

Extended Activities

1. Divide into groups and describe the flow of information from one IP process to another IP process connected by means of an ATM network. Include in your description the following (discuss with group members):
   a. Packets to the ATM switch
   b. ATM layers and how packets might be divided
   c. ATM cells to the Physical Layer at the sending station
   d. ATM network-to-network connectivity
   e. ATM cells across an ATM network
   f. ATM cells from the Physical Layer to the IP layer at the receiving computer

Lesson 3—ATM Devices

Standard WAN devices cannot be used to implement an ATM network, because ATM is a connection-oriented technology. ATM devices must cooperate to establish, maintain, and release virtual channels, unlike connectionless WAN devices that are only concerned with forwarding one data frame at a time.

Objectives

At the end of this lesson you will be able to:

*   Explain how ATM networks are constructed
*   Describe the function of ATM routers, channel service units/data service units (CSU/DSUs), network interface cards (NICs), and switches

 **Key Point**

ATM provides high-speed, connection-oriented, cell-switching services.

Categories of ATM Devices

Devices used to create ATM networks fall into five separate categories:

*   Routers
*   CSUs/DSUs
*   NICs
*   Switches
*   Intelligent hubs

Routers

Routers take LAN packets and convert the frame to an ATM cell when attached to an ATM switch. A router also takes cells from the ATM switch, converts the cells into LAN frames, and forwards the frames to the correct LAN segment. The ATM and Routers Diagram illustrates this relationship.

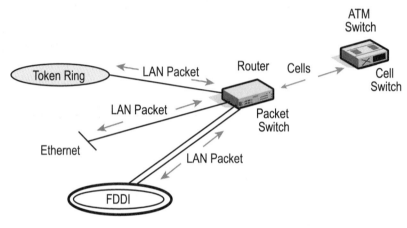

ATM and Routers

It is important to note that the router switches packets, not cells. Data is reformatted to and from cells only at the interface to the ATM switch. As a result, routers function as ATM access devices that allow non-ATM LANs to connect to an ATM network.

CSU/DSUs

ATM DSUs use the ATM Data Exchange Interface (DXI) to convert LAN packets to cells, making it possible to connect a router (without a hardware ATM interface) to an ATM switch. This concept is illustrated on the ATM With CSU/DSUs and Routers Diagram. ATM-compatible DSUs require that LAN routers use DXI, which creates a variable-length, frame-based ATM interface between data terminal equipment (DTE) (router) and the ATM CSU/DSU, to format LAN packets. The DSU can then convert the information to fixed-length ATM cells.

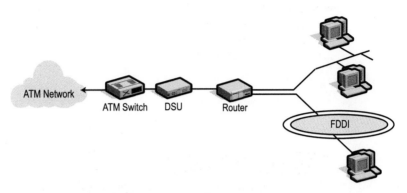

ATM with CSU/DSUs and Routers

NICs

ATM NICs (adapter cards) provide ATM connectivity at the desktop. These are available for most high-end systems and personal computers (PCs). Cells are transmitted directly from a workstation to the ATM switch and out over the network. The ATM NICs Diagram illustrates the use of NICs in an ATM network.

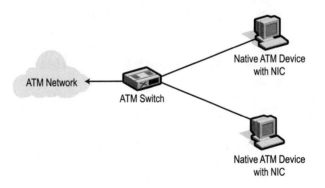

ATM NICs

Switches

Switches are fundamental components in an ATM network. They are used to route cells between input ATM switch ports and output ports. They must also buffer data, and in some cases, translate header address information. There are two different types of ATM switches:

- VP switch

- VC switch

VP switches route VPs; a VP routes multiple VCs simultaneously. A VP switch is intended for MAN and WAN implementation where a multiplexed group of VCs is switched along the same route.

The VPI identifies each separate VP from all other VPs sharing the same transmission path in the network. A transmission path is a Physical Layer point-to-point link between two ATM devices. As with a frame relay data link connection identifier (DLCI), the VPI only has local significance. The VPI for a particular virtual path connection (VPC) changes as the VPC passes through different switches and across different transmission facilities.

A VC switch routes individual VCs. Because VCs are contained within a VP, a VC switch must be able to demultiplex individual VCs from an inbound VP, and switch them to different outbound VPs.

Intelligent Hubs

An intelligent hub permits ATM LANs to be constructed in a star topology; nodes are attached to the central hub through point-to-point links. There are two approaches for deploying ATM in intelligent hubs:

- The hub can contain a very high-speed backplane bus that is shared by all port cards. An ATM interface module provides connectivity between the port cards attached to the high-speed bus and an ATM network.

- The hub can contain a native ATM backplane. With this approach, ATM is used across the interface between each port card and the backplane, and each port card has a dedicated ATM connection to an ATM switching module.

The Intelligent Hub With an ATM Backplane and ATM Switching Module Diagram illustrates the second of the two approaches.

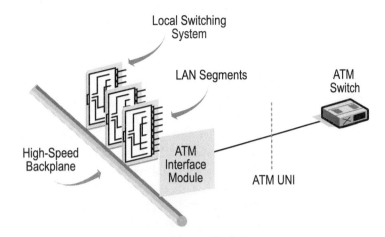

**Intelligent Hub With an
ATM Backplane and ATM Switching Module**

ATM Networks

ATM can be used as a WAN solution or in a LAN environment. The ATM Network Diagram shows ATM in a LAN environment. In this diagram, the ATM switch is the "collapsed" corporate backbone. It provides connectivity to end devices residing on Ethernet and Token Ring networks.

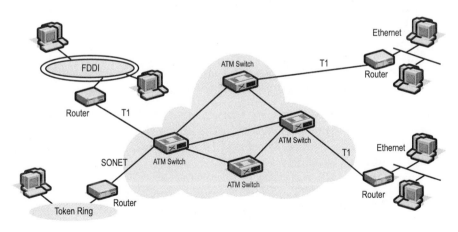

ATM Network

Activities

1. How does an ATM CSU/DSU allow routers without native ATM interfaces to be used on an ATM network?

    _____

    _____

    _____

    _____

2. List and describe the two types of ATM switches.

    _____

    _____

    _____

    _____

3. Where is ATM currently found in computer networks? What is the trend in ATM implementation?

    _____

    _____

    _____

    _____

Extended Activity

Visit the ATM Forum Web site at **http://www.atmforum.com/** for the current progress on ATM specifications and current technologies.

Lesson 4—SMDS

SMDS is a metropolitan-area data service available through LECs only. It was designed to provide connections between LANs in a citywide region, within a single LATA. SMDS was developed by Bellcore (now Telcordia, formerly an AT&T subsidiary). Several Bell operating companies have made SMDS available within their areas.

Objectives

At the end of this lesson you will be able to:

*   Show how the SMDS protocol stack relates to the OSI model

*   Describe the type of traffic SMDS is best suited to transport, and explain why

*   Explain how traffic passes from a LAN, through a router and DSU, and into an SMDS network

Key Point

SMDS is a connection-oriented, cell-switched service that delivers data rates up to 45 Mbps.

SMDS Operation

The basic characteristics of SMDS are largely described by its name.

Switched,

Switched Multibit Data Service (SMDS)

SMDS is a public-switched network, similar to frame relay. To the networks that connect to it, SMDS has no "distance." In other words, like the public telephone system, all that is required to send a packet to another SMDS-connected network is the user's address. To a subscriber's LAN, SMDS looks like another subnet. All internal nodes of the SMDS "cloud" are hidden from the subscriber.

SMDS is a connectionless, best-effort service; it is not necessary to set up an end-to-end connection before sending data. SMDS is also a cell-relay system. Like ATM, it uses 53-byte cells that each carry a 48-byte payload; however, SMDS uses a different format for its 5-byte cell header.

Multimegabit

SMDS falls in the same performance range as frame relay (T1/E1 to T3/E3), potentially overlapping the low end of B-ISDN. It can provide up to 45 Mbps of bandwidth, because each pair of SMDS switches is connected by two one-way T3 lines (typically fiber optic cable).

SNI

The SMDS protocol specifies how to connect customer premises equipment (CPE) with an SMDS network. The point at which the CPE interfaces with the SMDS network is called the "Subscriber Network Interface (SNI)." This interface, connecting a customer to the SMDS cloud, is usually implemented by means of T1 or T3 lines, as shown on the SMDS Network Example Diagram.

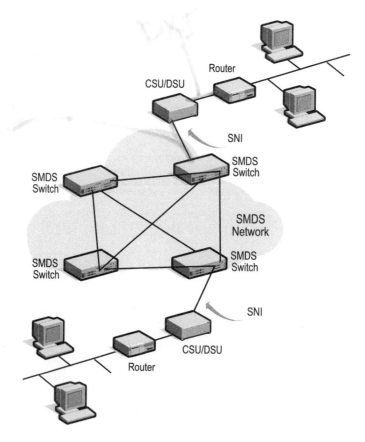

SMDS Network Example

SMDS Protocols

SMDS protocols were defined by the Regional Bell Operating Companies (RBOCs), based on the IEEE 802.6 standard for MANs. This standard was originally known as Queued Packet Synchronous Exchange (QPSX), and is now called "DQDB." Each DQDB end station has two buses: one for incoming traffic and one for outgoing traffic. Thus, DQDB provides full-duplex communication between any two nodes. However, an SMDS network supports only connectionless data traffic.

The interface with SMDS is the Logical Link Control (LLC) sub-layer of the OSI Data Link Layer, as shown on the SMDS Layers Diagram. Thus, while SMDS uses cell relay internally, it is technically a frame-switching facility because LLC deals with frames. You are not likely to hear it called that, however.

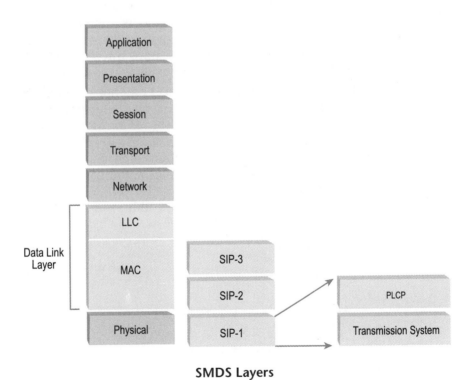

SMDS Layers

SIP

The SMDS protocol stack is known as the SMDS Interface Protocol (SIP). This stack consists of internal SMDS protocols called "SIP-1", "SIP-2," and "SIP-3."

SIP-1

SIP-1 corresponds to the OSI Physical Layer. SMDS uses cell relay at Layer 1, relaying 53-byte cells similar to ATM; however, the format of the 5-byte header is different.

The SIP-1 layer is divided into two sublayers:

- The Physical Layer Convergence Protocol (PLCP) sublayer defines how the SMDS 53-byte cell is mapped to the specific transmission system described at the lower sublayer.

- The Transmission System sublayer describes the digital carrier used for SNI. This includes DS1 (T1), DS3 (T3), SONET, and High-Speed Serial Interface (HSSI).

SIP-2

SIP-2 corresponds to the lower part of the OSI Medium Access Control (MAC) sublayer. SIP-2 defines the network interface. At the sending end, it segments frames into 53-byte cells. At the receiving end, it reassembles individual cells into frames.

SIP-2 uses Queued Arbitrated (QA) functionality, which allocates cells to each data transmission on an as-needed basis. This approach is most appropriate for connectionless transmissions that are not time sensitive.

SIP-3

SIP-3 corresponds to the upper part of the OSI MAC sublayer. SIP-3 transports data from the upper-layer protocols. It is also responsible for error correction and data addressing. The SIP-3 data unit is the PDU, which can be as large as 9,188 bytes.

DXI

The SMDS Interest Group (SIG) created the DXI protocol to provide a standard interface between a router and the DSU used to access an SMDS network. DXI only exists to move data between a router and CSU/DSU; it is not used in every network. The SMDS and DXI Diagram illustrates this relationship.

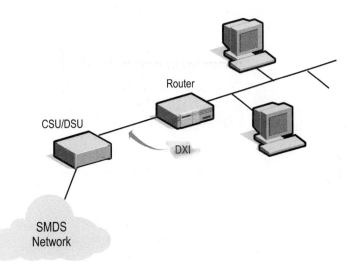

SMDS and DXI

DXI specifies how various SIP-layer tasks are distributed between the router and DSU. The SMDS Network Interface Points Diagram presents the protocols associated with the router, and protocols associated with the DSU. As we can see on the diagram, DXI is divided into the DXI link and DXI physical layers.

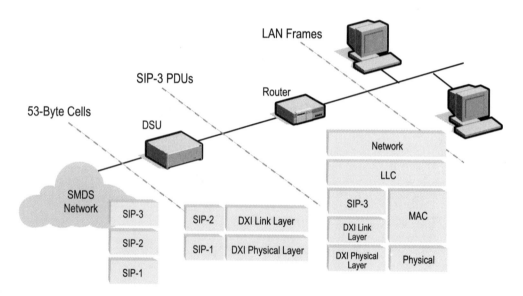

SMDS Network Interface Points

Router Functions   When frames are transmitted from a LAN to a router, a router converts the MAC layer protocol (such as Ethernet) to a SIP-3 PDU for delivery to the DSU. The DXI link layer encapsulates each PDU between a header and trailer, creating a frame. The purpose of this frame is to move PDUs across the physical link between the router and DSU. DXI link layer protocols are based on the High-Level Data Link Control (HDLC) protocol, thus the format of the frame is very similar to HDLC.

The DXI physical layer defines a connection between a router and DSU. The most common DXI physical layer protocols are HSSI, V.35, and X.21.

DSU Functions

A DSU receives the DXI link layer frames. It removes SIP-3 PDUs from the frames, and then converts them into cells for transmission across the SNI to the SMDS switch.

The opposite happens when cells are received. The DSU converts cells to PDUs, then encapsulates them into frames. The frames are transmitted across the DXI to the router. The router removes PDUs from the frames, and then converts PDUs back into frames for the LAN. This process is summarized on the SMDS Encapsulation Diagram.

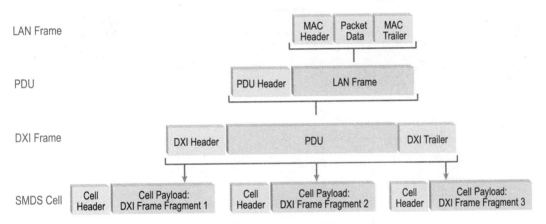

SMDS Encapsulation

Advantages and Disadvantages

Like frame relay, SMDS is ideal for data transfers, and citywide client/server computer networks with many-to-many communications. In other words, if many locations must exchange data with one another (not just back to the home office), SMDS can be an effective solution. It is especially cost-effective if the locations must transfer data at data rates higher than T1.

Although SMDS scales down, its maximum throughput limits the technology's ability to scale up beyond 45 Mbps (higher speeds are being tested). This makes it only useful for businesses already using T1 circuits.

SMDS is not a good choice for WANs that cross LATA boundaries, because of the restrictions placed on LECs in the 1984 Modified Final Judgment (MFJ). This rule has limited SMDS to a metropolitan-area service only, which is not attractive to business customers who want to exchange data with locations outside their LATAs. To set up this sort of interLATA network with SMDS, a LEC must partner with an interexchange carrier (IXC).

Even though SMDS is a cell-based technology, it does not perform very well for interactive real-time video or voice, or pay-per-view movies. This is because it is also a connectionless technology. Thus, while data travels in same-size cells, the cells may take multiple paths through the network, and that can cause delays at the destination end. The best-effort approach of connectionless services means that SMDS cannot guarantee delivery of each cell, which is imperative for voice and video communications. Thus, despite its potential for faster throughput, SMDS is best suited for data transport.

Activities

1. List the Physical Layer standards shown on the SMDS Network Example Diagram in this lesson, and the likely cable types associated with each.

    _____

    _____

    _____

2. For each device shown on the diagram, list the services that would most likely be provided.

    _____

    _____

    _____

3. Given the following diagram, describe the movement of information from Client A to Client B and back. In your discussion, describe what protocols are used at each device and across the WAN.

    _____

    _____

    _____

    _____

    _____

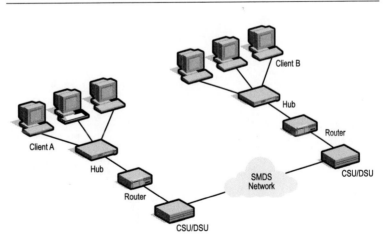

Extended Activities

1. Compare the protocols below to SMDS. Describe the differences and similarities to SMDS based on the way connections are established, the size and type of frame or packet, and where each is most often used.

   a. X.25

       _____

       _____

   b. Frame relay

       _____

       _____

   c. Point-to-point T1

       _____

       _____

   d. ISDN

       _____

       _____

   e. Point-to-Point Protocol (PPP)

       _____

       _____

Lesson 5—IEEE 802.16: The Wireless Last Mile

Wireless technologies provide network connectivity without the cost and effort incurred when using wired solutions. The IEEE 802.16™ —2001 Air Interface for Fixed Broadband Wireless Access Systems standard describes the Data Link and Physical Layer components of an emerging broadband WirelessMAN™ service intended to connect both urban and rural remote users and networks to MAN, WAN, and Internet backbone networks. The 802.16 standard specifies a connection-oriented, point-to-multipoint wireless access solution that promises high-bandwidth, multiple service network connectivity in applications where wired network access is impractical or unavailable.

Objectives

At the end of this lesson you will be able to:

- Explain basic characteristics of 802.16 wireless technologies

- Describe the functions and components of the IEEE 802.16 protocol layers

Key Point

Broadband wireless networks extend the service provider's reach beyond the limitations of the physical cable plant.

The Promise of Broadband Wireless Networks

The IEEE 802.16 standard specifies the Medium Access Control (MAC) and Physical (PHY) Layer protocols that support a stationary point-to-multipoint broadband wireless access (BWA) solution supporting multiple higher layer services, such as data and voice communications, over a shared medium. The MAC layer specifies the addressing, medium access control, quality of service (QoS), and security functions, while the Physical Layer specifies a short wavelength, high bandwidth (10-66 GHz), line-of sight, radio-based transmission medium. The Wireless Internet Access Diagram shows an example of an 802.16 standards-based network.

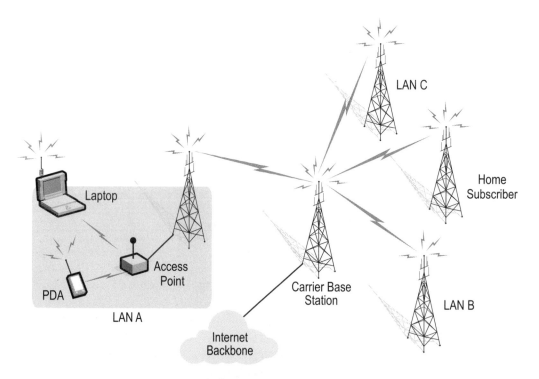

Wireless Internet Access

Wireless MAN technology promises network connectivity in locations where building a high-speed, wired network backbone is too time consuming or costly to be practical. For example, a developing country could provide its citizens wireless Internet access at a fraction of the cost of building a nationwide fiber optic network.

In other applications, wireless MAN, WAN, and Internet access provide alternatives to traditional copper and fiber-based last-mile solutions. The 802.16 standard can be a complementary technology to the 802.11a/b/g wireless LAN standards, providing the backhaul path to the Internet for wireless hotspots, home offices, and enterprise networks.

802.16 Equipment

The 802.16 standard defines two pieces of equipment:

- **Base station (BS)**—A BS is the central wireless hub to which all subscriber stations (SS) connect. This is located at the carrier's or ISP's facilities. The BS performs admission control, bandwidth allocation, and provides QoS either as an aggregate of all service flows or on a per-flow basis.

- **Subscriber station (SS)**—An SS consists of the individual 802.16 network endpoints connecting the subscriber equipment (access point, router, and so forth) to the base station. These endpoints are located at the subscriber's facility. The SS acts on behalf of the client devices (whether they are a set of networked workstations, an ATM switch, or an IP router) to request the necessary bandwidth and QoS needed to service the aggregate or individual service flows.

The BS radio connects to an antenna mounted on top of a tall building or mast and operates in the 10 to 66-GHz frequency range. The radio signal is limited to line-of-sight connectivity at these frequencies, although the use of sectorized antennas can propagate the signal to cover 4 to 9 square kilometers or more. Sectorized antennas divide the transmission channel into smaller frequency ranges or coverage patterns; each sector services a portion of the 360-degree coverage area of a traditional omni-directional antenna. A channel's bandwidth is typically about 25 to 28 Mhz.

SSs are located at the edge of a wired or wireless LAN or home network, and can replace traditional wireline xDSL, cable modem, leased line, frame relay, and ATM links. The 802.16 standard provides mechanisms for mapping traditional LAN and WAN technology characteristics, such as addressing, QoS, and virtual LAN (VLAN) IDs, into 802.16 MAC layer Protocol Data Units (PDU), and can transport these characteristics end-to-end across the wireless link. The standard is designed to support real-time, delay-sensitive traffic, such as VoIP, with the same service levels provided by wired networks. In fact, low-latency and high data rate connections exceeding 100 Mbps are possible. A single BS can support hundreds of SSs.

The 802.16 Protocol Layers

IEEE 802.16 specifies two protocol layers: the MAC layer and the PHY Layer. The MAC layer consists of three sublayers:

- **Service Specific Convergence Sublayer (CS)**—The service-specific CS maps higher layer protocol data, such as IP packets and ATM cells, to service flows, either individually or as an aggregate of like traffic. A service flow designates a QoS treatment for a particular higher layer network service. When provisioned, service flows are assigned 32-bit Service Flow Identifiers (SFIDs), which uniquely identify them from all other service flows provisioned on the link. Admitted and active service flows are also assigned Connection Identifiers (CID).

- **MAC Common Part Sublayer (MAC CPS)**—The MAC CPS builds MAC PDUs (frames). These MAC PDUs carry higher layer data, and transport contention control, bandwidth allocation, and connection establishment and maintenance messages. The MAC CPS can schedule different BS-SS polling intervals by service CIDs so that it can provide appropriate service flow-specific QoS over the PHY layer.

- **Privacy Sublayer**—The privacy sublayer handles authentication, data encryption, and encryption key exchange. Privacy is optional, but when implemented, it encrypts MAC PDU payloads to protect them from theft. Additionally, privacy prevents unauthorized access to wireless services. The vendor supplies a unique digital certificate to each SS that is used for authenticating the SS to its associated BS.

The PHY Layer performs signal encoding and decoding, synchronization, and radio transmitter and receiver functions. The 802.16 standard specifies a PHY operating in the 10 to 66-GHz frequency range.

The CS

The CS supports two types of higher layer network data: ATM cells and packetized data.

ATM CS

The Asynchronous Transfer Mode (ATM) CS classifies ATM cells to connections and service flows by either the virtual path identifier (VPI)—if VP switched—or by the cells' individual VPI/virtual channel identifier (VPI/VCI) values—if VC switched. A 16-bit Connection Identifier (CID) identifies each classified flow.

The ATM CS may perform payload header suppression (PHS) to reduce the amount of redundant data passed across the link. ATM cells may be packed, which means more than one cell is transported in a MAC PDU. These cells may share the same VPI or VCI values. PHS masks this redundant cell header information on transmission, and re-creates it at the receiver. A PHS Identifier (PHSI) is inserted between the MAC header and the data, replacing the masked cell header information. The receiver reads the PHSI and the associated CID and uses this information to unmask the received cell headers.

Packet CS

The packet CS classifies packet-based protocols, such as IP packets, VLAN tags, and PPP and Ethernet frames. Just as the ATM CS maps cells, the packet CS maps packets and frames to service flows. PHS may be used as well, if the MAC PDU packs packets or frames.

The 802.16 standard specifies several packetized traffic classifiers:

- **IEEE Std 802.3/Ethernet CS classifiers**—Classifies 802.3 Ethernet frames by either Logical Link Control (LLC) parameters (source or destination MAC address or Ethertype) or for IP over Ethernet, the LLC and IP header information (Type of Service [ToS] bits or protocol field).

- **IEEE Std 802.1Q-1998 CS classifiers**—Classifies frames by the 802.1p/Q VLAN (VLAN) tag and priority. LLC and IP header parameters may also by used.

- **IP classifiers**—Classifies packets by the IP header and protocol fields.

The MAC CPS

The MAC CPS is responsible for controlling access to the shared medium (the uplink channel). An 802.16 network operates in a point-to-multipoint fashion, which means the BS is the hub, and the SSs are the spokes. The BS may use a sectorized antenna to simultaneously service multiple sectors, or cells, and multiple SSs within a sector can attempt to simultaneously access the BS. A sectorized antenna can create multiple cells radiating around the antenna's pole, increasing the signal's coverage area significantly over that of a single 360-degree cell.

During its transmission time period, the BS is free to broadcast messages to the SSs without concern for contention. All SSs in the sector hear the broadcasted messages, listen for their CIDs, and disregard those messages not addressed to them. In the reverse direction, the SSs share the uplink within their sector and channel; therefore, the SSs must gain permission to transmit. Polling mechanisms handle contention by scheduling when each connection may transmit and for how long, depending on the QoS provided it.

Connection Establishment

Before it can request service flows and connections, an SS must determine the channel on which it will operate and then register with a BS. It locates its channel by exchanging a series of ranging messages with the BS. These messages help the SS to choose the correct transmit power levels and to fine tune signal timing and frequency. The SS sends its 48-bit MAC address as a component of the ranging request (RNG-REQ) message. The BS maps this MAC address to two of three SS-specific management flow CIDs, a basic CID and a primary management CID. After ranging is completed, the SS uses the primary management CID to request registration (REG-REQ) with the BS. The BS authenticates and authorizes the SS and then supplies the SS with its third management flow CID, the secondary management CID.

After it has the secondary management CID, the SS uses Dynamic Host Configuration Protocol (DHCP) to establish Internet Protocol (IP) connectivity. The DHCP server supplies the SS with a Trivial File Transfer Protocol (TFTP) server address and configuration file name that the SS uses to download additional configuration information. The SS and BS coordinate the time of day, and the SS downloads the configuration file. This configuration file contains preprovisioned service information that the SS uses to establish service connections.

To establish a service flow, the SS generates a Dynamic Service Addition request (DSA-REQ) message and forwards it to the BS. Included are the primary management CID, a transaction ID used to track the messages, and the requested service flow parameters. The BS responds with a message received (DSA-RVD) message.

The BS returns a DSA response (DSA-RSP) message indicating the requesting SS's primary management CID, the newly assigned SFID (if it adds the service flow) and CID (if the connection is admitted or becomes active). Also included are the transaction ID, the connection's QoS parameters, and if the connection failed, the connection parameters that caused it to fail.

The SS returns to the BS a DSA acknowledgment (DSA-ACK). Included in this message is the SS's primary management CID and the transaction ID taken from the DSA response message. The Simplified BS-SS Connection Establishment Diagram illustrates the process flow.

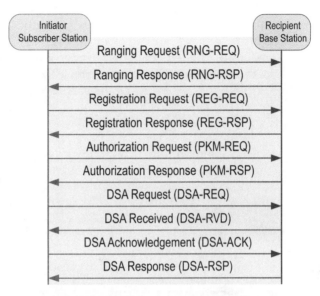

Simplified BS-SS Connection Establishment

Service Flow Changes

An initiator can change the parameters of a connection using a Dynamic Service Change request (DSC-REQ) message. This message identifies the SS's primary management CID, the corresponding SFID, and the newly requested service flow parameters. The receiver may either acknowledge or deny the requested parameters by returning a DSC response (DSC-RSP) message. A DSC-RSP denying the request identifies those service flow parameters that caused the request to fail. The initiator of the change returns a DSC acknowledgment (DSC-ACK) message.

Ending Service Flows and Connections

After a connection is no longer needed, an SS or BS generates a Dynamic Service Deletion request (DSD-REQ) message indicating the SFID it wishes to terminate. The receiver sends a DSD response (DSD-RSP) message, indicating the dropped SFID. This series of actions drops the corresponding connection.

MAC PDUs
    The 802.16 MAC defines two PDU types: the Generic MAC PDU, which transports CS data and link management information, and a Bandwidth Request PDU, which changes service flow bandwidth parameters. The Generic MAC PDU consists of three components: the generic MAC header and the optional payload and CRC, shown on the Generic MAC PDU Diagram.

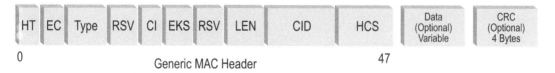

0   Generic MAC Header   47

Generic MAC PDU

The generic MAC header fields are as follows:

- **Header type (HT)**—1 bit. Set to 0 in a management or data PDU. Set to 1 in a Bandwidth Request PDU header.

- **Encryption control (EC)**—1 bit. If set to 1, indicates that the payload is encrypted. A 0 indicates no payload encryption.

- **Type**—6 bits. Indicates the type of payload. These bits depend on the message, subheaders, and its direction, uplink or downlink.

- **Reserved**—1 bit.

- **CRC Indicator (CI)**—1 bit. If set to 1, Indicates a CRC is appended to the PDU. A 0 indicates no CRC.

- **Encryption Key Sequence (EKS)**—2 bits. Traffic Encryption Key and Initialization Vector indexes used for payload encryption. Ignored if EC equals 0.

- **Reserved**—1 bit.

- **Length (LEN)**—11 bits. Designates the MAC PDU length in bytes.

- **CID**—16 bits.

- **Header Check Sequence (HCS)**—8 bits. Used to detect errors in the header.

The payload can range in size from 0 to 4,048 bytes in length, and can consist of ATM cells, IP packets, and other higher layer network data. The CRC is a 4-byte checksum used for error detection.

The MAC CPS also specifies several subheaders, which, if used, are inserted immediately following the generic MAC header. These subheaders control fragmentation, bandwidth grants, and packing. Management messages are used for connection management and are carried as the payload within a Generic MAC PDU.

The Bandwidth Request PDU Diagram shows the bandwidth request header used to request additional bandwidth from the BS.

0   47

Bandwidth Request PDU

No payload is included with a Bandwidth Request PDU. The Bandwidth Request Header fields are as follows:

- **HT**—1 bit. Set to 1.

- **EC**—1 bit. Always 0.

- **Type**—6 bits. Indicates the bandwidth request header type.

- **Bandwidth request (BR)**—16 bits. Represents the number of uplink bandwidth bytes the SS requests for the specified CID.

- **CID**—16 bits.

- **HCS**—8 bits.

An SS disregards any Bandwidth Request PDUs received from a BS.

The Privacy Sublayer

A concern surrounding wireless networks is their vulnerability to service theft and hacking. The 802.16 standard specifies security procedures designed to protect the network from service theft and ensure the safety and integrity of transported data.

Packet data encryption is used to secure the MAC PDU payload. Using digital certificates and public key encryption techniques, the BS authorizes and authenticates each SS and encrypts subsequent data. The BS and SS create three security associations (SAs), primary, static, and dynamic. The primary SA is created at SS initialization. The BS creates static SAs and either a BS or an SS can create dynamic SAs as they create or delete service flows. The BS authorizes the SS using its basic CID, digital certificate, and the SS-specified cryptographic capabilities. During operation, the BS periodically reauthorized the SS. Service flow SAs are mapped to the flows' CIDs.

The PHY

The PHY provides the physical carrier for the MAC layer PDUs. The 802.16 standard specifies a PHY operating in the 10 to 66-GHz licensed and nonlicensed frequency bands. It also specifies two different structures for uplink and downlink channels. The uplink PHY uses both Demand Assigned Multiple Access (DAMA) and Time Division Multiple Access (TDMA) techniques to divide the uplink channel into time slots. TDMA divides the available channel bandwidth into a sequence of frames, and DAMA allows the BS to assign these frames to uplink connections on demand, allowing for more efficient use of the available bandwidth. After the connection is released, the bandwidth is made available for other connections.

The downlink PHY uses time-division multiplexing (TDM) to multiplex SS data into a continuous stream simultaneously received by all stations. Because it does not share downlink bandwidth with any other station, the BS need not concern itself with contention in the downlink path. The downlink may also use DAMA-TDMA techniques to support bursty traffic, such as IP data. Techniques that are or may be used in both directions are: Forward Error Correction (FEC); Quadrature Phase Shift Keying (QPSK); 16-Quadrature Amplitude Modulation (QAM), which is mandatory in the uplink and optional on the downlink PHY; and 64-QAM, which is optional in both the uplink and downlink PHY. To support full duplex SSs, Frequency Division Duplexing (FDD) provides for separate uplink and downlink channel frequencies.

802.16 Network Example

The Sample 802.16 Network Diagram illustrates a potential 802.16 standards-based wireless network application.

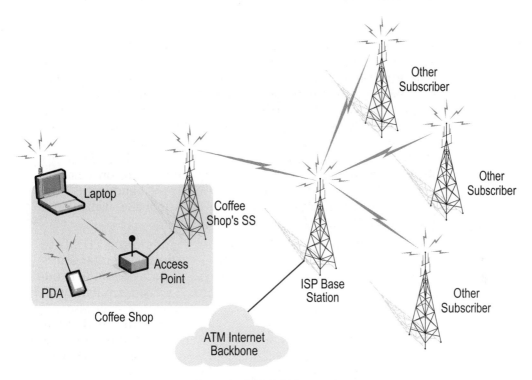

Sample 802.16 Network

A chain of coffee shops provides its customers a wireless Internet hotspot. Customers bring their palmtop or laptop computers to the store, sit down, order a cup of coffee, and request a connection to the store's IEEE 802.11b wireless LAN. The LAN access point then connects over a wired connection to the store's 802.16 SS. All customer Internet connections share a common SFID and CID and receive best effort service from the 802.16 uplink. Internet traffic to and from each client is identified by the client's IP address, included as part of the MAC PDU payload.

The BS is located two miles away at a local ISP's facility. Using sectorized antennas, this BS supports SSs scattered over several square miles. The coffee shop SS's basic, primary, secondary, and service flow CIDs uniquely identify its traffic from among the other traffic sharing the same channel and sector. The BS connects to the ISP's network over an ATM backbone.

The coffee shop's customers access the Internet just as they would over any wired connection. After the shop's 802.11b wireless LAN authorizes the customers' connections, they are able to transfer files, send and receive e-mail, and even make Internet telephone calls. Because of the 802.16 network's built-in encryption, customers can feel confident that their sensitive information will not be intercepted and stolen. In fact, the store's customers could use tunneling protocols to further secure connections to their office networks, adding additional insurance against data theft.

Activities

1. Which technology allows an 802.16 network to support full duplex SSs?

    a. 64-QAM

    b. TDMA

    c. FDD

    d. QPSK

2. What does an SS do with a bandwidth request header it receives from a BS?

    a. Sends a bandwidth request acknowledgement

    b. Checks the BS's digital certificate before processing the request

    c. Disregards any bandwidth request frames received from a BS

    d. Assigns the requested bandwidth automatically

3. An 802.16 service specific CS can map which of the following higher layer data characteristics to QoS treatments? (Choose three.)

    a. VLAN ID

    b. IP address

    c. SFID

    d. ToS bits

4. The 802.16 MAC CPS performs which of the following functions? (Choose two.)

    a. Maps higher layer data to service flows

    b. Transports connection establishment messages

    c. Encrypts MAC PDU payloads

    d. Schedules QoS specific polling intervals

5. Which message does an SS use to establish a new service flow?

    a. DSA-REQ

    b. DHCP-REQ

    c. DSA-RVD

    d. RNG-REQ

Extended Activities

1. The IEEE 802.16 working groups is developing a number of amendments to the basic standard. Research these amendments and describe how they alter or improve the original standard.

   _____

   _____

   _____

   _____

   _____

   _____

2. How does the 802.16 standard improve upon the well-publicized security vulnerabilities of the 802.11 wireless LAN standards?

   _____

   _____

Lesson 6—Sample Network

This lesson provides an overview of a network in use today. Primary functions of the example company LAN are file sharing, device sharing such as printers, access to the customer and project tracking databases, access to the company WAN for electronic mail (e-mail) and file sharing with remote locations, access to the Internet and company intranet, and remote dial-in access.

Objectives

At the end of this lesson you will be able to:

- Understand how T1, frame relay, and ATM are incorporated in a medium-sized business

- Understand a business's general connectivity strategy

Key Point

Most networks consist of multiple LAN and WAN technologies.

Role of the Network in the Organization

The example company is project-based, designing, installing, and maintaining Layer 1, 2, and 3 devices for LANs, WANs, and MANs. The network provides project tracking of approximately 3,500 projects annually. Projects originate from, and are managed by, 10 regional offices in the western United States, as well as from corporate headquarters. The network serves human resources in recruiting, and accounting in financial tracking and reporting. Sales and marketing information is distributed, Internet connectivity is used for browsing, and e-mail is provided with a single connection company-wide. Computer-aided design and documentation (CADD) is provided for internal and external customers.

The LAN does not have a high-level, mission-critical function. Uses of the network are for daily operations and communication, none of which involve online supervision of systems or direct revenue generation, such as point of purchase, call center, or online order placement. The Sample Network Diagram illustrates the example network that is the subject of this lesson.

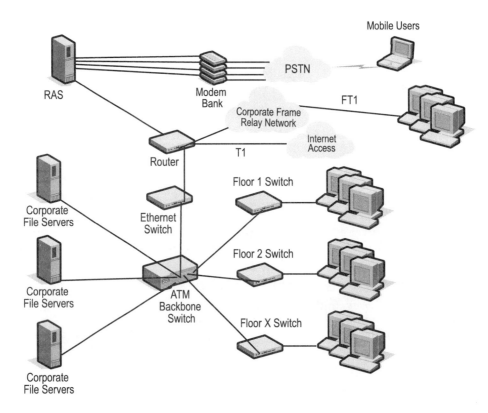

Sample Network

Primary Applications Used by the Organization

The primary applications of our example network use company-wide include Lotus Notes, Microsoft Outlook and Exchange, Oracle financial programs, and Microsoft Office. Additional applications are used by groups or individuals for specialized functions. These include AutoCad for customer network design and documentation, PageMaker for desktop publishing of sales collateral material, and FrontPage for World Wide Web (Web) site production and hosting. Network operating systems (NOSs) are Microsoft Windows NT and Novell NetWare.

General Connectivity Strategy

The strategy for the example LAN is to provide universal connectivity for all employees to applications, file sharing, printer sharing, and e-mail, for the purpose of minimizing WAN traffic and preventing catastrophic failures of the network for more than several hours.

Service to remote locations is scalable according to the number of employees and whether there is a sales or operational function, or both. All offices have migrated beyond dial-in access. The smallest regional offices have dedicated 56-kilobits-per-second (Kbps) service to the frame relay cloud.

Initially, regional offices are set up as clients to servers at area offices or headquarters. As offices grow in number of employees or become both sales and operations centers and traffic grows, servers are set up and applications such as the Lotus Notes project tracking program become resident on those servers. Additional local resources, such as CADD, are added as needed.

Overall WAN/LAN Topologies

The LAN is actually part of a campus network in the headquarters building. Approximately 50 workstations are used by headquarters employees. Workstations and devices such as printers are connected by Category 5 unshielded twisted pair (UTP) cable to ports on an Ethernet switch.

The "campus" is a six-floor office building. Each floor is served with a switch. (Only three switches are shown on the Sample Network Diagram.) These Ethernet switches are connected to an ATM 155-Mbps backbone. Routers and gateways are centrally located on the lower level of the building.

A router connects the LAN to the WAN, which is a frame relay service. The architecture for the LAN includes TCP/IP and Ethernet 802.3. Routers use the Interior Gateway Routing Protocol (IGRP), a routing protocol used to determine the best path between routers, for support of IP and Internetwork Packet Exchange (IPX) Novell clients.

Remote office connectivity to the frame relay cloud is performed using dedicated access circuits. Headquarters is served by a T1 access circuit. Remote offices are served by DS0 and fractional T1s (FT1s) from 128 to 384 Kbps. The virtual private circuit committed information rates (CIRs) range from 1 to 64 Kbps.

Future Growth Plans and Migration Strategies

Plans for future growth revolve around sizing the area and regional offices by the number of employees, number of projects in progress, and whether CADD is to be provided in the office. An important growth driver is videoconferencing, which is being considered to save personnel time and travel costs. The frame relay service for the WAN is easily scalable according to actual and projected traffic needs.

Activities

1. What applications are found in your organization?

    _____

    _____

    _____

    _____

2. How does the network play a role in your use of each application?

    _____

    _____

    _____

    _____

3. Describe the ATM, frame relay, and T1 elements of the sample network in terms of function.

    _____

    _____

    _____

    _____

4. In the example network in this lesson, why is the company trying to minimize WAN traffic?

    _____

    _____

    _____

    _____

5. Do you think videoconferencing is specific only to organizations such as this, or is it a widespread need in today's organizations?

_____

_____

_____

_____

6. How does videoconferencing benefit an organization?

_____

_____

_____

_____

Extended Activities

1. Draw a diagram of a network using the following number of users, servers, and technologies:

   a. Two sites connected by means of an ATM WAN using SONET. The WAN is a service provided by a long-distance carrier.

   b. Each site consists of a switched backbone Ethernet network. There are four workgroups attached to the backbone switch, each workgroup contains its own server and 20 clients. The backbone is 100 Mbps, and the workgroups are 10-Mbps switched to the desktop. There are also three servers attached to the backbone that all clients can access.

   c. Each site is connected to the Internet by means of frame relay.

Summary

B-ISDN uses a form of cell relay called "ATM." ATM operates at Layer 1 with small cells, rather than the large frames used by T-carrier technology. B-ISDN provides T3 and SONET speeds, which are now generally available.

ATM technology is gaining widespread acceptance in LAN, MAN, and WAN environments. ATM's ability to transfer many different types of information at high speeds gives it the capability to handle virtually any type of end-user traffic.

SMDS is a connectionless, cell-switched service. Like ATM, it uses 53-byte cells that each carry a 48-byte payload; however, SMDS uses a different format for its 5-byte cell header. Its data rate (T1 to T3) takes over where frame relay leaves off. However, SMDS is not a good choice for WANs that cross LATA boundaries, because federal law limits SMDS to metropolitan-area service only.

Higher-layer WAN protocols work together to provide LAN, MAN, and WAN connectivity for large and small businesses. By combining the different technologies, businesses can build a cost-effective, reliable enterprise network spanning tens, hundreds, or thousands of miles and serving thousands of users.

The IEEE 802.16 standard, which specifies a broadband, wireless, last-mile connectivity solution for MANs, WANs, and Internet connections. The standard specifies two protocol layers, the MAC and PHY layers. The MAC layer specifies three sublayers; the Convergence Sublayer (CS), the MAC Common Part Sublayer (MAC CPS), and the Privacy Sublayer.

The CS maps higher layer data, such as ATM cells and IP packets, to service flows and connections, providing end-to-end QoS for each mapped flow. A combined SFID and CID identify each admitted and active service flow. The MAC CPS builds MAC PDUs (frames) for transporting data and management messages across the wireless link. The Privacy Sublayer authenticates and authorizes SSs and encrypts the data payloads.

The PHY handles radio frequency and time slot assignments, signal modulation and error detection and correction. The 802.16 standard connections can take the place of traditional wireline services, such as xDSL, Cable Modem, or ATM.

Unit 6 Quiz

1. ATM is used in which of the following situations?

   a. Wide-area networking

   b. Backbone connectivity

   c. Desktop-to-networking device (such as an ATM switch) connectivity

   d. All of the above

2. Why can ATM effectively carry multiple types of information?

   a. It uses cells to transfer information.

   b. It uses SONET as a transmission medium.

   c. It uses T3 as a transmission medium.

   d. It transfers data in a connectionless fashion.

3. Which of the following is true of both ATM and frame relay?

   a. They are both connection-oriented.

   b. They were both developed for voice and data.

   c. They were both introduced by IEEE.

   d. They both use cells to transmit information.

4. Which of the following is a disadvantage of using a connection-oriented service?

   a. Real-time applications cannot use connection-oriented services.

   b. The setup time for connection-oriented services is longer than connectionless services.

   c. A connection-oriented service is unable to efficiently carry multimedia.

   d. A connection-oriented service offers a lower speed of information transfer.

5. Which of the following best describes the use of the ATM layer of ATM?

   a. Map Network Layer protocols into ATM cells

   b. Map Transport Layer protocols into PDUs

   c. Map cells onto the physical media

   d. Add the ATM header before transmission to the next node in the network

6. The AAL is divided into which two sublayers?

   a. AAL and convergence sublayers

   b. Convergence and ATM sublayers

   c. Convergence and SAR sublayers

   d. AAL and ATM sublayers

7. Which of the following does the VCI in the ATM header identify?

   a. Virtual channel

   b. Virtual circuit

   c. Virtual communication

   d. Valid channel

8. Which of the following is true concerning ATM?

   a. VPs can contain multiple ATM networks.

   b. Virtual channels can contain multiple VPs.

   c. VPs can contain multiple virtual channels.

   d. Permanent paths can contain multiple virtual channels.

9. Which of the following is not a networking transfer mode?

   a. STM

   b. PTM

   c. ATM

   d. FTM

10. Which of the following are functions of ATM cells?

    a. Efficient switching

    b. Prioritization of time-sensitive traffic

    c. Simplification of ATM switch design

    d. All of the above

11. Which of the following voice communication technologies is being replaced by the other three, which are considered alternative technologies?

    a. TCP/IP

    b. Frame relay

    c. ATM

    d. Leased lines

12. To which of the following does the concept of tunneling refer?

    a. Putting information inside IP packets to be transferred across the Internet

    b. Putting IP packets inside PPP packets for transfer across the Internet

    c. Putting IP packets inside IPX packets for transfer across the Internet

    d. Using the Internet for security purposes

13. Which of the following protocols is considered Physical Layer only?

    a. ATM

    b. T1

    c. IP

    d. Frame relay

14. Which of the following protocols was initially designed for multimedia (voice, video, and data)?

    a. Frame relay

    b. T1 and T3

    c. ATM

    d. SONET

15. To which of the following might a FRAD refer?

    a. A device used to send voice technology over an IP network

    b. A router used to connect LANs using frame relay

    c. A switch that interfaces ATM to an Ethernet network

    d. A frame relay application

16. Which factors effect an xDSL line's performance? (Choose two.)

    a. The standards supported by the connecting modems

    b. The number of B-channels provisioned on the xDSL link

    c. The number of splices and noise on the local loop

    d. Mismatched wire gauges between the CO and the subscriber

17. Which two are services offered by X.25? (Choose two.)

    a. SVCs

    b. PVCs

    c. Virtual connections

    d. Physical connections

18. Which X.25 protocol manages connections between DCE and DTE anywhere in a network?

    a. LAPB

    b. LAPD

    c. X.21

    d. PLP

19. A PAD serves what purpose on an X.25 network?

    a. It assigns frames locally significant DLCIs as they traverse the network switches

    b. It accepts byte streams from synchronous DTE and assembles them into X.25 packets

    c. It provides an interface between the PSTN and the packet network

    d. It accepts data from an asynchronous DTE and assembles that data into X.25 packets

20. Which are the three X.25 virtual circuit stages? (Choose three.)

    a. Call setup

    b. Call cancel

    c. Data transfer

    d. Call clearing

21. For which reasons might you choose Frame relay over X.25 WAN connectivity? (Choose two.)

    a. Frame relay can support greater bandwidths than can X.25

    b. Frame relay provides higher reliability than does X.25

    c. Frame relay requires less overhead than does X.25

    d. Frame relay requires no virtual channel, only physical circuits

22. The point at which the CPE interfaces with the SMDS network is called which of the following?

    a. SNI

    b. UNI

    c. SIP

    d. PLP

23. Which SMDS specification provides a standard interface between a router and the CSU/DSU?

    a. DXI

    b. SNI

    c. SIP

    d. UNI

24. Which U.S. Department of Justice action limits SMDS to inter-LATA-only communications?

    a. Telecommunications Act of 1996

    b. MFJ

    c. Hush-a-Phone Decision

    d. Federal Communications Act of 1954

25. Which PBX feature can provide the appearance of two lines when only one telephone number is provisioned?

    a. Call park

    b. Call forwarding

    c. Call accounting

    d. Call waiting

26. A cell differs from a packet and frame in which of the following ways?

    a. A cell is much slower than a frame or packet.

    b. A cell is used in connectionless networks.

    c. A cell can be used to transfer analog information.

    d. A cell is a fixed-length entity.

27. Which of the following protocols was initially designed for multimedia?

    a. Frame relay

    b. T1 and T3

    c. ATM

    d. SONET

28. Which IEEE standard specifies the MAC and Physical Layer protocols for a fixed wireless MAN service?

    a. 802.3

    b. 802.11

    c. 802.16

    d. 802.66

29. The 802.16 standard specifies a wireless network operating in which frequency range?

    a. 1to 11MHz

    b. 10 to 66MHz

    c. 10to 66GHz

    d. 2 to 11GHz

30. An 802.16 BS authenticates and authorizes an SS with which vendor-assigned component?

    a. SFID

    b. Digital certificate

    c. Security association

    d. MAC address

31. Which of the following is the 802.16 network component that connects user equipment to the wireless links?

    a. Access point

    b. Subscriber station

    c. Base station

    d. Wireless hub

32. How long is an 802.16 SS's MAC address?

    a. 8-bits

    b. 16-bits

    c. 32-bits

    d. 48-bits

    e. 64-bits

33. SMDS is best suited for data transport. True or False

34. SMDS is designed to support WAN communications. True or False

35. Frame relay is always a more cost-effective solution than T1. True or False

36. The Internet is a relatively inexpensive way to provide WAN connectivity. True or False

37. ATM, SONET, T1, and frame relay can be used within the same network. True or False

Unit 7
Convergence of Communications Over WAN Technologies

This unit discusses how wide area network (WAN) technologies support and help implement converged communications, voice, video, and data, all transported over the same physical network topologies. Increasingly, companies are investigating and installing these combined services, and vendors are finding new and better ways to support the diverse reliability and bandwidth requirements each service demands. WAN technologies carrying this converged traffic include Asynchronous Transfer Mode (ATM), frame relay, Digital Subscriber Line (DSL), and Integrated Services Digital Network (ISDN) circuits.

We will investigate components key to integrating public-switched telephone network (PSTN) and data communications. We will examine the market drivers pushing the demand for converged technologies. We will also look at more traditional PSTN offerings, and how they can help enterprises meet their communications requirements now and in the future.

Lessons

1. Voice Over Alternative Technologies

2. Fundamental VoIP Network Components

3. Factors Driving the Demand for Packet Telephony

4. Private VPNs

5. PSTN Remote Access

Terms

access concentrator—An access concentrator is a network device used to combine multiple communications lines onto a single, high-speed output link.

Adaptive Differential Pulse Code Modulation (ADPCM)—ADPCM is a form of PCM that produces the digital signal at a lower bit rate than does standard PCM. ADPCM records only the difference between samples rather than sample the entire waveform. ADPCM can reduce the resultant signal's digital bandwidth by one-half that of PCM.

application programming interface (API)—An API is a software interface that formats requests from an application software to a NOS. Telephony APIs, such as TAPI, TSAPI, and JTAPI, format requests from application software to a telephone system, such as a PBX.

Automatic Call Distributor (ACD)—An ACD is a programmable system that controls how inbound calls are received, held, delayed, treated, and distributed to call center agents.

Automatic Route Selection (ARS)—ARS is a private branch exchange (PBX) feature that enables the system to automatically choose the least cost route to the destination. ARS is also known as least cost routing (LCR).

bearer circuit—A bearer circuit is a basic communication channel as defined in signaling hierarchy. In a VoIP network, a bearer circuit is a particular end-to-end media stream from the PSTN to the gateway, or across the packet network between communicating nodes.

call agent—See media gateway controller (MGC).

Digital Subscriber Line (DSL) access multiplexer (DSLAM)—A DSLAM is a mechanism at the LEC's CO that links many customer DSL connections to a single high-speed ATM line.

drop-and-insert equipment—Drop-and-insert equipment is used by a carrier circuit's subscriber to demodulate the circuit (drop) at some intermediate point and add information (insert) for transmission on the same circuit. An ATM ADM is an example of drop-and-insert equipment.

European Telecommunications Standards Institute (ETSI)—
ETSI is an international, nonprofit organization that produces telecommunications standards used in Europe and elsewhere. For more information, visit **http://www.etsi.org**.

extranet—An extranet is a broader form of a private intranet. Extranets are private TCP/IP networks that are shared between closely aligned organizations, and are not available to the general public.

frame tagging—Frame tagging is a technique used to identify a frame's membership in a VLAN segment. As a frame is forwarded through the network, frame tagging places a unique identifier in the frame's header. Each network switch that understands the tagging protocol ensures that only those switches, routers, or end nodes that compose the VLAN's membership receive the frame. Once the tagged frame leaves the VLAN (for example, by means of a routed link), the edge device removes the tag.

G.711—G.711 is one of a series of ITU-T voice digitizing algorithms. G.711 transfers digitized audio at 48, 56, and 64 Kbps.

G.722—G.722 is one of a series of ITU-T voice digitizing algorithms. G.722 transfers digitized audio at 32 Kbps.

G.723—G.723 is one of a series of ITU-T voice digitizing algorithms. G.723 transfers digitized audio at 5.3 or 6.3 Kbps.

G.728—G.728 is one of a series of ITU-T voice digitizing algorithms. G.728 transfers digitized audio at 16 Kbps.

G.729—G.729 is one of a series of ITU-T voice digitizing algorithms. G.729 transfers digitized audio at 8 Kbps.

gatekeeper—A network device or process that controls data flow on a transmission channel or allocates transmission bandwidth among multiple competing signals is referred to as a gatekeeper.

H.225—H.225 is an ITU-T recommendation that specifies the messages used by H.323 endpoints to control call admissions, registration, bandwidth, status, and call signaling.

H.245—H.245 is an ITU-T recommendation that specifies the H.323 call control messages that govern how endpoints operate across the half-duplex logical connections. H.245 messages control endpoint capabilities exchange, opening and closing of logical channels, flow control, and so forth.

H.248/Megaco—Megaco, in conjunction with ITU-T H.248, is the signaling protocol used between the MGCP, MG, and MGC.

H.261—H.261 is an ITU-T video coding algorithm designed to support link data rates of 64 Kbps.

H.263—H.263 is an ITU-T video coding algorithm designed to support link data rates of under 64 Kbps.

H.310—H.310 is the ITU-T multimedia conferencing recommendation for voice and video terminals supporting end-to-end conversations over broadband connections, such as ATM.

H.320—H.320 is the ITU-T multimedia conferencing recommendation for voice and video terminals supporting end-to-end conversations over narrowband connections, such as ISDN-BRI.

H.321—H.321 is the ITU-T recommendation for adapting the H.320 recommendation to broadband ATM networks.

H.322—H.322 is the ITU-T multimedia conferencing recommendation for video conferencing over LANs providing QoS.

H.323—H.323 is the ITU-T recommended set of standards and protocols used to support multimedia conferencing on packet-based, best effort networks, such as the Internet and IP LANs. Included in the recommendation are several protocols that control call set up and tear down and voice and video signal conversion and compression.

H.324—H.324 is the ITU-T recommendation for multimedia conferencing over low speed connections, such as dial up modem links. H.263 and G.723 are the video and voice codecs specified.

incumbent local exchange carrier (ILEC)—An ILEC is the same as a LEC or RBOC.

Intelligent Information (II) Digits—II Digits is a two-digit string used with ANI to identify an incoming call type over ISDN-PRI services. Subscribers can detect, route, and block calls based on II Digit information.

intermediate distribution frame (IDF)—An IDF is an equipment room or closet that provides intermediate connectivity between the MDF and individual end device wiring. The network backbone runs between the MDF and IDF.

International Softswitch Consortium (ISC)—The ISC is an organization of more than 130 members that supports the development of applications that provide multimedia communications across IP networks. Learn more about the ISC at **http://www.softswitch.org**.

Internet Engineering Task Force (IETF)—IETF is the official standards body responsible for the development and adoption of many Internet-based standards.

Internet telephony service provider (ITSP)—An ITSP is a provider of Internet-based telephony services, supplying packetized voice interfaces to the local and remote PSTN.

Java Telephony Application Programming Interface (JTAPI)—JTAPI is a telephony-to-computer API using Java, a programming language developed by Sun Microsystems. Java transcends proprietary or machine-specific computer languages. A Java program will run on any Java-compliant machine with no, or only slight, modification.

latency—Latency is the transmission delay created as a device processes a frame or packet. It is the duration from the time a device reads the first byte of a frame or packet, until the time it forwards that byte.

listed directory number (LDN)—The LDN is a subscriber's or device's main telephone number. An LDN is the primary service number for an end device.

main distribution frame (MDF)—An MDF is an equipment room or closet that connects the outside plant network cabling to the inside plant cabling, such as connecting a local VoIP network to an ISP's network.

media gateway (MG)—The MG is the MGCP component that provides the interface between the public switched telephone network (PSTN) and the packet network and is responsible for converting voice signals to packets, and vice versa.

media gateway controller (MGC)—An MGC, also known as a call agent, is the MGCP component responsible for call signal processing. The MGC converts PSTN signaling, either dual tone multi-frequency (DTMF) or Signaling System 7 (SS7) messages, to packetized data. The MGC controls the MG.

Media Gateway Control Protocol (MGCP)—MGCP is described by RFC 2705 as a protocol and set of components for processing voice over IP calls. MGCP uses MGs to convert analog voice to packetized voice, and separate MGCs that handle call signaling. Compared to H.323, this process simplifies the media gateway component by offloading call signal processing to the MGC.

multipoint control unit (MCU)—MCUs are hosts that coordinate multipoint conferences of three or more terminals that use the H.323 packet multimedia standards. All H.323 terminals participating in a conference must establish a connection with the MCU.

network control point (NCP)—An NCP is an SDN node on which the user's VPN database resides. The NCP determines whether calls remain on the VPN, or must leave the VPN to travel over standard PSTN services.

network management system (NMS)—An NMS consists of the servers, workstations, and software that enable network monitoring, management, and configuration.

network service provider—A network service provider is a company that provides network services, such as Internet access, frame relay, ATM, and others, through its own private network infrastructure.

packet telephony—Packet telephony is voice telephone service provided over connectionless packet networks, instead of the public-switched telephone service.

Q.SIG (or QSIG)—Also known as PSS1, Q.SIG is an ISO standard that defines the ISDN signaling and control methods used to link PBXs in private ISDN networks. The standard extends the "Q" point in the ISDN logical reference model, which was established by ITU-T in its Q.93x series of recommendations that defined the basic functions of ISDN switching systems. Q.SIG signaling allows certain ISDN features to work in a single or multivendor network.

Regional Bell Operating Company (RBOC)—An RBOC is one of seven companies formed from AT&T's 22 local telephone companies during the breakup of the Bell system. An RBOC makes telephone connections to subscribers' homes and businesses, provides telephone services, and collects fees for those services. The original seven RBOCs were Ameritech, Bell Atlantic, Bellsouth, New York New England Telephone Company (NYNEX), Pacific Telesis, Southwestern Bell Communications, and USWest. The terms RBOC, Local Exchange Carrier (LEC), and Incumbent Local Exchange Carrier (ILEC) are equivalent.

Remote Monitoring (RMON)—RMON is a protocol that gathers network information at a central workstation. RMON defines additional management information bases (MIBs) that provide more detailed information about network usage and status than MIBs defined by SNMP.

Resource Reservation Protocol (RSVP)—RSVP is a new Internet protocol developed to enable the Internet to support specified QoSs. By using RSVP, an application is able to reserve resources along a route from source to destination. RSVP-enabled routers schedule and prioritize packets to fulfill the QoS.

Session Initiation Protocol (SIP)—SIP is the RFC 2543-recommended Application Layer protocol for simplified signaling on multimedia IP network sessions.

Simple Network Management Protocol (SNMP)—SNMP is a TCP/IP Application Layer protocol used to send and receive information about the status of network resources on a TCP/IP network. Data networks frequently support SNMP functionality, while traditional voice networks do not.

Software Defined Network (SDN)—SDN is AT&T's 4ESS switch-based Virtual Private Network (VPN) product used to create private corporate voice networks over public facilities. An SDN operates as a private line, but has lower costs.

T1-emulated tandem tie trunks—Using certain T1 signaling techniques, T1 circuit channels can emulate analog tie trunks or tandem tie trunks. A tandem tie trunk connects PBXs by means of an intermediate PBX. The intermediate PBX acts as a relay between the source and destination PBXs.

Telephony Application Programming Interface (TAPI)—TAPI is an API introduced in 1993 by Microsoft and Intel, to add telephony features to the family of Windows products. The first version of TAPI focused largely on first-party call control. The current version (TAPI 3.0) supports third-party control and features such as media streaming. An increasing number of vendors are offering products that support both TSAPI and TAPI.

telephony gateway—A telephony gateway is a specially equipped computer or router that forms the interface between a telephone network and IP network, converting voice telephone calls to IP data, or packetized calls to standard telephone signals.

Telephony Server Application Programming Interface (TSAPI)—TSAPI is an API developed by Novell and Lucent Technologies to allow LAN-connected CTI applications third-party control. In this API, a data link between the telephone system and a server on a LAN provides telephony applications on the LAN the ability to control various telephone and computer functions. An increasing number of vendors are offering products that support both TSAPI and TAPI.

tunneling—Tunneling is a technology that lets a network protocol carry information for other protocols within its own packets (for example, carrying IPX packets inside IP packets). The packets may be secured using data encryption techniques.

type of service (ToS)/quality of service (QoS)—Users of the Transport Layer specify QoS or ToS parameters as part of a request for a communications channel. QoS parameters define different levels of service based on the requirements of an application. For example, an interactive application that needs good response time would specify high QoS values for connection establishment delay, throughput, transit delay, and connection priority. However, a file transfer application needs reliable, error-free data transfer more than it needs a prompt connection, thus it would request high QoS parameters for residual error rate/probability.

unified messaging—Also known as integrated messaging, unified messaging allows you to receive, send, and interact with all your messaging sources (voice, e-mail, fax, voice mail, and so on) from a single central location.

uniform (universal) dial plan—A uniform dial plan is a private network numbering system that assigns unique extension numbers to each user, regardless of location. If locations in different cities are linked in a private telephone network, a uniform dial plan allows employees in different cities to dial each other using only extension numbers.

Universal Service Fund (USF)—The USF is a component of the Telecommunications Act of 1996. It is designed to provide discounted telecommunications services to certain schools, libraries, and rural hospitals, and serves to subsidize telephone service to high-cost rural areas and low-income households.

vector directory number (VDN)—A VDN is an extension number used in automatic call distributor (ACD) software to connect calls to a vector for processing. The VDN by itself may be dialed to access the vector from any extension connected to the switch.

virtual local area network (VLAN)—A VLAN is a group of computers in a large LAN that behave as if they are connected to their own small, private LAN. We create VLANs using special switches and software, and can assign computers to different VLANs without changing their physical configuration.

virtual private network (VPN)—A VPN is a connection over a shared network that behaves like a dedicated link. VPNs are created using a technique called "tunneling," which transmits data packets across a public network, such as the Internet or other commercially available network, in a private "tunnel" that simulates a point-to-point connection. The tunnels of a VPN can be encrypted for additional security.

Voice Activity Detection (VAD)—VAD is a method of detecting pauses in speech and saving bandwidth by not transmitting these pauses with the voice intelligence.

voice-capable router (vrouter)—A vrouter is a voice-capable router that provides inside interfaces to both local data and voice networks and an outside interface to a WAN. A vrouter packetizes voice data for transmission over the WAN, and can provide QoS functions.

voice frame relay access device (VFRAD)—A VFRAD is a device that encapsulates voice packets into frame relay frames. A VFRAD is located between the voice network and frame relay network, where it multiplexes voice, fax, and data traffic, and can provide essential voice over frame relay services, such as echo cancellation, compression, and encryption.

Voice over Internet Protocol (VoIP)—VoIP is a technology that consists of telephone signals transmitted as IP packets. See packet telephony.

Wildfire—Wildfire is a voice-activated virtual personal assistant created by Wildfire Communications, Inc. See **http://www.wildfire.com** for more information.

Worldwide Intelligent Network (WIN)—According to AT&T, WIN is the largest, most sophisticated communications network in the world. Over this network of SONET OC-192 backbone links, AT&T carries more than 675 terabytes of data and 300 million voice calls in an average day.

Lesson 1—Voice Over Alternative Technologies

Advances in telecommunications technology have reached a point of convergence between networks and services that historically have been separate. Traditionally, businesses have used multiple networks to carry various types of traffic, such as voice and data. Combining these various networks into one, and running a single, cost-efficient technology capable of supporting voice and data has been a long-term goal.

Although the idea of a single network has been around for years, it has not been until recently that advances in technology have ignited general interest from the business marketplace. Understanding network and technological alternatives, and deciding which one is most advantageous for a particular business, is the challenge.

Objectives

At the end of this lesson you will be able to:

- Name alternatives for sending voice over different technologies

- Explain market drivers of voice over alternative technologies

- Name three principle alternatives and their advantages and limitations

Key Point

New voice over technologies are gaining tremendous popularity.

History

Imagine a large multinational corporation with multiple domestic facilities as well as international facilities. Each location is connected by means of a variety of separate networks (on public and private carriers), to carry voice, data, and video transfer traffic. Imagine a mid-size manufacturing company with several locations across the United States. What do these scenarios have in common? Both are typical of many organizations today, in that they are using multiple networks, facilities, and technologies to carry their voice and data traffic between locations. In the past, organizations have been forced to use divergent networks, depending on their telecommunications application. Voice traffic would traditionally traverse the PSTN. Data would ride on a private network of dedicated connections, or possibly a public-switched data network. The older data networks were often low-speed analog connections susceptible to network-induced errors with questionable dependency. Businesses incurred costs for each network connection, as well as for traffic sent over each.

Market Drivers

One of the primary market drivers for voice over alternative technologies is the need to reduce telecommunications costs. The majority of business customers are looking for ways to cut communications expenditures, while maintaining quality and functionality. The desired result is to lower costs, open up network resources for new applications, and make the network more responsive to increasingly demanding business needs. In addition, there is interest in gaining the capabilities of sophisticated, multimedia applications that are possible by means of new, high-capacity, fiber-based data networks.

With the evolution of technology, voice traffic can now be transported over packet data networks using the Internet Protocol (IP). Although this seems relatively minor, it is critical in the push for cost reduction by means of IP solutions. This is because IP data traffic is tariffed differently than conventional voice traffic over switched-circuit networks. In the United States, IP data services are considered special services, and do not fall under normal telephony tariffs. Conversely, switched-circuit telephony rates are regulated by national and local governments, protecting local monopolies from price competition. This makes international connections particularly expensive.

Over the years, communication networks have become very reliable. In addition, devices communicating between sites have become more intelligent, enabling them to more readily accommodate network delay, and the need to recover from and retransmit lost data. Unlike most data communications that can tolerate delay, voice communication must be performed in near real time. This means transmission and network delays must be kept small enough to remain imperceptible to a user. Until recently, packetized voice transmission was unattainable due to voice bandwidth requirements and transmission delays associated with packet-based networks.

Human speech is burdened with a tremendous amount of redundant information that is necessary for communication to occur in the natural environment; however, the redundant information is not necessary for a conversation to occur over a communications network. Analysis of a representative voice sample shows that only 22 percent of a typical dialog consists of essential speech components that need to be transmitted for complete voice clarity. This information is presented on the Speech Components Diagram. The balance is made up of pauses, background noise, and repetitive patterns.

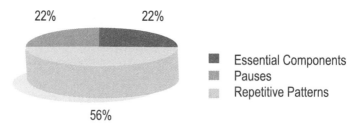

22%   22%

■ Essential Components
▨ Pauses
▨ Repetitive Patterns

56%

Speech Components

Packetized voice is possible and low bit rates are achieved by analyzing and processing only the essential components of the voice sample, rather than attempting to digitize the entire voice sample (with all the associated pauses and repetitive patterns). Current speech processing technology takes the voice digitizing process several steps further than conventional encoding methods.

Voice Over the Internet

For several years, a variety of companies have tried to capitalize on the capabilities of the Internet network, and the idea of Internet telephony evolved. These companies offered products that ran on multimedia computers and required the party on each end to use the same software and have similarly equipped computers (with microphones and sound cards) and flat-rate Internet access. The basic problem with this setup was that the quality tended to be below par, and sounded more like citizens band (CB) communications between truckers than a traditional telephone call over the PSTN.

Many people are drawn to the idea of voice over the Internet, and the idea of making calls for "free." This is a fallacy, because there are many associated costs, such as additional network capacity, equipment, equipment upgrades, software, and so on.

The next phase of development deals with gateways. Gateways bridge the traditional circuit-switched telephone network with that of the Internet. A gateway user places a voice call to a service provider's local "point of presence" (POP) or central office (CO). Here the call is received by the gateway, which authorizes the voice signal to be changed into data messages and sent over the Internet (or another packet-based network such as frame relay). As gateways develop, they will be able to interconnect with business-grade telephone systems and offer a wide degree of functionality, such as traditional dialing and calling features. For corporate customers, and especially carriers and other service providers who plan to incorporate the Internet for delivery of voice calls, gateways are critical.

Quality of service (QoS) appears to be equally or more important than cost for many customers. This is especially true given that the price of traditional public-switched services has dropped to near commodity levels. Analyst interviews with Fortune 1,000 customers (Yankee Group, 1997) reflect that impacts to call quality would be unacceptable for "mission-critical" communications with customers. The quality of a call is influenced by bandwidth availability, latency management, echo cancellation, and lost packet reconstruction. The Internet, which was not designed for voice data, offers no means of specifically addressing these needs. However, the Internet Engineering Task Force (IETF) is working to define standards that support this technology (for example, Resource Reservation Protocol [RSVP] that allows users to reserve bandwidth). Because these standards are only recommendations, it may take a significant amount of time before they are incorporated into equipment and software. Widespread deployment of these capabilities may take even longer. Yet without these capabilities, the quality of a voice call is jeopardized. Just as there is a cost for quality, there is a price for reduced quality if it impacts a company's customers, productivity, and/or image.

VoFR

Frame relay is a high-speed interface standard for connection to packet-based network services. Dynamic bandwidth allocations support the characteristically "bursty" traffic of business environments. Performance often relies on high-quality lines that decrease the need for error checking and control functions. Voice over frame relay (VoFR) technology offers the possibility to consolidate voice and voice-band data (for example, fax and analog modems) with data services over the frame relay network.

Just as Internet users want to use their existing Internet bandwidth, so do those businesses that have frame relay connections. Through the years, frame relay has proved to be a highly dependable, scalable, and versatile way to transfer data. To send a voice signal over frame relay it must first be converted to a data packet. This is done by means of a frame relay access device (FRAD). A FRAD must be attached to all endpoints of the network that want to transmit or receive VoFR packets. There are a variety of companies that make FRADs. FRADs can be routers or other customer premises equipment (CPE) that are attached between the local area network (LAN) and WAN.

It is expected that most companies will add voice to an existing frame relay port already transporting data applications. In this scenario, companies will need to upgrade their FRAD (or router) with voice-supported software and possibly hardware. For new implementations of frame relay, companies will purchase newer routers and FRADs that already support voice, fax, and data.

In a small-office scenario, customers will connect a telephone directly into an analog voice port on a router or FRAD. Larger set-ups will connect the private branch exchange (PBX) directly into the router by means of a T1 interface port. Fax machines will connect either directly to the router/FRAD or through the PBX.

The VoFR Diagram illustrates a typical VoFR implementation.

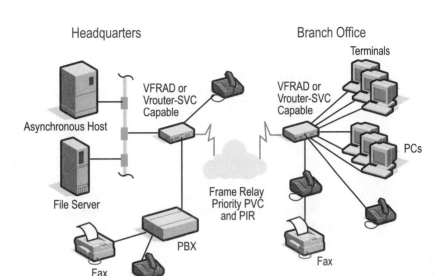

VoFR

Although implementation agreements for carrying VoFR are progressing within organizations such as the Frame Relay Forum's Technical Committee, there is currently no uniform standard or implementation agreement defined for vendor equipment interoperability or the transport of voice across a carrier's public frame relay network. In the absence of such an agreement, many equipment vendors have developed proprietary methods for integrating voice onto frame relay networks. Customers must choose carefully which vendor to select. A proprietary solution could either make their network flexible and scalable for future growth, or lock them into a system that could soon be outdated. One of the major responsibilities of the Frame Relay Forum is to establish industry standards for VoFR, such that greater interoperability would exist between different hardware and equipment vendors.

Another consideration of passing voice traffic over frame relay is proper sizing of the network. Many telecommunications carriers and FRAD suppliers recommend prioritization of voice channels to ensure available capacity and minimize the chance for delay. By designating separate permanent virtual circuits (PVCs) for data and voice packets, a business can engineer their frame relay network to optimize use and reduce the possibility of network congestion inhibiting transfer of either data or voice packets.

Voice Over ATM

ATM is a communications protocol suite for a desktop, LAN, campus backbone network, and WAN. It is based on international standards for cell-switched data transmission that allows voice, video, and data communications over a single virtual network. Inherent in the design standards of ATM is the ability to transfer voice and data together. So why hasn't everyone jumped on this technological bandwagon?

The answer lies in standards and costs. True widespread development and implementation of ATM services has been thwarted by constantly changing standards. The ATM Forum, similar to the Frame Relay Forum, is striving to establish industry standards for voice over ATM. One of the biggest problems is that various vendors are embattled in promoting their version of the ATM protocol and platform to be set as the standard. As a result of this lack of unity among ATM switch vendors, many companies are reluctant to make the significant capital expenditures required to move to the ATM platform. In addition, many companies have pushed forward with implementation of frame relay networks, rather than wait for ATM. ATM services are also generally unavailable in the market in low-bandwidth ranges. Frequently, the lowest access speed supported is T1 (1.536 megabits per second [Mbps]).

The reality is that some businesses today are implementing voice over ATM. It is gaining popularity, but will not be widespread until firm standards are established and accepted by the market, and access cost is driven down to a point where it can be considered competitive with traditional services.

Market Direction and Trends

The use of data networks for voice delivery is still a relatively new trend. With the exception of ATM, neither the Internet nor frame relay were designed with voice traffic in mind. Technology to deliver voice traffic over these two forms is being retrofitted, so to speak, to fit the transport medium (and not the other way around). In addition, there is still the question of standards. Although standards for frame relay and the Internet are relatively mature, standards for ATM seem to be in a constant state of fluctuation. This constant state of change applies to the technologies transferring voice traffic over IP-based networks as well.

As these three network technologies have developed, there has been a tendency toward the development of similar functionality (for example, access speeds, support of multimedia applications, and so on). In most cases, user requirements necessitated these changes. And now, business customers are less interested in which particular network they are using than in getting the functionality they require. In turn, service providers are seeing that a combination of technologies (for example, frame relay/ATM service) may be a better way to meet users' needs and expectations. The job is then figuring out how to make them work together.

Voice over alternative technologies is still not a tried-and-true service. The hardware and software that supports it is still not at the reliability level of circuit-switching technology, nor is the voice quality always compatible. There are still standards to be set, benchmarks to be established, and a myriad of technological details to be worked out and debugged. However, in many instances, voice over the Internet, frame relay, and ATM are currently up and functioning within organizational environments, both large and small. Groups such as the Frame Relay and ATM Forums continue to drive development and set standards among members and within the industry. Recently, the Voice on Net (VON) Coalition announced its incorporation, with the purpose to educate regulators, legislators, media, and consumers worldwide about VON technologies. Almost every major network hardware vendor is designing products to enable voice transmission over traditional data networks, because that is where the market is pushing. Businesses need to decide at what point they will embrace this technology enterprise-wide, and how it will benefit their overall corporate telecommunications direction. Voice over alternative technologies is truly a trend of the future and will only grow with time.

Activities

1. Where do you think voice networking will be in 10 years?

   _____

2. What are the problems with using the Internet for real-time voice conversations?

   _____

   _____

3. Which technology would you pick for your organization's voice network and why?

   _____

   _____

4. List and describe three alternatives for carrying voice traffic.

   _____

   _____

   _____

   _____

   _____

Extended Activities

1. Visit the following Web sites and find information on sending voice over each. Summarize your findings.

   a. ATM Forum: **http://www.atmforum.com**

   b. Frame Relay Forum: **http://www.frforum.com**

   _____

   _____

   _____

   _____

   _____

   _____

Lesson 2—Fundamental VoIP Network Components

Several components compose a Voice over IP (VoIP) network. The International Telecommunication Union-Telecommunications Standardization Sector (ITU-T) H.323 packet multimedia standard specifies terminals, multipoint control units (MCUs), gateways, and gatekeepers. The Media Gateway Control Protocol (MGCP) fundamental components include the media gateway, gateway controller, switches/routers, and PSTN. Some of these components are used in all VoIP network implementations.

Objectives

At the end of this lesson you will be able to:

- Name and describe the fundamental H.323 components found in VoIP networks

- Name and describe the fundamental MGCP components found in VoIP networks

Key Point

H.323 provides for multimedia transmission across packet networks.

Overview of the ITU-T H.323 Standard

The H.323 standard specifies the components, protocols, and procedures for transmitting real-time audio, video, and data communications over packet-based networks. Packet-based networks include IP-based (including the Internet) or Novell (Internetwork Packet Exchange [IPX])-based LANs, enterprise networks, metropolitan area networks (MANs), and WANs.

H.323 can be applied in a variety of ways, depending on the type of traffic to be transmitted:

- Audio only (IP telephony)

- Audio and video (videotelephony)

- Audio and data

- Audio, video, and data

- Multipoint-multimedia communications (audio or video conferencing)

Because H.323 provides a myriad of services, it can be applied in a wide variety of areas, including consumer, business, and entertainment applications.

Version 1: Videophone

Version 1 of the H.323 standard was accepted in October 1996. It defined visual telephone systems and equipment for LANs that provide a nonguaranteed QoS. As this suggests, Version 1 was heavily weighted toward multimedia communications in a LAN environment.

Version 2: Packet-Based Multimedia

The emergence of VoIP applications, also called "IP telephony," was not guided by any standard. The absence of a standard resulted in incompatible IP telephony products, and necessitated a revision of H.323.

VoIP introduced new requirements, such as providing communication between a personal computer (PC)-based telephone and a telephone on the switched circuit network (SCN) of the public telephone system. Version 2 of H.323 accommodated these additional requirements, and was accepted in January 1998.

Version 3: Under Development

New features are currently being added to the H.323 standard, which will evolve to Version 3 shortly. The features being added include fax-over-packet networks, gatekeeper-to-gatekeeper communications, and fast-connection mechanisms.

Other Standards of the H.323 Family

The H.323 standard is part of the H.32x family of recommendations specified by ITU–T. The other recommendations of the family specify multimedia communication services over different networks:

- H.324—SCNs such as the public telephone system
- H.320—ISDN
- H.321 and H.310—Broadband-Integrated Services Digital Network (B–ISDN)
- H.322—LANs that provide guaranteed QoS

One of the primary goals in the development of the H.323 standard was interoperability with other multimedia services networks. This interoperability is achieved through the use of a gateway, which is a node that performs any translation necessary for traffic to pass between two dissimilar networks.

H.323 Network Components

The ITU-T H.323 packet multimedia standard specifies four kinds of components, which most VoIP solution vendors have adopted as fundamental building block components. When networked together, these components provide the VoIP network's point-to-point and point-to-multipoint multimedia communications services:

- Terminals (client end stations)
- MCUs
- Gateways
- Gatekeepers

Not all of these components are required in every VoIP network. Furthermore, gatekeepers, gateways, and MCUs are logically separate VoIP network functions, but can be implemented within a single physical device.

Terminals

Used for real-time bidirectional multimedia communications, an H.323 terminal can either be a PC or a stand-alone device running an H.323 protocol stack and the desired multimedia applications. A terminal must support audio communications, and can optionally support video or data communications. Because the basic service provided by an H.323 terminal is audio communication, this kind of terminal plays a key role in IP telephony services.

The primary goal of H.323 is to interwork with other multimedia terminals. Therefore, H.323 terminals are compatible with terminals that comply with the other members of the H.32x family of standards, listed above.

MCUs

MCUs coordinate multipoint conferences of three or more H.323 terminals. All terminals participating in a conference must establish a connection with the MCU. The MCU manages conference resources, negotiates between terminals to choose the audio or video coder/decoder (codec) to use, and may handle the media stream. If multipoint conferencing is not used in an H.323 network, an MCU is not required.

Gateways

At some point, all LAN-based telephony systems need to connect to the PSTN. Gateways convert a voice signal's format between packet-switched and circuit-switched transmissions. In general, an H.323 gateway provides connectivity between an H.323 network and a non-H.323 network. A gateway is not required, however, for communication between two terminals on the same H.323 network.

A gateway provides communication between an H.323 terminal and the PSTN. This dissimilar network connectivity is achieved by translating protocols for call setup and release, converting media formats between different networks, and transferring information between the networks connected by the gateway.

The gateway converts packetized voice (sound that has been digitized and placed into a LAN or WAN packet and frame) to a format the PSTN can accept. Because the digitization format for voice on the packet network is often different than on the PSTN, a gateway can also convert each format to the other; thus, these devices are often called "transcoding gateways." Gateways also pass PSTN signaling information, including dial tone. Gateways support four types of connections:

- Analog (standard telephone)

- T1 or E1

- ISDN, generally Primary Rate Interface (PRI)

- ATM, at speeds of optical carrier (OC)-3c and higher

Gatekeepers

A gatekeeper can be considered the brain of the H.323 network. It is the focal point for all calls within the H.323 network. Although it is not a required component, a gatekeeper provides important services, such as addressing, terminal and gateway authorization and authentication, accounting, billing, and charging. Gatekeepers can also provide call control and voice switching services.

The gatekeeper's most important function is to limit the number of real-time network connections so they do not exceed the available network bandwidth. Real-time applications register themselves with the gatekeeper before attempting to bring up a session. The gatekeeper may refuse a request to bring up a session, or grant the request at a diminished data rate. This function is most important for video connections, which can consume vast amounts of bandwidth for a high-quality connection.

A gatekeeper is not required; however, if one is available on the network, terminals must use its services. All terminals, gateways, and MCUs managed by a single gatekeeper are referred to as an H.323 zone. A zone may be independent of network topology and composed of multiple network segments connected using routers or other devices. The H.323 Zones Diagram illustrates the zone concept.

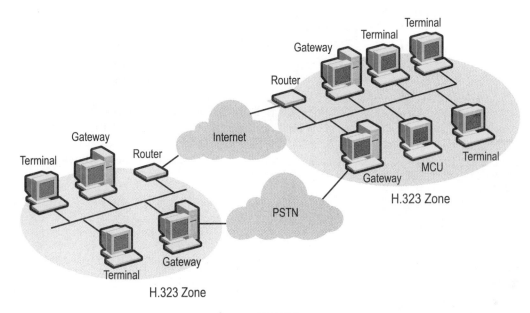

H.323 Zones

MGCP

Media Gateway Control Protocol (MGCP) is originally defined in the IETF informational RFC 2705. MGCP defines protocols used to move the call signaling functions from the VoIP gateways to external call control elements called Media Gateway Controllers (MGC) or call agents.

These external call control elements synchronize to send call control commands to their controlled Media Gateways (MG). The call agents serve as the masters in the MGCP master/slave architecture, sending commands to the slave gateways. The gateways handle the audio processing functions, while the call agents present themselves as H.323 gatekeepers or endpoints.

MGCP Network Components

The MGCP components include:

- media gateways (MGs)
- media gateway controllers (MGCs)

The MGCP Network Components Diagram illustrates these devices and their placement on the network.

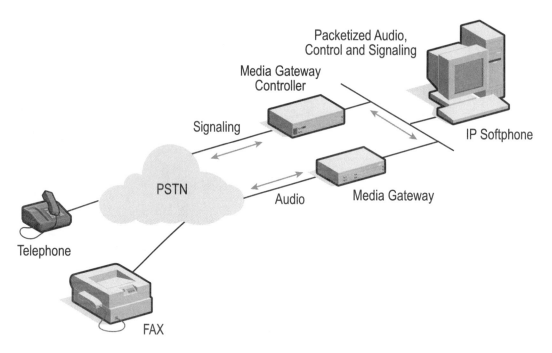

MGCP Network Components

MGs

The Media Gateway (MG) is the MGCP network component that serves to simply convert non-packet voice traffic to and from packetized voice traffic. Because the call agent is responsible for converting complex signaling protocols, the MG can concentrate on encoding and decoding speech. Hence, the MGCP endpoint can be much less complex and costly than an H.323 gateway or terminal.

Located at the packet telephony network's edge, the MG includes several key functions:

- **Endpoints**—An MGCP endpoint is the voice traffic flow/ MGCP network point of entry and exit. MGCP endpoints can be either physical, such as a Plain Old Telephone Service (POTS) service termination point, or virtual, in the form of an IP softphone installed on a desktop PC.

- **Residential gateways**—An MGCP residential gateway terminates a residential POTS line and provides access to a carrier's MGCP network over IP trunks, such as ADSL or Cable Modem connections.

- **Connections**—An MGCP connection is an association between endpoints either on the same or different MGs. For example, we could establish a connection between two POTS endpoints located on the same MG for the purpose of completing a VoIP call; this is called a point-to-point connection. We could also establish connections between a POTS endpoint, an IP softphone, and an IP trunk interface, all located on different MGs. This is called a multi-point connection. The call agent normally establishes these connections dynamically, though we can also establish permanent connections in special cases that require permanent circuits between endpoints.

- **Calls**—MGCP groups connections between endpoints as calls. A point-to-point connection is a call between two endpoints, while a multipoint connection is a call between three or more endpoints. A call can be active, that is, carrying media between endpoints, or inactive, where a connection exists between the endpoints, but no media is transferred. The call agents control the call's state.

MGCs

The MGC, also known as the call agent, is the MGCP network node that performs call control functions. As mentioned earlier, the MGC offloads the call signaling functions from the MG. An MGC controls one or more MGs, and performs call and connection control and network resource management.

The MGC initiates and terminates calls, maintains call status information, tracks MG resource usage, and directs the MG to reserve or release resources. An MGC can act as an H.323 gatekeeper, and can provide an interface to the PSTN Signaling System 7 (SS7) network.

MGCP Call Control Transactions

MGCP implements the MG control interface as a set of transactions. The transactions are composed of a command and a mandatory response. There are eight types of commands:

- CreateConnection—Sent by the MGC to the MG to create a connection between endpoints

- ModifyConnection—Sent by the MGC to the MG to modify a call's parameters, such as the resources it requires

- DeleteConnection—Sent by the MGC to the MG to release a call and its resources

- NotificationRequest—Sent by the MGC to the MG to request specified endpoint event notification messages

- Notify—Sent by the MG to the MGC to indicate a specified event occurred

- AuditEndpoint—Sent by the MGC to the MG to determine an endpoint's status

- AuditConnection—Sent by the MGC to the MG to retrieve a connection's parameters

- RestartInProgress—Sent by the MG to the MGC to indicate an endpoint startup, line initialization, restart, or out-of-service condition

Activities

1. An MGCP MGC is also known as a _____.

    a. Terminal agent

    b. Call agent

    c. Call terminator

    d. MCU

2. Match the H.323 device with its description.

    a. Terminal

    b. Gateway

    c. Zone

    d. Gatekeeper

    e. MCU

    Considered the brain of the H.323 network _____

    Organization of H.323 devices managed by a single gatekeeper _____

    Provides communications between H.323 terminals and the PSTN _____

    Coordinates conferences between H.323 terminals _____

    Limits the number of real-time network connections to preserve bandwidth _____

    Performs transcoding between voice signal formats _____

    Can either be a stand-alone device or a PC running the H.323 protocol stack _____

3. Name and describe the MGCP MG components.

    _____

    _____

    _____

Extended Activities

1. Using the Internet and a World Wide Web (Web) browser, research additional information on the following topics:

   a. H.323 terminals

   b. H.323 MCUs

   c. H.323 gateways

   d. H.323 gatekeepers

   e. Real-Time Transport Protocol (RTP)

Lesson 3—Factors Driving the Demand for Packet Telephony

Several long-term trends are driving the growth of packet telephony services. The ongoing convergence of voice and data into open, standards-based platforms has encouraged independent software vendors to develop cost-effective voice- and data-enabled applications. Broadband access technologies, such as cable modems and DSL, promise to deliver huge levels of bandwidth to the network's edge. Among telecommunications carriers, packet telephony is emerging as a key technology for bypassing the higher-priced, long-distance telephone system. In an enterprise, packet telephony is emerging in applications where the added value can be clearly demonstrated.

Objectives

At the end of this lesson you will be able to:

- Identify packet telephony market drivers and applications that provide added value to clients

- Explain how VoIP services protect a company's communications infrastructure investment

- Explain how VoIP services enable better system and network management, including reduced operating costs

- Explain how VoIP services add flexibility and scalability to the voice network

- Explain how VoIP services provide access to new enterprise applications

 **Key Point**

Business demand for convergence is driving new technological developments and interoperability.

Long-Term Trends

Despite the challenges packet telephony implementations present, several long-term trends are driving the growth of VoIP and Fax-over-IP services.

Open Standards, Open Market

Converged, standards-based, open voice and data platforms have resulted in cost-effective voice- and data-enabled applications. Examples of these services range from unified messaging (the bundling of voice and electronic mail [e-mail]) to commodity voice mail and personal agent services, such as Wildfire.

The H.323 standard was originally designed to support end-to-end video conferencing, and its complexity limited the success of early VoIP products. Vendors attempted to adapt the standards to VoIP applications, but the result was often that vendor's interpretation of the standards, which prevented their product from working with other vendors' products. Early product interoperability issues limited multivendor deployments that supported anything beyond basic call setup. Customers had to choose between advanced features and product interoperability.

A recent Miercom VoIP vendor survey (**http://www.mier.com**) indicates that vendors are now agreeing somewhat on the protocols and standards that will allow multivendor VoIP network deployments. These include:

- ITU-T H.323v2

- IETF Session Initiation Protocol (SIP)

- IETF MGCP

- International Softswitch Consortium (ISC) specifications

- ITU-T H.248/Megaco

According to a Network World (**http://www.nwfusion.com**) VoIP industry survey reported on January 29, 2001, most vendors agree that H.323 will become the enterprise legacy standard, with MGCP and H.248/Megaco used between carrier call agents and other gateways. Many vendors believe that SIP will be the standard for call control between call agents and residential IP telephones. These opinions indicate that the equipment's network location will determine the protocols used.

More Bandwidth

Broadband access technologies, such as cable modems and DSL, promise to deliver huge bandwidth amounts to the edges of networks. They also promise to create a new category of utility providers. For example, Media One, an unregulated subsidiary of Qwest Communications, is conducting trials of coaxial cable-based broadband services as a means of faster home Internet access. If they succeed, they will be ideally positioned to also provide packet-based telephony or conferencing services.

Advanced signal conditioning techniques, such as high compression codecs and noise reduction, reduce the amount of data carried across the network, conserving precious bandwidth. For example, Adaptive Pulse Code Modulation (ADPCM) coding techniques can reduce standard PCM voice bandwidth from 64 Kbps to as little as 16 Kbps. Some codecs, such as the G.723.1 codec, provides advanced data compression algorithms which can remove redundant data characters from the digital voice stream, reducing bandwidth usage to nearly 5 Kbps. Voice Activity Detection (VAD) can reduce the amount of silence transmitted in each direction by as much as 40 to 50 percent.

Carrier Applications

Among telecommunications carriers, packet telephony is emerging as a key technology for bypassing the higher-priced, long-distance telephone system. A new class of carriers, called "Internet telephony service providers (ITSPs)," is building packet-based WAN networks to carry voice traffic. Even some traditional long-distance carriers are experimenting with packet-based WANs, primarily for service outside their regulated markets. New partnerships and consortia are emerging as these carriers attempt to create worldwide packet-based telephony networks.

Enterprise Applications

In an enterprise, packet telephony is emerging in applications where the value proposition can be clearly articulated. This is likely to begin with specific multimedia and multiservice applications in large organizations, such as applications using the joined delivery of data and voice over a single infrastructure. Examples include Internet call centers, new voice logging systems, and unified messaging.

In addition to cost savings, call centers have new opportunities to enhance customer-agent interaction using innovative services that take advantage of telephony, PC technologies, and the benefits of workgroups, by linking up all of the IP-based services. The IP Layer Diagram illustrates how IP supports these services.

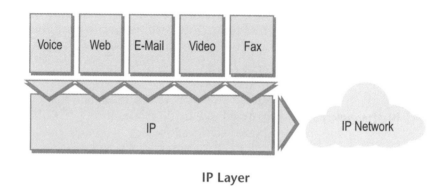

IP Layer

Voice Rides for Free

Thus far, most packet telephony is used for toll bypass. Organizations are purchasing VoIP gateways to combine telephone and data traffic over a WAN, thus reducing the cost of calling countries with high long-distance rates. Organizations with large branch office systems (such as banks), and a capillary data infrastructure to reach those branches, are also carrying voice over WANs. In an odd reversal of the metaphor that sold T1 multiplexers (MUXs) for years ("voice pays for the circuit; data rides for free"), these customers have already installed and justified their data networks and are using spare capacity to carry intracorporation voice traffic.

Additional cost benefits that companies glean from VoIP implementations include reduced infrastructure costs. By carrying voice traffic over the data network, organizations greatly reduce or eliminate the need to support two separate voice and data networks. Hence, VoIP users reduce Open Systems Interconnection (OSI) model Layer 1 costs throughout the company's network. Organizations also realize savings by combining their voice and data support organizations. VoIP gateways allow companies to maintain their legacy PBX systems, phasing them out as they reach the end of their life cycles rather than throwing them away just to implement the new technology.

Transparent Technology

Delivery of telephony services across packet- and circuit-switched networks is becoming more transparent. Some packet telephony providers have won customers by exploiting the lower cost of packetized voice; however, this market will be short-lived as more long-distance carriers become deregulated and pricing disparities collapse. In fact, telephony service providers may offer a range of service quality choices, each at an appropriate cost. Ultimately, users will not care how a call is transported (as a packet, circuit, or cell), as long as the call gets to the recipient with acceptable quality and at a competitive price.

Improved Network Management

In a typical organization, support personnel use separate management interfaces to manage their data and voice devices. The PBX vendor typically supplies either a terminal-based management console or a vendor proprietary management application, from which system administrators generate reports and monitor system performance and health.

On the other hand, data network administrators typically use open management systems based on Simple Network Management Protocol (SNMP) and Remote Monitoring (RMON) applications and agents, allowing centralized data network device management and monitoring. IP-enabled PBXs, and native VoIP systems, provide SNMP and RMON agents for system alarm and error monitoring, performance measurements, and configuration. Support personnel can easily perform all these management and support tasks from a centralized network management system (NMS), such as HP OpenView or Tivoli NetView, from where their data systems can be managed as well.

VoIP systems can provide Web-based management consoles, from where support personnel can centrally administer either a single system or an enterprise VoIP cluster. Additionally, VoIP gateways, gatekeepers, and terminals can also provide Web-based management interfaces. These all serve to reduce the number of vendor-specific management applications dispersed throughout the enterprise.

Network Flexibility and Scalability

Traditional PBX systems associate end-user extensions to physical switch ports. This demands that technicians and engineers maintain precise documentation, so that when users physically relocate within the facility support personnel can move their associated extension with them. This physical mapping of users to ports means that when performing Moves, Adds and Changes (MACs), support technicians must often lift and punch down wires on the cross connects, risking removing other non-associated extensions from service. Adding users might require adding additional circuit packs and cabling additional ports.

IP PBXs, on the other hand, associate users to logical addresses such as IP addresses. When an IP telephone is moved, it maintains its IP address and so its user mapping. Support personnel merely unplug the telephone, move it to its new location, and plug it in to an active data port on the same subnet or Virtual LAN (VLAN). On an IP PBX, moving and adding users is frequently a "plug and play" proposition. This logical addressing helps simplify contact center management, for example, in instances where agents may move from position to position, depending on manning, workload, and other criteria. By designing the network with VLAN-aware switches and routers, network administrators can control network traffic and security while enabling user mobility within the enterprise.

VoIP can consolidate accounting systems, placing all call accounting functions on a central gatekeeper or SIP controller. Additionally, it can eliminate network points of failure, replacing dedicated point-to-point voice circuits with redundant, connectionless packet paths.

Access to New Applications

Enterprises desiring to gather and track customer data and handle inbound and outbound calls by combining traditional PBX systems with PC- and server-based applications have been hampered somewhat by the complexity of converting analog call information to digital. These traditional configurations require the CTI application both perform the analog-to-digital conversion process and process the caller information. VoIP, through its use of open application programming interfaces (APIs), moves the voice and signaling information conversion process to the network's gateways and gatekeepers. Inside the network, CTI components work with calls and data in the same digital format as any other network data.

For example, on a traditional PBX-connected IVR system, the IVR must interpret and act upon DTMF tones supplied by the caller in response to the IVR's prompts. In a VoIP network, the gateway or gatekeeper collects all the customer information, performs the analog-to-digital conversion processes, and sends the digitized information to the IVR as packetized data. The IVR no longer needs to convert the analog caller information to digital, and so can perform its primary job of responding to callers.

UM is another example of a CTI application that benefits from VoIP. UM provides a means for network users to work with their voice mail, email, fax, and other multimedia applications from a central interface. The IP PBX sends voice and fax messages across the network in packetized digital format. In turn, a centralized UM server can collect information from these diverse sources, store them in a central location, and serve them to the user from a central message store. Again, the gateway or gatekeeper digitizes analog information, and saves this information as digitized audio files. These files may then be attached to email messages and forwarded to other users. Regardless of the application, VoIP moves the analog-to-digital conversion process from the CTI application to the network's edge.

VoIP opens the enterprise voice network to new applications, enabling network managers to quickly and easily introduce new voice services. Rather than taking down the voice system to install new features, network support personnel can add a new server to the network, and experiment with new features in a controlled, test environment. Once testing is complete, the application can be put in service on the production network. VoIP enables enterprises to grow voice applications beyond the limitations imposed by the PSTN and traditional voice services, instead allowing them to deploy new services limited only by data network and application technology development.

Activities

1. Which three VoIP network benefits will help you sell a converged network solution to a potential customer? (Choose three.)

   a. Better service-level agreements

   b. Reduced wiring requirements

   c. Reduced toll call costs

   d. Centralized network management

2. Converged networks use which two technologies to reduce call bandwidth over that required by PCM voice? (Choose two.)

   a. Bandwidth on demand

   b. Comfort noise generators

   c. Voice encoding and compression

   d. VAD

3. Which three data network management technologies and protocols does convergence enable on the voice network? (Choose three.)

   a. Simple Network Management Protocol

   b. Terminal-based Management Consoles

   c. Remote Network Monitoring

   d. Network Management System

Extended Activities

1. Your job is to sell your school, church, or employer on a converged network solution. What VoIP benefits and advances would you highlight, and what improvements would you suggest they make to their existing network to implement these changes?

   _____

   _____

   _____

   _____

   _____

2. Research Internet VoIP carriers, and compare their rates and service quality with your local PSTN services. Are the trade-offs in call quality justified by the potential savings? Start with the following Universal Resource Locators (URLs):

   http://www.net2phone.com

   _____

   _____

   _____

   http://www.dialpad.com

   _____

   _____

   _____

Lesson 4—Private VPNs

In the realm of telephony, a private virtual private network (VPN) is an interconnected group of communications systems (PBXs), marketed by IXCs such as AT&T with its Software Defined Network (SDN), MCI with its Vnet service, and Sprint with its VPN service. People within each system, called "local users," can exchange voice and data with other individuals at communications systems in the network, called "nonlocal users." The systems in a private VPN may be located on the same campus, or separated by thousands of miles using facilities provided by international partners. This lesson reviews general concepts necessary to understand private VPN creation.

Objectives

At the end of this lesson you will be able to:

*   Explain the issues you must consider when performing telephony integration over a private VPN

 **Key Point**

A private PBX network can carry long-distance traffic over private lines.

Private Communications Networks

When organizations have several locations in different regions, they often implement a PBX system at each branch office, then use the PSTN to handle communications between those systems. This approach is shown on the Public Communications Network Diagram.

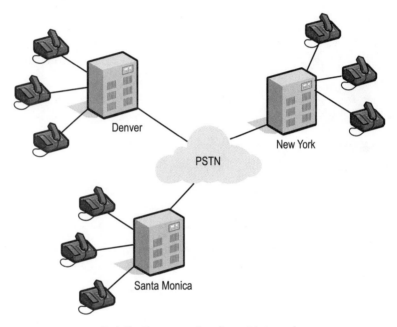

Public Communications Network

This arrangement works well, as long as the volume of interlocation telephone traffic is fairly low. For companies that require a higher level of long-distance traffic, it makes more sense to connect regional offices with private leased lines. The Private Communications Network Diagram illustrates this approach.

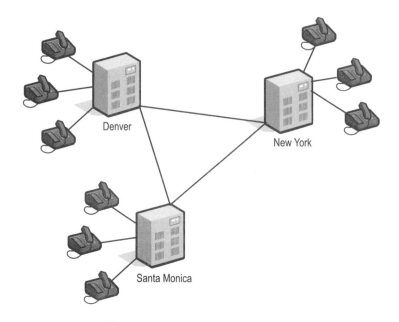

Private Communications Network

In a private network, the separate communications systems are linked by private transmission facilities. These lines/trunks may be analog tie trunks, T1-emulated tie trunks, or ISDN-PRI trunks.

When a company needs the control of a private network combined with the flexibility of a public network, the answer may be a voice VPN. AT&T's SDN is a flagship VPN product in the AT&T nodal architecture, giving customers a corporate VPN implemented over the AT&T public-switched network facilities.

SDN is a customer's VPN that resides in the AT&T 4ESS-based switched Worldwide Intelligent Network (WIN). It provides features and management capabilities that are usually not found in private networks, such as customized routing, advance numbering plans, call screening, authorization codes, remote access, security codes, and customized billing.

Each SDN includes a network control point (NCP), on which the company's unique VPN database resides. This database determines whether the call is on-net (remains within the VPN) or off-net (leaves the VPN at some point), and determines the path over which the call will travel. The SDN serving office, which receives and processes the call, maintains the VPN. The VPN service fully supports analog data transmission up to 28.8 Kbps, and end-to-end digital data transmission at 56 or 64 Kbps.

SDN is compatible with most private networks and PBXs, thus protecting these existing investments. Because SDN does not require a sophisticated PBX base, businesses can choose dedicated access (T-carrier or ISDN) or dial-up access. Traveling users can get dial-up access to the SDN by providing a valid authorization code.

Regardless of how it is implemented, private networks are distinct from the worldwide PSTN. A private network carries calls within an organization, while PSTN lines and trunks carry calls to local and long-distance parties outside the organization. When properly implemented, a private PBX network can achieve significant cost savings and improved efficiency, increased user satisfaction, and improved security, as well as added network scalability and flexibility.

Cost Savings

Private VPNs can reduce both toll charges and the costs of leased private lines. Since the VPN uses public lines within the carrier's network, VPN users pay only for the bandwidth they use, not for the lines. Carriers bill VPN users by call duration, depending on the time of the day in which the call was placed. For example, a call placed during normal business hours would cost more per minute than one placed after hours. Customers agree to a minimum network traffic commitment, and per-minute rates vary depending on whether or not the customer meets this commitment. Rates can increase significantly if the customer fails to meet their minimum traffic commitment. However, since the VPN is configured across shared lines within the carrier's network, the carrier can quickly provision and reconfigure the VPN bandwidth based on the customer's changing needs.

VPNs are best suited to meeting the communications needs of small- and mid-sized businesses with moderate voice communications needs. Large enterprises with more demanding communications needs, such as moving multimedia (voice, video, and data) traffic between sites would do better to obtain private network services.

Users realize savings in the following ways:

- All on-net calls between company locations bypass the PSTN, eliminating toll charges. For example, if a company has locations in Dallas and Cincinnati, the private network carries all calls between those cities. Users can dial any company extension, anywhere in the network, just as they would dial an extension on their own local system. Using Automatic Route Selection (ARS), the system transparently routes the call over the correct trunks or service providers. The NCP makes these decisions based on both the originating call location and dialed number.

- Off-net calls, that is, calls to destinations outside the company, can use the private network to reduce toll charges. For example, consider a company with locations in Seattle and Orlando. A call from Seattle to Miami first travels free over the company network to Orlando. Then the Orlando PBX transfers the call to the PSTN for routing to Miami. The company is only billed for long-distance service between Orlando and Miami. To avoid off net long distance toll charges altogether, a subscriber could install foreign exchange (FX) trunks between the off net sites and a VPN terminating CO. In this case, the subscriber pays only a fixed monthly mileage charge for the FX trunk rather than per minute long distance charges.

- Leased trunks are cheaper than full-service switching. A company can order a point-to-point T1 circuit from a service provider, then use system programming to set it up for tandem ISDN-PRI services. The telecommunications service provider provides amplification (repeaters) for PRI trunks when the distance between networked systems is great enough to distort signals. However, the service provider does not supply higher-cost switching services.

- The VPN can incorporate the customer's existing voice services, such as an onsite PBX or Centrex service. The subscriber can tie their PBX into the carrier's network over dedicated tie lines, or the carrier can configure the customer's Centrex service to pass calls between sites over the VPN.

Improved Efficiency

Private PBX networks can also improve efficiency:

- Leased trunks can be used for much more than voice calling. A company can tailor its use of PRI B channels by using drop-and-insert equipment that allows fractional use of T1 channels for data/video communications between sites, while keeping the remaining T1 channels for PRI voice or data traffic. T1 channels can support a mix of T1-emulated tandem tie trunks for voice or data communications at 56 Kbps per B channel, while allowing data transfers over two or more channel-bonded B channels.

- When appropriate, a company's incoming call traffic can be spread over the entire private network. By configuring calling groups, overflow calls from one location can be routed to other locations, increasing the number of coverage points and sharing personnel and resources between systems.

- A centralized voice messaging system can provide additional savings by not requiring a separate voice messaging system at each location in the private network.

Enhanced User Satisfaction

When a private PBX network is implemented to function as a single system, it offers its users simpler operation and a wider range of features:

- A uniform (or universal) dial plan establishes a single numbering system for all company users. Each telephone within the private network is assigned a unique seven-digit number, which may differ from the device's listed directory number (LDN). Within the private network, all calls appear to be local.

- When switches are linked with ISDN connections and the Q.SIG interswitch protocol, the network can offer the full range of ISDN and Q.SIG supplementary services, such as calling party ID or call forwarding.

VPN subscribers can add or subtract locations as needed, while only incurring the costs associated with terminating the sites at the nearest servicing CO. The carrier assumes responsibility for routing the new locations' calls within the network. Additionally, private VPN users benefit from the carrier network's built in redundancy, rather than dealing with the management burden and expense of leasing and configuring multiple private lines between sites.

Activities

1. Which three of the following are true statements concerning voice VPNs? (Choose three.)

   a. FX lines are allowed as a voice VPN component.

   b. Voice VPNs route calls based on the calling party's ANI.

   c. Voice VPNs route calls based on the originator's location and the dialed number.

   d. Voice VPN on-net calls bypass the PSTN, eliminating toll charges.

2. Which two statements are true concerning voice VPNs? (Choose two.)

   a. Voice VPNs can work with an existing Centrex system.

   b. Voice VPNs are more failure prone than private leased lines.

   c. Per minute call rates depend on the customer meeting minimum average call traffic commitments.

   d. Large sites with intense voice and video communications needs will realize a large cost savings.

3. When might a company choose a voice VPN over a private, leased-line network?

   a. When they want to maintain network management responsibilities

   b. When most calls are projected to be placed off-net

   c. When they want quick network provisioning and reconfiguring

   d. When they need to connect multiple sites with high data traffic

Extended Activities

1. Would a company located remotely, without direct connectivity to an IXC network, benefit from a voice VPN? Where would most of this customer's calls likely route, off-net or on-net?

   _____

   _____

   _____

2. Research voice VPN offerings from the major carriers, such as MCI Worldcom, Sprint, and AT&T. To whom do they market these products?

   _____

   _____

   _____

Lesson 5—PSTN Remote Access

In recent years, organizations have become more mobile and geographically dispersed. Accordingly, many network designs have included remote access technologies. Organizations use these technologies to provide telecommuters, remote employees, and mobile workers network access. This lesson discusses PSTN services that enable remote access technologies.

Objectives

At the end of this lesson you will be able to:

- Identify and analyze PSTN remote access technologies, including dial-up, ISDN, and DSL access

Key Point

As corporate work forces become more mobile, remote access technologies are critical converged network components.

Remote Access Applications

Organizations often include remote offices such as branch offices, sales offices, manufacturing sites, warehouses, and other remote locations as part of their enterprise networks. Remote offices can also be located at a business partner, vendor, or supplier site. Telecommuters and mobile users also require remote access to enterprise applications such as e-mail, Web browsing, order entry, and calendaring. Remote users may need to download bandwidth-intensive applications such as software and software updates, file backup and storage, product demonstrations, and online classes.

The PSTN supplies several remote access-enabling technologies:

- Dial-up access
- ISDN access
- DSL access

Dial-Up Access

Despite the recent growth in digital technologies, such as DSL and wireless, the majority of remote users still use modems for remote access. Modems are inexpensive, and allow communications between the two devices transmitting digital information over analog PSTN local loops. A common analog modem misconception is their maximum real operating speed is 56 Kbps. Theoretically, these modems can average 56 Kbps unrestricted throughput; however, the Federal Communications Commission (FCC) limits download speeds to 53 Kbps. Additionally, the PSTN analog network infrastructure limits ITU V.90 standard modem upload speeds to a maximum throughput of approximately 33.6 Kbps.

ISDN Access

ISDN provides a number of services not previously available to data communications users. Many of these are similar to voice network services, because they are both made possible by the same Signaling System 7 (SS7) signaling protocol used by the voice network. For example, ISDN-Basic Rate Interface (BRI) automatically provides a caller's telephone number as part of incoming calls. This feature, called "Automatic Number Identification (ANI)," is similar to Caller ID, but cannot be blocked by the caller.

With ISDN, a user can block incoming calls, transfer a call to another ISDN subscriber, and connect to multiple ISDN subscribers (similar to a PSTN conference call). An example of an ISDN-provided service is Information Indicator (II)-digits, available with AT&T ISDN-PRI service and bundled with ANI. II-digits are a two-digit string used to identify an incoming call type. II-digits allow subscribers to detect, route, or block calls based on the following conditions:

- Assign call priority to calls placed from pay telephones, cellular telephones, and other line types.

- Detect pay telephone calls placed with the intention to avoid detection and tracking by collection agencies or dispatching services.

- Route calls to specific vector directory numbers (VDNs) based on the originating line type.

Incoming ISDN-PRI calls can have II-digits associated, as can incoming ISDN-PRI tie trunks.

An example of II-digit usage is an instance where a call center might receive repeated threatening calls over incoming ISDN-PRI tie trunks. The call center's PBX is configured to examine the call II-digits. In examining the call records, the switch administrator finds all the threatening call II-digits are set to 29. This indicates the calls are originating from a prison/inmate service, and closer call examination indicates the calls come from a local state prison. The call center supervisor uses this information to administer the PBX to block these calls, and notifies the state prison board as well. The II-Digits Summary Table lists a summary of existing II-digit set descriptions.

II-Digits Summary

Code	Use
00	Identified line—no special treatment
01	Multiparty—ANI cannot be provided
02	ANI failure
06	Hotel/motel—directory number not accompanied by automatic room ID
07	Special operator handling required
23	Coin or non-coin—line status unknown
24	800 service
27	Coin call
29	Prison/inmate service
30-32	Intercept
34	Telephone company operator-handled call
40-49	Locally determined by carrier
52	OutWATS
61	Type 1 cellular
62	Type 2 cellular
93	Private VPN

DSL Access

DSL comes in a variety of speeds, which makes it attractive to the consumer. However, speed depends on the following physical conditions of the copper local loop:

- Reach (loop length)—Each DSL service has a maximum reach, or distance, the service can be offered from the CO. Typically, the range of DSL is between 12,000 and 26,000 feet. Customers located beyond the service's reach cannot receive the service.

- No devices on the line—The copper wires between the CO and customer must be free of electronic devices, such as repeaters. This is a problem because most copper that extends more than 6,000 feet from the CO contains some kind of electronic repeater to boost the analog signal. It is also essential that the line does not contain loading coils, which were typically installed on analog lines to filter out high-frequency noise by cutting off all frequencies above 4 kilohertz (kHz). The ADSL Bandwidth Diagram shows that such a device will block the wide frequency range DSL uses.

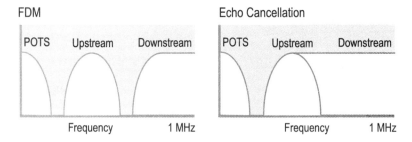

ADSL Bandwidth

Thus, an incumbent local exchange carrier (ILEC) must first remove these devices before it can provide DSL service to many of its customers. This increases the time and cost of many DSL installations.

- Good wiring—The copper loop must also be in good physical condition, well-installed, with no mismatched wire gauges. The age of the average copper wire plant makes this unlikely. Bellcore estimates the typical U.S. telephone line crosses 22 splices, which allows line noise and crosstalk to reduce effective data rates. In addition, effective data rates are reduced by other problems throughout the telephone system, such as overlong loops that attenuate signals, nonterminated wire pairs, and crosstalk between wires.

ADSL

ADSL is called "asymmetric" because its downstream data rate is much faster than its upstream rate. This type of DSL is one of the most attractive solutions for home users and telecommuters, because it matches typical Internet usage patterns. For example, a Web surfer only sends approximately 10 keystrokes upstream to bring a large Web page downstream.

ADSL upstream speeds range from 16 to 640 Kbps. Individual products today incorporate a variety of speed arrangements, from a minimum set of 1.544/2.048 Mbps downstream and 16 Kbps upstream to a maximum set of 9 Mbps downstream and 640 Kbps upstream. All of these arrangements operate in a broad frequency band above the 4,000-Hertz (Hz) POTS voice band, leaving POTS independent and undisturbed even if a premise's ADSL modem fails.

Many home and home office users do not subscribe to a minimum downstream data rate of 1.544 Mbps. Instead, carriers supply services in fractions of the minimum data rate the ADSL Data Rates Table lists. Carriers break out the minimum data rate with devices called "Digital Subscriber Line Access Multiplexers (DSLAMs)." The DSLAM serves as an interface point between the subscriber premises and carrier network, multiplexing multiple customer data packets into one or more high-speed circuits. Carriers split the high-speed circuits' available bandwidth across several customers, charging each depending on their subscribed bandwidth.

ADSL Data Rates

Data Rate (Mbps)	Wire Gauge (AWG)	Distance (feet)	Wire Size (millimeter)	Distance (kilometer)
1.5 or 2	24	18,000	0.5	5.5
1.5 or 2	26	15,000	0.4	4.6
6.1	24	12,000	0.5	3.7
6.1	26	9,000	0.4	2.7

Activities

1. Which three of the following are PSTN-supplied remote access technologies? (Choose three.)

   a. Dial-up access

   b. T1 access

   c. ISDN access

   d. DSL access

2. An ISDN service, bundled with ANI, that identifies incoming call types is called _____.

   a. PRI

   b. BRI

   c. II-digits

   d. ANI digits

3. Which II-digit string designates an 800 service call?

   a. 24

   b. 27

   c. 29

   d. 30

4. A call center receives continuous inbound threatening calls. The call center's carrier helped them trace the calls to a local prison. Which II-digit set would you ask the carrier to block on your inbound trunks?

   a. 27

   b. 34

   c. 52

   d. 29

5. Which PSTN service provides constant, on-demand remote network access for voice, video conferencing, and e-mail services?

   a. SW56

   b. WATS

   c. ISDN-BRI

   d. DDS

6. Which remote access technology provides telecommuters with simultaneous voice and data access over existing twisted pair local loop lines?

    a. ISDN-PRI

    b. ADSL

    c. DID

    d. FX

Extended Activities

1. Go to **http://www.webopedia.com** and research the following technologies:

    a. ISDN

    b. ADSL

    c. SDSL

2. Which technologies are available in your area? Which would be the best choice if you had to support remote network users in your organization?

    _____

    _____

    _____

    _____

    _____

Summary

This unit reviewed some of the technology alternatives available for deploying and upgrading a network. We began by looking at sending voice over alternative technologies. We looked at how technologies such as frame relay and ATM can be used to transport voice conversation over what is typically thought of as a data network.

We learned that the ITU-T H.323 recommended standard provides the processes and protocols needed to carry multimedia traffic over packet-switched networks. H.323 specifies four components: terminals, MCUs, gateways, and gatekeepers. Terminals are the H.323 endpoints. MCUs coordinate multipoint conferences between H.323 terminals. Gateways provide a communication interface between the PSTN and packet network. Gatekeepers authorize and authenticate H.323 connection requests, allowing or denying connections and controlling how each connection accesses the available network bandwidth.

MGCP provides a means of controlling a telephony gateway from an external device, called an "MGC" or "Call Agent." MGCP defines a master/slave environment where a master MGC controls the slave MG. The MGC performs the gatekeeper function in an H.323 network.

Factors driving converged technologies on the enterprise include widespread availability of high-bandwidth WAN connections, such as those provided by T-carriers, ATM, and DSL services. Standards, such as H.323 and SIP, have opened the door to more and better converged products, each capable of interoperating with those marketed by other vendors. ITSPs are building WANs capable of reliably transporting voice-over technologies. Reduced tariffs and regulations have kept VoIP costs low, and increased Internet usage has made the technology acceptable among both corporate and private users. TCP/IP network management functions, such as those provided by RMON and SNMP, allow carriers to centrally monitor and manage their voice-over networks. The inherent network scalability WAN technologies provide ensures that converged networks can grow to meet user demands.

IXCs provide private VPNs to aid corporate users in reducing their communications costs, while increasing voice network features and management capabilities. Users can purchase such advanced features as customized routing plans, call screening, and customized call billing solutions. A carrier-maintained centralized database maintains call routing information, determining when to route a call on-net or off-net. Private VPNs support T-carrier, ISDN, and even analog voice lines and trunks. Private VPN users realize toll savings when calls remain on-net, and can also reduce long-distance toll charges by implementing least cost routing (LCR) to send off-net calls over the VPN to the on-net PSTN gateway nearest the call's destination. A uniform dialing plan can make all on-net calls appear as local, even though the caller and receiver are cities or states apart.

Finally, WAN technologies provide telecommuters and remote offices remote network access services. ISDN, DSL, and even dial-up lines can carry voice, video, and data traffic between users and sites. Such advanced services as II-digits and ANI allow ISDN telecommunications network administrators to better control and monitor remote network access services. DSL technologies provide the bandwidth remote users need to access converged services remotely, running over the existing POTS cable plant. Even dial-up services provide infrequent remote network access for file sharing, collaboration, conferencing, and messaging.

Unit 7 Quiz

1. Which of the following four voice communications technologies is being replaced by the other three, which are considered alternative technologies?

   a. TCP/IP

   b. Frame relay

   c. ATM

   d. Leased lines

2. An MG consists of which two of the following components? (Choose two.)

   a. Controllers

   b. Call agents

   c. Endpoints

   d. Connections

3. The H.323 component that provides such capabilities as billing, authentication, and accounting is a(n) _____.

   a. Gateway

   b. Gatekeeper

   c. Agent

   d. Terminal

4. Which MGCP command message directs an MG to release a call?

   a. DeleteConnection

   b. AuditEndpoint

   c. RestartInProgress

   d. NotificationRequest

5. Which MGCP command message directs an MG to return an endpoint's status?

   a. DeleteConnection

   b. AuditEndpoint

   c. AuditConnection

   d. NotificationRequest

6. Which MGCP command message indicates to the MGC that a line is initializing?

    a. RestartInProgress

    b. AuditEndpoint

    c. AuditConnection

    d. NotificationRequest

7. MGCP is also known as what type of protocol?

    a. Master/slave

    b. Peer-to-peer

    c. Point-to-point

    d. Transcoding

8. Which two of the following are benefits of a converged voice and data network? (Choose two.)

    a. Cheaper international long-distance service

    b. Better voice quality on international calls

    c. Increased network equipment reliability

    d. Ease of network and system management

9. Which three of the following are VoIP network market drivers? (Choose three.)

    a. Open standards

    b. Network scalability

    c. New applications

    d. Extensive regulation

10. Which two of the following provide the cost savings subscribers gain from VoIP technologies? (Choose two.)

    a. Voice calls bypassing the Internet

    b. Reduced IP efficiency

    c. Increased social acceptance

    d. Reduced regulation

11. How much bandwidth can VAD conserve?

    a. 10 percent

    b. 30 percent

    c. 40 percent

    d. 70 percent

12. What is the device in a voice VPN that stores the company's VPN database?

    a. NCP

    b. SDN serving office

    c. Virtual Control Point

    d. Signaling Transfer Point

13. A voice VPN supports which of the following data rates? (Choose two.)

    a. 56 Kbps analog data

    b. 28.8 Kbps analog data

    c. 56/64 Kbps digital data

    d. 128 Kbps digital data

14. Which two of the following are functions the VPN database performs? (Choose two.)

    a. Determines a call's path

    b. Receives and processes a call

    c. Decides whether a call is on-net

    d. Implements the VPN to PSTN gateway

15. IXCs can provision VPNs over which three of the following carriers? (Choose three.)

    a. Cellular

    b. ISDN

    c. T1

    d. Dial-up

16. What is the maximum theoretical download speed at which a single POTS remote access line can run?

    a. 28.8 Kbps

    b. 33.6 Kbps

    c. 56 Kbps

    d. 128 Kbps

17. What remote access technology allows sufficient bandwidth for both acceptable quality voice and data transmissions on existing twisted pair local loops?

    a. T1

    b. FX

    c. ISDN-PRI

    d. ADSL

18. What function does the H.323 gatekeeper perform when an IP device initializes and makes contact?

    a. Registration

    b. Admission

    c. Housekeeping

    d. Status

19. Which three choices are MGCP commands? (Choose three.)

    a. DeleteEndpoint

    b. AuditEndpoint

    c. RestartInProgress

    d. CreateConnection

20. H.323 gateways support which of the following connection types? (Choose two.)

    a. ATM

    b. SMDS

    c. Analog

    d. ADSL

21. Which statement best describes an H.323 terminal?

    a. It is an endpoint for an H.323 communications session

    b. It controls which devices can establish connections over the network

    c. It converts PSTN voice traffic to packetized voice

    d. It controls multimedia conferences

22. Which VoIP network components can consolidate call accounting functions? (Choose two.)

    a. Call agent

    b. Gateway

    c. SIP controller

    d. Gatekeeper

23. Unified messaging provides users with which converged network capabilities? (Choose three.)

    a. Integrated voicemail

    b. Integrated e-mail

    c. Telephone e-mail access

    d. PBX administration

24. Which are voice VPN features? (Choose two.)

    a. Caller ID over Q.SIG protocols

    b. Economical call routing in remote locations

    c. Economical call routing using ARS

    d. Separate numbering systems for each site

25. When might a company choose to use dial up remote access over ISDN or ADSL services?

    a. When cost is an issue in the service selection process

    b. When cost is not an issue in the service selection process

    c. When high speed, multimedia communications is necessary

    d. When they need to block calls originating from a specific source

26. A legacy PBX is designed to provide support for system monitoring and management using SNMP and RMON. True or False

27. VoIP solutions simplify network maintenance and management. True or False

COURSE QUIZ

1. What is the major difference between a LAN and a WAN?
   a. Type of cabling used to configure the network
   b. Distance between nodes in the network
   c. Type of devices used to connect workstations to the network
   d. Type of NIC used

2. What is SLIP commonly used for?
   a. Serial connectivity to the Internet
   b. Connectivity to a backbone
   c. Modem-to-LAN connectivity
   d. LAN-to-WAN connectivity

3. Which of the following is the fastest line speed?
   a. T1
   b. SONET
   c. 256 Kbps
   d. 512 Kbps

4. What technology uses a CIR to state the average circuit rate?
   a. X.25
   b. Frame relay
   c. ATM
   d. SONET

5. Which of the following describes a simple point-to-point network?

   a. Network where all computers use a single cable type

   b. Network that consists of one type of computer, such as a PC or Macintosh

   c. Network where a single physical connection links local and remote stations

   d. Network where all computers connect to a single logical bus

6. Which of the following describes how a connectionless network operates?

   a. No connection is established between endpoints.

   b. No physical path exists between any two points in the network.

   c. A circuit-switched network is used.

   d. All nodes attached to the physical media receive the transmission.

7. Which of the following refers to the copper cabling that connects many homes and businesses to the first CO?

   a. Local loop

   b. Trunk lines

   c. Digital loop

   d. Leased lines

8. What is the name of the document used to describe a service offered by a telecommunications vendor?

   a. Tariff

   b. Specification

   c. Telecommunications map

   d. Service document

9. Which of the following parts of a telecommunications network can carry an analog signal? (Choose two.)

   a. Trunks

   b. Local loop

   c. RS-232 cable

   d. V.35 cable

10. Which of the following was the original telecommunications network designed to carry?

    a. Low bandwidth voice signals

    b. High bandwidth voice signals

    c. Low bandwidth data signals

    d. High bandwidth data signals

11. In which of the following types of telecommunications circuits would the information always travel the same path and distance?

    a. Circuit-switched circuit

    b. Packet-switched circuit

    c. Dial-up connection

    d. Leased line

12. Which of the following would not be considered DCE?

    a. ISDN-interface device

    b. Modem

    c. MUX

    d. PC

13. Which of the following is a modem function? (Choose two.)

    a. Amplify analog signals

    b. Convert digital signals to analog signals

    c. Repeat digital signals

    d. Convert analog signals to digital signals

14. Which of the following best describes the function of a codec?

    a. Converts voice signals to digital signals

    b. Converts digital signals to electrical signals

    c. Amplifies digital signals on the local loop

    d. Provides ISDN connectivity

15. Which of the following types of information typically require the most bandwidth?

    a. Digital voice communication

    b. Document imaging

    c. Compressed video

    d. Full-motion video

16. Which of the following best describes ADSL?

    a. Analog-to-digital conversion at the local loop

    b. Digital-to-analog conversion at the local loop

    c. High speed to the subscriber, low speed from the subscriber

    d. High-speed data transfer from the subscriber, low-speed transfer to the subscriber

17. Which of the following is a disadvantage of using satellite communications for voice transmission?

    a. Propagation delays

    b. Low bandwidths

    c. High error rates

    d. Unpredictable equipment behavior

18. Which of the following protocols is normally used to communicate data over a satellite network?

    a. HDLC (or an HDLC subset)

    b. LAPD

    c. xDSL

    d. ADSL

19. Which of the following is the purpose of compression?

    a. Create less expensive telecommunications equipment

    b. Make more efficient use of telecommunications facilities

    c. Create a more secure network

    d. Provide for permanent communications facilities

20. Which of the following best describes ADSL?

    a. It is an analog service.

    b. It is a permanent service.

    c. Information travels from subscriber to CO only.

    d. Information travels in one direction faster than in another direction.

21. FT1 consists of multiples of which of the following?

    a. 64-Kbps channels

    b. 58-Kbps channels

    c. T1 channels

    d. T3 channels

22. Which of the following technologies supports DDS?

    a. Satellite communications

    b. Digital modems

    c. Analog modems

    d. Codecs

23. Which of the following best characterizes DTE?

    a. Network node requiring communications services

    b. Communicating device maintained by a telephone company

    c. High-speed switch

    d. CSU/DSU

24. A T1 line type is equivalent to the _____ standard.

    a. DS0

    b. ISDN-BRI

    c. DS1

    d. E1

25. How could the transmission rate of data traveling across a T1 channel be 56 Kbps?

   a. A portion of a T1 channel is used for in-band signaling for voice communications.

   b. A speed of 56 Kbps is the highest theoretical rate for data communications across a T1.

   c. T1 only transmits information at 56-Kbps rates.

   d. It is the most efficient means of using the T1 channel.

26. Which of the following is the purpose of a MUX?

   a. Map low-speed input signals to a high-speed output signal

   b. Map high-speed input signals to a low-speed output signal

   c. Convert analog signals to digital signals

   d. Convert digital signals to analog signals

27. Which of the following is the building block for SONET? (Choose two.)

   a. STS-1

   b. 51.84 Mbps

   c. 48 Kbps

   d. 64 Kbps

   e. Both a and b

28. What would the physical transport be when ATM is carried at 155-Mbps rates?

   a. DDS

   b. T1

   c. T3

   d. SONET

29. What is the primary difference between STS and OC signals?

   a. STS is digital, OC is analog.

   b. STS is low-speed, OC is high-speed.

   c. STS is electrical, OC is optical.

   d. STS is binary, OC is octal.

30. What is the purpose of the HDLC protocol?

    a. Transmit information across a telecommunications link

    b. Frame data for point-to-point networks

    c. Transmit messages from process to process

    d. Transmit application information from client to server

31. Which two of the following operate at the highest OSI model layer? (Choose two.)

    a. Packet switching

    b. X.25 packet switching

    c. Frame relay

    d. Cell relay

32. In which of the following ways does a cell differ from a packet and frame?

    a. A cell is much slower than a frame or packet.

    b. A cell is used in connectionless networks.

    c. A cell can be used to transfer analog information.

    d. A cell is a fixed-length entity.

33. A packet is found at which layer of a protocol stack?

    a. Physical

    b. Data Link

    c. Network

    d. Transport

34. A frame is found at which layer of a protocol stack?

    a. Physical

    b. Data Link

    c. Network

    d. Transport

35. SONET is found at which layer of a protocol stack?

    a. Physical

    b. Data Link

    c. Network

    d. Transport

36. Considering the overall frame and cell lengths of the following technologies, which is most efficient?

    a. Frame switching

    b. Cell switching

    c. Packet switching

    d. Frame relay

37. Which 802.16 Convergence Sublayer (CS) classifies traffic by VPI or VPI/VCI?

    a. MAC

    b. ATM

    c. Packet

    d. Privacy

38. Which of the following statements concerning 802.16 networks is true?

    a. They support both fixed and mobile equipment

    b. They can protect data payloads from theft

    c. They are designed to provide LAN services

    d. The CS builds MAC layer PDUs

39. Which 802.16 CS feature removes redundant payload information from a series of higher layer PDUs transported within the same MAC PDU?

    a. PHS

    b. SFID

    c. Encryption

    d. Packing

40. An 802.16 Service Flow ID (SFID) is how many bits long?

    a. 8

    b. 16

    c. 32

    d. 64

41. Which component of a DSA request message identifies the initiating device?

    a. Primary management CID

    b. Secondary management CID

    c. SFID

    d. Transaction ID

42. A typical use of SW56 services is as a backup route if primary route failures occur. True or False

43. Multiple SW56 lines can be used together to obtain higher bandwidths. True or False

44. All layers of the SONET protocol relate to the Physical Layer of the OSI model. True or False

45. An ATM cell could consist of multiple SONET frames. True or False

46. The Control field of an HDLC information frame is used for flow control and information acknowledgment. True or False

47. A CO is also referred to as a local exchange. True or False

48. A trunk link connects COs. True or False

49. Transmission of digital signals uses four wires to support half-duplex communications. True or False

50. DDS is all digital with the exception of the local loop. True or False

51. A MUX can take multiple simultaneous digital input streams and put them onto a single digital output stream. True or False

52. A MUX can take a high-speed digital bit stream and divide it into multiple digital output streams. True or False

53. A codec performs the same basic operation as a modem. True or False

54. The physical media used to transmit information at the highest rates is fiber optic cable. True or False

55. A satellite facility is often used to provide connectivity for real-time information transfer. True or False

GLOSSARY

ABAM—ABAM is a designation for 22-gauge, 110-ohm, plastic-insulated, twisted pair Western Electric cable normally used in COs.

access concentrator—An access concentrator is a network device used to combine multiple communications lines onto a single, high-speed output link.

Adaptive Differential Pulse Code Modulation (ADPCM)—ADPCM is a form of PCM that produces the digital signal at a lower bit rate than standard PCM. ADPCM records only the difference between samples rather than sample the entire waveform. ADPCM can reduce the resultant signal's digital bandwidth by one-half that of PCM.

add/drop multiplexer (ADM)—An ADM is a MUX that extracts and inserts lower-rate signals from a higher-rate, multiplexed signal without having to demultiplex the higher-rate signal. An OADM is an optical ADM.

adjacent channel interference—Adjacent channel interference is interference caused when a signal exceeds its assigned frequency band and "spills over" into the band assigned to another signal.

Alternate Mark Inversion (AMI)—AMI is a T1 line-coding format in which successive 1 bits, or marks, are alternately inverted. A 0 bit is represented as zero amplitude.

American National Standards Institute (ANSI) standard T1. 403-1989—This ANSI standard defines the use of the ESF T-carrier frame format with digital channel banks.

American Standard Code for Information Interchange (ASCII)—ASCII is one of the most widely used codes for representing keyboard characters on a computer system. ASCII uses 7 bits to represent 128 elements. For example, when the character "A" is pressed on the keyboard, the ASCII binary representation is 1000001. The other major encoding system is EBCDIC. See Extended Binary Coded Decimal Interchange Code (EBCDIC).

amplitude modulation (AM)—AM imposes a signal pattern on a carrier wave (consistent electrical signal) by varying the height of the wave, or how far from the center it swings.

analog—Analog signals are waves of electrical current. Variations in the human voice, when mixed with an analog signal by means of a telephone handset, produce a new signal that represents the human voice as a unique electrical wave.

application programming interface (API)—An API is a software interface that formats requests from an application software to a NOS. Telephony APIs, such as TAPI, TSAPI, and JTAPI, format requests from application software to a telephone system, such as a PBX.

Asymmetric Digital Subscriber Line (ADSL)—ADSL is a relatively new technology used to delivery high-speed digital communications across the local loop.

Asymmetric Digital Subscriber Line (ADSL) Lite—Also known as G.lite, ADSL Lite is a simplified version of ADSL that requires no splitters installed on the customer premises, and can deliver downstream speeds up to 1.5 Mbps.

asynchronous—An asynchronous operation is one in which characters are not transmitted on any strict timetable. The start of each character is indicated by transmitting a start bit. After the final bit of the character is transmitted, a stop bit is sent, indicating the end of the character. The modems must stay synchronized only for the length of time it takes to transmit the character. If their clocks are slightly out of synchronization, data transfer will still be successful.

Asynchronous Transfer Mode (ATM)—ATM is a cell-switching network that consists of multiple ATM switches that forward each individual cell to its final destination. ATM can provide transport services for audio, data, and video.

AT&T Accunet T1.5—AT&T Accunet T1.5 service is one of several AT&T digital services. Accunet T1.5 provides for the transmission of 1.544-Mbps digital signals over terrestrial channels, and uses one of two types of framed DS1 signal formats, D4 or ESF.

AT&T Publication 43801—AT&T Publication 43801 specifically defines Digital Channel Bank's use and operation. It is one of many AT&T documents designed to specify a carrier technology's operation.

attenuation—The weakening of a signal over distance is referred to as attenuation.

automated attendant—An automated attendant is a device that automatically answers incoming calls and allows callers to route themselves to an extension in response to a recorded voice prompt.

Automatic Call Distributor (ACD)—An ACD is a programmable system that controls how inbound calls are received, held, delayed, treated, and distributed to call center agents.

automatic protection switching (APS)—APS is a SONET architecture designed to allow SONET to perform network management and error detection from any point in the signal's path.

automatic repeat request or automatic retransmission request (ARQ)—ARQ is a method commonly used by communicating devices to verify data upon receipt. The sender calculates and encodes an error-detection field and sends it with the data. The receiver then recalculates the field, and compares it with that which was received. If they match, the receiver acknowledges receipt (ACK); if the match fails, the receiver negatively acknowledges the data's receipt (NAK), and the sender retransmits. The sender must store the transmitted data until it receives either an ACK or NAK.

Automatic Route Selection (ARS)— ARS is a private branch exchange (PBX) feature that enables the system to automatically choose the least cost route to the destination. ARS is also known as least cost routing (LCR).

backward explicit congestion notification (BECN)—BECN is a frame relay framing bit that a frame relay device sets in transmitted frames traveling away from frames that have experienced congestion.

bandpass filter—A bandpass filter is an electronic device that accepts, or passes, a particular band of frequencies and blocks all others. Bandpass filtering is the basis of FDM.

baseband—A baseband modem is a modem that does not modulate a signal before transmission, thereby transmitting the signal in its native form. Baseband signaling is the transmission of either digital or analog signals at their original frequencies.

base station (BS)—A BS is the 802.16 network component that operates as the central network connection point and provides connection management for a number of subscriber stations. A single BS can service several hundred subscriber stations.

bearer circuit—A bearer circuit is a basic communication channel as defined in signaling hierarchy. In a VoIP network, a bearer circuit is a particular end-to-end media stream from the PSTN to the gateway, or across the packet network between communicating nodes.

Binary Eight Zero Substitution (B8ZS)— B8ZS is a T1 channel encoding method that inserts two consecutive 1s, called a "BPV," into a signal whenever eight consecutive 0s are transmitted. This represents a timing mark to the receiver, maintaining synchronization between the sender and receiver. This allows the circuit to provide the entire 64 Kbps of available data bandwidth to each DS0 channel.

bipolar violation (BPV)—In T1 coding formats, a BPV occurs when two consecutive 1 bits have the same polarity.

bits per second (bps)—Bps is a measurement of the number of binary bits transmitted per second. Common modem speeds are 28,800 and 56,000 bps (28.8 and 56 Kbps, respectively).

bit stuffing—Also known as zero bit insertion, bit stuffing allows binary data to be transmitted on a synchronous transmission line. Within each frame are special bit sequences that identify addresses, flags, and so forth. If the information (data) portion of the frame also contains one of these special sequences, a 0 is inserted by the transmitting station and removed by the receiving station.

broadband—Two methods are used to transmit signals between nodes: baseband and broadband. A broadband system is one that transmits signals into separate carrier channels simultaneously over cable, similar to television or stereo cable. In the context of LANs, broadband refers to analog transmission of digital signals, and baseband refers to digital transmission of digital signals.

broadband digital cross-connect—A broadband digital cross-connect interfaces SONET and DS3 signals. It accesses STS-1 signals, and switches at this level. It is the equivalent of a DS3 digital cross-connect, but for SONET.

Broadband-Integrated Services Digital Network (B-ISDN)—ISDN line rates come in three basic varieties: basic, primary, and broadband. Basic or "narrow" ISDN consists of two bearer (B) channels and one data (D) channel. Each B channel can carry one PCM voice conversation or data at a transmission rate of 64 Kbps. The ISDN-PRI consists of twenty-three 64-Kbps B channels for carrying voice, data, and video, and one 64-Kbps D channel for carrying signaling information; it is similar to T1 signaling. B-ISDN, also called "wide ISDN," has multiple channels above the primary rate. In addition to B and D channels, there are a number of additional channels defined, including the A, C, and H series of channels.

bursty—A network traffic pattern in which a lot of data is transmitted in short bursts at random intervals is referred to as bursty.

busy hour—Busy hour refers to the one hour during which a network or office telephone system carries its greatest traffic. A telephone network should be designed to provide enough transmission capacity to carry most busy-hour traffic, so that only some, but not many, callers are put on hold or receive busy signals.

call agent—See media gateway controller (MGC).

Call Detail Report (CDR)—A CDR is an itemized report of all calls and their durations, used for call accounting purposes. A Call Detail Recording feature, as part of a PBX or provided by a carrier, collects the data presented in the report.

carrier—A carrier is a company that provides communications circuits. The digital communication services, designated T1, T2, and so on, are also referred to as carriers.

C band—The C band is a portion of the electromagnetic spectrum ranging in frequency from 4 to 6 GHz, used for satellite communications.

central office (CO)—A CO is a telephone company facility where local loops are terminated. The function of a CO is to connect individual telephones through a series of switches. COs are tied together in a hierarchy for efficiency in switching. Other terms for a CO are local exchange, wiring center, and end office.

Certificate Authority—A CA is an organization that creates digital certificates for individuals and Web servers after verifying the identity of those persons or sites. A CA signs each digital certificate with its own digital signature, thus vouching for the identity and trustworthiness of the owners of the certificates.

channel—Generically speaking, a channel is a communications path between two or more communicating devices. Channels are also referred to as links, lines, circuits, and paths.

channel service unit (CSU)—A CSU is a device that connects customer equipment to digital transmission facilities, such as a T1 circuit. The CSU is the device that actually generates the transmission signals on the local loop, that is, the telephone channel. CSUs are normally coupled with DSUs in a device called a "CSU/DSU." See data service unit (DSU).

characters per second (cps)—The acronym cps is typically used to describe the number of characters a printer can print per second.

circuit—A circuit is the physical connection between two communicating devices.

class of restriction (CoR)—CoRs control call origination and termination on PBX trunks or trunk groups. CoRs control call routing, identification, and other trunk details.

class of service (CoS)—In the telecommunications world, CoS is the collection of privileges and services assigned to a particular extension. In the data world, CoS defines the prioritization or other differentiating treatment of particular data traffic classes, such as VoIP or video conferencing.

coder-decoder (codec)—A codec is a hardware device that takes an analog signal and converts it to a digital representation of the signal.

collapsed backbone—When a network's backbone, connecting all the network segments, is contained within a hub, switch, or router, it is considered a collapsed backbone. In an Ethernet network, the bus is collapsed within a hub, and the network devices connect to the bus using UTP cable.

committed burst size (CBS)—CBS is the number of bits a circuit can transfer over a period of time.

committed information rate (CIR)—CIR is the guaranteed average data rate for a frame relay service.

common channel signaling (CCS)—Digital telecommunications systems require a method to set up and maintain calls. CCS, which dedicates a separate communications channel to control signaling, is becoming the predominant method of carrying signaling information between devices, thus eliminating problems associated with control signaling within the voice channel.

competitive access provider (CAP)—A CAP is a company that provides fiber optic links to connect urban business customers to IXCs, bypassing the LEC. Once these fiber optic links are in place in major metropolitan areas, CAPs can begin to expand their service offerings.

competitive local exchange carrier (CLEC)—CLECs are telecommunications resellers or brokers that sell services bought from ILECs. CLECs resell data service, such as Internet access and local toll calling, to business and residential customers.

Compressed Serial Line Interface Protocol (CSLIP)—CSLIP is an Internet protocol that reduces the overhead TCP communications imposes on data traffic. For example, in a simple character-based terminal communication, TCP and IP headers can add almost 4,000 percent overhead, considering an ASCII character is 1 byte long, and each character can be carried in a single packet. Each packet carries 20 bytes of TCP header information, and another 20 bytes of IP information. CSLIP reduces the TCP header portion to 3 to 5 bytes, reducing overhead to approximately 300 percent.

connection identifier (CID)—CID is a 16-bit code used to identify service flows on an 802.16 network.

Consultative Committee for International Telegraphy and Telephony (CCITT)—CCITT is a subcommittee of ITU, responsible for standards used in communications, telecommunications, and networking. CCITT standards include X.25, V.42, and the ISDN I-series recommendations.

convergence technologies—Convergence technologies are protocols and systems that allow different types of media to be transported over the same network. One of the best examples of a convergence technology is ATM, providing for the prioritization and transport of different types of media, such as voice, data, and video.

crosstalk—Crosstalk is interference experienced on a communications circuit imposed by adjacent circuits. Crosstalk is affected by cable placement, shielding, and transmission techniques.

customer premises equipment (CPE)—CPE, which also stands for customer-provided equipment, refers to telephone equipment that resides at a customer site.

Cyclic Redundancy Check (CRC)—CRC is the mathematical process used to check the accuracy of the data being transmitted across a network. Before transmitting a block of data, the sending station performs a calculation on the data block and appends the resulting value to the end of the block. The receiving station takes the data and the CRC value, and performs the same calculation to check the accuracy of the data.

data circuit-terminating equipment (DCTE)—See data communications equipment (DCE).

data communications equipment (DCE)—DCE devices are OSI model Layer 1 devices that are responsible for properly formatting the electrical signals on a physical link, and performing signal clocking and synchronization.

Data Exchange Interface (DXI)—A DXI defines the interaction between network devices and an SMDS CSU/DSU. A DXI is also considered the interface between DTE and an ATM CSU/DSU.

data link connection identifier (DLCI)—A DLCI is part of a frame relay frame. It is a 10-bit address that identifies the virtual circuit the frame belongs to. The DLCI identifies the logical channel between a user and network, and has no network-wide significance.

Dataphone Digital Service (DDS)—DDS, also known as Digital Data Service, is a series of services, provided by a telephone company, that provide digital facilities for data communication. DDS is available in several speeds, including 2.4, 4.8, 9.6, and 56 Kbps.

data service unit (DSU)—A DSU is a device that takes data from a LAN device and creates digital information suitable for public transmission facilities. A DSU is necessary to connect CPE to digital transmission facilities, such as a T1 circuit. It is normally used in conjunction with a CSU in a device called a "CSU/DSU." See channel service unit (CSU).

data terminal equipment or data termination equipment (DTE)—DTE is equipment, often a computer, that executes Layer 2 and higher processes. DTE depends on the services of the DCE to connect to a communications link.

DB-9—A DB-9 connector is the 9-pin, D-shaped connector specified by the EIA/TIA 574 serial communications standard. A DB-9 connector can either use female (receptacle) or male (plug) pin configurations.

DB-25—A DB-25 connector is the 25-pin, D-shaped connector specified by the EIA/TIA RS-232-C serial communications standard. A DB-25 connector can either use female (receptacle) or male (plug) pin configurations.

Demand Assigned Multiple Access (DAMA)—DAMA is a method of controlling access to the radio channel and involves time slots that are assigned to the subscribers as needed, rather than dedicated to specific devices. In this manner, the channel can dynamically adapt to changing user bandwidth requirements.

dense wavelength-division multiplexing (DWDM`—DWDM uses multiple light wavelengths to transmit signals over a single optical fiber. Each wavelength, or channel, carries a stream of data at rates as high as 2.5 Gbps and higher. It can use over 50 channels.

Dial-on-Demand Routing (DDR)—DDR is a technique used with circuit-switched links that allows a router to initiate a connection only when information is present at the router interface. The router drops the connection after transmission ends.

differential phase-shift keying (DPSK)—DPSK represents digital data by encoding digital values as shifts in the analog signal's phase. The data is represented as a change in the phase, rather than as a specific signal phase.

digital access cross-connect switch (DACS)—A DACS is a telephone company device that establishes semiperma-nent (not switched) paths for voice or data channels. All physical wires are attached to the DACS once, then electronic connections between them are made by entering software instructions. Depending on the manufacturer, a DACS may also be called a "DCS."

digital certificate—A digital certificate is a unique electronic file used to authenticate a user, program, provider, service, or transaction. The certificate usually consists of a file containing a copy of the user's or service's public encryption key, along with the signature of a trusted person verifying that the key does, indeed, belong to the user or service claimed. A Certificate Authority (CA) creates a certificate, and the certificate is encrypted in a way that makes it impossible to forge.

digital cross-connect (DSX)—A DSX is a cross-connect frame that allows technicians to manually cross-connect T1s with patch cords and plugs. See digital access cross-connect switch (DACS).

digital signal level 0 (DS0)—DS0 is a 64-Kbps channel that provides the bandwidth required for one analog voice telephone line. The DS0 signal is the fundamental building block of the North American digital signal hierarchy.

Digital Subscriber Line (DSL) access multiplexer (DSLAM)—A DSLAM is a mechanism at the LEC's CO that links many customer DSL connections to a single high-speed ATM line.

Direct Inward Dialing (DID)—DID is a process by which a PBX routes calls directly to a particular extension (identified by the last four digits). Incoming trunks must be specifically configured to support DID.

Direct Inward System Access (DISA)—DISA is a method of dialing into a telephone system over either toll or toll-free lines, to gain access to internal telephone system services and features. For example, remote users can dial into a company PBX over a toll-free DISA line, and gain access to the company's long-distance service. Breaking into a PBX over DISA lines is one technique hackers use to commit toll fraud.

Direct Station Selector (DSS)—A DSS is a PBX auxiliary device that allows an operator to call an extension by merely touching a button. The operator can quickly observe an extension's status by looking at the state of the extension's indicator.

discard eligibility (DE) bit—The DE bit is a bit set in a frame relay frame that indicates the frame may be dropped to free bandwidth for higher-priority frames in times of network congestion.

Distributed Queue Dual Bus (DQDB)—DQDB is the IEEE 802.6 standard for MANs. See Switched Multimegabit Data Service (SMDS).

drop-and-insert equipment—Drop-and-insert equipment is used by a carrier circuit's subscriber to demodulate the circuit (drop) at some intermediate point and add information (insert) for transmission on the same circuit. An ATM ADM is an example of drop-and-insert equipment.

dumb terminal—A terminal that totally depends on a host computer for processing capabilities is referred to as a "dumb" terminal. Dumb terminals typically do not have a processor, hard drive, or floppy drives; they have only a keyboard, monitor, and method of communicating to a host (usually through some type of controller).

duplex—Duplex refers to the process of transmitting data in two directions simultaneously. This is also referred to as duplex transmission or full-duplex.

Dynamic Host Configuration Protocol (DHCP)—DHCP provides configuration parameters to Internet hosts. DHCP consists of two components: a protocol for delivering host-specific configuration parameters from a DHCP server to a host and a mechanism for allocation of network addresses to hosts. DHCP is built on a client/server model, in which designated DHCP server hosts allocate network addresses and deliver configuration parameters to dynamically configured hosts.

E1—E1 carrier standards are the European standards that are similar to the North American T-carrier standards. E1 is similar to T1; however, it specifies a 2.048-Mbps data rate and supports 30 communications channels.

E and M signaling—E (ear) and M (mouth) signaling is a telephony signaling arrangement where separate circuit leads, the E and M leads, are used for circuit supervision and signaling. The near end applies -48 V DC to the M lead, which applies a ground to the far end E lead. The M lead indicates the near end's desire to activate the circuit, and the far end's E lead indicates this to the receiver.

echo cancellation—Echo cancellation is a method of creating two transmission channels. This method enables two stations to both transmit on the same band. Each station subtracts, or cancels, its own transmission from the combined signal. This action causes each station to receive only the signal transmitted by the other station.

EIA/TIA-562—EIA/TIA-562 specifies an unbalanced, electrical-only serial communications standard similar to RS-232 but providing greater bandwidth (64 Kbps). EIA/TIA-562 can interoperate with RS-232 drivers and receivers in many applications.

EIA/TIA-574—EIA/TIA-574 was developed to alleviate confusion arising between the official RS-232 interface and the popular 9-pin version developed by IBM. This standard specifies the DB-9 interface, and recommends the use of the EIA/TIA-562 standard instead of RS-232 electrical levels. EIA/TIA-574 supplies the minimum number of communications lines for nonsynchronous serial data transfer between DTE and DCE.

Electronic Industries Association/Telecommunications Industry Association (EIA/TIA)—EIA and TIA represent companies providing communications, materials, products, systems, distribution services, and professional services around the world.

end office—An end office is a telephone company facility where local loops are terminated. The function of an end office is to connect individual telephones through a series of switches. End offices are tied together in a hierarchy for efficiency in switching. Other terms for end office are local exchange, wiring center, CO, and public exchange.

Ethertype—Ethertype is the type field in an Ethernet frame header used to designate the layer 3 protocol the frame transports.

European Telecommunications Standards Institute (ETSI)—ETSI is an international, nonprofit organization that produces telecommunications standards used in Europe and elsewhere. For more information, visit **http://www.etsi.org**.

excess burst size (EBS)—EBS is the maximum amount of uncommitted data (in bits) in excess of the CBS that a frame relay network can attempt to deliver during a time interval. This data is generally delivered with a lower probability and is treated as discard eligible.

excess information rate (EIR)—The frame relay EIR is a data rate over and above the CIR. The data exceeding the CIR is given best effort delivery by the carrier and is considered discard eligible.

Extended Binary Coded Decimal Interchange Code (EBCDIC)—EBCDIC is the IBM standard for binary encoding of characters. It is one of the two most widely used codes to represent characters, such as keyboard characters. (ASCII is the other.) See American Standard Code for Information Interchange (ASCII).

Extended Superframe (ESF)—Extended Superframe is a method of arranging T1 channel samples in groups of 24 frames. Each frame is 193 bits long, consisting of 24 eight-bit samples plus one framing bit.

extension—Voice terminals connected to a PBX/switch by means of telephone lines are referred to as extensions. The term also defines the three-, four-, or five-digit numbers used to identify the voice terminal to the PBX/switch software for call routing purposes.

extranet—An extranet is a broader form of a private intranet. Extranets are private TCP/IP networks that are shared between closely aligned organizations, and are not available to the general public.

Facility Data Link (FDL)—FDL is the enhanced link diagnostics, network reporting and control, and other circuit monitoring functions enabled by ESF. FDL is allowed 4 Kbps of the ESF T1 signaling channel.

fade—The gradual weakening of a signal over distance, often called "attenuation," is referred to as fade.

fast-packet switching—Fast-packet switching is a packet-switching technology that operates at the Physical and Data Link Layers of the OSI protocol stack. Because fast-packet switching is located at these lower layers (only a small amount of processing is needed) and is associated with small packet sizes, it operates at very high speeds.

Federal Communications Commission (FCC)—The FCC is an independent U.S. government agency that was established by the Communications Act of 1934, and is directly responsible to Congress. The FCC is charged with regulating interstate and international communications carried by radio, television, wire, satellite, and cable. The FCC's jurisdiction covers the 50 states, the District of Columbia, and United States' possessions.

Fiber Distributed Data Interface (FDDI)—FDDI is a LAN standard specifying a 100-Mbps token-passing network using fiber optic cable.

flow control—Flow control is a method of controlling the amount of frames or messages sent between two computer systems. Practically every data communication protocol contains some form of flow control to keep the sending computer from sending too many frames or packets to the receiving node.

foreign exchange (FX)—An FX is a trunk service that lets businesses in one city operate in another city by allowing customers to call a local number. The number is connected, by means of a private line, to a telephone number in a distant city.

foreign exchange office (FXO)—The FXO is the CO providing the FX service.

foreign exchange subscriber (FXS)—The FXS is the subscriber side of an FX service.

Forward Error Correction (FEC)—FEC is an error detection and correction technique that sends redundant bits along with the data payload. The receiver uses this redundant information to recreate lost or corrupted data without requesting retransmission.

forward error correction (FEC)—FEC is a technique of error detection and correction in which a transmitting host computer includes some number of redundant bits in a frame's data payload. These redundant bits allow the receiving device to re-create and recover from transmission errors, eliminating the need to retransmit.

forward explicit congestion notification (FECN)—FECN is a frame relay framing bit that a frame relay device sets in transmitted frames to indicate to the receiving devices that congestion has occurred in the frame's path from the source to the destination.

fount—Fount is another term for Customer-Controlled Reconfiguration of a digital access cross-connect.

frame relay—Frame relay is a wide-area data transmission technology that normally operates at speeds of 56 Kbps to 1.5 Mbps. A frame relay is essentially an electronic switch. Physically, it is a device that connects to three or more high-speed links and routes data traffic between them.

frame relay access device (FRAD)—A FRAD is a frame relay network device required for connecting to a network, such as a switch or router.

frame tagging—Frame tagging is a technique used to identify a frame's membership in a VLAN segment. As a frame is forwarded through the network, frame tagging places a unique identifier in the frame's header. Each network switch that understands the tagging protocol ensures that only those switches, routers, or end nodes that compose the VLAN's membership receive the frame. Once the tagged frame leaves the VLAN (for example, by means of a routed link), the edge device removes the tag.

Frequency Division Duplexing (FDD)—FDD is a radio transmission technique that supports full duplex stations by allowing them to transmit and receive on separate frequencies.

frequency modulation (FM)—FM is a method of modifying a signal so that it can carry information. The carrier (original sine wave) has its frequency modified to correspond to the information being carried.

frequency shift—Frequency shift is an FM method of transmitting a binary bit stream over an analog carrier wave. A binary 0 is represented by a lower frequency, while a 1 is represented by a higher frequency.

frequency-shift keying (FSK)—FSK is a method of representing a digital signal with analog waveforms. FSK represents a 0 as a specific frequency, and a 1 as another frequency.

G.711—G.711 is one of a series of ITU-T voice digitizing algorithms. G.711 transfers digitized audio at 48, 56, and 64 Kbps.

G.722—G.722 is one of a series of ITU-T voice digitizing algorithms. G.722 transfers digitized audio at 32 Kbps.

G.723—G.723 is one of a series of ITU-T voice digitizing algorithms. G.723 transfers digitized audio at 5.3 or 6.3 Kbps.

G.728—G.728 is one of a series of ITU-T voice digitizing algorithms. G.728 transfers digitized audio at 16 Kbps.

G.729—G.729 is one of a series of ITU-T voice digitizing algorithms. G.729 transfers digitized audio at 8 Kbps.

gain—Gain is the increase in a signal's power, voltage, or current. Signal amplifiers create gain.

Gallium Arsenide Field Effect Transistor (GaAs-FET)—A GaAs-FET is a field effect transistor composed of gallium arsenide. A FET is a transistor designed to provide an output signal even when supplied with an input signal near zero power.

gate—A gate is a digital device designed to generate a binary output, that is a 1 or a 0, based on the state of one or more digital inputs.

gatekeeper—A network device or process that controls data flow on a transmission channel or allocates transmission bandwidth among multiple competing signals is referred to as a gatekeeper.

geostationary—Satellite communications systems transmit signals from earth stations to satellites located in space. Antennas located on earth are pointed at a geostationary satellite (also referred to as geosynchronous) that is located in an orbit of approximately 22,300 miles (35,800 km), and is at a fixed point in the sky.

geosynchronous—See geostationary.

gigahertz (GHz)—One GHz is the measurement for a signal that cycles 1 billion times per second.

guardband—A guardband is a band of unused frequencies that prevents overlap between adjacent transmissions. For example, the frequency bands assigned to two adjacent radio stations are separated by a transmission-free guardband.

Gunn diode—A Gunn diode is a microwave oscillator that operates based on the negative differential resistance properties of gallium arsenide. The Gunn diode is named after John Battiscombe Gunn.

H.225—H.225 is an ITU-T recommendation that specifies the messages used by H.323 endpoints to control call admissions, registration, bandwidth, status, and call signaling.

H.245—H.245 is an ITU-T recommendation that specifies the H.323 call control messages that govern how endpoints operate across the half-duplex logical connections. H.245 messages control endpoint capabilities exchange, opening and closing of logical channels, flow control, and so forth.

H.248/Megaco—Megaco, in conjunction with ITU-T H.248, is the signaling protocol used between the MGCP, MG, and MGC.

H.261—H.261 is an ITU-T video coding algorithm designed to support link data rates of 64 Kbps.

H.263—H.263 is an ITU-T video coding algorithm designed to support link data rates of under 64 Kbps.

H.310—H.310 is the ITU-T multimedia conferencing recommendation for voice and video terminals supporting end-to-end conversations over broadband connections, such as ATM.

H.320—H.320 is the ITU-T multimedia conferencing recommendation for voice and video terminals supporting end-to-end conversations over narrowband connections, such as ISDN-BRI.

H.321—H.321 is the ITU-T recommendation for adapting the H.320 recommendation to broadband ATM networks.

H.322—H.322 is the ITU-T multimedia conferencing recommendation for video conferencing over LANs providing QoS.

H.323—H.323 is the ITU-T recommended set of standards and protocols used to support multimedia conferencing on packet-based, best effort networks, such as the Internet and IP LANs. Included in the recommendation are several protocols that control call set up and tear down and voice and video signal conversion and compression.

H.324—H.324 is the ITU-T recommendation for multimedia conferencing over low speed connections, such as dial up modem links. H.263 and G.723 are the video and voice codecs specified.

half-duplex—Half-duplex transmission refers to the process of transmitting data in both directions, but not simultaneously.

handshaking—Handshaking refers to the initialization process that two or more computers go through before they are able to communicate. It is the first part of each and every data communications protocol, and is used to establish initial setup parameters.

harmonic distortion—A harmonic frequency is a multiple of a lower frequency. For example, 4,000 and 6,000 Hz are both harmonics of 2,000 Hz. Harmonic distortion describes the tendency to amplify and transmit harmonics of an input signal. Amplifier feedback, the shrieking sound caused by a microphone too close to a loudspeaker, is a type of harmonic distortion.

hertz—One hertz is one cycle of a sine wave (electrical wave) in one second. One million hertz (megahertz) (1 MHz) is 1 million cycles per second.

High-Level Data Link Control (HDLC)—HDLC is an ISO communications protocol that represents a wide variety of Data Link Layer protocols, such as SDLC, LAPB, and LAPD. The operation of HDLC consists of the exchange of different types of frames, including information frames, supervisory frames, and unnumbered frames. Two communicating computers exchange commands and responses by means of the three different types of frames.

High-Level Data Link Control (HDLC) information frame—An HDLC information frame is an HDLC frame that carries data between two computers. See High-Level Data Link Control (HDLC), HDLC supervisory frame, and HDLC unnumbered frame.

High-Level Data Link Control (HDLC) supervisory frame—An HDLC supervisory frame is an HDLC frame that two computers exchange to control the flow of data between them. For example, by inserting the appropriate codes in the supervisory frame, a computer can acknowledge the receipt of data, or request a retransmission. See High-Level Data Link Control (HDLC), HDLC information frame, and HDLC unnumbered frame.

High-Level Data Link Control (HDLC) unnumbered frame—An HDLC unnumbered frame is a frame that exchanges control information between two communicating computers. For example, by inserting the appropriate codes in the supervisory frame, a computer can change operating modes or request a disconnect. See High-Level Data Link Control (HDLC), HDLC information frame, and HDLC supervisory frame.

High-Speed Serial Interface (HSSI)—HSSI is a serial data communications interface designed to support data rates up to 52 Mbps.

hunt group—A group of trunks/agents selected to work together to provide specific routing of special-purpose calls is referred to as a hunt group.

hybrid fiber coax (HFC)—HFC is a network design method, common in the cable television industry, that combines optical fiber and coaxial cable into a single network. Fiber optic cables run from a central site to neighborhood hubs. From those hubs, coaxial cable serves individual homes.

Hypertext Markup Language (HTML)— HTML is a text-based language used to generically format text for Web pages. HTML tags different parts of a document in terms of their function rather than their appearance. A Web browser reads an HTML document and displays it as indicated by the HTML formatting tags and browser's default settings.

IEEE 802.1p—IEEE 802.1p is the IEEE extension to the 802.1D MAC bridges standard. It allows for the prioritization of MAC layer frames on the network. The 802.1p standard uses a portion of the 802.1Q VLAN tag to represent one of eight possible priority values, each mapped to one of eight traffic classes.

IEEE 802.1Q—IEEE 802.1Q is a vendor-neutral standard for VLAN implementation. The standard specifies a 2-byte VLAN tag that includes a 12-bit VLAN identifier, which is used by the network switches or bridges to decide to which network segment they should forward each frame. The last switch to handle the tagged frame before passing it to the destination node strips the header from the frame.

IEEE 802.11—The IEEE 802.11 standard is the IEEE standard that specifies medium access and Physical Layer specifications for 1 Mbps and 2 Mbps wireless connectivity between fixed, portable, and moving stations within a local area.

IEEE 802.11a—The IEEE 802.11a standard is an extension to 802.11 for wireless LANs at speeds up to 54 Mbps in the 5GHz band.

IEEE 802.11b—The IEEE 802.11b standard is the "High Rate" amendment ratified by the IEEE in September 1999, which added two higher speeds (5.5 and 11 Mbps) to 802.11. The original 802.11 standard defines the basic architecture, fea-tures, and services of 802.11b. The 802.11b specification affects only the Physical Layer, adding higher data rates and more robust connectivity. At this writing, the 802.11b standard is the dominant technology used in WLANs (wireless LANs). 802.11b is also referred to as 802.11 High Rate or Wi-Fi.

IEEE 802.11g—The IEEE 802.1g standard is a draft wireless network standard designed to provide the bandwidth of 802.11a networks while maintaining backward compatibility with 802.11b networks. The 802.11g standard operates in the 2.4-GHz Industrial Scientific Medical (ISM) band.

IEEE 802.16—The IEEE 802.16 standard is the IEEE WirelessMAN™ standard for wireless WAN and MAN connectivity. The 802.16 standard operates in the 10to 66-GHz licensed and nonlicensed frequency range.

impedance—In an AC circuit, impedance is the circuit's total resistance to current flow. The lower the impedance, the better quality the circuit. Impedance in telecommunications circuits varies by frequency.

incumbent local exchange carrier (ILEC)—An ILEC is the same as a LEC or RBOC.

initialization vector (IV)—An IV is a randomly generated code used to start an encryption algorithm and ensure that no two coded strings created with the same key and algorithm begin with the same series of characters.

Institute of Electrical and Electronics Engineers (IEEE) 802.6—This IEEE standard is for MAN protocols. DQDB, the protocol upon which SMDS is based, is defined by IEEE 802.6.

Integrated Digital Network (IDN)—A network that integrates both digital transmission and digital switching into a single digital network, such as ISDN.

Integrated Services Digital Network (ISDN)—ISDN is a digital multiplexing technology that can transmit voice, data, and other forms of communication simultaneously over a single local loop. It provides the following services:

- Access to the telephone network from a local loop.

- Access to communications channels of varying capacities suitable for various uses (for example, voice, data, and video). Access is possible from a single local loop connection to the network. The ISDN provider takes care of multiplexing the various channels for long-distance transmission.

- "On demand" establishment of any kind of communications link, with tariffs based on use.

Integrated Services Digital Network-Basic Rate Interface (ISDN-BRI)—ISDN-BRI provides two "bearer" channels (B channels) of 64 Kbps each, plus one control channel (D channel) of 16 Kbps. See Integrated Services Digital Network-Primary Rate Interface (ISDN-PRI).

Integrated Services Digital Network-Primary Rate Interface (ISDN-PRI)—ISDN-PRI is also called "T1 service." It offers 23 "bearer" channels (B channels) of 64 Kbps each, plus 1 control channel (D channel) of 64 Kbps. See Integrated Services Digital Network-Basic Rate Interface (ISDN-BRI).

Intelligent Information (II) Digits—II Digits is a two-digit string used with ANI to identify an incoming call type over ISDN-PRI services. Subscribers can detect, route, and block calls based on II Digit information.

Interactive Terminal Interface (ITI)—ITI is an informal telecommunications term for the combined ITU-T X.3, X.28, and X.29 recommendations.

Interactive Voice Response (IVR) unit—See Voice Response Unit (VRU).

interexchange carrier (IXC)—An IXC is a long-distance company, such as AT&T or MCI, that provides telephone and data services between LATAs.

interference—Interference refers to any energy that interferes with the clear reception of a signal. For example, if one person is speaking, the sound of a second person's voice interferes with the first. See noise.

intermediate distribution frame (IDF)—An IDF is an equipment room or closet that provides intermediate connectivity between the MDF and individual end device wiring. The network backbone runs between the MDF and IDF.

International Softswitch Consortium (ISC)—The ISC is an organization of more than 130 members that supports the development of applications that provide multimedia communications across IP networks. Learn more about the ISC at **http://www.softswitch.org**.

International Standards Organization (ISO)—ISO is a voluntary organization, chartered by the United Nations, that defines international standards for all fields other than electricity and electronics, which are handled by IEC.

International Telecommunication Union (ITU)—ITU Telecommunications Standardization Sector (ITU-T) is a sector of ITU, which sets network standards for public telecommunications.

International Telecommunication Union-Telecommunications Standardization Sector (ITU-T)—ITU-T is an intergovernmental organization that develops and adopts international telecommunications standards and treaties. ITU was founded in 1865 and became a United Nations agency in 1947.

Internet Engineering Task Force (IETF)—IETF is the official standards body responsible for the development and adoption of many Internet-based standards.

Internet service provider (ISP)—An ISP is an organization Internet users must go through to access the Internet backbone.

Internet telephony service provider (ITSP)—An ITSP is a provider of Internet-based telephony services, supplying packetized voice interfaces to the local and remote PSTN.

ITU-T I.430—ITU-T I.430 is the ITU Layer 1 specification for the ISDN-BRI S/T interface. Each BRI frame is 48 bits long and repeated 4,000 times per second for a total line bit rate of 192 Kbps.

ITU-T I.431—ITU-T I.431 is the ITU Layer 1 specification for the ISDN-PRI operating at 1.544 Mbps (North America) or 2.048 Mbps (Europe).

ITU I.451—ITU I.451 is the ISDN specification for the UNI basic call control at the Network Layer. See ITU Q.931.

ITU Q.920—ITU Q.920 is the ISDN specification for the general aspects of UNI at the Data Link Layer. See ITU Q.921.

ITU Q.921—ITU Q.921 is the ISDN specification for UNI at the Data Link Layer. See ITU Q.920.

ITU Q.930—ITU Q.930 is the ISDN specification for the general aspects of UNI at the Network Layer. See ITU Q.931.

ITU Q.931—ITU Q.931 is the ISDN specification for the UNI Network Layer basic call control. See ITU Q.930.

Java—Java is an interpreted, platform-independent, high-level programming language developed by Sun Microsystems. Java is a powerful language with many features that make it attractive for the Web.

Java Telephony Application Programming Interface (JTAPI)—JTAPI is a telephony-to-computer API using Java, a programming language developed by Sun Microsystems. Java transcends proprietary or machine-specific computer languages. A Java program will run on any Java-compliant machine with no, or only slight, modification.

jitter—Jitter is a signal distortion caused when a carrier signal is not synchronized to its reference timing positions. Jitter can cause transmission errors and loss of synchronization for high-speed synchronous communication links.

Ka band—The Ka band is a portion of the electromagnetic spectrum ranging in frequency from 20 to 30 GHz, used for satellite communications.

keep alive bits—Keep alive bits, also known as fill bits or stuff bits, are sent across a communications link to maintain synchronization between end devices when no data is traveling across the link. Without keep alive bits, the circuit's receiver will time out and drop or error out the circuit.

Ku band—The Ku band is a portion of the electromagnetic spectrum ranging in frequency from 11 to 14 GHz, used for satellite communications.

latency—Latency is the transmission delay created as a device processes a frame or packet. It is the duration from the time a device reads the first byte of a frame or packet, until the time it forwards that byte.

leased line—Because of the noise associated with early analog telephone lines, it became common practice for telephone companies to "lease" lines to companies for continuous, unswitched use. These leased lines are also referred to as dedicated circuits or nailed lines.

least-cost routing—In data networks, least-cost routing describes the methods routers use to determine the lowest cost link between networks. Least-cost routing makes these determinations based on cost factors, such as bandwidth, delay, and cash costs.

line overhead (LOH)—The SONET LOH is that portion of the SONET frame that controls reliable payload transport between network elements.

line terminating equipment (LTE)—SONET LTE are devices that operate at the SONET line layer, such as ADMs. PTE performs the functions of LTE.

Link Access Procedure Balanced (LAPB)—LAPB is a Data Link Layer protocol implemented from the HDLC standard. Primarily used in X.25 networks, LAPB provides an error-free link between two connected devices.

Link Access Procedure for D Channel (LAPD)—LAPD (or LAP-D) is part of the ISDN layered protocol. It is very similar to LAPB, and operates at the Data Link Layer as well. LAPD defines the protocol used on the ISDN D (signaling) channel to set up calls and other signaling functions.

Link Control Protocol (LCP)—LCP is a transmission protocol used by PPP to set up and test a serial connection.

listed directory number (LDN)—The LDN is a subscriber's or device's main telephone number. An LDN is the primary service number for an end device.

local access and transport area (LATA)—LATAs are the geographic calling areas within which an RBOC may provide local and long-distance services. LATA boundaries, for the most part, fall within states and do not cross state lines, although, one state may have several LATAs.

local exchange carrier (LEC)—A LEC is a company that makes telephone connections to subscribers' homes and businesses, provides telephone services, and collects fees for those services. The terms LEC, ILEC, and RBOC are equivalent.

local loop—A local loop or subscriber line loop is the wiring that extends from a home or business to the CO. It is also referred to as the "last mile."

Local Number Portability (LNP)—LNP is an SS7 service, mandated by the Telecommunications Act of 1996, that allows a subscriber to change service providers while maintaining the same telephone number. LNP assigns each telephone number a network address, and network devices work together to quickly locate the destination, regardless of the carrier on which the address resides.

local significance—Local significance means that an address only identifies a point-to-point link, not an entire end-to-end connection. Frame relay DLCI and ATM VCI have local significance.

Logical Link Control (LLC)—LLC is a Data Link Layer protocol used to control the flow of information across a physical link. LLC is often used in Ethernet networks that use the IEEE frame type, which does not include a type field. LLC provides a "steering" mechanism to move information from a Data Link Layer protocol, such as Ethernet, to the correct Network Layer protocol, such as IP.

low-pass filter—A low-pass filter is a device designed to pass only signals below a certain point, and cut off those frequencies above the highest passable frequency.

main distribution frame (MDF)—An MDF is an equipment room or closet that connects the outside plant network cabling to the inside plant cabling, such as connecting a local VoIP network to an ISP's network.

media gateway (MG)—The MG is the MGCP component that provides the interface between the public switched telephone network (PSTN) and the packet network and is responsible for converting voice signals to packets, and vice versa.

media gateway controller (MGC)—An MGC, also known as a call agent, is the MGCP component responsible for call signal processing. The MGC converts PSTN signaling, either dual tone multi-frequency (DTMF) or Signaling System 7 (SS7) messages, to packetized data. The MGC controls the MG.

Media Gateway Control Protocol (MGCP)—MGCP is described by RFC 2705 as a protocol and set of components for processing voice over IP calls. MGCP uses MGs to convert analog voice to packetized voice, and separate MGCs that handle call signaling. Compared to H.323, this process simplifies the media gateway component by offloading call signal processing to the MGC.

meet-me conference—A meet-me conference is a calling arrangement where conference members dial a specified number and enter a security access code, allowing them access to the conference.

meshed—A meshed network is a network that consists of multiple physical paths between endpoints.

modem—Short for modulator/demodulator, a modem is used to convert binary data into analog signals suitable for transmission across a telephone network.

Modified Final Judgment (MFJ)—The MFJ is the agreement reached between the U.S. Department of Justice and AT&T on January 8, 1984, that settled a 1974 antitrust case of the U.S. versus AT&T. The MFJ created the seven RBOCs, divesting AT&T of its local exchange business. The RBOCs were restricted from providing long-distance service. AT&T retained long-distance service and its manufacturing business.

modulation—Modulation is the process of modifying the form of a carrier wave (electrical signal) so that it can carry intelligent information on a communications medium.

Modulo—Modulo is the term used to describe the maximum states for a counter. For example, in a satellite communications link, modulo 128 indicates that the packet counter can track 128 outbound and inbound packets before the receiver must send an acknowledgment.

After the counter reaches its maximum count, it resets to 0.

multipath reflection—Multipath reflection refers to a situation in which a single radio signal is reflected from several obstacles, causing multiple signals to arrive at a receiving antenna. Because the true signal and reflected signals travel different distances, they arrive at different times, causing audio echoes or video "ghosting." This term is also referred to as multipath reception.

multiplexer (MUX)—A MUX is computer equipment that allows multiple signals to travel over the same physical media.

multipoint control unit (MCU)—MCUs are hosts that coordinate multipoint conferences of three or more terminals that use the H.323 packet multimedia standards. All H.323 terminals participating in a conference must establish a connection with the MCU.

network control point (NCP)—An NCP is an SDN node on which the user's VPN database resides. The NCP determines whether calls remain on the VPN, or must leave the VPN to travel over standard PSTN services.

Network Control Protocol (NCP)—NCP is a protocol that allows PPP to simultaneously support multiple Layer 3 protocols over a single connection.

network interface (NI)—An NI is the interconnection point between a subscriber's equipment and the carrier's network, located on the subscriber's premises.

network interface card (NIC)—A NIC is an expansion board inserted into a computer to enable the computer to be connected to a network.

network interface unit (NIU)—An NIU is an electronic device that acts as the demarcation point between the carrier's network and CPE. An NIU can include protective devices that disconnect the circuit in the case of a lightning strike, and can conduct an automatic loopback to test the line's integrity.

network management system (NMS)—An NMS consists of the servers, workstations, and software that enable network monitoring, management, and configuration.

network service provider—A network service provider is a company that provides network services, such as Internet access, frame relay, ATM, and others, through its own private network infrastructure.

network termination type 1 (NT1)—An ISDN NT1 multiplexes TE1 and TE2/TA devices at the OSI model Physical Layer and interfaces the local loop.

network termination type 2 (NT2)—An ISDN NT2 usually resides at the carrier's facility as a PBX or switch. The NT2 provides Layer 2 and 3 services.

network termination type 12 (NT12)—An ISDN NT12 is a device that performs both the NT1 and NT2 functions.

Network-to-Network Interface (NNI)—NNI describes the connection between two public frame relay services. Providers use NNI to monitor the frame relay network's status. An NNI is also an ATM network interface.

noise—Noise refers to any undesired signal or signal distortion. Noise is often caused by electrical interference. See interference.

omni-directional antenna—An omni-directional antenna is a common wireless network antenna type, which propagates radio signal in a 360 degree pattern around the antenna pole.

operation, administration, maintenance, and provisioning (OAM&P)—The specific functions of managing a system or network, such as those that provide alarm indications, management messages, and configuration interfaces.

optical carrier (OC)—OC is the term used to specify the speed of fiber optic networks conforming to the SONET standard. OC designates the optical characteristics of SONET technologies.

overreach—When a radio signal is transmitted from a sending antenna to a receiving antenna by means of an intermediate repeater antenna, overreach occurs when the receiving antenna receives the signal from both the sender (directly) and the repeater. This causes signal interference because the signal received from the repeater is slightly delayed by processing.

packet assembler/disassembler (PAD)—A PAD is an X.25 network device that takes characters from a terminal or host and frames them into packets for transport across the network. The receiver then removes the characters from the packets for transmission to the destination terminal or host.

Packet Layer Protocol (PLP)—PLP is an OSI model Layer 3 protocol that manages connections between DCE and DTE anywhere in an X.25 network. PLP accepts data from a Transport Layer process, breaks the data into packets, assigns the packets a Network Layer address, and takes responsibility for error-free delivery of the packets to their destination. PLP estab-lishes virtual circuits and routes packets across the circuits. PLP also handles packet multiplexing.

packet switching—Packet switching is the process of sending data in packets over a network to some remote location. Frame relay and X.25 are examples of packet-switching networks.

packet telephony—Packet telephony is voice telephone service provided over connectionless packet networks, instead of the public-switched telephone service.

Packet Transfer Mode (PTM)—PTM is a method of information transfer by means of packet transmission and packet switching that permits dynamic sharing of network resources among many connections. Ethernet, FDDI, and frame relay are examples of PTM.

pair gain—Pair gain is the multiplexing of a given number of telephone conversations over a lesser number of physical telephone lines. Lucent Technologies' SLC is one example of pair gain technology, where devices on each end of a line use multiplexing techniques to combine up to 96 analog local loops onto two wire pairs.

path overhead (POH)—The SONET POH is that portion of the SPE that carries the OAM&P information for end-to-end network management.

path terminating equipment (PTE)—SONET PTE consists of network elements that originate and terminate transported services.

payload header suppression (PHS)—PHS is a technique used to mask redundant cell, frame, or packet header information when one or more of the same type of higher layer data PDUs are transported as the payload of an 802.16 MAC PDU.

payload header suppression identifier (PHSI)—A PHSI is a mask used by 802.16 nodes to identify which redundant payload cell, frame, or packet header information is suppressed within a service flow.

permanent virtual circuit (PVC)—A PVC is a connection across a frame relay network, or cell-switching network such as ATM. A PVC behaves like a dedicated line between source and destination endpoints. When activated, a PVC will always establish a path between these two endpoints.

phase modulation (PM)—PM is a type of modulation that uses phase changes to encode information onto a carrier. For example, if a wave is traveling up, a phase change sends the wave back down to its negative value (creating two wave "troughs" in a row, instead of a trough and then a crest).

phase-shift keying (PSK)—PSK represents digital data over an analog carrier by varying the signal's phase, or time displacement. PSK can represent more than 1 bit, depending on the number of phase shifts implemented.

Physical Layer Convergence Protocol (PLCP)—PLCP is the SMDS SIP Level 1 sublayer that adapts a transmission facility to handle DQDB functions. The PLCP sublayer defines how the SMDS 53-byte cell is mapped to the specific transmission system described at the lower sublayer.

PKZip—PKZip is a file compression utility marketed by PKWARE, Inc.

plain old telephone service (POTS)—POTS is a term used to describe basic analog telephone service provided by a LEC or CLEC.

point of presence (POP)—A POP is the physical transfer point between two networks. In most cases, the POP is a CO switch located in the same building as the LEC CO; however, it also refers to an ISP's Internet access node for a city or area code.

Point-to-Point Protocol (PPP)—PPP is a protocol that allows a computer to use TCP/IP by means of a point-to-point link. PPP is based on the HDLC standard that deals with LAN and WAN links, and operates at the Data Link Layer of the OSI model.

port—There are two primary ways the term "port" is used in networking. Port can refer to a physical port in a device, such as a port on a switch or MUX. Port can also refer to a software port, a number typically used to identify a software process within a computer.

private branch exchange (PBX)—A PBX is a device that connects telephone users of a private network, such as a business, to outside lines available from a telephone company. Today's PBXs are fully digital, not only offering very sophisticated voice services, such as voice messaging, but also integrating voice and data.

private network—A private network is a network consisting of private lines, switching equipment, and other networking equipment provided for the exclusive use of one customer. In other words, the network and its associated services are not intended for use by the general public.

protocol data unit (PDU)—A PDU is a datagram created by a particular layer of an open system reference model. A PDU is used to provide peer-to-peer communications between local and remote processes.

provisioning—In the context of telecommunications, provisioning is the process of conditioning a telecommunications circuit for use by an organization.

public key encryption—Public-key encryption is a cryptographic system that uses two mathematically related keys. One key is used to encrypt a message, and the other to decrypt it. People who need to receive encrypted messages distribute their public keys, but keep their private keys secret.

public network—A public network is a network available to the public for transmission of voice, data, and other types of services.

public-switched telephone network (PSTN)—PSTN is the worldwide voice telephone network accessible to anyone with a telephone.

Pulse Code Modulation (PCM)—PCM is a method of converting an analog voice signal to a digital signal that can be translated accurately back into a voice signal after transmission. A codec samples the voice signal 8,000 times per second, then converts each sample to a binary number that expresses the amplitude and frequency of the sample in a very compact form. These binary numbers are then transmitted to the destination. The receiving codec reverses the process, using the stream of binary numbers to re-create the original analog wave form of the voice.

Q.SIG (or QSIG)—Also known as PSS1, Q.SIG is an ISO standard that defines the ISDN signaling and control methods used to link PBXs in private ISDN networks. The standard extends the "Q" point in the ISDN logical reference model, which was established by ITU-T in its Q.93x series of recommendations that defined the basic functions of ISDN switching systems.

Q.SIG signaling allows certain ISDN features to work in a single or multivendor network.

Quadrature Amplitude Modulation (QAM)—QAM is a signal modulation technique that combines Amplitude Shift Keying (ASK) with PSK. ASK turns the signal off and on to represent digital data. By combining these techniques a single carrier can represent a number of digital bit combinations. For example, 64-QAM represents a total of 64 sets of unique binary bit patterns (000000-111111), or states, with a combination of phase shifts and amplitude changes.

Quadrature Phase Shift Keying (QPSK)—QPSK is a phase shift keying (PSK) technique that uses four phases. PSK is a signal modulation technique that changes a radio signal's phase to represent digital data.

quantization—Quantization is a process in which the continuous range of values of an analog signal is sampled and divided into nonoverlapping (but not necessarily equal) subranges, and a discrete, unique value is assigned to each subrange.

An application of quantization is its use in pulse-code modulation. If the sampled signal value falls within a given subrange, the sample is assigned the corresponding discrete value for purposes of modulation and transmission.

quantization noise—Quantization noise is the difference between information contained in an analog signal and that contained in its digital form. Also referred to as quantizing distortion, quantization noise occurs when an analog signal is converted to digital, or digital to analog. The more accurate the conversion, the less quantization noise is contained in the signal.

quantized—An analog signal is quantized when it is converted to a digital format.

queue—A queue is a collection point where calls are held until an agent or attendant can answer them. Calls are ordered as they arrive and are served in that order. Depending on the time delay in answering the call, announcements, music, or prepared messages may be employed until the call is answered.

Queued Arbitrated (QA) functionality—QA is an SMDS time slot type that supports asynchronous data traffic. Data is carried on a best effort basis.

queued packet synchronous exchange (QPSX)—QPSX is the predecessor to DQDB, a protocol for communications over MANs.

rain attenuation—Rain attenuation is the weakening of a radio signal caused by water droplets (rain or fog) in the air. This attenuation increases with the density of fog and rain.

Rate-Adaptive Digital Subscriber Line (RADSL)—RADSL is a transmission technology that allows for adaptive, high-speed data transfer over existing twisted pair telephone lines. RADSL uses intelligent DSL modems that sense the local loop's performance characteristics and dynamically adjust the transmission speed accordingly. RADSL supports downstream transmissions up to 7 Mbps, and bidirectional transmissions up to 640 Kbps.

Regional Bell Operating Company (RBOC)—An RBOC is one of seven companies formed from AT&T's 22 local telephone companies during the breakup of the Bell system. An RBOC makes tele-phone connections to subscribers' homes and businesses, provides telephone services, and collects fees for those services. The original seven RBOCs were Ameritech, Bell Atlantic, Bellsouth, New York New England Telephone Company (NYNEX), Pacific Telesis, Southwestern Bell Communications, and USWest. The terms RBOC, Local Exchange Carrier (LEC), and Incumbent Local Exchange Carrier (ILEC) are equivalent.

Remote Monitoring (RMON)—RMON is a protocol that gathers network information at a central workstation. RMON defines additional management information bases (MIBs) that provide more detailed information about network usage and status than MIBs defined by SNMP.

request for comment (RFC)—RFC documents are working notes of the Internet research and development community. A document in this series can be on essentially any topic related to computer communication, from a meeting report to the specification of a standard.

Resource Reservation Protocol (RSVP)—RSVP is a new Internet protocol developed to enable the Internet to support specified QoSs. By using RSVP, an application is able to reserve resources along a route from source to destination. RSVP-enabled routers schedule and prioritize packets to fulfill the QoS.

Robbed Bit Signaling—Robbed bit signaling is technique used on certain T1 circuits, such as emulated tie trunks, where bits are robbed from the T1 frames to indicate signaling, such as off-hook, on-hook, ringing, and so forth. These robbed bits leave only seven bits per channel for carrying digitized voice or data.

RS-232-C—Also known as RS-232 and EIA/TIA-232-E, the RS-232-C specification details the electrical, functional, and mechanical interface between computers, terminals, and modems. The standard defines what the interface does, circuit functions, and their corresponding connector pin assignments.

RS-232-D—RS-232-D defines RS-232 serial communications using an RJ-45 connector. The pin assignments for RS-232-D are as follows:

Pin 1—DCE Ready, Ring Indicator

Pin 2—Received Line Signal Detector

Pin 3—DTE Ready

Pin 4—Signal Ground

Pin 5—Received Data

Pin 6—Transmitted Data

Pin 7—Clear to Send

Pin 8—Request to Send

section overhead (SOH)—The SONET SOH is that portion of the SONET frame dedicated to the transport of status, messages, and alarm indications for SONET link maintenance.

section terminating equipment (STE)—SONET STE are those devices that operate at the SONET section layer, such as SONET regenerators. PTE and LTE perform STE functions as well.

sectorized antenna—A sectorized radio antenna is divided into two or more parts to allow it to simultaneously support several radio cells. The antenna divides a 360-degree omni-directional signal into equal parts, making each part better able to focus the signal on a more restricted coverage area. Signal gain with an omni-directional antenna is greater than with an omni-directional antenna.

security association (SA)—An SA is created by 802.16 network devices (before a secure connection is established) wishing to communicate by exchanging security information. Such information includes digital certificates for identification and the encryption method and encryption keys to be used.

Serial Line Internet Protocol (SLIP)—SLIP is not an official Internet standard, but a de facto standard included in many implementations of TCP/IP. It was originally developed to provide remote connectivity to UNIX TCP/IP hosts.

service flow—Service flow is a specific category of higher layer network data carried across an 802.16 wireless link. Each service flow is identified by a Connection ID (CID). An SS can support up to 64,000 service flows in each direction.

service flow identifier (SFID)—An SFID is a 32-bit identifier assigned to each service flow by the BS, in part to identify the QoS the flow receives on the link. When a service flow is admitted and when it is active, the BS associates the SFID with a corresponding CID.

Session Initiation Protocol (SIP)—SIP is the RFC 2543-recommended Application Layer protocol for simplified signaling on multimedia IP network sessions.

sideband—A sideband is a range of frequencies below or above a signal's carrier-wave frequency (AM) or center frequency (FM). The total bandwidth of a signal is the carrier (center) frequency plus its upper and lower sidebands. Single sideband is an inherent property of FM.

signaling—Signaling is the method a telephone system uses to represent the status of a call. Signaling sets up and breaks down calls, and also represents call progression through the various switching offices and PBXs involved in the call's handling.

Signaling System 7 (SS7)—SS7 is a telecommunications protocol defined by ITU as a way to offload PSTN data traffic congestion onto a wireless or wireline digital broadband network. SS7 is characterized by high-speed packet switching and out-of-band signaling. Out-of-band signaling does not take place over the same path as the data transfer (or conversation); a separate digital channel is created, called a "signaling link" where messages are exchanged between network elements. SS7 architecture is set up so that any node can exchange signaling with any other SS7-capable node, not just between directly connected switches.

simple and efficient adaptation layer (SEAL)—SEAL, also known as AAL 5, is used as a simplified adaptation layer for local, high-speed LAN implementations. SEAL is intended for connectionless or connection-oriented variable-bit-rate services.

Simple Network Management Protocol (SNMP)—SNMP is a TCP/IP Application Layer protocol used to send and receive information about the status of network resources on a TCP/IP network. Data networks frequently support SNMP functionality, while traditional voice networks do not.

simplex—Simplex transmission refers to the process of transmitting data in only one direction.

slamming—Slamming is the illegal practice of switching a customer's long-distance service from one IXC to another, without the customer's knowledge or permission.

sliding window—The term windowing is also referred to as a sliding window. Windowing provides a method for protocols such as TCP to control the flow of data. It also allows multiple packets or frames of data to be acknowledged with a single response.

smart jack—A smart jack is a device a carrier can attach to the end of a T-carrier circuit to enable the carrier to test the line's condition without the need to manipulate the CPE. The smart jack appears as an RJ-48 jack, and can plug directly into the CSU.

Software Defined Network (SDN)—SDN is AT&T's 4ESS switch-based Virtual Private Network (VPN) product used to create private corporate voice networks over public facilities. An SDN operates as a private line, but has lower costs.

spoofing—Spoofing means that a router responds to a local host in lieu of sending information across a WAN link to a remote host. The local host thinks the response came from the remote host/network, when it really came from the router.

Station Message Desk Interface (SMDI)—SMDI is an integration protocol controlling integration information exchange over a serial interface. SMDI is typically used by CO switches.

Station Message Detail Reporter (SMDR)—Also known as Station Message Detail Recording, SMDR is a recording of all calls received or generated by a telephone switching system.

statistical time-division multiplexing (STDM)—STDM is a more flexible method of TDM. TDM allocates a fixed number of time slots to each channel, regardless of whether the channel has data to send. In contrast, a statistical MUX analyzes transmission patterns to predict gaps in a channel's traffic that can be temporarily filled with part of the traffic from another channel.

stutter tone—Stutter tone, also known as stutter dial tone, is a broken-up dial tone sent by a PBX or CO to indicate to a user that he or she has a voice mail message waiting to be heard. This is commonly used on telephones not equipped with a message waiting indicator.

Subscriber Line Carrier (SLC)—Lucent Technologies' SLC is a method of using T1 multiplexing technology to carry more lines over existing wires. See pair gain.

Subscriber Network Interface (SNI)—SNI is an SMDS term describing CPE access to an SMDS network over a dedicated circuit.

subscriber station (SS)—An SS is the 802.16 network component that provides user connectivity to the 802.16 network. An SS can simultaneously service many different user connections.

Superframe (SF)—Superframe is a method of arranging T1 channel samples in groups of 12 frames. Each frame is 193 bits long, consisting of 24 eight-bit samples plus one framing bit.

Switched Multimegabit Data Service (SMDS)—SMDS is a high-speed cell-switched data communications service offered by telephone companies that enables organizations to connect geo- graphically separate LANs into a single WAN or MAN.

Switched Multimegabit Data Service (SMDS) Interface Protocol (SIP)—SIP is used for communications between CPE and SMDS carrier equipment. SIP consists of three levels: SIP Level 3 operates at the top of the OSI model Layer 2 MAC sublayer; SIP Level 2 operates at the lower portion of the MAC sublayer; and SIP Level 1 corresponds to the OSI model Physical Layer.

switched services—Switched services refer to transmission provided over a network of nondedicated lines. A switched connection is a temporary transmission path created when needed, and then released. Basic telephone service is an example of a switched service.

switched virtual circuit (SVC)—An SVC is a temporary connection established through a switched network. During data transmission, an SVC behaves like a wire between the sender and receiver. ATM VCs and telephone connections are both examples of SVCs.

synchronous—A synchronous operation is one in which two communicating devices closely synchronize their internal timing circuits (usually by transmitting a burst of bits of a fixed length before the data). To transmit data, a sending device, such as a modem, puts a 1 or a 0 on the line every so often. A receiving device samples the line on the same timetable as the sending device to receive the information accurately. The devices must stay synchronized to communicate without errors.

Synchronous Data Link Control (SDLC)—SDLC is a subset of the HDLC standard. It is a Data Link Layer protocol most often found in SNA networks.

Synchronous Digital Hierarchy (SDH)—
SDH is an international standard for synchronous data transmission over fiber optic cables, equivalent to the North American SONET standard. SDH defines a standard rate of transmission at 155.52 Mbps, which is referred to as STS-3 at the SONET electrical level and as STM-1 for SDH. STM-1 is equivalent to SONET's OC level 3.

Synchronous Optical Network (SONET)—
SONET is the standard for connecting fiber optic transmission systems. SONET was proposed by Bellcore in the mid-1980s and is now an ANSI standard.

synchronous payload envelope (SPE)—
The SONET SPE is the portion of the SONET frame that carries the payload data.

Synchronous Transfer Mode (STM)—STM is a B-ISDN transport-level technique that uses TDM and switching across a UNI. Data communications occurs with an associated clock.

Synchronous Transport Signal level 1 (STS-1)—STS-1 is the building block of SONET bandwidth at 51.84 Mbps. STS designates the electrical characteristics of the SONET standard. The STS-1 rate was chosen for its ability to transport the entire bandwidth of a DS3 (T3) signal, which is approximately 45 Mbps.

Synchronous Transport Signal level 3, concatenated (STS-3c)—STS-3c is the cell mapping that occurs in the ATM TC sublayer that aligns by row every ATM cell within the SONET frame payload capacity. In the STS-3c mapping, the entire payload of an STS-3c frame is filled with ATM cells yielding a transfer capacity of 149.760 Mbps. Although the SONET STS-3c frame payload is 2,349 bytes, and an ATM cell is 53 bytes, an integer number of ATM cells will not fit into an STS-3c frame.

Synchronous Transport Signal level 12, concatenated (STS-12c)—STS-12c is cell mapping that occurs in the ATM TC sublayer that aligns, by row, every ATM cell within the SONET frame payload capacity. In STS-12c mapping, the entire payload of an STS-12c frame is filled with ATM cells yielding a transfer capacity of 622.08 Mbps.

Systems Network Architecture (SNA)—
SNA is IBM's architecture for computer networking. SNA was designed for transaction processing in mission-critical applications. SNA networks usually involve a large number of terminals communicating with a mainframe.

T1—In 1962, the Bell System installed the first "T-carrier" system for multiplexing digitized voice signals. The T-carrier family of systems, which now includes T1, T1C, T1D, T2, T3, and T4 (and their European counterparts E1, E2, and so on), replaced FDM systems, providing much better transmission quality.

T1-emulated tandem tie trunks—Using certain T1 signaling techniques, T1 circuit channels can emulate analog tie trunks or tandem tie trunks. A tandem tie trunk connects PBXs by means of an intermediate PBX. The intermediate PBX acts as a relay between the source and destination PBXs.

tariff—Tariffs are documents filed by regulated telecommunications companies in accordance with FCC requirements. A tariff details the services, equipment, and pricing offered by a common carrier to all potential customers. A tariff is a public document, accessible by all.

telephony—Telephony refers to the transmission of voice signals over a distance (for example, using telephone equipment such as switches, telephones, and transmission media).

Telephony Application Programming Interface (TAPI)—TAPI is an API introduced in 1993 by Microsoft and Intel, to add telephony features to the family of Windows products. The first version of TAPI focused largely on first-party call control. The current version (TAPI 3.0) supports third-party control and features such as media streaming. An increasing number of vendors are offering products that support both TSAPI and TAPI.

telephony gateway—A telephony gateway is a specially equipped computer or router that forms the interface between a telephone network and IP network, converting voice telephone calls to IP data, or packetized calls to standard telephone signals.

Telephony Server Application Programming Interface (TSAPI)—TSAPI is an API developed by Novell and Lucent Technologies to allow LAN-connected CTI applications third-party control. In this API, a data link between the telephone system and a server on a LAN provides telephony applications on the LAN the ability to control various telephone and computer functions. An increasing number of vendors are offering products that support both TSAPI and TAPI.

terminal adapter (TA)—A TA is a hardware interface between a non-ISDN TE2 and an ISDN network.

terminal equipment type 1 (TE1)—A TE1 is an ISDN device providing a four-wire, twisted pair, native ISDN digital interface.

terminal equipment type 2 (TE2)—A TE2 is a device connected to an ISDN network, but which does not understand ISDN protocols. A TE2 requires a TA to connect to an ISDN network.

TIA/EIA-568—The TIA/EIA-568 standard addresses telecommunications wiring within a commercial building.

tie line, tie trunk—A tie line (tie trunk) is a dedicated circuit that links two points without having to dial a telephone number. Many tie lines provide seamless background connections between business telephone systems.

Time Division Multiple Access (TDMA)—TDMA is a technique used to divide up a transmission channel into frames and time slots. The technique allows multiple subscribers shared access to the channel. A series of time slots are assigned to a frame, and the sender and receiver reference a shared time slot map to determine where in the data stream frames begin and end.

time-division multiplexing (TDM)—TDM is a multiplexing technology that transmits multiple signals over the same transmission link, by guaranteeing each signal a fixed time slot to use the transmission medium.

time slice—In TDM, a time slice (or time slot) is a fixed period of transmission time allotted to traffic from one process, application, or user.

Traffic Encryption Key (TEK)—TEK is a component of the 802.16 network data encryption function used to indicate the encryption pattern the BS and SS use to secure the MAC PDU contents.

transponder—A transponder is a device carried onboard a satellite that receives a weak microwave signal and amplifies, conditions, and retransmits it back to earth.

Trivial File Transfer Protocol (TFTP)—TFTP is the TCP/IP protocol for file transfer with minimal capability and overhead. TFTP depends on the unreliable, connectionless, datagram delivery service, UDP.

trunk—Trunk lines are the physical connections between the end offices of a telephone network.

tunneling—Tunneling is a technology that lets a network protocol carry information for other protocols within its own packets (for example, carrying IPX packets inside IP packets). The packets may be secured using data encryption techniques.

type of service (ToS) bits—ToS bits are the set of eight bits in an Internet Protocol (IP) packet header used to designate the type of service a packet is provided across a network. QoS services used for delay-sensitive, bandwidth-intensive services, such as video and Voice over IP (VoIP) modify these bits to suit their needs. Network devices all along the packet's route must recognize these bit settings, and provide the appropriate network services.

type of service (ToS)/quality of service (QoS)—Users of the Transport Layer specify QoS or ToS parameters as part of a request for a communications channel. QoS parameters define different levels of service based on the requirements of an application. For example, an interactive application that needs good response time would specify high QoS values for connection establishment delay, throughput, transit delay, and connection priority. However, a file transfer application needs reliable, error-free data transfer more than it needs a prompt connection, thus it would request high QoS parameters for residual error rate/probability.

unified messaging—Also known as integrated messaging, unified messaging allows you to receive, send, and interact with all your messaging sources (voice, e-mail, fax, voice mail, and so on) from a single central location.

uniform (universal) dial plan—A uniform dial plan is a private network numbering system that assigns unique extension numbers to each user, regardless of location. If locations in different cities are linked in a private telephone network, a uniform dial plan allows employees in different cities to dial each other using only extension numbers.

uninterruptible power supply (UPS)—UPS is an emergency backup power source that instantly takes over when the regular electrical power fails.

Universal Asynchronous Receiver/Transmitter (UART)—A UART is a portion of a serial interface that performs parallel to serial conversion; adds start, stop, and parity bits; monitor's the port's status; controls circuit timing; buffers data; and then reverses the process on the receiving end.

Universal Service Fund (USF)—The USF is a component of the Telecommunications Act of 1996. It is designed to provide discounted telecommunications services to certain schools, libraries, and rural hospitals, and serves to subsidize telephone service to high-cost rural areas and low-income households.

User-Network Interface (UNI)—UNI specifies the procedures and protocols between user equipment (FRAD) and the frame relay network. UNI also defines the interface between an ATM network device and the ATM network.

V.10—V.10 is an ITU recommendation for serial communications over unbalanced circuits.

V.11—V.11 is an ITU recommendation for serial communications over balanced circuits.

V.22bis, V.32bis, V.34bis, V.42bis—The V series includes ITU-T standards for sending data, by means of a modem, over the telephone network:

- V.22bis is an older modem standard for transfer rates up to 1,200 bps.

- V.32bis defines full-duplex, dial-up capabilities up to 14.4 Kbps.

- V.34bis is an improved standard that uses compression techniques to achieve speeds up to 33.6 Kbps.

- V.42bis is a group of protocols that provide error correction by allowing the receiving device to request retransmission of corrupted data.

V.24—ITU-T V.24 defines interface characteristics for serial data interchange between DTE and DCE, similar to RS-232-C.

V.35—The CCITT (ITU) V.35 recommendation specifies a balanced, electrical serial modem communications interface that operates up to 48 Kbps. ITU rescinded V.35 in 1988, and specified the V.10 and V.11 standards as its replacement.

V.90—V.90 is the ITU-T standard for PCM modems running at up to 56 Kbps. V.90 allows for downstream (toward the user) data rates of 56 Kbps (limited to 53 Kbps by FCC regulations) and upstream rates of up to 33.6 Kbps.

vector directory number (VDN)—A VDN is an extension number used in automatic call distributor (ACD) software to connect calls to a vector for processing. The VDN by itself may be dialed to access the vector from any extension connected to the switch.

very high-bit-rate Digital Subscriber Line (VDSL)—VDSL is a version of ADSL service that delivers up to 52 Mbps downstream, and 1.5 to 2.3 Mbps upstream.

very small aperture terminal (VSAT)—A VSAT is a small-diameter (approximately 1.5 to 3 meter) satellite antenna, used for satellite point-to-multipoint communications.

V.FC—V.FC is a modem communications protocol that supports speeds up to 28.8 Kbps.

virtual channel identifier (VCI)—A VCI is a value in an ATM cell header that uniquely identifies one ATM VC. Each VC is one data transmission from a source node to a destination node.

virtual circuit—A virtual circuit is a communications path that appears to be a single circuit to the sending and receiving devices. A virtual circuit can traverse multiple physical circuits.

virtual local area network (VLAN)—A VLAN is a group of computers in a large LAN that behave as if they are connected to their own small private LAN. We create VLANs using special switches and software, and can assign computers to different VLANs without changing their physical configuration.

virtual path identifier (VPI)—A VPI is a value in an ATM cell header that identifies a group of ATM VCs moving from the same source to the same destination.

virtual private network (VPN)—A VPN is a connection over a shared network that behaves like a dedicated link. VPNs are created using a technique called "tunneling," which transmits data packets across a public network, such as the Internet or other commercially available network, in a private "tunnel" that simulates a point-to-point connection. The tunnels of a VPN can be encrypted for additional security.

virtual tributary (VT)—A VT is a lower-level channel that has been multiplexed to become part of a higher-capacity channel. For example, 28 T1 (DS1) channels can be multiplexed to form 1 T3 (DS3) channel; each of the T1 channels is considered a tributary of the T3.

Voice Activity Detection (VAD)—VAD is a method of detecting pauses in speech and saving bandwidth by not transmitting these pauses with the voice intelligence.

Voice over Internet Protocol (VoIP)—VoIP is a technology that consists of telephone signals transmitted as IP packets. See packet telephony.

Voice Response Unit (VRU)—Also known as an IVR unit, a VRU is an interface technology that allows outside callers to control a computer application and input information using their telephone keypads. All VRUs can speak back the results of the computer application, and some can also be programmed to fax back the results.

wavelength—A signal's wavelength is the distance an electrical or optical wave travels in a single cycle. Wavelength is inversely proportional to frequency; the greater the wavelength, the shorter the frequency.

wavelength-division multiplexing (WDM)—WDM uses multiple light wavelengths to transmit signals over a single optical fiber. Each wavelength, or channel, carries a stream of data at rates as high as 2.5 Gbps and higher.

white noise—The term white noise refers to random electrical noise or static. See noise.

wideband digital cross-connect—A wideband digital cross-connect is similar in function to a broadband digital cross-connect, except it switches at the VT (or DS1) level.

Wildfire—Wildfire is a voice-activated virtual personal assistant created by Wildfire Communications, Inc. See **http://www.wildfire.com** for more information.

wireless hotspot—A wireless hotspot is a public place, such as a coffee shop, airport lounge, or hotel lobby that provides wireless network connectivity for paying customers or the general public to use.

Worldwide Intelligent Network (WIN)—According to AT&T, WIN is the largest, most sophisticated communications network in the world. Over this network of SONET OC-192 backbone links, AT&T carries more than 675 terabytes of data and 300 million voice calls in an average day.

X.3—X.3 is the ITU recommendation that describes the operation of the X.25 PAD in a public packet-switched network. X.3 defines the parameters that govern PAD control over asynchronous terminal operation.

X.21—ITU X.21 defines the interface between DTE and DCE in synchronous operations across a public data network. X.21 is only used for link establishment and connection control functions.

X.21bis—X.21bis is the CCITT recommendation that specifies the V.series modem serial interface.

X.25—X.25 has been a long-time standard for packet switching. The X.25 interface lies at OSI Layer 3, rather than Layer 1. X.25 defines a protocol stack as having three layers.

X.28—ITU X.28 defines the terminal-to-PAD interface for DTE accessing a public-switched network's PAD facility.

X.29—ITU X.29 specifies the procedures for handshaking and user data transfer between a PAD and a packet mode DTE or another PAD.

X.75—X.75 is an international standard and ITU-T recommendation for linking X.25 networks. X.75 defines the connection between public networks and the terminal and transit control procedures to be used when transferring data between public networks.

X.121—ITU X.121 is the recommendation for packet mode data device numbering systems. X.25 uses the X.121 protocol.

X.400—X.400 is an ISO and ITU standard for addressing and transporting e-mail messages. It conforms to Layer 7 of the OSI model and supports several types of transport mechanisms, including Ethernet, X.25, TCP/IP, and dial-up lines.

zero bit insertion—Bit stuffing allows binary data to be transmitted on a synchronous transmission line. Within each frame are special bit sequences that identify addresses, flags, and so forth. If the information (data) portion of the frame also contains one of these special sequences, a 0 is inserted by the transmitting station and removed by the receiving station.

WestNet's Related Titles

The WestNet Advantage

When creating its courseware, WestNet raised the bar on how content is written and delivered. From distance learning to instructor-led courses, WestNet provides a value not found in any other curriculum or certification preparation program. With each course, students receive a fully illustrated textbook, CD-ROM, and access to an interactive online course, with pre- and post-assessment exams, online help from data and telephony experts, and student activity guides.

WestNet offers an exclusive, integrated stream of courses ranging from the core courses of networking and telephony fundamentals and architectures, to the complex structures of converging technologies and network implementation. Additionally, WestNet courses offer comprehensive content about each subject of study, as well as presenting clear, concise, and updated information and technologies.

WestNet's exclusive Signature Series courseware includes a variety of tools to assist students with their education. These unique features are not found in any other IT curriculum providers' material.

The most popular Signature Series courses are described on the following pages.

Introduction to Networking

Course Overview
Introduction to Networking provides an introductory overview of the fundamental concepts of networking and data communications. This course is designed for those with basic experience using a computer, who want to understand how networks move information between computers.

In this course, students will learn how signals travel across different types of physical network structures, and how those signals carry useful data from one device to another. As they will see, the same key principles and components form the foundation of all networks, from the smallest peer-to-peer systems to the worldwide Internet. The knowledge students gain in this course will serve as a firm foundation for continued study in data networking.

Key Topics
- Physical transmission media: copper wires, optical fibers, and radio waves
- Analog and digital signaling
- Communication protocols and services
- The OSI Reference Model
- Common transmission technologies for local area networks
- Popular network operating systems
- Networking devices
- Linking networks across a wide area

Course Objectives
- Identify the different types of networking hardware and software
- Explain how signals are transmitted over wires, fiber optic cables, and wireless systems
- Describe what protocols are, and why they are necessary
- Describe the different types of addresses that computers use to send and receive information
- Learn how information flows between two communicating computers
- Describe the technologies used in local area networks (LANs) and wide area networks (WANs)
- Identify the common types of networking devices, and explain the purpose of each one
- Build a small peer-to-peer network

Introduction to Telecommunications

Course Overview
This course is a telecommunications primer that will give students a thorough, but non-technical, understanding of the worldwide telecommunications network. Students will learn about the basic signaling and switching systems that make the telephone system work, and gain an appreciation of the complex technologies necessary for reliable phone service. This course will also explain the business aspects of the telecom industry, and introduce the various types of companies that now compete for commercial and residential customers. Students will explore the issues and trends that are fueling the explosive growth in the telecommunications industry, and gain a firm understanding of the state of the industry today.

Key Points

- Evolution of the U.S. telecommunications industry
- Structure of the telephone network
- Local Exchange Components
- Customer Premise Equipment Analog voice services
- Digital data services: T1, ISDN, and DSL

Course Objectives

- Understand the technical and political evolution of the U.S. telecom industry
- Discuss how the Telecommunications Act of 1996 led to today's complex telephone market
- Explain, in non-technical terms, the process of making a telephone call
- Describe the differences of the three main types of transmission media
- Describe the most commonly used switching systems for business phones
- Explain the difference between analog and digital signals
- Describe how digital signals are carried by analog connections, and vice-versa
- Explain the relationship of the Internet to the telecommunications system
- Name the reason for the telecom system's endless "need for speed"

Introduction to Local Area Networks

Course Overview The *Introduction to Local Area Networks* course explains the concepts, technologies, components, and protocols used in local area networking (LAN) environments. Students will learn about the popular LAN protocols of Ethernet, Token Ring, and asynchronous transfer mode (ATM), with emphasis on all speeds of Ethernet. This course also introduces the most widely used network operating systems: Novell NetWare, Windows NT, and Windows 2000.

Participants will see how computers work together in both peer-to-peer and client/server networks. They will also learn the first principles of network design, as they learn how to use hubs, bridges, switches, and routers to optimize network traffic.

When students complete this course, they will have a solid understanding of the fundamental concepts of LAN operation. This knowledge provides a clear advantage when taking other courses to learn how to administer specific network operating systems.

Key Topics

- Client/server remote procedure calls
- Characteristics of physical media
- Operation of Ethernet, Token Ring, and ATM LANs
- Ethernet configurations and topologies
- Novell NetWare
- Microsoft Windows NT and Windows 2000
- LAN testing and analysis

Course Objectives

- Explain the characteristics of the three types of physical media used in LANs
- Compare and contrast the operation of Ethernet, Token Ring, and ATM networks
- Identify the different types of Ethernet networks, and explain their relationship to each other
- Explain the basic approaches of traffic isolation and broadcast containment in Ethernet LANs
- Describe the concept of a virtual LAN
- Identify the components of the OSI 8802 (IEEE 802) protocol suite, showing their relationship to one another

Introduction to TCP/IP

Course Overview   In the *Introduction to TCP/IP* course, students will learn the underlying applications, components, and protocols of transmission control protocol/Internet protocol (TCP/IP) and its necessary link to the Internet. This course will also help students learn how to identify TCP/IP layers, components, and functions. Navigation tools, TCP/IP services, and troubleshooting methodologies are also covered in this course.

Key Topics

- Usage of TCP/IP applications such as TCP, browsers, email and network management
- Structure of TCP/IP and IP routing
- TCP/IP addressing and subnetting
- How TCP/IP addresses are discovered and used in computer networks
- IP routing and router usage
- Moving information from source to destination across a TCP/IP network
- How TCP/IP applications work

Course Objectives

- Recognize TCP/IP layers, components, and functions, and map these to the OSI model
- Describe and implement TCP/IP application services that support electronic mail, remote terminal access, network management, Web access, and file transport across routed networks
- Explain TCP/IP protocols used to transport data over intranets, extranets, and the Internet
- Identify and utilize Internet navigation and searching tools such as Web browsers (HTTP) and file transfer services (FTP, TFTP)
- Design and implement subnetworks
- Design and implement Classless Interdomain Routing (CIDR)
- Choose a routing protocol based on network size and service requirements, including QoS/ToS routing, VLSM, and link redundancy
- Describe TCP/IP support services, including DNS and DHCP
- Use TCP/IP tools to troubleshoot and isolate internetwork communications failures

Internet Technologies

Course Overview   In the *Internet Technologies*, students will review the Internet, its history, organization and structure, and learn how to access the Internet, both as an individual user and as a group of users. Students will learn how to create basic Internet Web pages and build a Web server to host these pages. Additionally, students will review the applications used for retrieving information or providing information across this global network of networks.

Key Topics

- Internets, intranets and extranets
- Getting connected to the Internet
- Web clients and Web servers
- Building a Web server
- Creating a Web page
- Operating systems used for Web servers
- Web server applications
- Using the Internet

Course Objectives

- Identify the organizations that manage the Internet
- Describe methods for accessing the Internet
- Build a Web server and understand its primary components
- Describe common operating systems used by Web servers
- Discuss common application servers used for Internet access
- Retrieve Internet information through a wide variety of applications
- Build basic Internet Web pages

Internetworking Devices

Course Overview

The *Internetworking Devices* course focuses on the issues encountered with network growth and the internetworking components that offer solutions to these issues. Students will identify and describe the components of repeaters, hubs, bridges, switches, routers and gateways. In addition, students learn when to use a router and when to use a switch, and discuss routing methodologies and routing protocols. They will also review Network Management and the Simple Network Management Protocol (SNMP).

Prerequisites

The *Introduction to Networking* course is a prerequisite for this course. An understanding of LAN and WAN protocols and technologies, as discussed in the *Introduction to Local Area Networks* and *Introduction to Wide Area Networks* courses is also helpful. As well, the participant should have a grasp on TCP/IP and related protocols.

Key Topics

- Repeaters function and usage
- Bridging two networks
- Switch function and usage
- Router protocols and configuration
- Gateways and Protocol converters
- Virtual Local Area Networks
- SNMP

Course Objectives

- Describe the use of repeaters and hubs in networks
- List the advantages of using switch technologies in computer networks
- Identify when to use a router and when to use a switch
- Discuss routing methodologies and routing protocols
- Identify the need for Virtual LANs
- Describe how protocols such as OSPF and RIP are used by routers
- List the functions of SNMP and describe how they are used in networking

Protocol Analysis

Course Overview

The *Protocol Analysis* course covers the underlying processes and protocols that form the foundation of today's networking infrastructure. Its primary focus is TCP/IP networking protocols and applications, with sections devoted to Novell's IPX/NCP, NetBIOS/NetBEUI/SMB, NFS, Microsoft's client/server operations, as well as network routing protocols. It presents the common frame formats found in LANs and WANs, including Ethernet Version 2, IEEE 802.3, SNAP, PPP, Frame Relay and ATM.

The course begins by discussing important concepts such as virtual circuits, layering, and service boundaries then proceeds to physical and logical network addressing as viewed from both LAN and WAN perspectives. Participants will understand the function of frame, packet and port addresses, and how these are deployed in the delivery of information to user applications. A Web browser/server conversation is covered from the DNS lookup to the subsequent transfer of the Web page across the network.

Prerequisites

Prerequisites for the *Protocol Analysis* course include *Introduction to Networking*, as well as *Introduction to Local Area Networks, Introduction to Wide Area Networks, Introduction to TCP/IP,* and *Internetworking Devices*.

Key Topics

- Network addressing
- Protocol Analyzer operations
- Reading and interpreting protocol traces
- LAN and WAN protocols
- TCP/IP Network and Application protocols
- IP Routing protocols
- Client/Server, Web browser, and Web server operations

Course Objectives

- Identify the most common protocols used in today's networks
- Analyze Data Link, Network, Transport, Session and Application Layer protocol headers and contents
- Describe the request/reply information transfer between a client and a server
- Understand the function of frame, packet and port addresses
- Analyze and trace network traffic with a protocol analyzer

Network Design

Course Overview

The *Network Design* course serves as a guide to gaining a more in-depth understanding of the methods used to analyze, design and manage LANs and point-to-point networks. Students will analyze a business issue and solve it by using a methodical process. Exercises and activities are geared toward learning the techniques necessary for network design and analysis. In addition, students will analyze and discuss network diagrams from several corporate networks.

Prerequisites

The *Introduction to Networking* course is a prerequisite for this course. Other suggested courses include *Introduction to Local Area Networks*, *Introduction to Wide Area Networks*, *Introduction to TCP/IP*, and *Internetworking Devices*.

Key Topics

- Analyzing technical requirements
- Traffic analysis
- Logical network design
- Physical network design
- Designing a small network

Course Objectives

- Understand the process of gathering technical requirements
- Understand the requirements analysis phase of network design
- Determine the root cause of a technical problem
- Describe the steps in traffic analysis
- List ways to measure networking traffic
- Evaluate networking equipment to solve a performance problem

Mastering the Web

Course Overview

The *Mastering the Web* course serves as a guide for understanding the numerous aspects of creating and managing Web sites. Understand the tasks and tools involved in building and maintaining a Web site. Review the WebMaster's responsibilities, including site management and administration, programming, security, content and design, and prepare for the challenges that this role brings.

Prerequisites

The *Introduction to Networking* course and the *Internet Technologies* course are prerequisites to this course.

Key Topics

- E-commerce
- Web servers
- Web page authoring and graphics
- Client-side Programming
- Server-side Programming with Perl
- CGI, Java and JavaScript
- Active Server Pages
- Web security

Course Objectives

- Identify Web server network operating systems
- Learn the important aspects of e-commerce business
- Describe the use of various Web server applications
- Understand where programming languages such as Java, CGI and Perl are used in Web servers
- Identify and describe the Web development team members and their respective responsibilities
- Understand Web site process and methodology
- Describe how database driven Web pages are generated
- Understand key aspects of Web security

Design and Implementation of Voice Networks

Course Overview

The *Design and Implementation of Voice Networks* course explains the structure and design of telecommunication networks, both large and small. It begins with an overview of the public telephone network, and describes the large networks and transmission facilities that switch telephone calls. The focus then narrows to the PBX switching systems that are essential to most businesses. Students will receive a thorough explanation of the components and functions of a typical PBX, with special emphasis on the architecture of the Lucent DEFINITY.

After introducing the public telephone network, the course introduces the digital transmission services that operate over that network. Students will be able to explain the operation, protocols, strengths, and weaknesses of point-to-point services, such as T1, and switched services, such as Frame Relay and ATM.

To explain the critical interface between the customer premises and the public network, the course concludes by introducing the science of traffic engineering. It introduces the three most common methods of estimating the optimum trunk capacity of a phone system, and offers practical advice for gathering the raw data necessary for traffic engineering calculations.

Course Objectives

- Explain the operation of the public switched telephone network
- Describe the typical components and functions of a PBX voice switching system
- Name the point-to-point and switched telecommunications facilities offered by telephone service providers, and describe how each one works
- Explain how to link multiple PBXs to form a private communication network
- Describe how calls are routed through private telecom networks
- Explain how an Automatic Call Distributor (ACD) works, and how it is typically used
- Briefly describe the most common methods of traffic engineering, and explain the proper application of each one
- Using standard industry reference tools, estimate the optimum number of communications channels for a business

567

Convergence of Technologies

Course Overview
Technology convergence is the trend toward creating single networks that support many different types of traffic: data, audio, video, and interactive multimedia. This course explains the functional requirements of a converged network, and shows how various technologies make convergence possible by providing each of those functions.

The *Convergence of Technologies* course first focuses on the critical need for increased bandwidth, by reviewing the standard LAN and WAN protocols used in the most common networking configurations. It then introduces several emerging protocols and technologies that promise to provide the quality of service necessary for the transmission of time-sensitive information. With this foundation in place, the remainder of the course concentrates on practical applications of convergence. Students will see how large call centers use close integration of data and voice networks to efficiently deliver high levels of customer service.

Course Objectives

- Describe the key network protocols that are emerging to support multimedia applications

- Name the wide-area digital services that are most suitable for converged networking, and explain their relative advantages and disadvantages

- Explain why bandwidth is so important to converged networks, and describe the most viable methods of increasing bandwidth in an existing LAN

- Describe the protocols and technologies that make it possible for telephone calls, faxes, and video conferencing to be transmitted over an IP network

- List the technologies needed in a call center environment, and explain how the best call centers implement computer telephony integration (CTI)

- Discuss what would be necessary to provide true converged networking to individual home users

IP Telephony Principles and Applications

Course Overview   *IP Telephony Principles and Applications* presents and explains the many and varied techniques, solutions, principles, and challenges both carriers and end users utilize, experience, and overcome in implementing Voice-over IP services. This course explores the various protocols involved, the QOS challenges we face and ways we can overcome them, engineering principles to consider when designing a VoIP solution, market drivers and applications, security issues, and carrier options.

More and more today, businesses want to consolidate different types of communication traffic, such as voice calls, data transmission, and video conferencing, onto a single network infrastructure. This can simplify the communications process (fewer lines and network providers to manage) and cut call costs.

IP Telephony is helping to make this possible, by allowing standard public-network calls to be carried over packet networks such as the Internet. Through IP Telephony, businesses can save significantly on both voice calls and fax services. Newer software now allows remote and traveling workers to take advantage of IP Telephony from either desktop or laptop computers.

**Course
Objectives**

- Recognize and resolve challenges Enterprises face when converging voice and data communications

- When presented with a network integration scenario, identify and correct integration obstacles such as load sharing and balancing, proxy use, Network Address Translation (NAT) and Coder/Decoders (codecs)

- Discuss the intricacies of such Quality of Service (QoS) enabling protocols and technologies as frame and packet tagging (802.1Q.p), Differentiated and Integrated Services (DiffServ and Intserv), Type of Service (ToS) settings, flow control, and policies

- Determine the appropriate QoS technology to solve a particular service quality issue, both at the network's edge and within the internal network nodes

- Apply to the converged network voice and data traffic engineering principles, planning the network's design and identifying and correcting traffic flow problems

NetWare 5.1 Administration

Course Overview

NetWare was the first non-UNIX network operating system to provide file sharing between PCs. Since then it has added a multitude of services and features to meet the demands of the technology industry. From basic file and print sharing to high-end security, to the Web and application services, Novell does it all.

The Certified Novell Administrator (CNA) is frequently the first credential earned by NetWare career professionals. CNA training provides the critical day-to-day maintenance and management skills needed to survive in the exciting world of NetWare 5.1.

This *Novell NetWare 5.1 Administration* course fulfills the CNA exam requirements by covering day-to-day administration tasks: setting up user accounts, writing login scripts, managing the file system, configuring security, setting up printing with NDPS, and managing the desktop environment with ZENworks. The objectives and management skills that students will need to excel in NetWare 5.1 are also covered.

In addition to the information needed to pass the CNA exam, students will also gain the hands-on administration skills and knowledge needed to walk into a new job or professional environment.

Prerequisites

WestNet's *Novell NetWare 5.1 Administration* course is an advanced networking course. Students will find it helpful to have developed, at the minimum, basic networking skills. WestNet's *Introduction to Networking* course is just one of the many courses available to help prepare NetWare 5.1 Administration students for this course.

Key Topics

- Novell Access
- Administration Tasks
- NDS Security
- The File System
- File System Security
- Drive Mappings and Login Scripts
- Novell Distributed Print Services
- ZENworks
- Server Installation

Implementation of Data Networks

Course Overview   *Implementation of Data Networks* explains how to design the physical layout of a computer network and organize an installation project. It assumes that a logical network design has already been completed, based on customer requirements. From that starting point, the course explains how to fulfill those requirements within the constraints of the real world.

Students will learn how a wide range of network factors—media, topology, protocols, and devices—can either enhance or degrade its performance. The course covers the technical standards and legal regulations that determine many aspects of a physical design, and thoroughly discusses the process of configuring a Windows NT network. Students are also introduced to the project management tools that are essential to complete a network project on time and within budget.

Course Objectives

- Describe the process of planning and implementing a data network, based on customer requirements and a project plan.

- Name the key standards and regulations that affect a network implementation project, and explain their relative importance.

- Name the project management tools that are required to organize a technology project, and provide examples of how to use each one.

- Describe the differences between LANs based on coaxial cable, twisted pair, and fiber optic.

- Discuss the major issues involved when implementing a Windows NT network.

- Explain how the architecture and physical topology of a network determines the options available for increasing its speed.

- Explain the key requirements of an Internet security strategy.

Notes

Overall Course Evaluation Survey

Congratulations on completing this course! We hope you enjoyed your learning journey.

This survey will help us identify where we can focus our strengths and improve our weaknesses. As a token of our appreciation for your time in completing this, we will send you a Certificate of Appreciation (if you tell us who you are!).

Introduction to Wide Area Networks

Course # (see book cover): _____

Location of course: _____

Instructor-led ☐   Self-paced ☐

Did you use the CD?   Yes ☐   No ☐   Comments: _____
_____

Did you access the online course?   Yes ☐   No ☐   Comments: _____
_____

Did you use the Web board for support?   Yes ☐   No ☐   Comments: _____
_____

Did you visit the student Web site?   Yes ☐   No ☐   Comments: _____
_____

What are this course's strengths? _____

What did you like best? _____
_____

What are this course's weaknesses? _____

What did you like least? _____
_____

Would you be interested in other titles from this publisher? _____
If so, what specific topics would you like to see addressed? _____
_____

Optional (must provide this information if you would like a Certificate of Appreciation):

Name: _____

Occupation/Title: _____

Company: _____

Address: _____

City/State/ZIP: _____

Country (if outside USA): _____

E-mail address: _____

Gender: Male ☐   Female ☐

Age: Under 25 ☐   26-40 ☐   41-60 ☐   61+ ☐

Please return this survey to: WestNet Learning Technologies, Attn: Executive Vice President, 5420 Ward Rd., Suite 150, Arvada, CO 80002 USA

Or fax to: 303-432-2565

|||||

BUSINESS REPLY MAIL
BULK RATE MAIL   PERMIT NO. 83   ARVADA CO

POSTAGE WILL BE PAID BY ADDRESSEE

WestNet
LEARNING TECHNOLOGIES

5420 WARD ROAD STE 150
ARVADA CO 80002-9929